Microsoft Fabric Analytics Engineer Associate Study Guide

Hands-On Practice and Expert Tips for Acing the DP-600 Certification Exam

Brian Bønk and Valerie Junk

Microsoft Fabric Analytics Engineer Associate Study Guide
by Brian Bønk and Valerie Junk

Published by O'Reilly Media, Inc., 141 Stony Circle, Suite 195, Santa Rosa, CA 95401.

O'Reilly books may be purchased for educational, business, or sales promotional use. Online editions are also available for most titles (*http://oreilly.com*). For more information, contact our corporate/institutional sales department: 800-998-9938 or *corporate@oreilly.com*.

Acquisitions Editor: Michelle Smith
Development Editor: Shira Evans
Production Editor: Aleeya Rahman
Copyeditor: Doug McNair
Proofreader: Rachel Rossi
Indexer: nSight, Inc.
Cover Designer: Susan Brown
Cover Illustrator: Monica Kamsvaag
Interior Designer: David Futato
Interior Illustrator: Kate Dullea

March 2026: First Edition

Revision History for the First Edition
2026-02-23: First Release

See *http://oreilly.com/catalog/errata.csp?isbn=9798341634817* for release details.

979-8-341-63481-7

[LSI]

Table of Contents

Part II. Implementing and Managing Semantic Models

Part III. Maintaining a Data and Analytics Solution

Foreword

When we started *Guy in a Cube*, our mission was simple: teach people the clicks and help people grow in their data journey. What began as a few scrappy YouTube videos has grown into a global community of creators, analysts, and dreamers who believe data should empower, not intimidate.

That's why we're so excited about this book. Brian Bønk and Valerie Junk have built something special; this book is not just a technical deep dive into Microsoft Fabric, but a roadmap for the modern data professional. Fabric brings together every layer of the analytics journey, from ingestion and transformation to modeling, visualization, and governance, all in one unified experience. This book doesn't just teach you *how* to use Fabric; it helps you understand *why* it matters.

The pace of innovation in data today can feel overwhelming. New tools, new patterns, new AI experiences...it's a lot to keep up with, even for us. But as you read these chapters, you'll see that the foundation remains the same: good data, good design, and good storytelling. Whether you're building your first semantic model or optimizing enterprise-scale analytics, the insights here will meet you where you are and help you level up.

We've always said that the best part of our journey has been the people: the community that learns, shares, and lifts one another up. This book is an extension of that spirit. So, dive in! Experiment. Break things. Learn something new. Because the next generation of data stories—the ones that will change how organizations think, act, and grow—might just start with the knowledge you gain here.

But enough of all this talking. Let's get into the book!

— *Adam Saxton and Patrick LeBlanc*
Guy in a Cube

Preface

Microsoft Fabric is the *software as a service* (SaaS) platform from Microsoft that covers all aspects of building a modern analytics platform. From ingestion to insights, from bulk loading to streaming, and from charts to functions, everything is seamlessly integrated into a unified platform.

Microsoft Fabric was first announced at the Microsoft Build conference back in 2023 as a public preview version of the platform. Before that, the platform had been in heavy testing and private preview under the working title of Trident.

It's based on previous work on *Azure Synapse Analytics*, which was the first big release from Microsoft to move the analytics workload from only using Structured Query Language (SQL) server binaries to having a segregated split between compute and storage.

Compute is still based on the base thought of the SQL engine, but with brand-new binaries and features. Storage is now based on *Azure Data Lake Storage*, which acts as a centralized, flexible storage system to store all kinds of file types. Most often, users will store the open source Parquet file format, but they can also store formats like (but not limited to) CSV, JSON, XML, and Microsoft Excel to be read from the compute engine.

In the first release of Microsoft Fabric, we also saw the name *Synapse* appear in some services on the platform, but in its latest release, that name is gone. We now have a fully new and standalone platform that embraces everything you need to build a full-blown analytics platform for an organization of any size, from a small business to the biggest enterprise.

Everything in the platform is based on existing services from Microsoft Azure (with a few exceptions),[1] packed into an easy-to-use graphical interface.

1 Activator is not a standalone service in Microsoft Azure.

The different services in Microsoft Fabric are shown in Figure P-1 and are as follows:

- Data Factory
- Data Engineering
- Data Warehouse
- Data Science
- Real-Time Intelligence
- Power BI
- OneLake

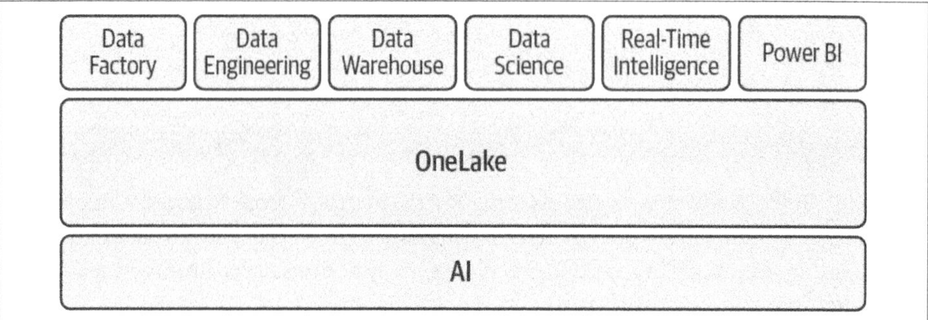

Figure P-1. The complete Fabric platform with all services

You can read more about each service in Chapter 1.

Who Should Take the Exam

Microsoft Fabric is used by technologists and business professionals, including business intelligence developers, data analysts, and business intelligence specialists, to integrate data, build semantic models, and understand and visualize important business data.

Whether you work in finance, manufacturing, sales, marketing, science, or professional services, data is the heartbeat of your business and data analysis is the key to your success. As a technical professional, certification in Microsoft Fabric will enhance your career prospects and professional credibility, providing many advantages that you'll need to excel in your field. Passing the Microsoft DP-600 exam and earning the Fabric Analytics Engineer Associate certification is key to showcasing your knowledge of and experience with the platform.

This book is based on the authors' expert knowledge and experience working in the Microsoft Fabric platform from the very beginning. You can use it as a learning resource to help you prepare for the certification exam and as a daily reference guide for working with Microsoft Fabric from an analytics and visualization point of view.

The Official Curriculum

The DP-600 certification exam tests you on a set of skills and knowledge from the perspective of a data analyst, a role that includes working with ingestions, transformations, and visualizations.

Given the rapid evolution of the Microsoft Fabric platform, the content of the certification exam might change over time. The content of this certification at the time of this writing is listed in the following text.

The exam measures your mastery of the following skills:[2]

- Maintaining a data analytics solution
  - Implementing security and governance
  - Maintaining the analytics development lifecycle
- Preparing data
  - Getting it
  - Transforming it
  - Querying and analyzing it
- Implementing and managing semantic models
  - Designing and building them
  - Optimizing enterprise-scale semantic models

The Purpose of This Book

This book covers all of the skills in the official curriculum in detail. It will give you an understanding of the exam and the content of the curriculum, and it will guide you on how to use theory in practice.

Please also note that the structure of this book does *not* follow the order of the list in the previous section. This is because we believe in a more implementation-based approach, and the first element of maintaining an analytics solution comes at the end of the list. The actual exam is also not structured in the same order as the list, so we'll present the questions in this guide to you in random order.

2 Read the complete exam details here: "Study Guide for Exam DP-600: Implementing Analytics Solutions Using Microsoft Fabric" (*https://oreil.ly/FHqUs*).

There's a key point to note when taking exams from Microsoft nowadays: you can't expect to pass them if all you've done is read a study guide like this one plus the documentation from Microsoft Learn. You also need to gain practical experience by working with the technology, so we'd like to encourage you to try out everything you read about in this book.

This book will help you understand the technical areas and knowledge you'll need to pass the DP-600 exam. It will walk you through the different areas of the exam, teach you how to get started, and introduce you to the baseline curriculum of the exam. You can use it as a study guide, a source of practice questions for the exam (see the question bank at the back of this book), and a reference source for future projects. But you also need practical, hands-on experience with real life implementations and projects in the Microsoft Fabric platform. In other words, passing the exam is not something you can just read your way to!

In the past, some of the Microsoft exams mainly tested candidates on their memory capabilities, the questions asked candidates to recall hard facts from the documentation, rather than how they would actually perform implementations in Microsoft's different technology areas. But more recently, the exams have shifted to measuring candidates' skill levels, and that means candidates need to have practical experience.

Book Summary

This book contains eight chapters spread over three sections. Chapter 1 provides an introduction to Microsoft Fabric, and Chapter 2 will guide you through the different ways to implement integration. Chapter 3 covers transformations, and Chapter 4 covers query and analytics capabilities. Chapter 5 shows you how to build semantic models, and Chapter 6 shows you how to manage enterprise scale models. Chapter 7 is a guide to governance and security, and Chapter 8 covers the lifecycle of development.

Chapter 9, the final chapter, is a question bank with 100 practice questions that you can work through to help prepare yourself for the exam. Note that none of these questions are the same ones you'll find on the actual exam; they're practice questions that are designed to help you test your skills and get used to taking test questions as they appear on the exam. Taking them will help you get familiar with the question types, how to read and understand the questions, and how to manage your time on the exam.

Each of the chapters is self-contained, and we've tried to make each chapter as independent of the others as possible. However, you'll see references to other chapters and sections throughout the book, to remind you of details and context. This will help you see the big picture when using this book as a reference guide.

We've also tried to make this book as accessible as possible for a broad range of readers with varying levels of experience with Microsoft Fabric. If you're new to the platform, we encourage you to start with Chapter 1 and read the book from start to finish. Or, if you're an experienced Microsoft Fabric user, feel free to jump around and focus on the chapters that will help you sharpen your existing skills.

With all of that said, we, Brian and Valerie, wish you the best of luck on the exam, and we hope this book serves you well in getting you started on your personal journey to certification.

Conventions Used in This Book

The following typographical conventions are used in this book:

Italic
: Indicates new terms, URLs, email addresses, filenames, and file extensions.

`Constant width`
: Used for program listings, as well as within paragraphs to refer to program elements such as variable or function names, databases, data types, environment variables, statements, and keywords.

`Constant width bold`
: Shows commands or other text that should be typed literally by the user.

`Constant width italic`
: Shows text that should be replaced with user-supplied values or by values determined by context.

This element signifies a tip or suggestion.

This element signifies a general note.

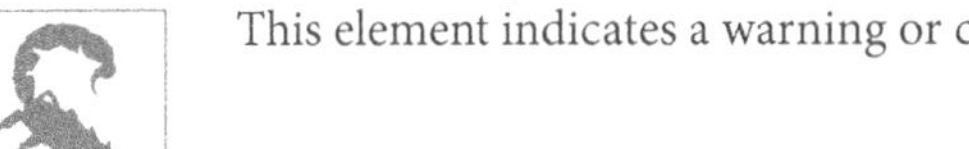

This element indicates a warning or caution.

O'Reilly Online Learning

For more than 40 years, *O'Reilly Media* has provided technology and business training, knowledge, and insight to help companies succeed.

Our unique network of experts and innovators share their knowledge and expertise through books, articles, and our online learning platform. O'Reilly's online learning platform gives you on-demand access to live training courses, in-depth learning paths, interactive coding environments, and a vast collection of text and video from O'Reilly and 200+ other publishers. For more information, visit *https://oreilly.com*.

How to Contact Us

Please address comments and questions concerning this book to the publisher:

O'Reilly Media, Inc.
141 Stony Circle, Suite 195
Santa Rosa, CA 95401
800-889-8969 (in the United States or Canada)
707-827-7019 (international or local)
707-829-0104 (fax)
support@oreilly.com
https://oreilly.com/about/contact.html

We have a web page for this book, where we list errata and any additional information. You can access this page at *https://oreil.ly/microsoft-fabric-analytics-study-guide*.

For news and information about our books and courses, visit *https://oreilly.com*.

Find us on LinkedIn: *https://linkedin.com/company/oreilly-media*.

Watch us on YouTube: *https://youtube.com/oreillymedia*.

Acknowledgements

From Brian

Writing a book has been on my wish list for a very long time, and I've finally fulfilled this ambition thanks to my collaboration with the talented Valerie Junk.

This project was only made possible through the opportunity provided by O'Reilly. I owe our editor, Shira Evans, a huge thank-you for her steadfast support and the many hours she spent keeping us on track and on time throughout the demanding schedule.

I also owe a substantial debt to the technical reviewers Nikola Ilic, Alexander Arvidsson, Ben Weissman, Reitse Eskens, and Johnny Winter, whose meticulous scrutiny of every page and testing of every code snippet ensured the accuracy required of a successful certification guide.

I also extend a massive thank-you to the fantastic crew behind *Guy in a Cube*, Adam Saxton and Patrick LeBlanc, for writing the foreword. Your work is truly an inspiration to the entire community.

This type of work is certainly a marathon, not a sprint. To my lifelong partner and spouse, Christa, thank you for the silent hours, the TV series we had to miss, and your unwavering belief in me no matter what endeavor I choose to pursue.

Finally, to you, the reader: I sincerely hope this guide helps you pass the DP-600 exam and, more importantly, unlocks your potential as a successful Microsoft Fabric Analytics Engineer.

From Valerie

Writing this book has been a valuable learning experience. Working on a project of this size together with Brian Bønk definitely pushed me to grow in new ways.

Thanks to O'Reilly for the opportunity, and to our editor, Shira Evans, for guiding us through every step. And thanks to the technical reviewers Alexander Arvidsson, Johnny Winter, Ben Weissman, Reitse Eskens, and Nikola Ilic, for taking the time to review all the content carefully.

A special thanks to my partner, Jochem van Iterson, for the support, tea, and snacks during long writing days. And thanks again to Alexander Arvidsson, who was a great sparring partner whenever I needed to talk things through.

CHAPTER 1
Introduction to Microsoft Fabric and the Certification Content

In this chapter, we'll introduce you to the Microsoft Fabric platform and give you an overview of all its bits and pieces. We'll give you a high-level view of the internal services in Microsoft Fabric, and we'll also introduce you to the certification path from Microsoft. In the subsequent chapters, we'll dive into specific details of each service as needed for the exam.

Key Components and Architecture

The Microsoft Fabric platform includes a list of services, as you'll see in Figure 1-1. These services are, as a joined group of services, the catalog of things you can do.

Some people are overwhelmed by the list of services and capabilities within Microsoft Fabric. But you don't need to use them all; they're merely options for you to choose from when building your own solutions, based on your specific needs.

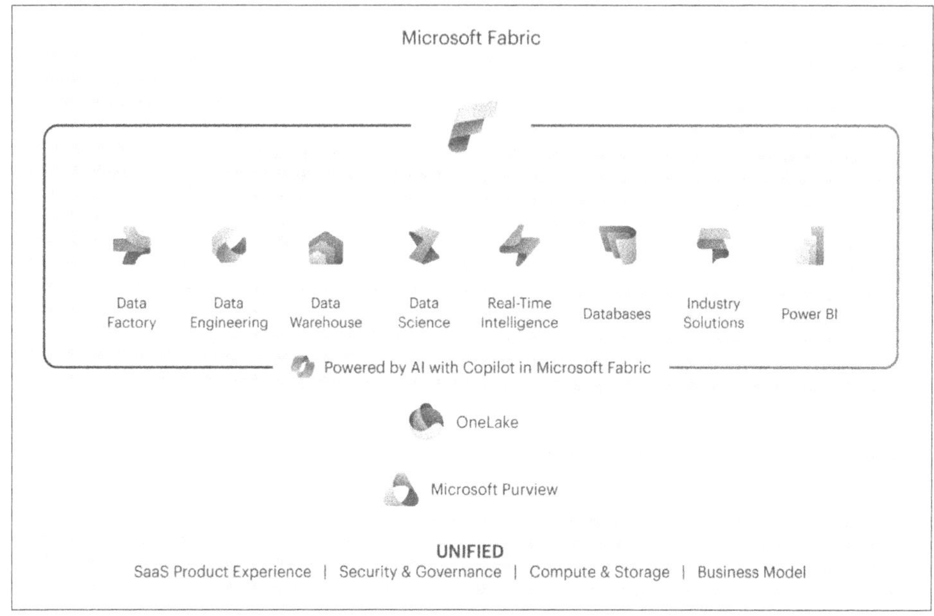

Figure 1-1. The complete Fabric platform with all services

Here, we list the icons in Figure 1-1 and provide a high-level description of the service each icon represents:

Data Factory
This service lets you access dataflows and pipelines, with which you can ingest, prepare, and transform data from a long list of sources, such as the built-in lakehouse, warehouse, and eventhouse.

Analytics
This service lets you create lakehouses, notebooks, Spark job definitions, and other elements to support the implementation of the process of collecting, storing, analyzing, and processing large volumes of data. This also includes options to create machine learning models, conduct experiments, and work with notebooks in both PySpark and Python to create your needed AI solutions. Here, you can also work with data agents and environments.

Databases
This is a built-in SQL database in Fabric that's based on the Azure SQL Database. It provides ease of setup and configuration, and with automated backup and storage in OneLake, it adds support for application-based storage known from the native SQL database.

Fabric IQ
With this service, you can define standards and semantics for your business and reuse them all over your company. You can also create and maintain the main definitions you use in your business, plus your internal business relationships. You can also use the elements from this service for data agents and other services inside Fabric.

Power BI
This service is the industry standard for reporting and analytics. With supporting services like dataflows, org apps, scorecards, dashboards, and paginated reports, you'll have a full stack of services to support your analytical needs.

Real-Time Intelligence
This service lets you handle data in motion with fast-paced zero-extract, transform, load (zero-ETL) transformations and very low latency. It will ingest all your telemetry data and let you handle it when you need to with underlying services like eventhouses, real-time dashboards, activators, rules, and event-driven actions.

OneLake
This is the one place for all your data in Microsoft Fabric. It offers an open storage model for all services and provides ease of sharing, securing, and managing your valuable data.

In Chapter 2, we'll dive into the details of these icons that are a part of the DP-600 exam.

This list of services is also supported by a list of main elements, which can be found in the main menu to the left of the Fabric GUI canvas, as shown in Figure 1-2.

The details of these main elements are as follows:

Workspaces
: You can click this icon to find the workspaces you have access to from the entire list of workspaces. There may be more workspaces across your organization, but this list will be filtered to only show the ones you have access to.

OneLake Catalog
: This is the entry point to getting an overview of the workspaces and items you can use. There's also an area called Govern that gives you an overview of some of the governance perspectives of Microsoft Fabric. We get into the details of governance later in this book.

Monitor
: Here, you can find an overview of and status updates on the jobs, notebook executions, pipeline runs, etc. that are going on inside your Fabric tenant.

Real-Time Hub
: This is your entry point for working with streaming data and data in motion. Here, you'll find pre-created items and objects you can interact with, and you'll also be able to create your own Fabric items and objects directly from this entry point.

Workloads
: Here, you can add a custom workload, which is a third-party provider that has created services in Fabric for you to use (some of which are paid services).

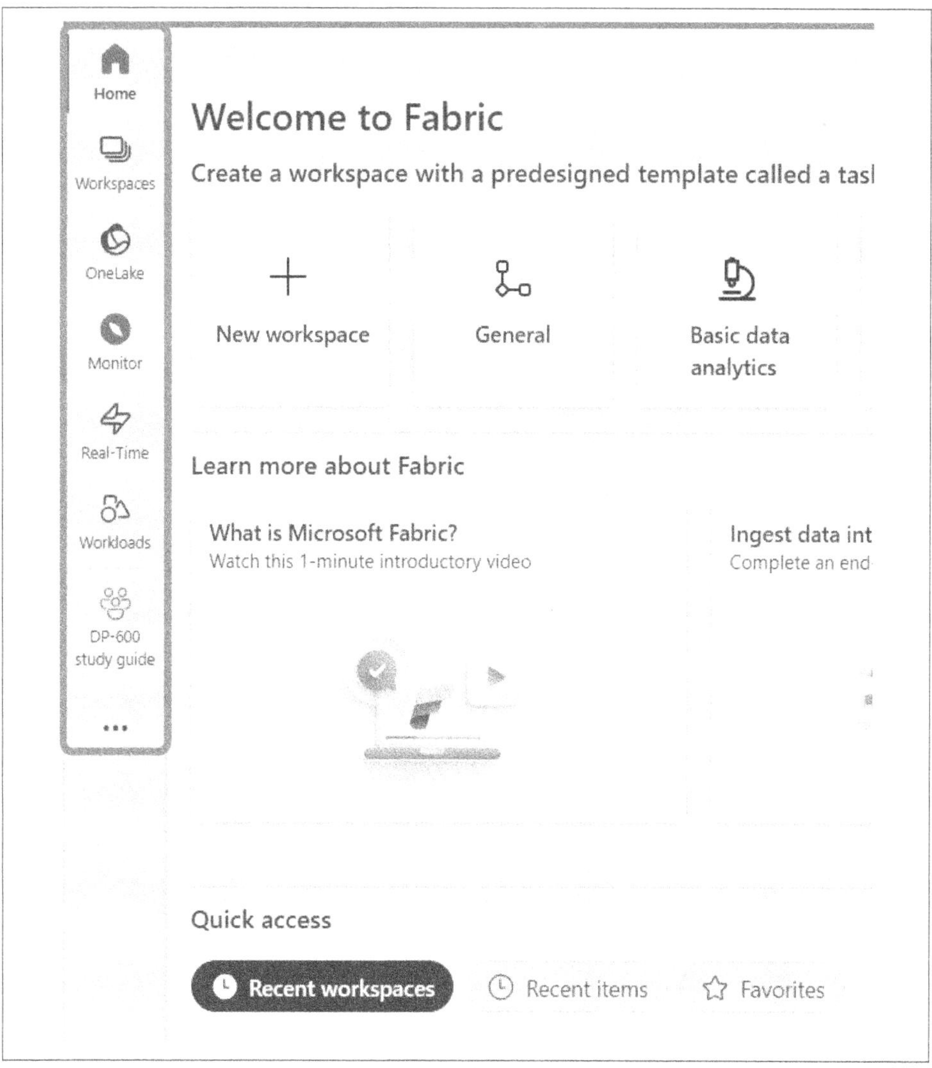

Figure 1-2. List of main elements in Microsoft Fabric

There are also the following additional options, which you can find in the overflow menu (the three dots at the bottom of the left-hand menu in Figure 1-2):

Apps
: Here, you can find any apps you have created and deployed to the app catalog.

Metrics

Here, you can directly work with scorecards and create metric sets, which are also called *goals*. The underlying engine maintains these goals to give you an over-time perspective on each of the metric sets. To maintain the over-time perspective of each goal, the engine automatically creates a new semantic model.

All these possibilities give any organization, from the small business to the largest enterprise, the opportunity to build an analytical solution tailored to fit its specific needs.

A Brief History of the Certification Content

When Microsoft Fabric hit the market, it didn't just make a splash, it arrived like a storm, transforming the landscape of the Microsoft Analytics ecosystem and redefining how we think about data platforms. With its seamless integration of services, powerful analytics capabilities, and end-to-end SaaS delivery, Fabric has truly taken the Microsoft data platform to the next level.

If you've been in the data world long enough to remember the days before cloud computing, when everything had to be installed and maintained on premises, then you've witnessed an incredible evolution. Back then, the idea of spinning up an entire analytics environment in the cloud in just minutes would have seemed like science fiction. But we've come a long way, from physical servers and manual patching to fully managed, cloud-native services that handle everything from ingestion to AI-powered insights. With each leap forward, we've completely reimagined the way we approach business intelligence, data engineering, integration, and visualization.

And through it all, Microsoft certifications have been right there with us, providing structure, direction, and validation for professionals looking to prove their expertise. Since the early '90s, the *Microsoft Certified Professional* (MCP) program has been a cornerstone of technical development. Back in 1992, certifications revolved around products like LAN Manager, Windows 3.1, and the early versions of SQL Server. These early certifications laid the groundwork for a culture of continuous learning and credentialing that remains strong to this day.

Since then, each new Microsoft platform release has been accompanied by a wave of certifications tailored to help IT professionals, developers, and data practitioners deepen their skills and demonstrate their capabilities, and Microsoft Fabric is no exception.

With the arrival of this powerful new platform came the introduction of a brand-new certification track. The first to launch was the DP-600: Microsoft Fabric Analytics Engineer Associate certification, which was designed specifically for professionals who want to showcase their knowledge and expertise in building, managing, and optimizing analytical solutions in Microsoft Fabric.

Soon after, Microsoft released another role-based certification for the platform. It was DP-700: Microsoft Fabric Data Engineer Associate, and as it entered the scene, it absorbed some of the infrastructure- and architecture-focused content that had initially been part of DP-600. This shift allowed curriculum developers to change DP-600's focus to put even more emphasis on analytics, governance, and data insights, solidifying its place as the go-to credential for analytics engineers working in Microsoft Fabric.

This study guide is built around the current DP-600: Microsoft Fabric Analytics Engineer Associate certification. Whether you're just getting started with Fabric or you're a seasoned business intelligence (BI) or data professional making the jump into this new platform, this guide is designed to support you every step of the way. It covers the full certification scope, from data ingestion and transformation, to designing and maintaining analytic solutions, to applying governance and security best practices across the platform.

More than just a test-prep resource, this guide is a source of practical insights, hands-on examples, and real-world context to help you not only prepare for the exam but also succeed as a Microsoft Fabric analytics engineer in your day-to-day work.

End-to-End Analytics Overview

Now that you have the basic information, we can begin to create an end-to-end analytics solution using the possibilities provided by Microsoft Fabric.

No matter what our end goal is, we need to build a solution that reads data from sources, manages the data in compliance with business requirements, and presents the data in an easy-to-understand manner that users and applications can employ in value-added activities.

Figure 1-3 shows an example of this process.

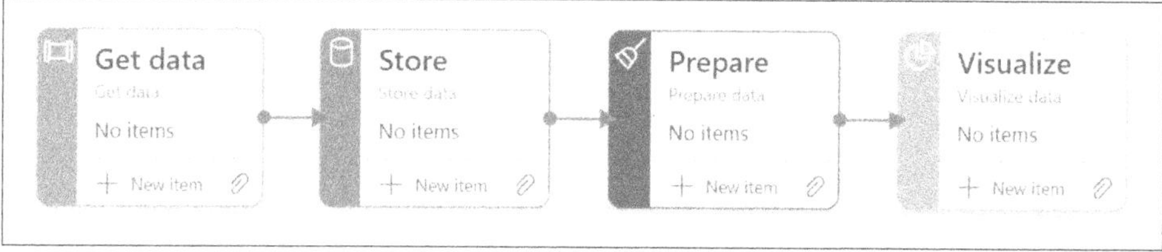

Figure 1-3. A simple illustration of an analytical process on a platform

To help us build a solution like the one in the figure (which we've used the task flow feature to illustrate), we have all the services from Microsoft Fabric to pick and choose from:

Getting data
: To help us get data, we have the Data Engineering, Data Factory, Data Science, Power BI, and Real-Time Intelligence services.

Storing data
: To store data, we can use the Databases, Data Warehouse, Data Engineering, Power BI, and Real-Time Intelligence services. The common denominator here is OneLake, with the exceptions of the import mode semantic models and Real-Time Intelligence (see the Note box for details).

Real-Time Intelligence and the eventhouse use a proprietary storage format in the Kusto engine (the underlying engine for Real-Time Intelligence storage). You can read more about the Kusto engine in Chapter 4. You can also create a copy of OneLake, and we'll cover that later in this book.

Preparing data
: The Databases, Power BI, Data Engineering, Data Warehouse, and Real-Time Intelligence services can all support the data preparation phase.

Visualizing data
: To visualize data, we have options from the Power BI and Real-Time Intelligence services.

We won't dive deeper into the architectural approach of building analytical solutions based on Microsoft Fabric, as that is part of the DP-700 certification.

When working with Microsoft Fabric and data in the platform, you may wonder about the governance aspect. Although the platform has some built-in features for governance, an enterprise-ready Microsoft Fabric platform implementation often also requires the Microsoft Purview service.

Microsoft Purview is a unified data governance, compliance, and risk management platform that helps organizations manage, protect, and get more value from their data. It's an open platform that not only embraces Microsoft services but also gives access to third-party services around the data and analytics platforms. This makes Purview a one-stop shop for managing governance, compliance, and risk.

Setting Up a Fabric Environment

In this study guide, we haven't included explicit labs for you to go through at your own pace. Instead, to get acquainted with the platform, we highly encourage you to try the official labs and drills from Microsoft Learn (*https://oreil.ly/xrXRV*). These lab drills are based on an existing Fabric environment, and to help you get started, we've included the following quick guide.

To use Microsoft Fabric, you need two things:

- A Fabric capacity
- A Power BI Pro license

You'll only need the Power BI Pro license if you want to use Power BI as a service. You can use Fabric without Power BI.

If you buy an F64 capacity or more, only your developers will need the Power BI Pro license. Your end users will be covered automatically by the F64+ capacity.

Fabric Capacity

The Fabric capacity is what drives all the compute operations when you're working with data and operations in the platform. Think of it as the CPU, memory, and network needed to load, read, and manipulate data.

A Fabric capacity comes in different sizes that are measured in stock-keeping units (SKUs), with the smallest one called F2 (with *F* standing for Fabric) and the currently largest one called F2048. A Fabric capacity can use the same number of SKUs as the number after the *F*.

How much capacity each service and process uses is measured in capacity units (CUs). The number of CUs a service uses can be any positive number, so for example, a service with an F2 capacity can run four parallel threads if each thread only uses 0.5 CUs.

The process of creating a Fabric capacity starts in the Azure portal (*https://oreil.ly/qCGRw*). Figures 1-4, 1-5, and 1-6 provide you with a quick guide to easily getting started on creating a Fabric capacity.

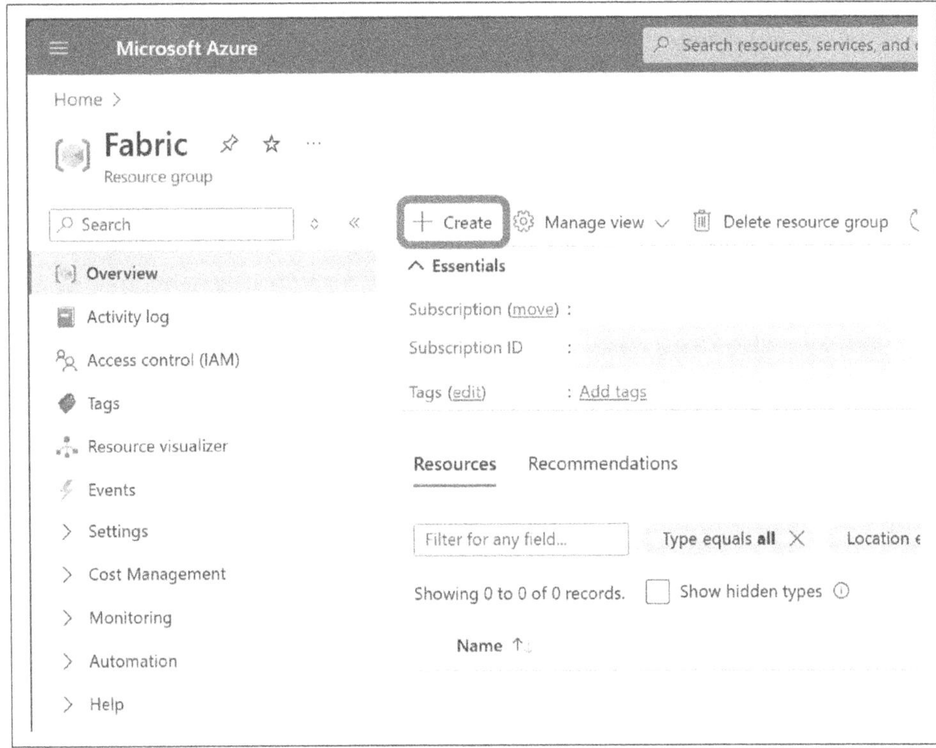

Figure 1-4. Select the + Create button in your resource group

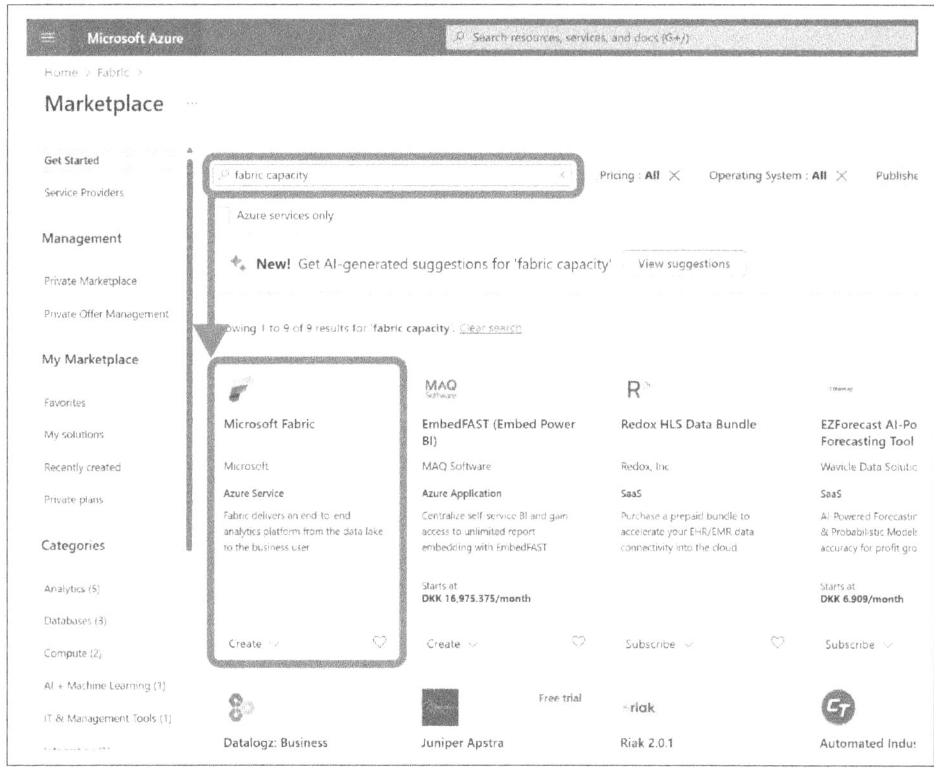

*Figure 1-5. Search for **fabric capacity** and select Create*

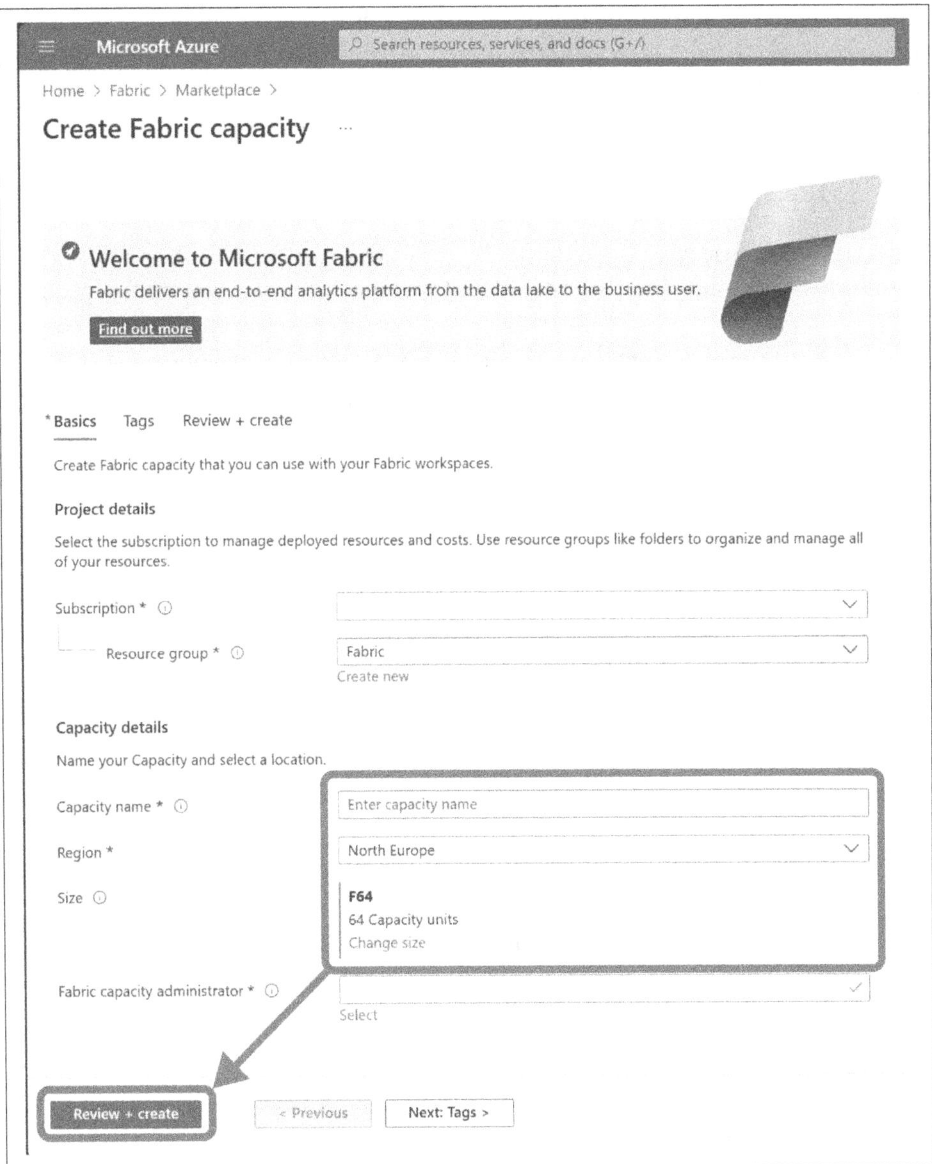

Figure 1-6. Give your capacity a name, choose a region and size, and configure the rest of the settings according to your needs

You can also create a trial capacity in Microsoft Fabric. This is automatically created when you begin to work with Fabric items in the Fabric portal (*https://oreil.ly/bDSdg*), and when you do so, you'll be prompted to start the trial capacity.

If you have a non-Fabric-enabled workspace and you're trying to create a Fabric-specific item for the first time, you'll automatically be upgraded to a trial license for Microsoft Fabric.

However, this license has a limitation of five trial capacities per tenant, so you may see a notification regarding limitation of Fabric trial capacities when you try this process.

A Fabric Trial is equivalent to an F64 capacity, without access to all features. For instance, you won't have access to Copilot when using a trial capacity, and a trial capacity is valid for 60 days from activation.

Throughout this book, we've provided guides, questions, and exercises from Microsoft Learn, which contains elements of an XML (XML for Analytics) endpoint in Microsoft Fabric. If you want to set this up before reading the rest of the book, please refer to Chapter 8 for details.

Creating a Fabric-Enabled Workspace

Every item in Microsoft Fabric is contained in a *workspace*, which is a consolidated placeholder or group of items that you can group by business area, technological area, or anything else to fit your business requirements. Workspaces can also work as a security context for access to data and insights. See Chapter 7 for more information about security and governance.

To create a workspace, find the Workspaces button in the main menu to the left of the Fabric portal, type in the name of your workspace, expand the Advanced section, and select either a Fabric capacity or a Trial capacity (see Figure 1-7).

Create a workspace
Name *
Name this workspace
Description
Describe this workspace
Domain
Assign to a domain (optional)
Learn more about workspace settings
Workspace image
Upload
Reset
Advanced
Contact list *
Enter users and groups
License mode
Pro
Select Pro to use basic Power BI features and collaborate on reports, dashboards, and scorecards. To access a Pro workspace, users need Pro per-user licenses. Learn more
Trial
Select Trial to assign this workspace to a Fabric trial capacity. A Microsoft Fabric trial capacity allows user to explore the capabilities of Microsoft Fabric like Data Factory, Data Engineering and Real-Time Intelligence among others. Learn more
Premium per-user
Select Premium per-user to collaborate using Power BI Premium features, including advanced dataflows, and datamarts. To collaborate and share content in a Premium per-user workspace, users need Premium per-user licenses. Learn more
Premium capacity
Embedded
Fabric capacity
Select Fabric capacity if the workspace will be hosted in a Microsoft Fabric capacity. With Fabric capacities, users can create Microsoft Fabric items and collaborate with others using Fabric features and experiences. Explore new capabilities in Power BI, Data Factory, Data Engineering, and Real-Time Intelligence, among others. Learn more

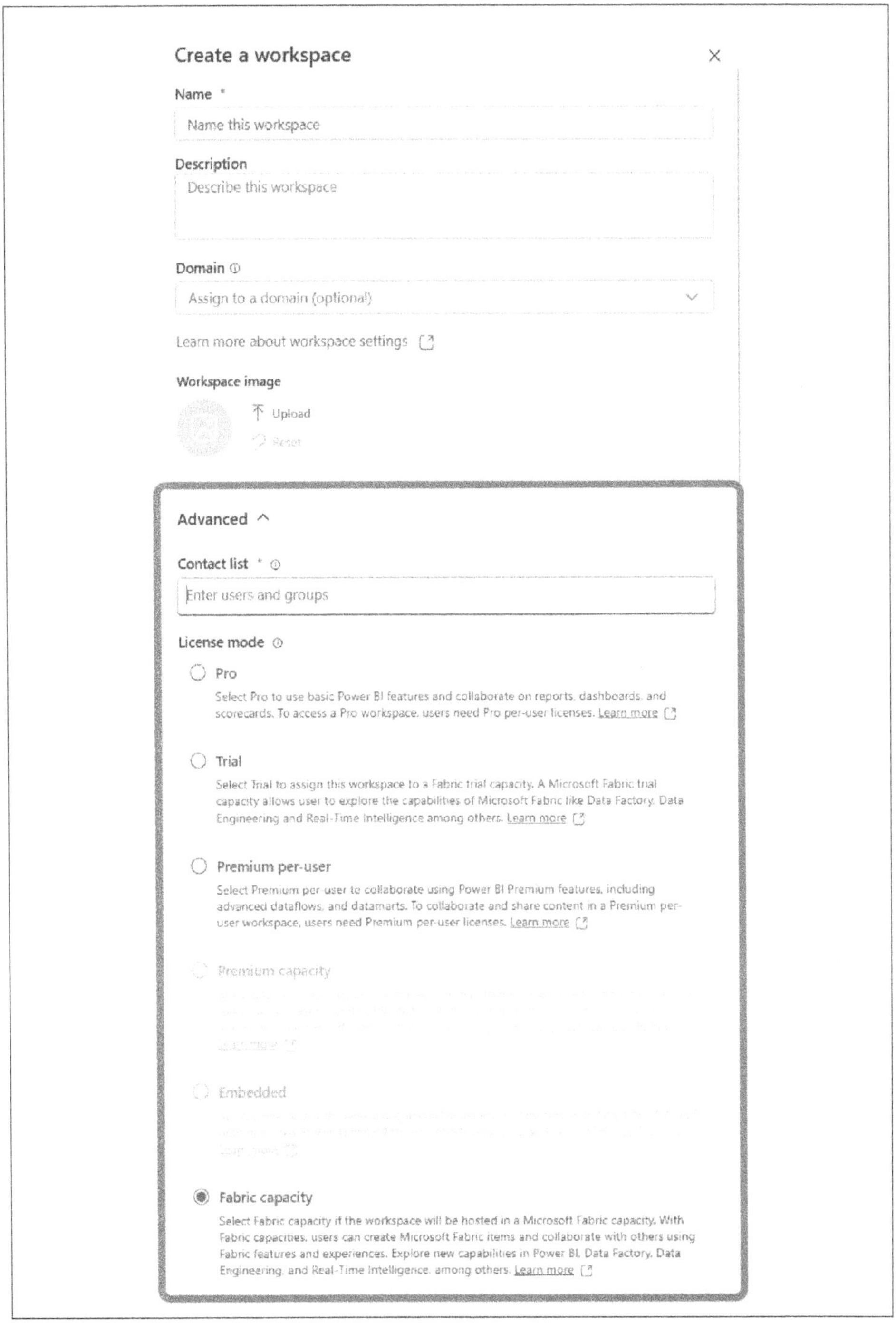

Figure 1-7. Selecting a Fabric capacity when creating a new workspace

For now, leave the rest of the settings as they are and click Apply.

Configuring a Workspace

After creating a given workspace in Microsoft Fabric, you'll have a list of options for configuring it. You can find the Workspace settings at the top of the workspace to the right. Figure 1-8 shows the main menu items in the workspace settings.

Workspace settings

General
License info
Azure connections
System storage
Git integration
OneLake
Workspace identity
Network security
Monitoring
Power BI
Delegated Settings
Data Engineering/Science
Data Factory

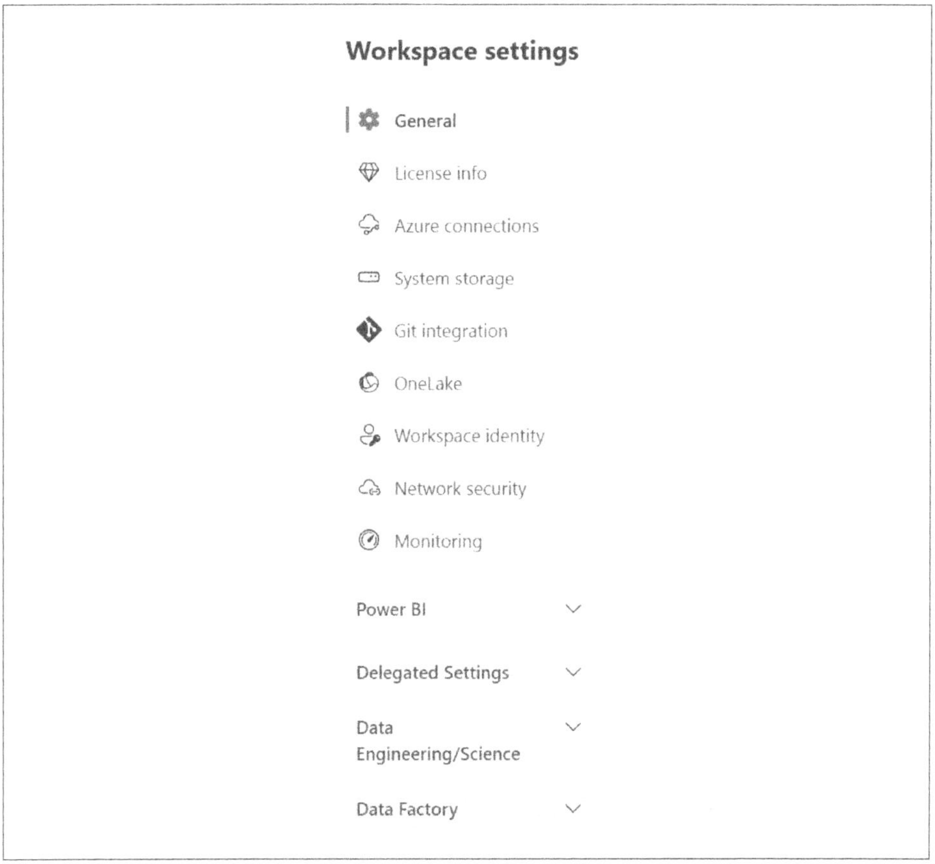

Figure 1-8. Main menu items in the workspace settings menu

Most of the settings in Figure 1-8 are out of scope for the content of this book. We'll cover the relevant ones in detail in Chapter 8, but we'll provide only high-level descriptions of the others, as you'll find in this section.

The key settings in Figure 1-8 are as follows:

General
: In this section, you can configure the main part of the workspace, including the name and workspace image. You can add a description, join it to a domain, edit the workspace contacts, add OneDrive security groups, and delete the workspace. Note that you'll rarely need to change General settings since they're high level.

License info
: Here, you can view and change the license information for the workspace. The license information is the configuration for capacity usage, and you can change the workspace's usage of Fabric capacity.

  You can also get the connection link for the workspace, which you'll use to connect third-party applications to the workspace and make programmatic changes to it (e.g., API and Graph connections).

Azure connections
: Here, you can configure the link to an Azure Data Lake Storage Gen 2 account to store the data from your dataflows (see Chapter 4), and you can also connect the workspace to a Log Analytics workspace so you can send logs there.

System storage
: Here, you can get a quick view of the system storage usage as a total and grouped by item name and size.

Git integration
: Here, to easily configure Git integration with your workspace, you can set up a connection to either GitHub or Azure DevOps. (Note that Git integration is not part of this book as it is out-of-scope for the exam.)

  If you're using GitHub, you must manually maintain personal access tokens (PATs). This is different from using Azure DevOps, which maintains the security connection through the single sign-on (SSO) functionality from Azure Entra ID.

OneLake
: Here, you can download the OneLake file explorer app, which gives you a fully integrated look at the raw files in the OneLake that's directly embedded in your normal local file explorer on your local computer.

  You can also enable caching for shortcuts (see Chapter 6). This cache will store some of the data from the shortcuts directly in the OneLake for the workspace, to speed up the reading of the data.

Workspace identity
: Here, you can configure the workspace identities for other applications outside of Microsoft Fabric to work with the items and processes within your workspace.

When you click the green + Workspace identity button, Fabric will create a managed service principal to be used outside of Fabric for application access.

Network security
: Here, you can create connections to private endpoints in Azure. You'll use *private endpoints* to connect to services in a virtual private network, and they enable Microsoft Fabric to read and write data and other information from those specific services.

Monitoring
: Here, you can set up workspace monitoring. You can use a standard set of workspace items to enable deep monitoring of what happens in your workspace, and that will create an eventhouse and an eventstream that will monitor the events in your workspace for further analysis.

Power BI
: In this section of the menu, you have access to three main areas:

  General
  : Here, you can configure access control for apps and templates (if enabled in the workspace), and you can enable or disable the option to work with a semantic model directly in the web user interface (see Chapter 3).

  Data connections
  : Here, you can enable an extra security feature that will disconnect the report from the underlying semantic model if the end user edits the report. This can, in some situations, help with the security and governance of the entire setup in the workspace.

  Embed codes
  : With Microsoft Fabric, you have the option of embedding a Power BI report in your own website without end users seeing the Fabric portal. If you have created an embedded Power BI report, you'll find the codes here to maintain that setup.

Delegated Settings
: In this section, you can enable or disable the option of letting users and applications access the workspace's OneLake by using a shared access signature (SAS) token.

Data Engineering/Science

Even though this section of the menu is not a part of the DP600 exam, we have added the details here to help you get a full perspective on the settings.

Here, you can specify options for the use of Spark in the Spark settings. You have five options:

Pool
: Here, you can specify the different Spark pool sizes of the Fabric environment. By default, there will be a *starter pool* that's faster to start than a manually configured Spark pool (which you can also configure here).

Environment
: Here, you'll have the option to configure the settings for environments in the workspace. A default environment comes with options to configure Spark properties, use of libraries, how notebooks will use Spark, and how the Spark job definitions handle processing of data. One of the best features here is the option to enable the Native Execution Engine (NEE), which will accelerate the speed of notebook execution. You can also configure standard Spark pools usage and setup, upload your own custom Spark libraries, and configure which standard libraries can be used in this specific workspace.

Jobs
: Here, you can configure the setup of execution in Spark jobs. This setting allows you to reserve the maximum number of cores for a Spark job to run, which will lower the number of parallel jobs available to run. You can also configure the timeout of the Spark pools, which will help you stop the Spark pools if they are not in use for the specified amount of time.

High concurrency
: Here, you can configure the option of running multiple notebooks on the same Spark session, which will help you optimize the exertion of parallel processes. You can do the same for notebooks running inside a pipeline (more on notebooks and pipelines later in this book).

Automatic log
: Here, you can enable the option to track machine learning models and experiments from notebooks on their metrics, parameters, and models.

Data Factory
: Here, you can configure the runtime settings for *Apache Airflow*, which is an orchestrator for execution of processes built using code. (Note that it's out of scope for this book.)

Summary

In this chapter, you read about the beginnings of the Microsoft Fabric platform, where it originated, and how the certification processes from Microsoft have emerged through time. We showed you how to set up your Fabric environment and configure your workspace settings, which are cornerstones of the environment for working with Fabric and set the baseline for the development cycle.

PART I
Preparing Data

An analytics platform, especially one as comprehensive as Microsoft Fabric, is fundamentally useless without a reliable, consistent flow of data. Getting data into the system is not just a necessary first step; it's a critical process that requires you to understand various source connections, ingestion methods, and optimal storage destinations. In a platform designed for end-to-end analytics, data can originate from countless systems, and you need to be proficient in utilizing a variety of tools, from simple connections in Power BI to sophisticated ingestion capabilities like dataflows. Moreover, with powerful, purpose-built storage services like the lakehouse, warehouse, and eventhouse, you need to choose the right place to put your data to maximize performance and govern your analytical workloads.

In this part, we'll explore how you can master all these tasks to build a solid data foundation in Fabric.

We begin by guiding you through the primary entry points into the Fabric portal, where you'll manage and create new data connections. Next, we cover the hands-on process of creating these new connections using both the familiar Power BI Desktop application and the Fabric portal web experience. After that, we introduce the two main pathways for discovering and monitoring your assets: the OneLake catalog and the Real-Time hub, which provide a high-level view of your data estate. We then cover the central OneLake service, the unified storage layer for nearly all your data, showing you how to use, share, and reuse data from this centralized location. Finally, we dive deep into the differences among the three primary storage services, the lakehouse, warehouse, and eventhouse, to help you choose the correct place for your data, and we conclude by showing you how to set up integration between OneLake and the eventhouse.

Building on this foundation, we transition from ingestion to data preparation. Because raw data often contains duplicates, missing values, or inconsistent formats, we explore a variety of techniques for cleaning, enriching, and transforming your data directly in Fabric. We start by showing you how to create reusable logic using views, functions, and stored procedures, allowing you to define transformations early in the process rather than waiting until the data reaches Power BI. We also cover essential operations like joins, aggregations, and filters, and we provide guidance on organizing your data into a star schema, a standard modeling pattern designed for fast, intuitive analysis and reporting.

In the final part of this journey, we move beyond preparation to focus on querying and analyzing the data you have built. We introduce the visual query editor, a web-based tool that allows you to alter and analyze data structures using a visual interface. For those who prefer code-based approaches, we dive into the Transact-SQL (T-SQL) world of Fabric to leverage the well-known SQL language for deep analysis. Finally, we introduce the KQL language used within Real-Time Intelligence to provide you with the skills to query and visualize streaming data within the Fabric environment.

CHAPTER 2

Getting Data

No analytics platform works without data. In this chapter, you'll learn how to ingest data by using various methods directly in the Fabric environment.

First, we'll guide you through the entry points in the Fabric portal, where you'll work with existing and new data connections. Next, we'll dive into the processes of creating new connections in different ways by using both the Power BI Desktop and the Fabric portal. Then, we'll guide you through the three data storing services: the lakehouse, warehouse, and eventhouse. Making the choice among these three can seem cumbersome and difficult, but we'll help you understand them so you can choose the correct place to store your data. To wrap up the chapter, we'll show you how to set up integration between OneLake and the eventhouse and connect this data with the semantic models in your data estate. We'll also cover the OneLake service, where you store all your data (with a single exception; more on that later), and we'll show you how to use, share, and reuse data from a centralized place.

Discovering Data with the OneLake Catalog and Real-Time Hub

In Microsoft Fabric, you have two entryways into a high-level view of your data estate: the OneLake catalog and the Real-Time hub, which have different uses.

The OneLake catalog gives you insights into the data that resides in the OneLake, but only the data you have access to. Even though there may be more data in the OneLake as an entire Fabric service, you, as the end user, can only see and discover the data you have a minimum of read access to.

The Real-Time hub gives you insights to the Real-Time artifacts in your tenant. Also, the security perspective of the Real-Time Hub is just like in the OneLake data hub: you only see what you have access to.

Now, let's dive into the details of each of them.

The OneLake Catalog

The OneLake catalog can be the first entry point for new business users who want to start working with reports and insights. It may also be the go-to starting point for many newcomers to Microsoft Fabric who want to find a specific item or browse to discover new ones. For some, the direct way of opening a workspace and beginning to work with items in the OneLake catalog is the easiest way to get started.

The OneLake catalog is also meant to be the entry point for the development of integrations, to get data from sources. It provides an overview of the data that's available, and it makes it easy to discover the existing elements found in the Fabric tenant.

Normally, any data analytics engineer would love to have access to everything, but sometimes, the reality is a bit different, as many organizations nowadays limit the developers' and engineers' access to data and items. So, each user who interacts with the OneLake catalog only sees a filtered view of all the items found in the tenant, based on their access levels to items and workspaces.

Figure 2-1 highlights the different areas of the OneLake catalog.

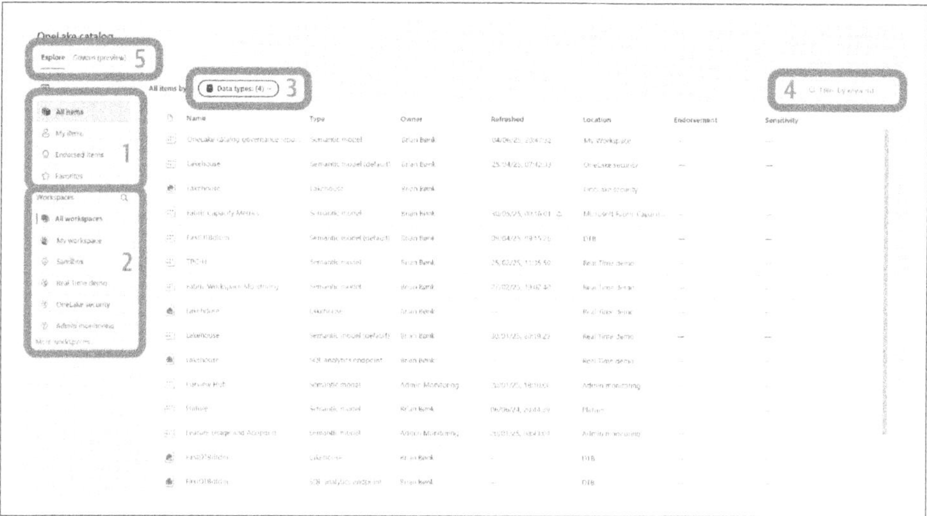

Figure 2-1. OneLake catalog overview

The details of these areas (numbered 1–5) are as follows:

Grouped items selector (area 1)
: Here, you can filter groupings of items based on their endorsement, your favorite items, or the items you are the owner of. You can also choose to see all items you have access to in the Fabric tenant.

Workspaces (area 2)
: This list shows you the workspaces you have access to. Here, you can either select the workspace you want to browse or search for the workspace by using the small magnifier icon to the right.

Filter (area 3)
: This selector and filter contains options to filter the view based on item types, which are grouped into five categories: Data, Insights, Processes, Solutions, and Configurations. In each category, you will find the specific item types you are searching for. It's also important to know that you can only select items from the same group of items, and you *can't* select items from two different groups at once.

Search bar (area 4)
: Here, you can search for anything, like item names, owners, workspaces, endorsements, and sensitivity. It's a free text search, and it works very quickly, with live filtering as you type.

Explore (area 5)
: Here, you'll find information about the governance status of your data. You'll get recommendations on actions you can take to improve the current governance status, and you'll also find links to tools for learning the governance features of Microsoft Fabric.

At the time of writing this book, there are two preview features in the OneLake catalog: the item grouping named Insights and the Govern part of the catalog. These two features are most likely to be added to the exam at a later stage, after their status has changed to generally available (GA).

The Real-Time Hub

The Real-Time hub (which is also found in the Fabric portal as Real-Time, in the left menu) is your one-stop shop for everything about streaming data. This includes connections, streams of data, event processing from the Fabric tenant, and the events happening in the Fabric capacity.

The Real-Time hub operates as the ingestion control plane within Microsoft Fabric's real-time data architecture. It supports the following:

- Connecting to CDC-enabled sources like Azure SQL DB and SQL Server through Event Hubs or Kafka
- Bridging ingestion from source systems to real-time consumers like eventstreams and eventhouses
- Working in conjunction with Azure Event Grid to ingest Fabric and Azure system events

The Real-Time hub in Microsoft Fabric offers a strategic capability for ingesting system-level events emitted by both Fabric and Azure services. These are not only limited to telemetry from user-defined applications; they also cover platform-generated events that signal state changes, health conditions, operational triggers, and resource lifecycles.

This system event ingestion is built on top of *Azure Event Grid,* which is a fully managed event routing service that enables reactive, event-driven patterns across distributed systems.

In this context, the Real-Time hub provides a powerful interface that surfaces relevant system events for discovery and routing, while Event Grid acts as the under-the-hood backbone that delivers those events from their source to consumers like an eventstream, eventhouse, or activator.

System events are structured messages that are automatically emitted by Microsoft Fabric or Azure services to indicate that something of significance has occurred, like 100% of the Fabric capacity having been used or a special file in the storage account having been deleted or changed. These system events include but are not limited to the following:

- Dataset refresh completion notices in Power BI
- Capacity utilization threshold warnings
- Workspace creation, modification, or deletion notices
- Dataflow failure alerts
- Eventstream deployment status updates

System events are standardized, contain rich context metadata, and follow consistent schemas. For example, a workspace creation event includes the workspace ID, creator identity, timestamp, and other useful operational attributes.

From a monitoring and orchestration perspective, these events are critical for building automation, enforcing governance, and triggering data pipelines in response to system changes.

When users open the Real-Time hub in Microsoft Fabric, they are presented with a curated interface that includes a category called *Fabric Events* and another called *Azure Events*. These are automatically populated with all the system events that the Real-Time hub can currently discover and ingest via Event Grid.

From there, users can do the following:

- Discover available system events across Fabric and Azure services.
- Enable routing of selected events to the eventstream for transformation or aggregation.
- Trigger rules using the activator to invoke actions (e.g., sending Teams alerts, starting pipelines) in response to specific events.

This simplifies what has historically been a complex event subscription process. Instead of manually wiring up Event Grid topics, endpoints, and event handlers, users can simply opt in to the event categories exposed by the Real-Time hub and configure routing with a few clicks.

OneLake Catalog versus Real-Time Hub

The main differences between the OneLake catalog and the Real-Time hub are found in Table 2-1.

Table 2-1. Differences between the OneLake catalog and the Real-Time hub

Topic	OneLake catalog	Real-Time hub
Discoverability	It gives the end user high-level insights into all existing items with deep search capabilities.	It gives the end user deep insights into the accessible items from Real-Time Intelligence in both Microsoft Fabric and in Microsoft Azure.
Creation of items	Users can't create items directly from the OneLake catalog.	Users can create all item types linked to Real-Time Intelligence and the activator.
Governance	From the Govern tab in the OneLake catalog, the user can get insights into the current state of all items in the tenant.	There's no built-in central governance overview, though some governance insights can be found in the details of each item.

Creating Connections and Ingesting or Accessing Data

When you create connections to data and either read it once or plan to permanently ingest it into the Fabric environment, you have several options for how to do so. We'll cover the following options from the perspective of the analyst role:

- Creating shortcuts to data from both inside and outside Fabric
- Implementing Dataflow Gen1 and Dataflow Gen2
- Creating data connections directly in Power BI
- Creating Connections to semantic models

There are more options than the ones mentioned here for ingesting data, such as Pipelines and notebooks. However, those options are out of scope for the DP-600 exam.

We'll go through each option in the following sections and describe the methods you need to know to work with them. We'll also cover some tips and tricks for some of the options.

Creating Shortcuts to Data from Inside and Outside Fabric

Microsoft Fabric has special connections to data called *shortcuts*. They don't move data to the place where you create the connection. Instead, they're pointers that indicate where data currently resides, and you can use them to read data when you need it.

The obvious benefit of this approach is that you don't need to move data and then create a copy of it. You merely read the data when you need it and always get the latest version.

These shortcuts exist in different flavors: from inside a single workspace, from outside the current workspace, and even from outside the tenant you are currently working in. And these shortcuts are not limited to other Fabric environments. You can also connect to Azure Data Lake Storage Gen2 and data environments from other vendors like Databricks, Snowflake, AWS, and other S3-compatible endpoints.

When creating *local shortcuts*, you can connect to the following items from both outside and inside your current workspace, if you have access to them:

- Kusto Query Language (KQL) databases
- Lakehouses
- Mirrored Azure Databricks catalogs
- Mirrored databases
- Semantic models
- SQL databases
- Warehouses
- Warehouse snapshots

Note that the shortcut functionality from KQL databases only works if the OneLake availability setting on the KQL database has been enabled. You can find the setting in Figure 2-2.

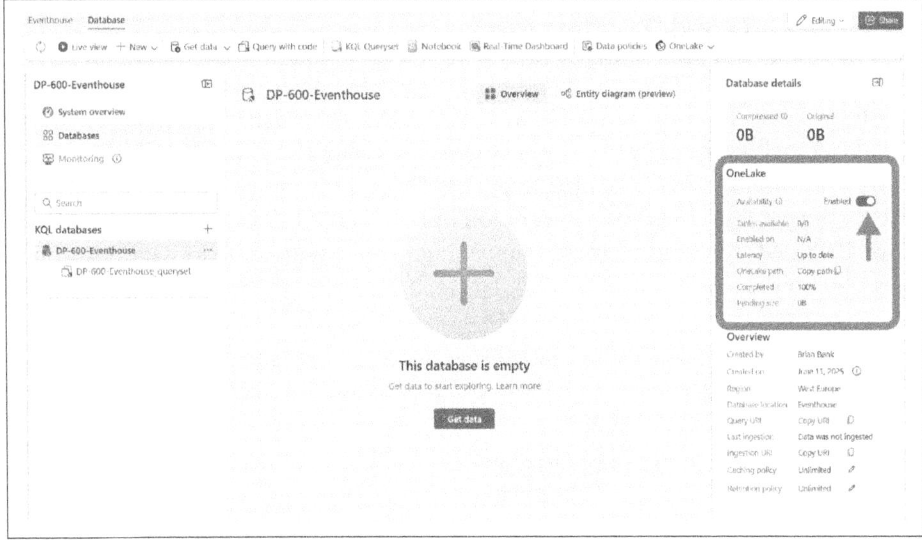

Figure 2-2. OneLake availability setting in KQL databases

When you create a shortcut, the user interface differs from item to item but the overall approach is the same: you create a connection to a data store without moving data based on the current user's or user principal's access to data.

All local shortcuts adhere to the current user's security context, and they filter the data based on this configuration. This also means that the developer can have one set of access configurations and the end user can have a different set of configurations. Each will still only see the data they have access to. This is the opposite of how external shortcuts work, and we discuss them next.

External shortcuts are the data we can set up to be read from outside Fabric. We can set up Amazon, Google, and Snowflake (to mention just a few) using *delegated authorization*, which means we can set up the shortcut and access to data but cannot inherit the current security context from that service. They are all configured using a specific set of credentials that are fitted to suit the external data provider.

This is a crucial difference between local shortcuts and external shortcuts. The security context will change when someone is using external shortcuts, and everyone will have access to the same data, no matter the user's specific security setting on the external data source.

Speaking of external data sources, there are other ways to work with them and ingest them directly into the Fabric environment. They are called *dataflows*, and we'll dive into them in the next section.

Dataflow Gen1 and Dataflow Gen2

When working with external data and the need to ingest, transform, and load it into Fabric, you have two UI-assisted options: Dataflow Gen1 and Dataflow Gen2. *Dataflow Gen1* has been in the Power BI area for years, and it was the first service to utilize the Power Query (or M) language directly in the browser. *Dataflow Gen2* is the new version of this UI-assisted integration option, and it brings custom destinations, more UI-based overview of what's happening, and options to load data faster than does Dataflow Gen1.

Dataflow Gen1 is slowly being replaced by Dataflow Gen2 in the entire exam. The features from Dataflow Gen1 are the same in Dataflow Gen2, with more features in Gen2.

We will start with Dataflow Gen1 and then transition to Dataflow Gen2.

Dataflow Gen1

Dataflow Gen1 is a UI-assisted approach that uses the Power Query language to read, transform, and save data in Fabric. Dataflow Gen1 consists of an ingestion engine with almost the same capabilities as the Power BI Desktop. It uses Power Query, and the destination resides inside the dataflow. It also uses a storage account behind the scenes, and you can configure this storage account to be an explicit one that you manage and create yourself from the Azure portal.

When you're creating new items, you'll find Dataflow Gen1 in the Get data and Prepare data sections of the Fabric menu (see Figure 2-3).

When you start to create a Dataflow Gen1 in Fabric, you'll see a screen asking you if you really want a Dataflow Gen1 and not a Dataflow Gen2 (see Figure 2-4).

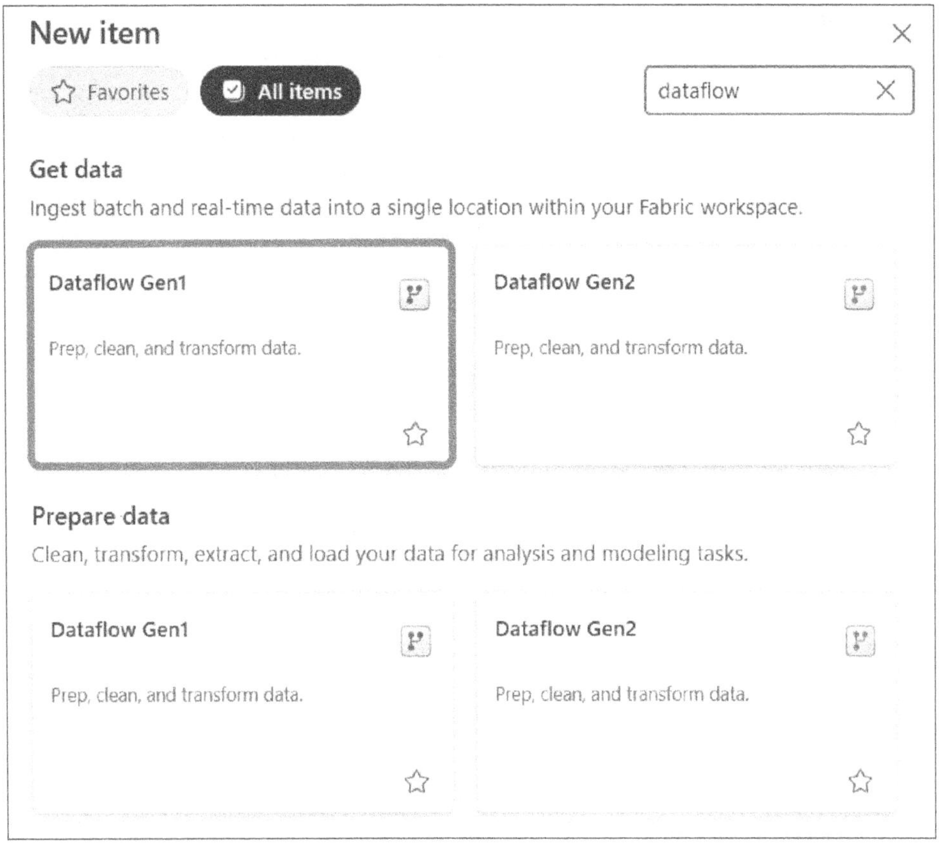

Figure 2-3. Fabric menu item for Dataflow Gen1

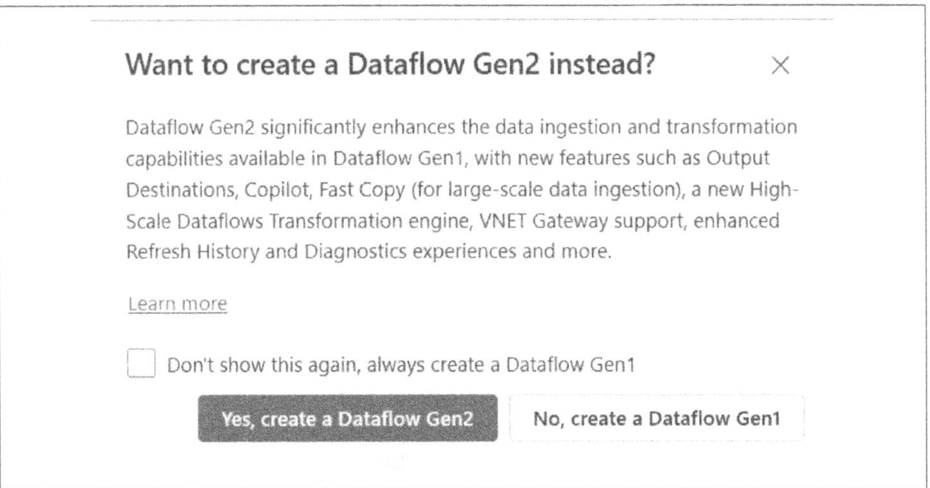

Want to create a Dataflow Gen2 instead?
Dataflow Gen2 significantly enhances the data ingestion and transformation capabilities available in Dataflow Gen1, with new features such as Output Destinations, Copilot, Fast Copy (for large-scale data ingestion), a new High-Scale Dataflows Transformation engine, VNET Gateway support, enhanced Refresh History and Diagnostics experiences and more.
Learn more
Don't show this again, always create a Dataflow Gen1
Yes, create a Dataflow Gen2
No, create a Dataflow Gen1

Favorites

Ingest batch and real-time data into a single location within your Fabric workspace.

Clean, transform, extract, and load your data for analysis and modeling tasks.

Figure 2-4. Splash screen when you start to create a Dataflow Gen1

Even though there's a newer version of Dataflow with more capabilities (as seen in Figure 2-4), we'll show you in what situations Gen1 can still be useful. Then, we'll detail the additional features of Dataflow Gen2.

Dataflow Gen1 is useful when you need to ingest data directly from an external source but can't use the shortcut method as described previously. This is because Dataflow Gen1 has a special capability to read data in direct query mode from the source and present it to the end user or application, which Dataflow Gen2 doesn't have. And if the shortcut feature doesn't work or doesn't apply to the scenario, then Dataflow Gen1 is a good choice.

In Table 2-2, you can see the differences between Dataflow Gen1 and Dataflow Gen2.

Table 2-2. Differences between Dataflow Gen1 and Dataflow Gen2

Features	Dataflow Gen1	Dataflow Gen2
Author dataflows with Power Query	Yes	Yes
Shorter authoring flow	No	Yes
Autosave and background publishing	No	Yes
Data destinations	No	Yes
Improved monitoring and refresh history	No	Yes
Integration with data pipelines	No	Yes
High-scale compute	No	Yes
Getting data via Dataflows connector	Yes	Yes
Direct query via Dataflows connector	Yes	No
Incremental refresh	Yes	Yes

If you click the No, create a Dataflow Gen1 button on the screen shown in Figure 2-4, it will bring up the screen in Figure 2-5.

There, you have the following four options:

- Defining new tables
- Linking tables from other dataflows
- Importing a model
- Attaching a Common Data Model folder (preview)

Note that the fourth option, Attach a Common Data Model folder, is in preview. It's been in preview for quite some time now, and because Dataflow Gen2 has been introduced, we're not sure if it will ever come out of preview. If it's still in preview when you take the exam, you won't be given any questions on it.

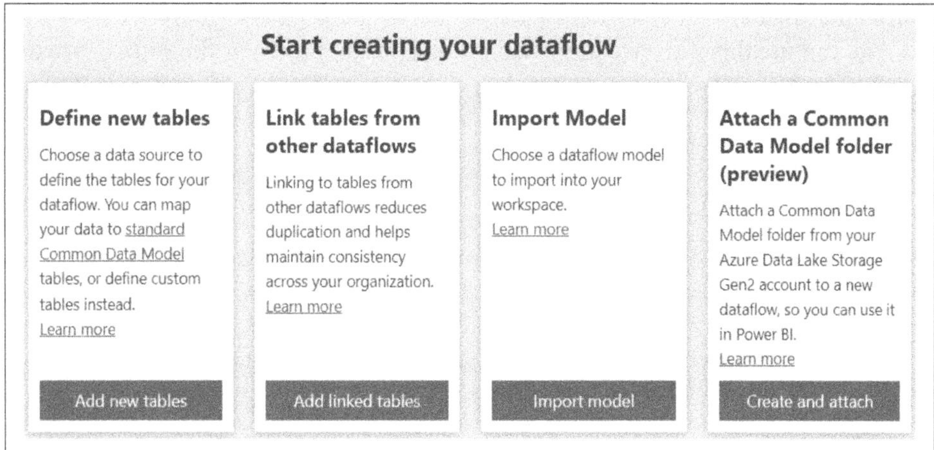

Figure 2-5. Welcome screen for Dataflow Gen1

Defining new tables. If you click the option to define new tables, you'll see the well-known UI for Power Query, and you'll be able to continue with the sources listed in Figure 2-6.

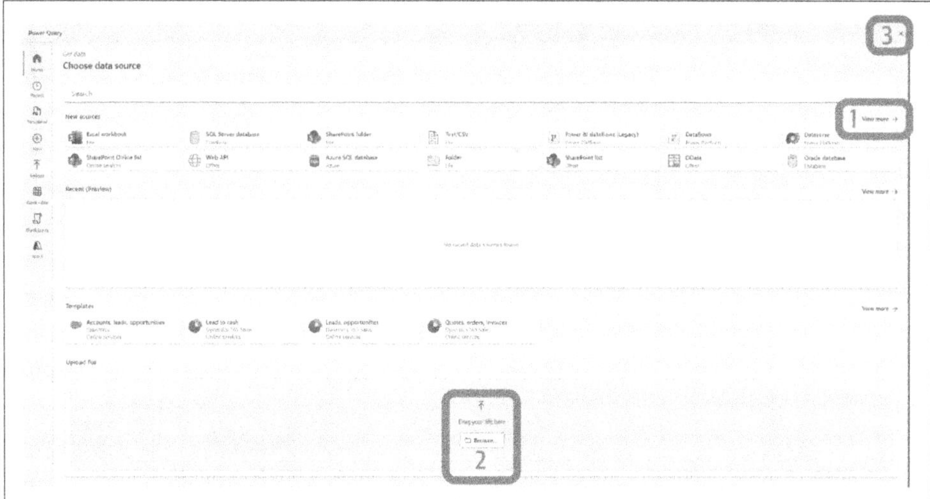

Figure 2-6. Screen for getting started with new tables

We've highlighted some specific areas (numbered 1, 2 and 3):

View more (area 1)
: You can click this option to view the entire selection of possible sources you can use. This list keeps expanding as Microsoft expands the options in Power BI and Fabric.

Upload file (area 2)

You can use this interface to upload a single file and use it as the source for your dataflow.

x (area 3)

We've highlighted this because it can be hard to find. You click it to close the UI if you don't want to save your work.

Once you've selected the source you want to use, you can connect to that source on the provided screen.

Each source has its own settings, so we won't dive into each of them here. It's also outside of the scope of the certification to know the network setup and the connectivity of the sources.

Next, we'll dive into the screen for data manipulation (see Figure 2-7).

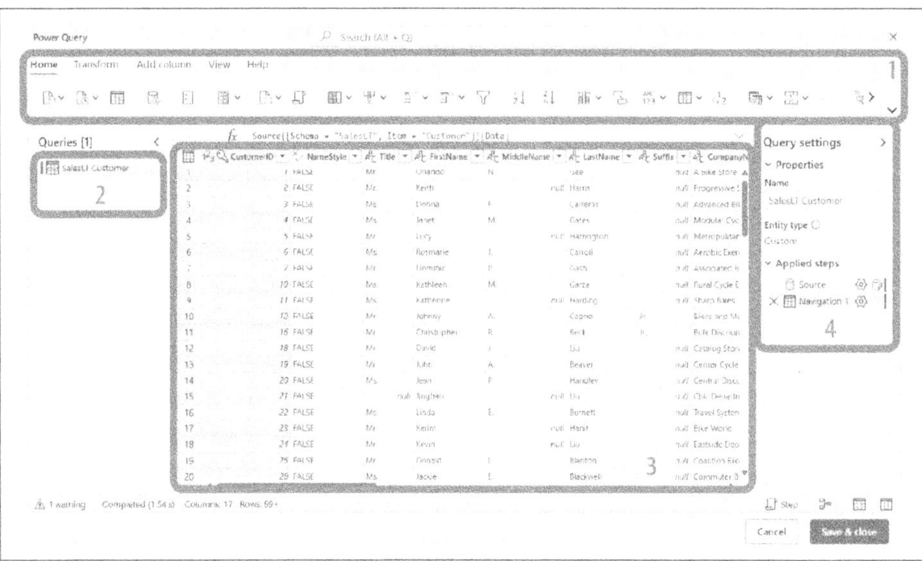

Figure 2-7. The Power Query UI in Dataflow Gen1

We've highlighted four areas of interest (numbered 1–4).

Menu bar (area 1)

This is almost the same menu bar you'll find in the Power BI Desktop version of Power Query (see later in this chapter). Here, you can select Power Query, Transform, Add column, View, and Help.

List of queries (area 2)

Here, you can find all the queries you have in the dataflow. Each dataflow can contain more than one query, and the end user of the dataflow will see them all. Then, the end user can connect to the item in Fabric.

Data preview (area 3)

In the data preview pane, you can see the current state of the data as a preview of the first 99 rows, and you can also scroll down with your mouse to see more rows. Here, you can modify your data by right clicking on a cell to replace values and right clicking on a column to execute any command shown in Figure 2-8.

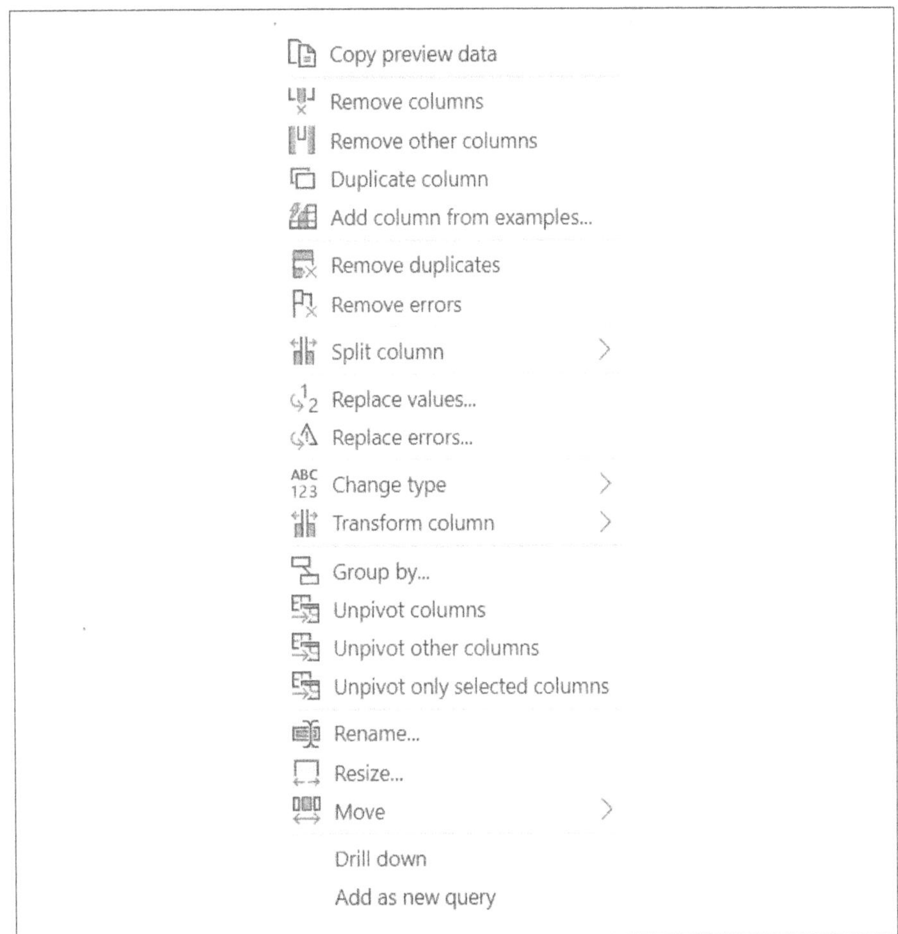

Figure 2-8. Complete context menu retrieved by right-clicking on a column in Dataflow Gen1

Query settings (area 4)

Every time you make changes to the data in the Power Query view, either with your mouse or through the formula bar, you'll see a new applied step in the "Query settings" area at the far right of the screen. You'll see the source you're connected to, the steps you've been creating, and the name of the table you're working with. This view also lets you click on any step and see the preview of that step in the preview pane, and that in turn enables you to work dynamically with your needs for data manipulation. It can also help you with debugging and further development of the data.

From some of the context menu items, you can also access a drop-down list of more options to choose from, and you can click each option to see details on it. For example, Figure 2-9 shows the details on the Split column action.

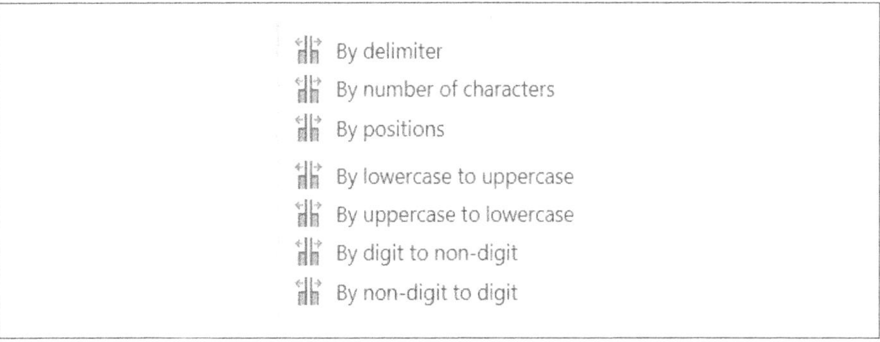

Figure 2-9. Details on Split column action

If you want to do your own coding and not use your mouse, you can write the M scripts you need in the formula bar just above the data preview.

In this book, we won't dive into the details of the M language. If you want to read more about it, you can find a complete reference guide on Microsoft Learn (*https://oreil.ly/iG4Jc*).

Linking tables from other dataflows. The "Link tables from other dataflows" section gives you the option to read data from already existing dataflows and use them as the source for your dataflow. This can be useful if you have some data you want to use and you also want to add more reference data, clean it, or aggregate it.

When you select this option, it will bring up the screen in Figure 2-10.

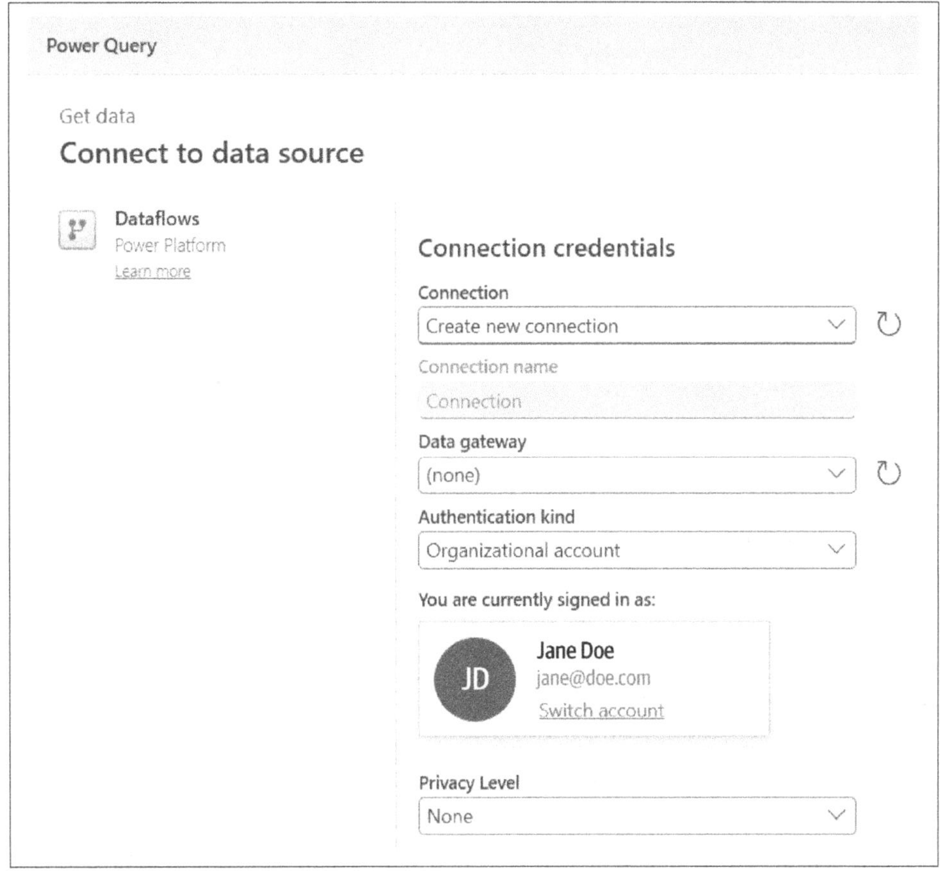

Figure 2-10. Screen for connecting to tables from other dataflows

Notice that the screen indicates you are signed in. This also means that you as the developer need to have access to the dataflow to be able to read it.

Importing a model. The Import Model option gives you the ability to import a predefined dataflow model into your dataflow and use it as your starting point. The format for Dataflow Gen1 is JSON, and you can get a copy of a dataflow by exporting it directly from the UI on an existing item (see Figure 2-11).

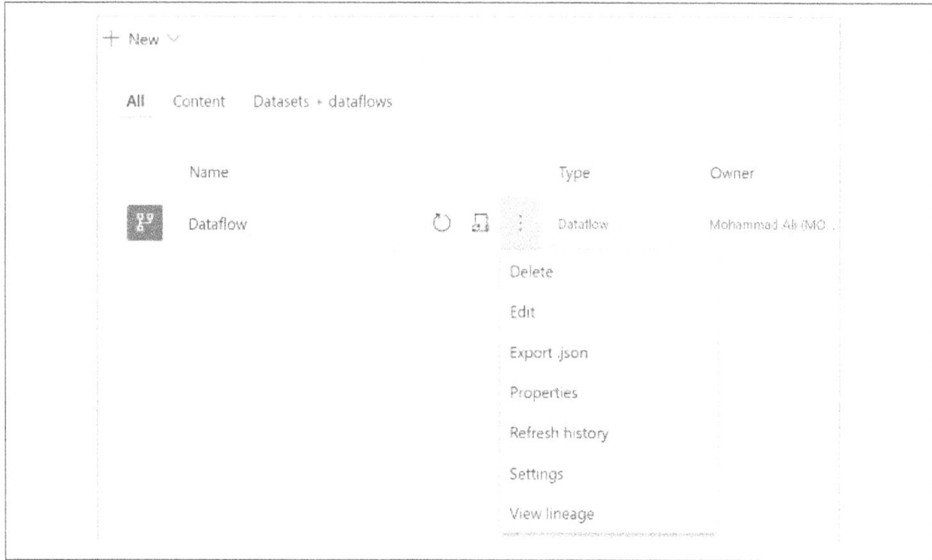

Figure 2-11. Exporting an existing Dataflow Gen1

This concludes the run-through of Dataflow Gen1. Next up is Dataflow Gen2.

Dataflow Gen2

The Dataflow Gen2 Fabric workspace item is the new and updated version of Dataflow Gen1 that brings in a lot of new features and capabilities. It comes with a completely new backend engine and even more options to work with and load data from different sources.

As with Gen1, you find Gen2 in the Get data and Prepare data sections of the New item screen (see Figure 2-12).

When you select the Dataflow Gen2 option, the next window will ask you for a name and give you the option to disable "Enable Git integration, deployment pipelines and Public API scenarios" (see Figure 2-13).

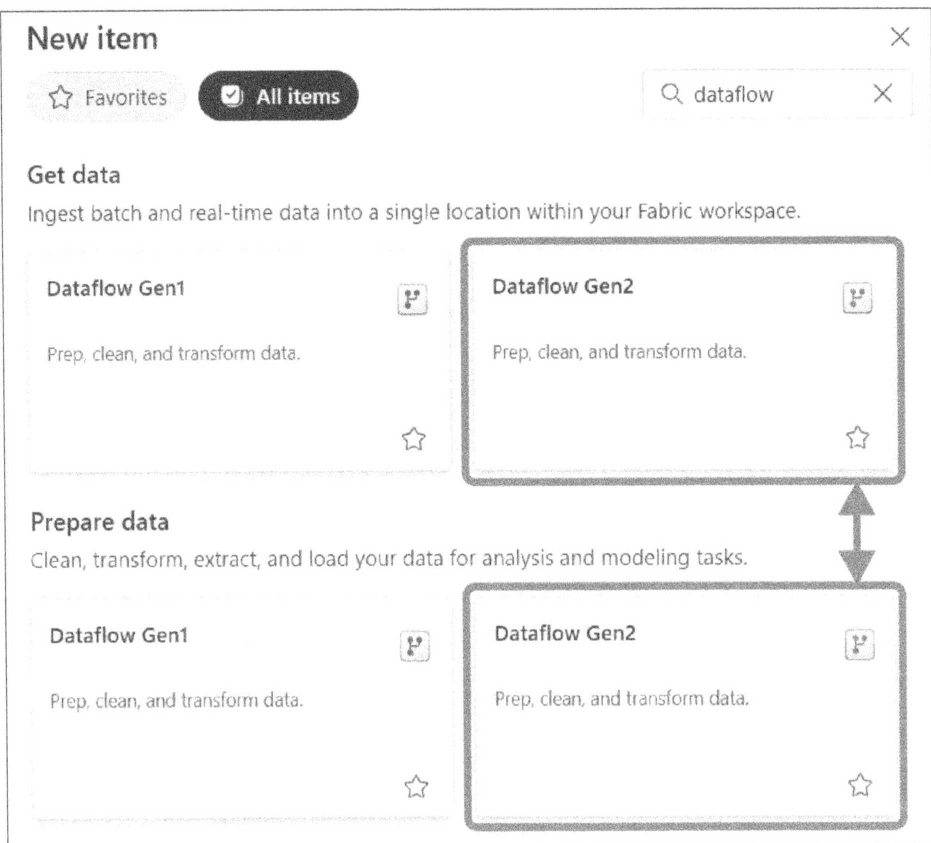

New item
Favorites
All items

Prep, clean, and transform data.

Figure 2-12. Dataflow Gen2 item creation

New Dataflow Gen2

Name

Dataflow gen 2

Enable Git integration, deployment pipelines and Public API scenarios

Create Cancel

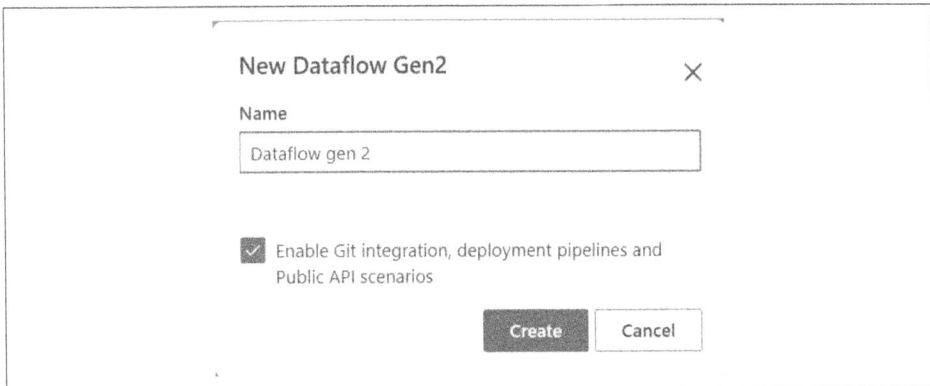

Get data
Ingest batch and real-time data into a single location within your Fabric workspace.
Dataflow Gen1
Prep, clean, and transform data.

Prep, clean, and transform data.
Prepare data
Clean, transform, extract, and load your data for analysis and modeling tasks.
Dataflow Gen1
Prep, clean, and transform data.

Figure 2-13. Name and options for Dataflow Gen2

This option has to do with enabling Git integration with Dataflow Gen2 and using a full CI/CD process to handle deployments of versions through the development cycles.

CI/CD and development cycles are outside of the DP-600 exam's scope, but if you want to learn more about them, you can read the complete blog post from Microsoft (*https://oreil.ly/xxcNX*).

When you finish creating your Dataflow Gen2, it will bring up a screen with five options (see Figure 2-14).

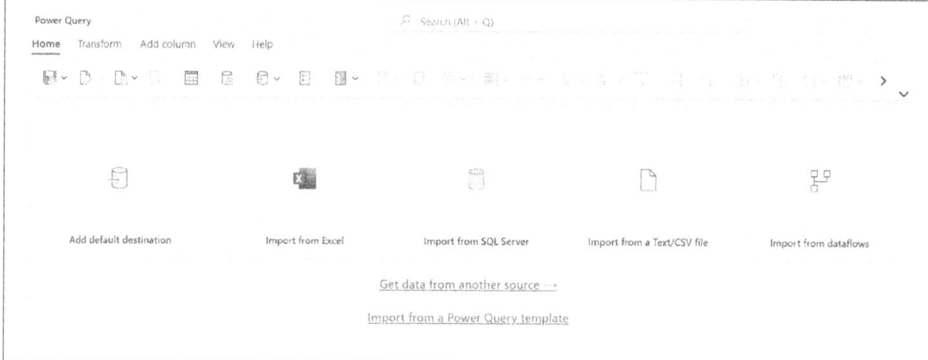

Figure 2-14. First screen that appears after creation of Dataflow Gen2

Here, you can directly add a default destination, import an Excel file, import data from a SQL server, import from a text or CSV file, and import from other dataflows. If that is not enough, then you can click "Get data from another source" to go to another screen that's (almost) the same as the "Choose data source" screen you worked with in Dataflow Gen1. It offers you the full selection of sources and options to handle data, but it's different in that it lets you read data from the OneLake catalog (see Figure 2-15), which we described earlier in this chapter.

In this view, you can find everything you need to connect to a source from the dataflow. As with Dataflow Gen1, you can find more sources if you click the "View more" option in the top right corner of the screen.

You'll also see some connectors that are marked in blue with the word *Preview*. These connectors are in preview and won't be a part of any exam for the DP-600 certification.

After you create a connection to the data you need and you load the data, you'll see the same data manipulation screen you saw in Dataflow Gen1, with a few changes (see Figure 2-16).

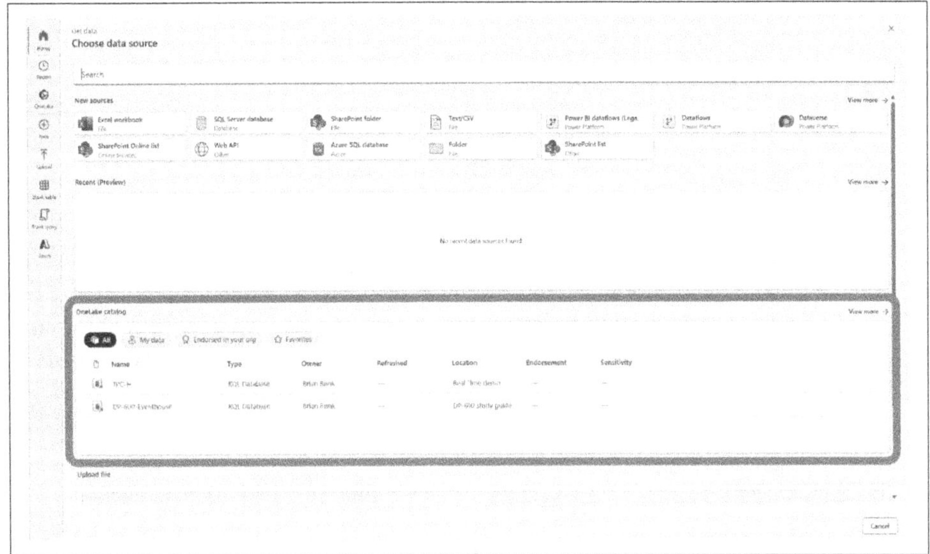

Figure 2-15. Source selection in Dataflow Gen2, with the OneLake catalog highlighted

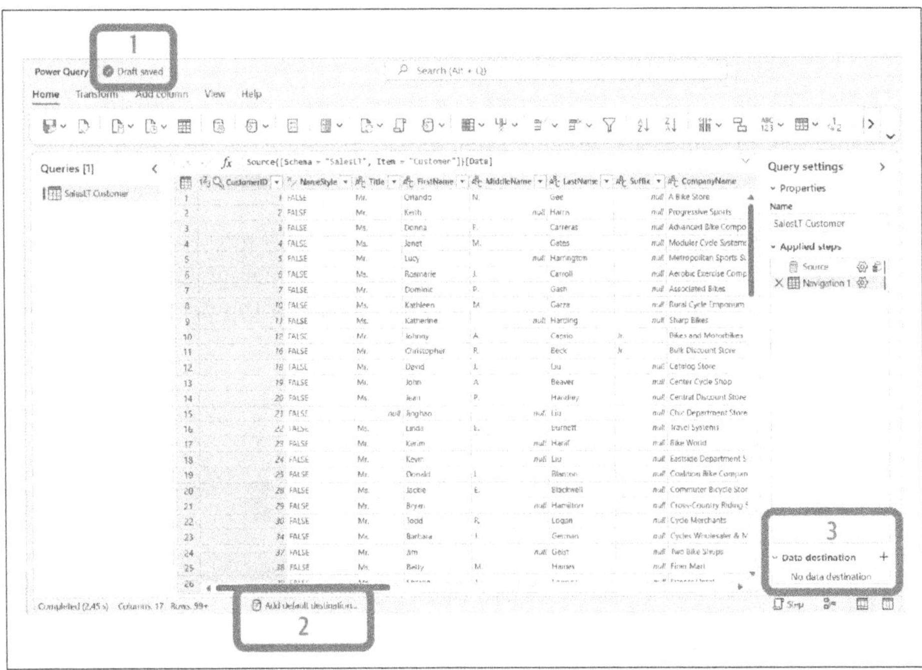

Figure 2-16. New elements on Dataflow Gen2 data manipulation screen

Here, we've highlighted three new areas of interest (numbered 1–3).

Draft saved (area 1)
This area indicates that your changes will be autosaved as you develop the dataflow. It changes to "Saving draft" immediately after you make a change, and once the change has been saved, you'll see the green icon again.

Add default destination (area 2)
This option has to do with the fact that you can add a default destination to the dataflow and all the data from the flow in that destination will always be the same. This is a good option to have, and it's perhaps the best one for making sure that all data is saved in the same place. See Figure 2-17 for the options available at the default destination.

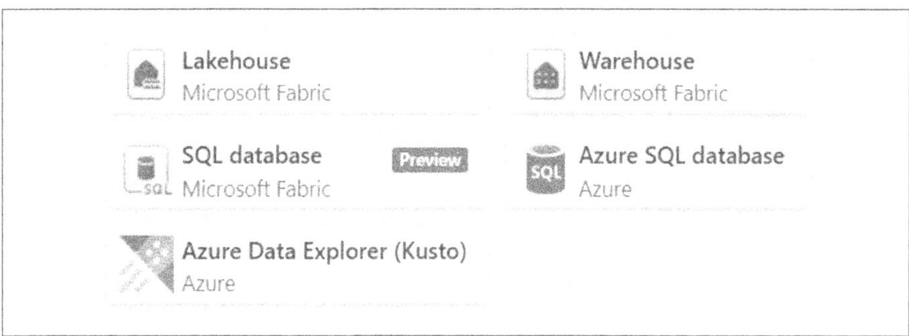

Figure 2-17. Default destination in Dataflow Gen2

Data destination (area 3)
This option lets you configure the specific destination for this specific table in the dataflow. Here, the options for connections are a bit different. You also have the SharePoint destination, which, at the time of writing of this book, is in preview (see Figure 2-18).

Figure 2-18. Destination list for individual tables in Dataflow Gen2

The ability to add custom destinations in Dataflow Gen2 is very useful. Now, we can save data where we want to, directly in the Fabric workspace item we require.

Note that the Azure Data Explorer (Kusto) connectors from both the default destination and the data destination support the eventhouse KQL database from Fabric. Even though it's not a part of the OneLake catalog in the selection of destinations, you can copy the URL from the KQL database and use it as a destination for your dataflow.

The rest of Dataflow Gen2 for development and coding capabilities is the same as described previously for Dataflow Gen1.

Now that we have covered both Dataflow Gen1 and Dataflow Gen2, it is a natural next step to create data connections with Power BI Desktop. In the next section, we'll dive into the details of how to create data connections to Power BI, both from external sources outside Fabric and internal sources such as OneLake, semantic models, and KQL querysets.

Data Connections from Power BI

When you work with data and want to build semantic models or visualizations, you have two options for getting started. On the one hand, you can use the Power BI Desktop application from Microsoft, which comes with a complete tool set to work with data connections, data manipulation, and data visualization. On the other hand, you can use the browser experience of Power BI within Microsoft Fabric, where you can get the same experience as from the desktop application. Which option is better for you depends on your approach to development. Also note that if you're a Mac user, you can't use the desktop application and must use the browser-based option. Windows users can use either.

You can grab the latest version of Power BI Desktop from either the Microsoft Store or the download link (*https://oreil.ly/WDt__*). Figure 2-19 shows the Power BI Desktop application from the Microsoft Store.

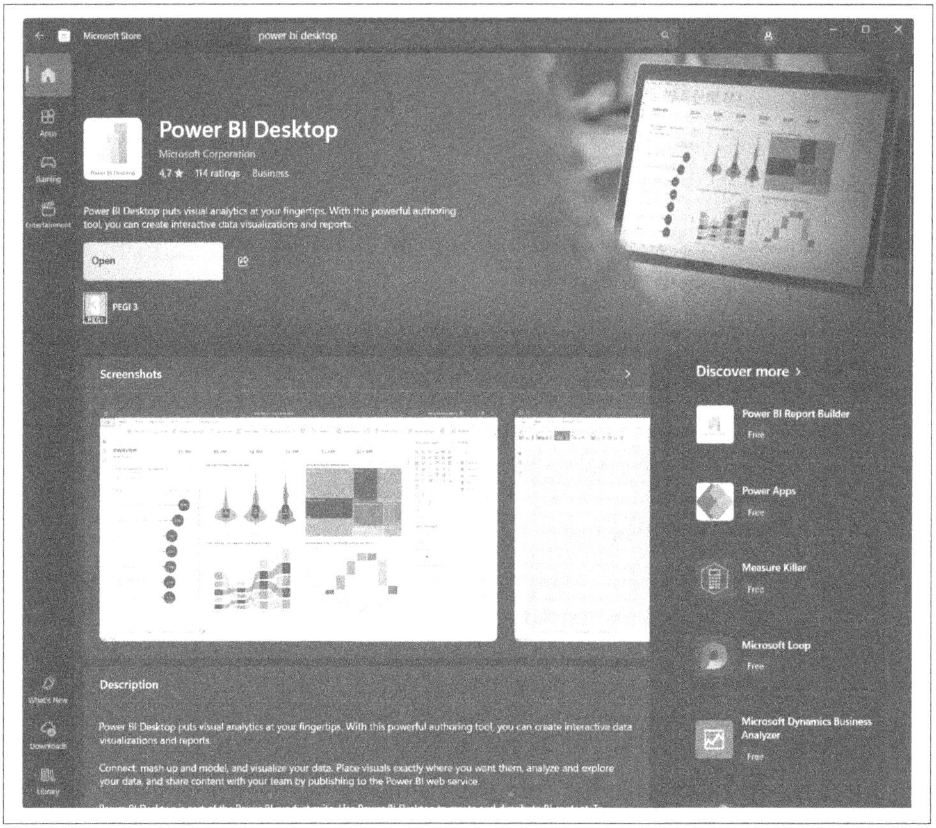

Figure 2-19. Power BI Desktop from the Microsoft Store

If you want to use the continuously updated version of Power BI Desktop, we highly recommend that you choose the version from the Microsoft Store since it will automatically update whenever a new version is released. If you use the version from the download link, you'll have to maintain the version upgrades yourself.

When you open Power BI Desktop, you'll see a welcome screen where you can connect to data sources at the top (see Figure 2-20).

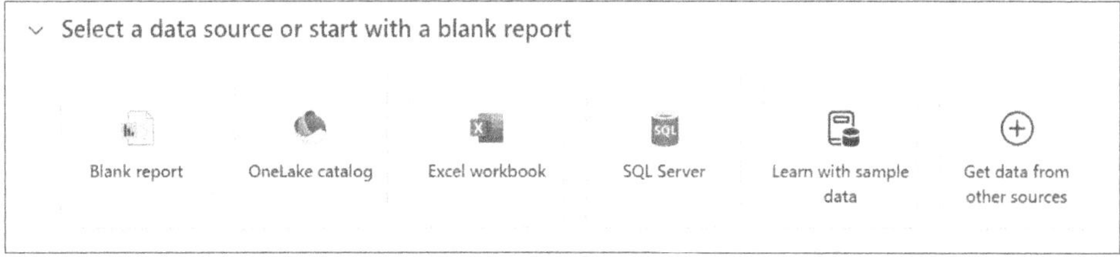

Figure 2-20. Top menu from Power BI Desktop for getting started with data connections

Here, you can easily get started and connect to data sources with a few clicks. If the options at the top of the screen aren't the ones you the needed, then click the "Get data from other sources" option and you'll see the list shown in Figure 2-21.

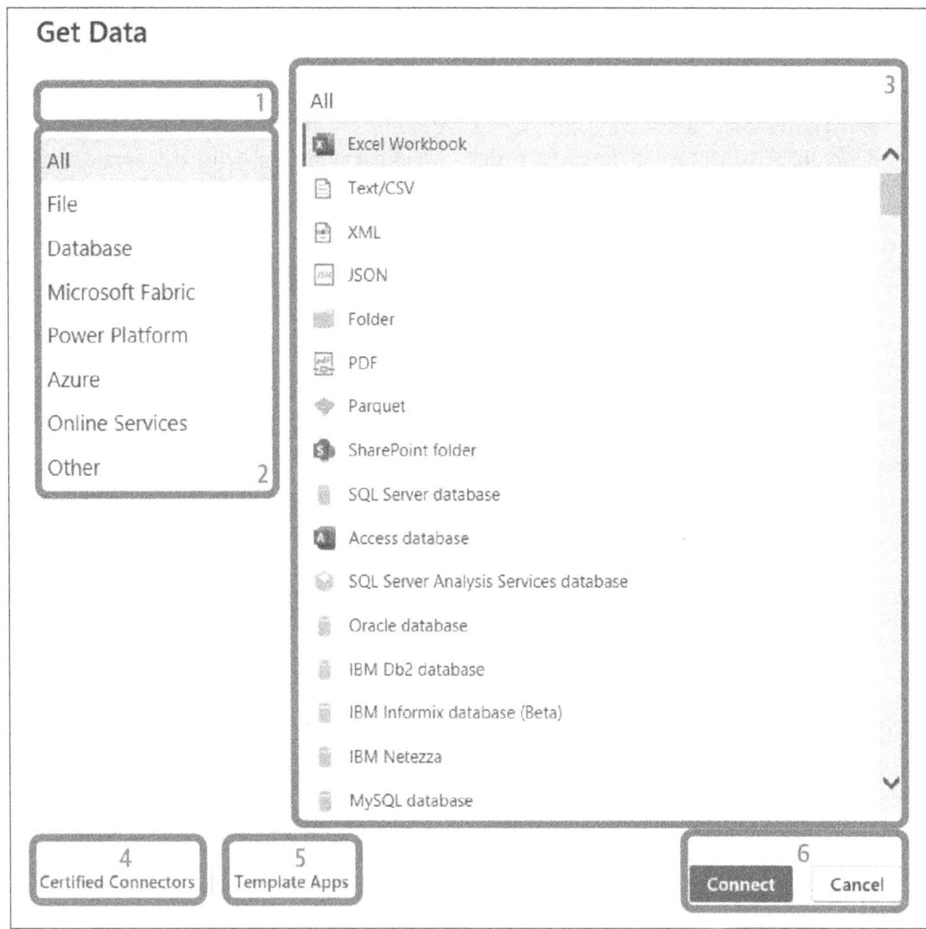

Figure 2-21. Get Data screen from Power BI Desktop

We've highlighted several areas of interest (numbered 1–6):

Search bar (area 1)
: Here, you can search for the connector you need. It's a free text search, and it helps you filter the content in area 3 very quickly.

Grouped filter (area 2)
: Here, you can select the group of connectors you are searching for. If you want to connect to the Power Platform but don't know the name of the connector, just

click Power Platform option on this list and the list of sources will automatically be filtered for you.

Source list (area 3)
: This is the complete list of connectors you can use. You'll find this list is very similar to those found in the Dataflow Gen1 and Dataflow Gen2, except that it has some extra connectors. This is because it's not limited to a web interface and Power BI can connect directly to local servers and infrastructure from your desktop. Also note that the sort order of the list is paired with the sort order of the grouped filter area.

Certified Connectors (area 4)
: A limited number of custom connectors are certified by Microsoft. There are strict rules for this certification. For instance, the connector cannot read data from web-based places other than the one it's connected to by the developer. This certification is out of scope for this exam, but if you want to read more about it, go to Data Factory Custom Activities on Microsoft Learn (*https://oreil.ly/msNrF*).

Template Apps (area 5)
: When you click this text, you're guided directly to the Fabric portal, which will give you the option to install a Power BI App from the app store from within Microsoft Fabric.

Buttons (area 6)
: When you've found your connector and are ready to continue, click the green Connect button to connect or click Cancel to cancel your work.

In the example shown in Figure 2-22, we've selected the SQL Server data source option and are ready to configure the connection.

In the top field, you can input the connection string for the database and, if you want, the name of the database. If you don't put in a name here, you'll be prompted later for a database name. As examples, we have put in `*<someserver>*.database.windows.net` for Server and `*<databasename>*` for database, but you should use your connection information from your environment.

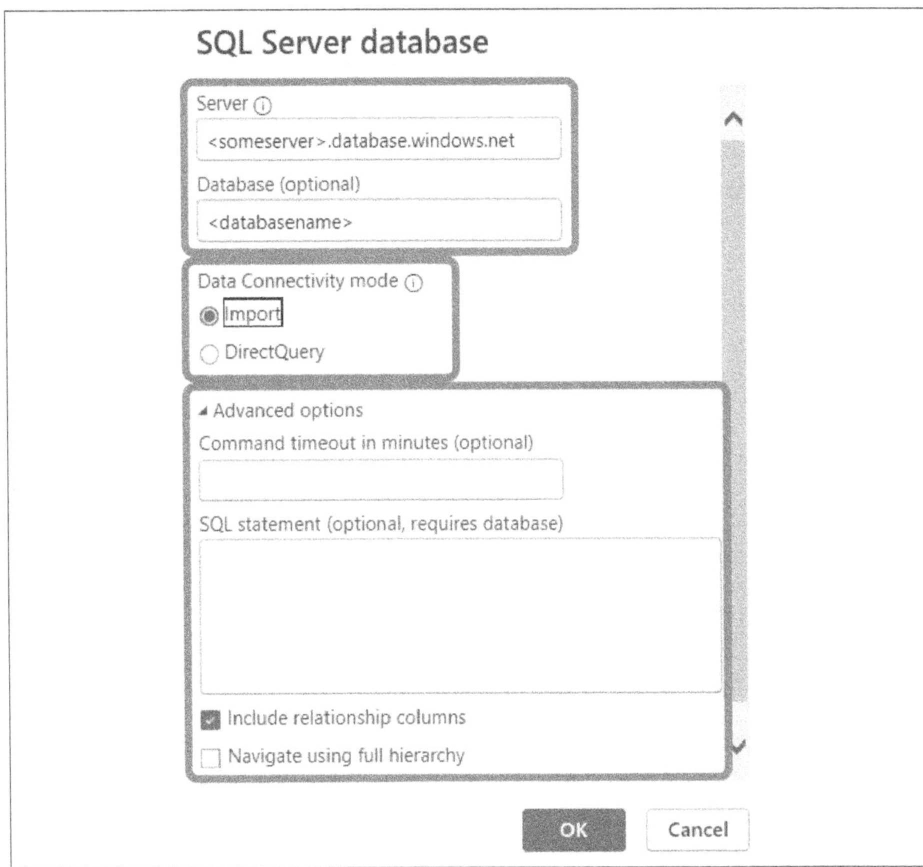

Figure 2-22. SQL Server database connection configuration screen

Even though we've shown you the way the SQL server database connection works, you're not limited to using that specific connection. There are other data connectivity modes, and you need to understand them so you can have a full understanding of connections in Power BI. You must choose between two modes: Import and DirectQuery:

Import

In this mode, Power BI reads all the data into memory and stores it in the underlying engine. This approach is slow at ingestion time, as the engine needs to read all the data, but it's very fast at query time, as all the data is stored in memory in columnar format and is ready to be queried using DAX expressions. You'll find out more about DAX expressions in Chapters 4 and 5.

DirectQuery
: In this mode, data is read at query time. When you filter a report or change anything that makes the engine need a new dataset, Power BI starts a query to get the data from the connected source. This option can be quite slow in some scenarios, like when you have a very large dataset in a SQL server database and the engine needs to filter that dataset based on a column from a different table. You'll learn more about star schemas and relationships in Chapter 5.

Even though Direct Lake is not an option for this type of connection, it's worth mentioning.

Direct Lake works by integrating the compute engine seamlessly with the structured data in OneLake. When a user interacts with a report or query, the connection first attempts to load necessary data chunks into the in-memory cache directly from the OneLake files. If the data is already cached, performance is instantaneous. If not, Direct Lake reads the file data on demand. Crucially, it monitors the Delta Lake transaction log for changes to the underlying data. When a new transaction is committed to the data lake, Direct Lake invalidates the corresponding cached data and automatically pulls the latest version of the Parquet files into the cache for subsequent queries. This process ensures data freshness without requiring a manual full dataset refresh, so it offers near real-time analytics directly on the lakehouse or warehouse tables within Fabric.

When working with connections to sources, you also have the option to connect to data that's already in Fabric and stored in the OneLake service. OneLake connectivity is the option in Figure 2-20 named OneLake catalog, and when you click that option, you'll be taken to the screen shown in Figure 2-23.

The screen will show you all the items you, as a developer, have access to. They may be workspaces you have access to or specific items in a workspace. You can connect to the following item types:

- KQL Databases
- Lakehouses
- Semantic models
- Metric sets
- SQL analytics endpoints
- SQL databases
- Warehouses

Based on which of the available items you select, you will either have direct access to the data source or need to select a profile to sign in with.

If you're prompted for a profile to sign in with, you'll see a screen similar to the one shown in Figure 2-24, with a navigator you can use to find the element or item you want to connect to.

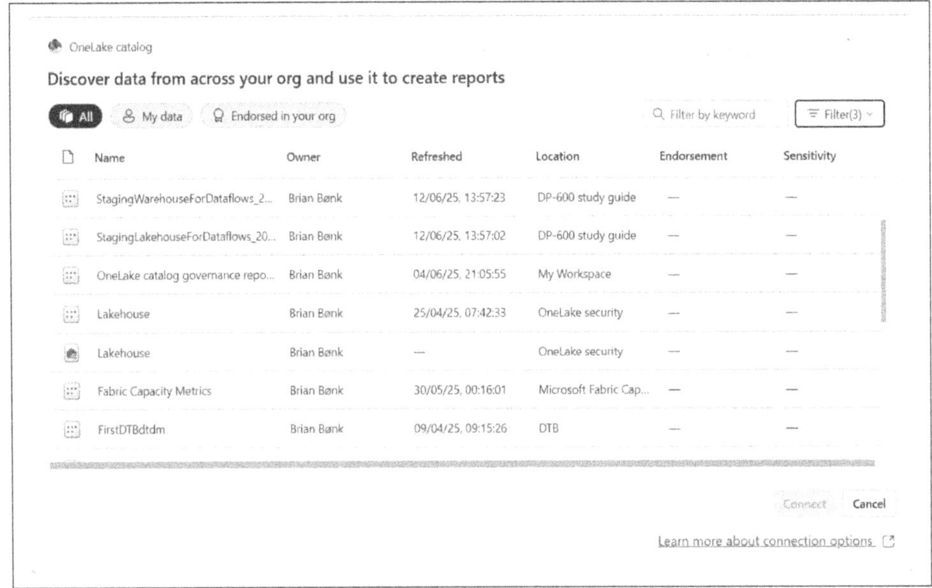

Figure 2-23. OneLake catalog screen for connection from Power BI Desktop

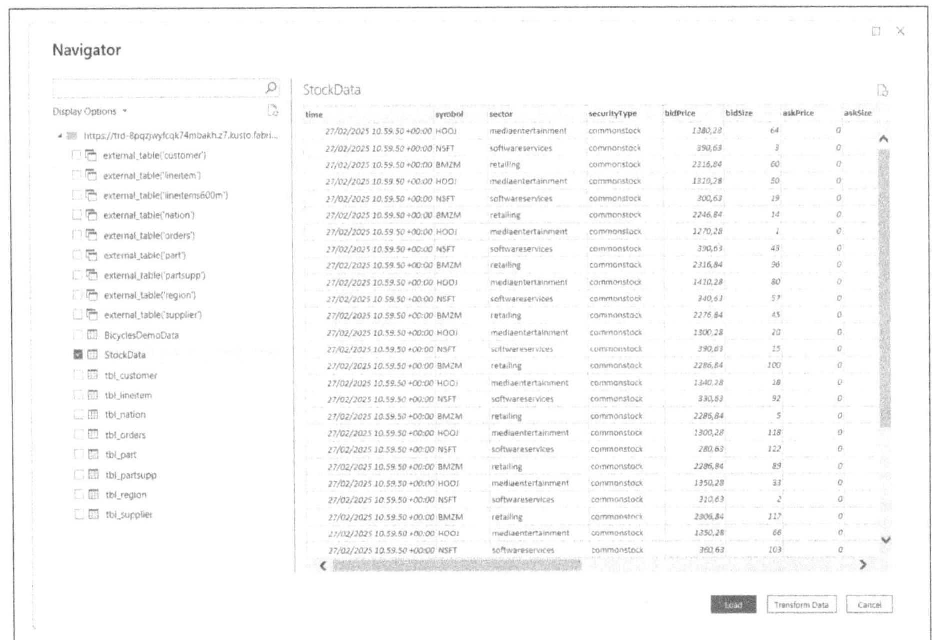

Figure 2-24. Navigator screen for selecting items after establishing a connection

Figure 2-24 shows a connection to a KQL database, and here, you need to choose a specific table to connect to. This is just like connecting to a SQL Server Database or any other object-oriented service from Microsoft.

You can then choose to either load the data directly, using the Load button at the bottom of the screen, or go through the Power Query experience by using the Transform Data button. We explained the Power Query experience in the previous section.

If you choose to connect to a semantic model from the OneLake catalog, then you'll be guided directly to the Power BI Desktop application, where there will be a full set of tables and measures on the right of the screen (see Figure 2-25).

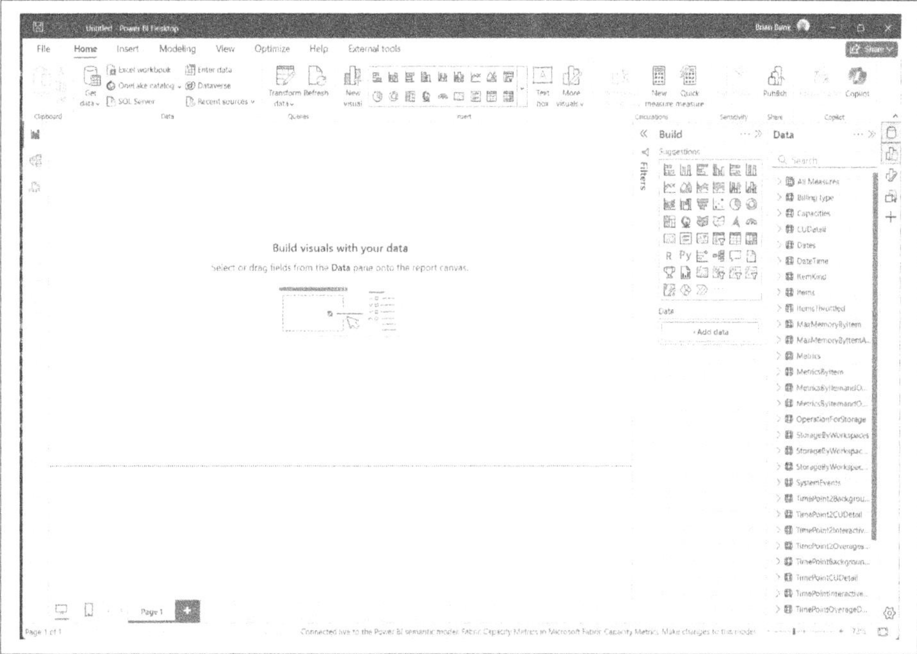

Figure 2-25. Power BI Desktop connected to a semantic model

Power BI Desktop has many features and functionalities you can use to ingest, manipulate, and visualize data, plus share reports with your organization. The application experience from Power BI Desktop is the full feature set from Power BI. Within Microsoft Fabric, there is also an experience based on the web interface when working with Power BI reports.

Data Connections to Power BI

When you're in a Fabric workspace, you can opt to create a Power BI report directly from within a new item list, as shown in Figure 2-25. When you select the Power BI report item, it will bring up the screen shown in Figure 2-26.

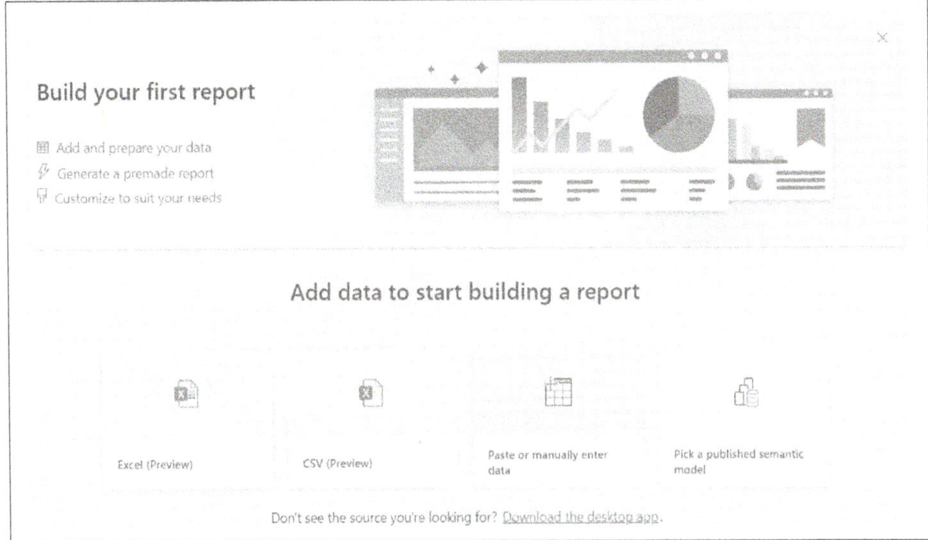

Figure 2-26. New Power BI report experience from the web user interface

Here, you can connect to Excel or CSV files, paste or type data manually, or connect to a published semantic model from a workspace you have access to.

In Figure 2-27, you can see the explorer options in the semantic model selector, which is similar to other connection screens we've presented in this book.

You can also filter by workspaces (on the left of the screen) or with the button for All (which shows all items you have access to), My data (which shows the items you are the owner of), or Endorsed in your org (which shows items that are endorsed in some way in your organization; it also automatically filters on the items you have access to).

Free text search is available in the top right-hand corner, while the middle of the screen shows your current filter context and lists the semantic models you can choose from.

When you select a semantic model, you have two options for creating a report: "Auto-create report" (which is the standard) or "Create a blank report" (which you can select from the drop-down list). The "Auto-create report" option uses a set of built-in templates and adds visuals to a report based on the existing content of the semantic model.

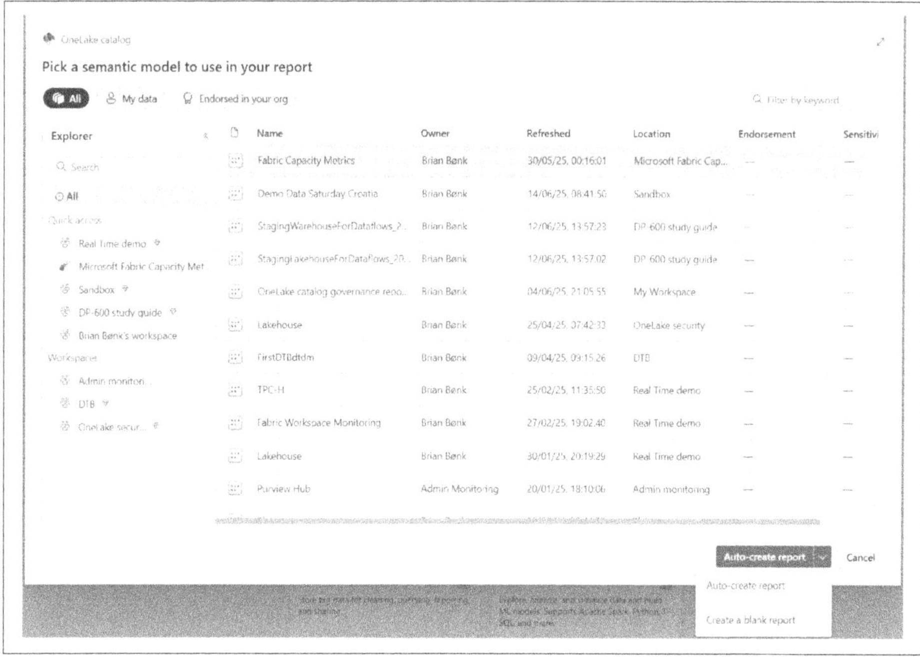

Figure 2-27. OneLake catalog explorer for semantic models

If you want to generate reports faster, you can use the splash screen shown in Figure 2-28. The option in Figure 2-28 might only be on screen for a few seconds, as the Fabric service is very fast at generating the report for us. So be quick to make a decision.

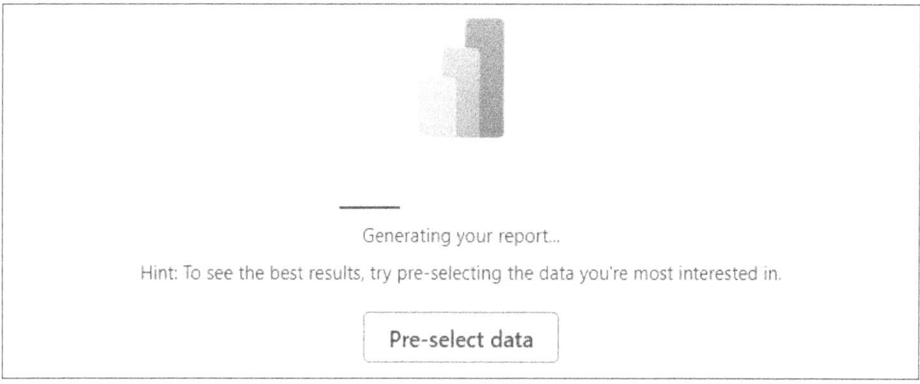

Generating your report...
Hint: To see the best results, try pre-selecting the data you're most interested in.
Pre-select data

Figure 2-28. Pre-selecting data for the autogenerated report

In our experience, using this option creates reports that look like the one in Figure 2-29 almost every time, with a few changes here and there.

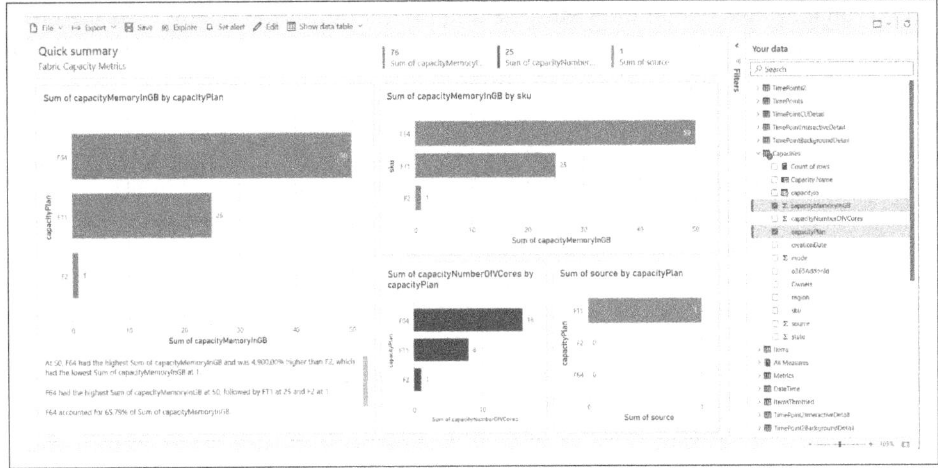

Figure 2-29. Results of using "Auto-create report" option in Power BI report web experience

You'll see the report, options for saving and exporting, other options at the top, and the entire content of the semantic model on the right on the screen. By default, the report is shown in "live" mode, and you can't edit it directly in the browser. Instead, you can click the Edit button at the top so you can edit the report and make it fit your needs for visuals, interaction, and other business requirements.

To add new elements to an existing visual, simply drag-and-drop them from the list of fields to the visual. To change a visual, you can do on-object editing by selecting it, and you'll see the properties pane at the right on the screen (see Figure 2-30).

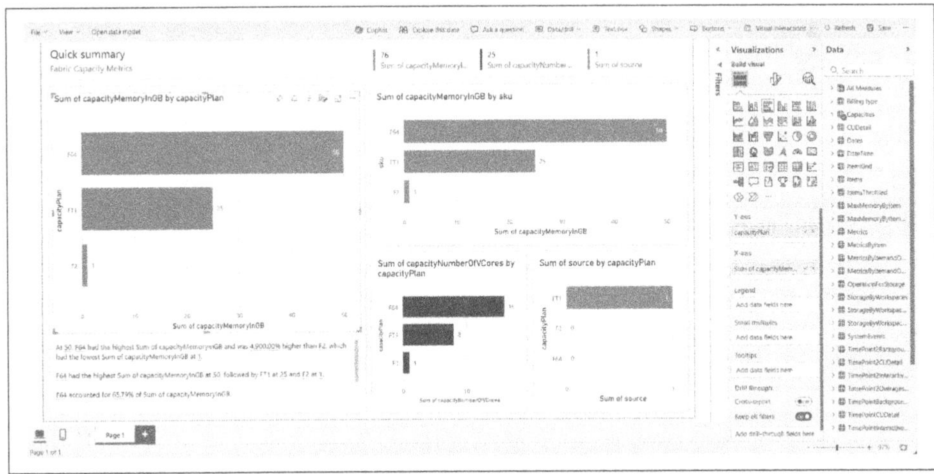

Figure 2-30. On-object editing from the Power BI web experience

Then, you'll be able to edit the visual the same way you can in the Power BI Desktop. You can add new visuals from the top menu and save and share the report to the organization. If you want to, you can also edit the mobile layout of the report, which you can find at the bottom left of the screen (see Figure 2-30). By default, the desktop layout is selected, and you can select the mobile layout and design the report to fit your needs when using a phone or tablet (see Figure 2-31).

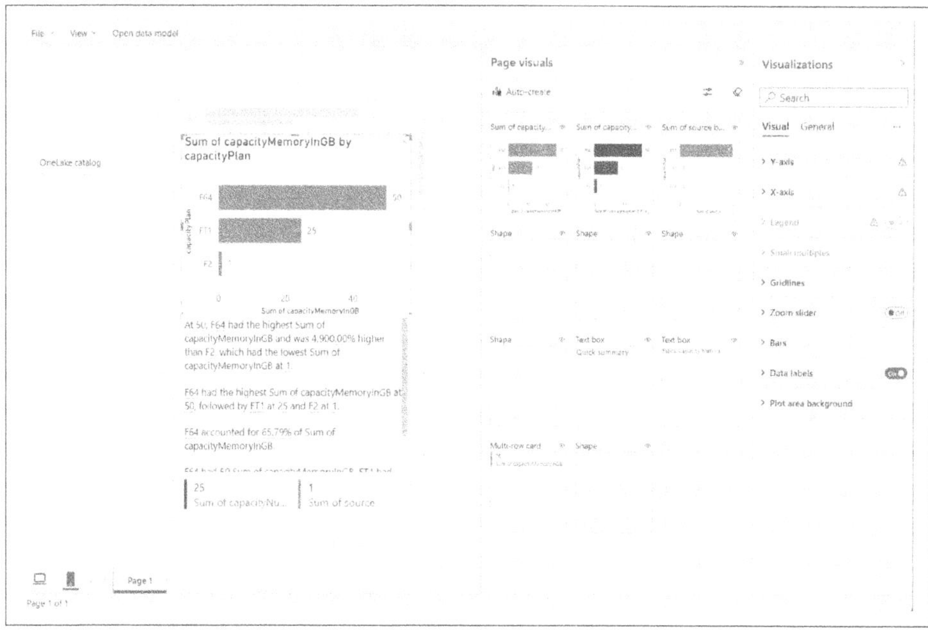

Figure 2-31. Mobile layout in Power BI web experience

You can also use the existing visuals from the desktop layout and drag-and-drop them to the canvas of the mobile layout. When you need to change the visual on the canvas, you can just select the item on the canvas and use the properties pane at the right of the screen.

KQL Queries to Power BI

We need to use a special implementation method of getting data when working with KQL queries to Power BI. The approaches when using the Power BI Desktop application and the Power BI web experience are a bit different, and we will cover both of them in the next sections.

KQL queries in Power BI Desktop. In the Power BI Desktop application, use the Get Data option and find the Azure Data Explorer (Kusto) connector in the list of connectors (see Figure 2-32).

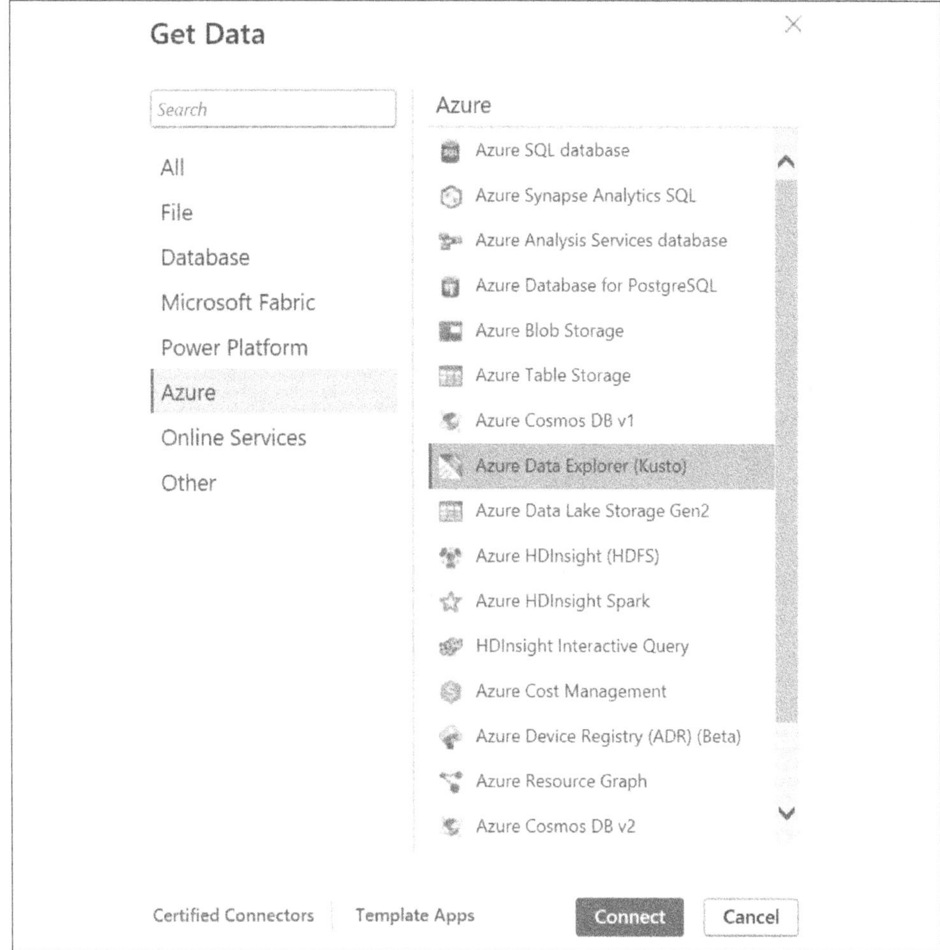

Figure 2-32. Azure Data Explorer (Kusto) connector in Power BI Desktop

When you select this connector, it will bring up a dialog box where you can enter your cluster name and the database name, and you'll have the option to paste a KQL query and use that as a source for your analysis work (see Figure 2-33).

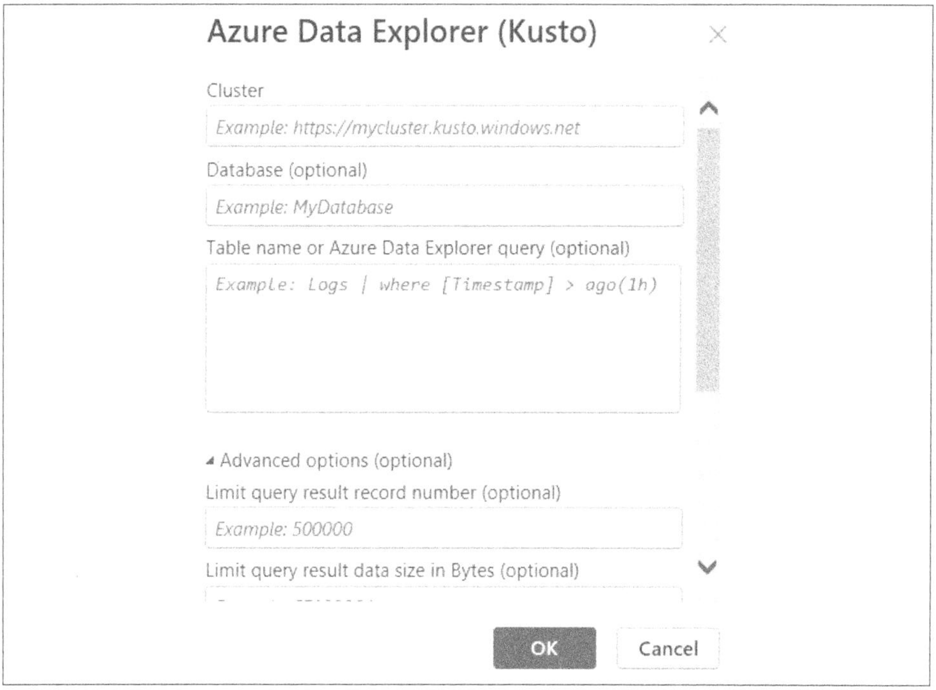

Figure 2-33. Azure Data Explorer (Kusto) connection dialog box

Next, scroll down and select the Direct Query data connectivity mode (see Figure 2-34).

You need to select the Direct Query mode because the KQL engine is much better at handling data queries from the database than Power BI is at handling the same amount of data. The KQL engine is built for very large datasets and can handle almost any query you want it to, and the connector does a very good job of *query folding* (translating what we're doing in Power BI into actual native KQL queries) for the KQL engine to execute. So, hesitate to select the Direct Query option in this scenario.

Now that you've got the entire connector configured, you can click OK to start working with the data in Power BI as you normally would.

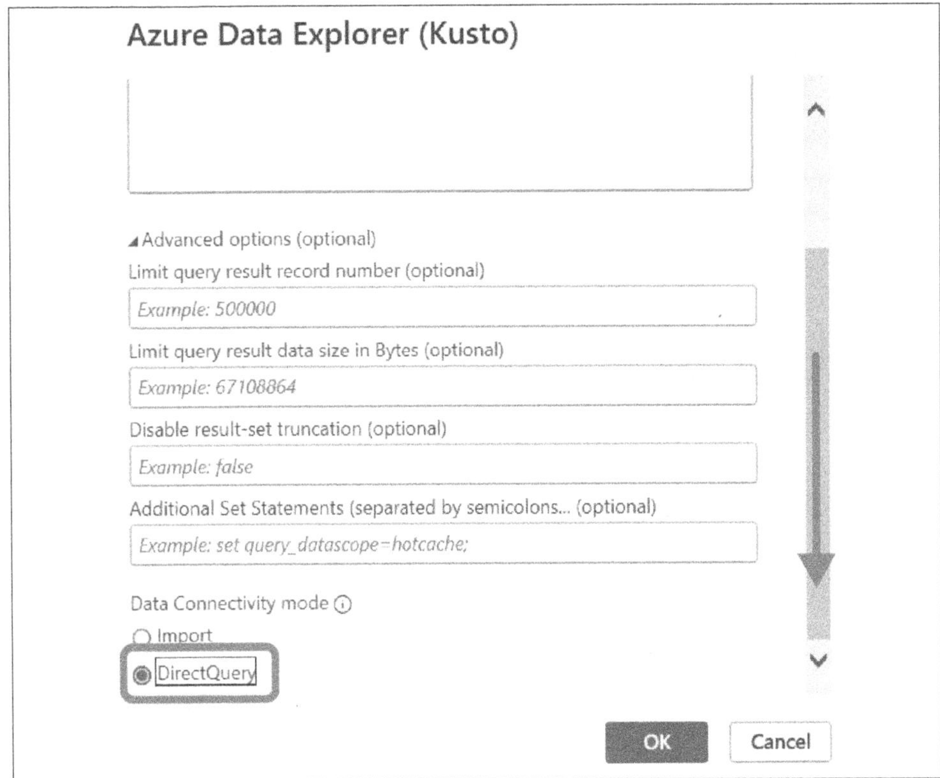

Figure 2-34. Selecting Direct Query as the data connectivity mode for the KQL query connection

KQL Queries in Power BI web experience. As we saw in the Power BI Desktop approach, it's easy to work with KQL queries if we remember to select the Direct Query option. But in Power BI web experience, we need to use a slightly different approach.

Here, we need to start at the eventhouse and KQL database level. In the KQL database, we have a standard attached *KQL queryset*, which is just a sort of a notebook to keep KQL queries as a part of the database.

Figure 2-35 shows the KQL database and the attached KQL queryset with a KQL script created. It is a very basic KQL script that takes a table and filters the rows based on a column.

When the KQL query is done and we're happy with the result set, we can go ahead and add it to a new Power BI report.

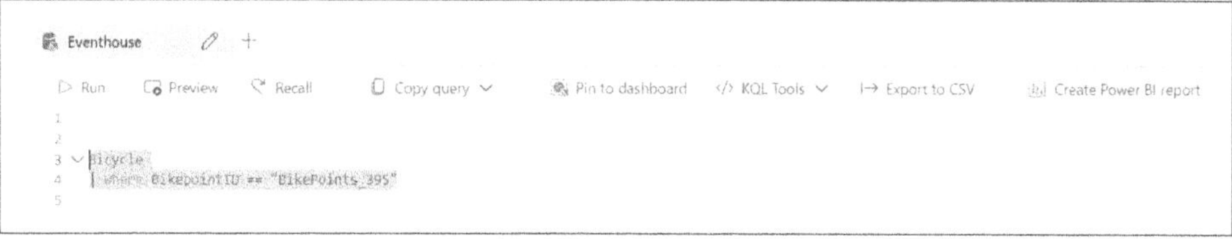

Figure 2-35. KQL queryset with a simple KQL script

Notice in the top menu in Figure 2-35 that the second-to-last menu item is Create Power BI report. This only gets enabled when a specific KQL query is selected in the queryset, and if no KQL query is selected, we cannot click this menu item. Note that in the figure, the KQL query is selected, so we can click Create Power BI report and get our data in the report.

When we click Create Power BI report, a screen will appear with Kusto Query Result on the right and the columns we can work with. We can then begin to create and design our report (see Figure 2-36).

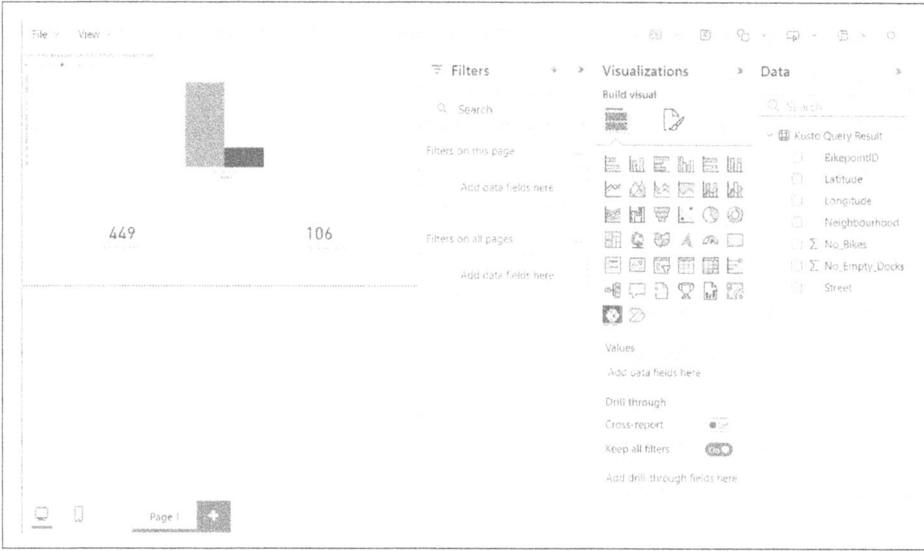

Figure 2-36. KQL query in Power BI web experience

In the figure, we've added some simple visuals, and we can continue to save the report and share it with our organization, as we've explained previously in this chapter.

At this point, we've covered all aspects of getting data to Power BI and ingesting data to Fabric. But what about the question of which service we should choose: a lakehouse, warehouse, or eventhouse? This is also a part of the DP-600 exam, so in the next section, we'll dive into how to choose among the three options.

Choosing a Lakehouse, Warehouse, or Eventhouse

Microsoft Fabric has three main services for storing analytical data: the lakehouse, the warehouse, and the eventhouse. But choosing the right service for the task can be difficult because none of them are one-size-fits-all. So here, we'll try to help you understand the different services and how to choose the right one for your use case.

The lakehouse and warehouse services are both built on top of the Delta Parquet file format approach stored in OneLake. Even though the underlying engines are different, they share some similar capabilities when storing data in OneLake.

The eventhouse can also store data in the OneLake service, but it does so as a selective mirror option directly on the KQL database or in each individual table in the KQL database.

Lakehouse

This service is built to support structured, semi-structured, and unstructured data from different sources. It is also built to be most effective using the notebook approach with the Spark, Scala, PySpark, Python SparkR, and SparkSQL scripting languages to ingest, manipulate, and handle data structures. It also delivers data in both the OneLake connection and a SQL analytics endpoint. However, it doesn't support multi-table transactions because the Warehouse service does, and it stores its data in folders and files grouped by databases and tables in the engine.

You can also use the Data Factory pipelines to ingest data to a lakehouse, but that's not in scope for the DP-600 exam.

Warehouse

This service also supports semi-structured and structured data in the storage, and it's built with Transact-SQL (T-SQL) as the primary language for data manipulation. It supports the use of functions and stored procedures as known from the SQL server. However, it's not on par with the lakehouse in functionality, as we'll cover in Chapter 3. On the other hand, the warehouse can use multi-table transactions with full atomicity, consistency, isolation, and durability (ACID) properties, while the lakehouse only has ACID properties in one table at a time. So basically, the warehouse has the same durability features you would get from the Microsoft SQL server.

Eventhouse

This service is built on a completely different engine from the lakehouse and warehouse. It uses the Kusto database engine as its main driver of compute and storage. The Kusto engine is widely used across the Azure ecosystem, in Log analytics, Azure Sentinel, and the implementation of the KQL database in the eventhouse.

The eventhouse supports unstructured, semi-structured, and structured datasets, supports the usage of both T-SQL and KQL, and is built to handle the time series–based data that we normally find in Internet of Things (IoT) devices, log events, and telemetry, just to mention a few.

Microsoft has written a complete and extensive guide on how to select the appropriate service for storage and compute, and you can find it at this link: Microsoft Fabric decision guide: choose a data store (*https://oreil.ly/30uWs*).

Table 2-3 compares the features of lakehouses, warehouses, and eventhouses.

Table 2-3. Comparison of lakehouse, warehouse, and eventhouse features

Features	Lakehouse	Warehouse	Eventhouse
Data volume	Unlimited	Unlimited	Unlimited
Types of data	Unstructured, Semi-structured, and structured	Structured and semi-structured (JSON)	Unstructured, Semi-structured, and structured
Primary developer personae	Data engineer and data scientist	Data warehouse developer, data architect, data engineer, and database developer	App developer, data scientist, and data engineer
Primary developer skill	Spark (Scala, PySpark, Spark SQL, and R)	SQL	No code, KQL, and SQL
Data organized by	Folders and files, databases, and tables	Databases, schemas, and tables	Databases, schemas, and tables
Read operations	Spark and T-SQL	T-SQL and Spark	KQL, T-SQL, and Spark
Write operations	Spark (Scala, PySpark, Spark SQL, and R)	T-SQL	KQL, Spark, and connector ecosystem
Multi-table transactions	No	Yes	Yes, for multi-table ingestion (*https://oreil.ly/Pu_v6*)
Primary development interfaces	Spark notebooks and Spark job definitions	SQL scripts	KQL queryset and KQL database
Security	Row-level security (RLS), column-level security (CLS), and table-level (*https://oreil.ly/HgPXW*) security (T-SQL) (but none for Spark)	Object-level security (OLS) (*https://oreil.ly/fRTk4*), RLS (*https://oreil.ly/x2pHm*), CLS (*https://oreil.ly/KwJ1x*), DDL/DML, and dynamic data masking (*https://oreil.ly/K64hi*)	RLS
Access data via shortcuts	Yes	Yes, via SQL analytics endpoint	Yes
Can be a source for shortcuts	Yes (files and tables)	Yes (tables)	Yes
Query across items	Yes	Yes	Yes
Advanced analytics	Interface for large-scale data processing, built-in data parallelism, and fault tolerance	Interface for large-scale data processing, built-in data parallelism, and fault tolerance	Time series–native elements and full geospatial and query capabilities
Advanced formatting support	Tables defined using PARQUET, CSV, AVRO, JSON, and any Apache Hive–compatible file format	Tables defined using PARQUET, CSV, AVRO, JSON, and any Apache Hive–compatible file format	Full indexing for free text and semi-structured data like JSON
Ingestion latency	Available instantly for querying	Available instantly for querying	Queued ingestion, and streaming ingestion has a couple of seconds' latency

Summary

In this chapter, we've gone through several features and shown examples of how to use the OneLake catalog and the Real-Time hub. We've also shown you how to ingest data with Dataflow Gen1 and Dataflow Gen2, and we've given you insights into how to create data connections in Power BI for both the desktop application and the web experience. Lastly, we showed you how to create connections to KQL queries from both experiences, and we gave you the knowledge to choose the storage and compute service for your analytical workloads.

CHAPTER 3

Transforming Data

Raw data is rarely ready for reporting or analysis right away. It often contains duplicates, missing values, and inconsistent formats, and sometimes, its relationships between tables aren't optimal. That's why we must transform data to make sure that the data we use in our final analyses is accurate and performs well.

In this chapter, we investigate different techniques in Fabric for cleaning, enriching, and transforming our data. We begin by exploring how to create views, functions, and stored procedures to reuse logic and simplify data preparation. Then, we look into how to enrich data by adding new columns or connecting related tables. Next, we cover working with joins, aggregations, filters, and data types, all of which are necessary to shape data to fit our business questions. We also explain how to handle duplicates, missing values, and NULLs. After cleaning our data, we learn about the *star schema*, which is a common modeling pattern that organizes data for fast and intuitive analysis. Finally, we discuss *denormalization*, which is the process of combining related tables into one.

Creating Views, Functions, and Stored Procedures

When working with structured data in a lakehouse or warehouse in Fabric, there are various methods you can use to apply transformations early in the process. Instead of importing raw data into Power BI and transforming it there, you can define transformations sooner, during the data preparation process (for example, in the Fabric warehouse). This approach is particularly beneficial when you're managing large volumes of data or when you need to reuse specific logic, maintain it centrally, or apply it consistently.

Views, functions, and stored procedures are useful options for defining SQL logic that transforms your data. You'll generally create these objects in a Fabric warehouse, which offers full T-SQL support. In a lakehouse, you can also create views by using the SQL analytics endpoint, but functions and stored procedures are not yet supported there.

For example, you can use a view to create a cleaned-up version of a disorganized table or to restrict access to sensitive columns for specific users. Functions can calculate business-specific metrics, while stored procedures can automate multiple transformation steps as part of a repeatable process.

In the following sections, we'll explore what views, functions, and stored procedures are, when and why to use them, and how to create each in a Fabric warehouse. All examples use SQL and are relevant to both lakehouses and warehouses, unless otherwise noted.

Views

A *view* is a virtual table built on top of a SQL query. It doesn't store any data itself unless it's materialized, and if it is, the query results are physically stored for faster access. Otherwise, a view returns the result of the underlying query each time you access it. You can think of a view as a saved `SELECT` statement that behaves like a table.

Views are particularly useful when your data is spread across multiple tables and you find yourself writing the same joins, filters, or calculated columns repeatedly. Rather than duplicating that logic in every query, you can define it once in a view. This not only keeps your queries cleaner and easier to maintain but also helps enforce consistency across reports and users. Views can also help simplify complex datasets for your end users. For example, if a table contains sensitive or irrelevant columns that shouldn't be exposed to certain users, you can use a view to return only the subset of data they are allowed to see. It acts as a controlled, filtered version of the original table that's tailored to meet the specific needs of a user or application. In addition, views behave like tables from a security perspective. You can assign `SELECT` permissions directly to a view and thus allow a user to query it even if they don't have access to the underlying tables. This provides a convenient way to enforce row- or column-level restrictions without exposing the full source data.

By using views, you can present users with a clean, purpose-built dataset that contains exactly the information they need, without requiring them to write joins, filters, or calculations themselves. Everyone who queries the view will see the same logic and structure, which helps reduce errors and improve trust in the data.

You may wonder what happens when the underlying data changes. Since a view is based on a live SQL query, it always reflects the latest state of the underlying tables. If the structure of your data changes—for instance, if you rename a column or add new logic—you update the view definition and all reports using that view will benefit from the updated logic instantly.

In Microsoft Fabric, you can create views directly within a lakehouse or warehouse by using the SQL analytics endpoint. Once you create views, you can query them interactively, use them in pipelines, and load them into Power BI by using either Import or Direct Lake mode, just like regular tables.

To illustrate how to create a view, we can access the SQL analytics endpoint of either our Fabric lakehouse or our Fabric warehouse. In this example, we use the sales sample data provided by Microsoft in a Fabric lakehouse. We want to create a view that combines the customer key and customer from the customer table with the profit and number of transactions from the sales table. We can achieve this by opening our Fabric lakehouse, clicking on New SQL Query, and writing the following code:

```
CREATE VIEW dim_customer AS
SELECT
    c.CustomerKey,
    c.Customer,
    SUM(fs.Profit) AS Profit,
    COUNT(fs.SaleKey) AS NumberOfTransactions
FROM fact_sale fs
JOIN dimension_customer c
ON fs.CustomerKey = c.CustomerKey
GROUP BY c.CustomerKey, c.Customer;
```

When we write this query and click on Run, we create a new view. We can find in the navigation pane on the left side of the lakehouse screen, which includes tables, views, and the query we used to create the views (see Figure 3-1).

Views are great when you want to simplify data access, abstract business logic, or control what information is shown to different users. However, views are limited to returning result sets; they don't accept parameters or perform row-by-row operations. When your data transformation needs to be more advanced—for example, when calculations depend on input values or you need to use them in different queries—is when functions come in.

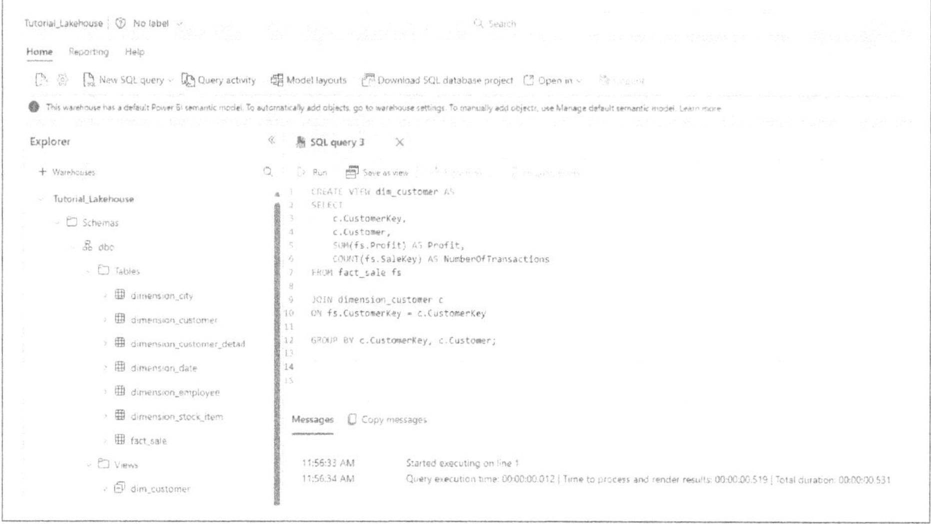

Figure 3-1. The SQL analytics endpoint of the Fabric lakehouse

Let's look at how functions work, what types exist, and how you can use them in a Fabric lakehouse or warehouse.

Functions

A *function* is a small, reusable block of SQL code. It takes an input (which is called a *parameter*), performs an operation on it, and returns a result. Functions are useful because they help you avoid repeating the same logic over and over again. If a certain calculation or transformation comes up often, turning it into a function means you only need to write and update it once.

There are two main function types: *scalar functions*, which return a single value, like a discount or a formatted date; and *table-valued functions*, which return a full table that you can use again in queries. While traditional SQL allows both scalar functions and table-valued functions, Fabric currently supports only *inline table-valued functions*. These functions return a result set, typically based on the input values, and are written as a single `RETURN SELECT` statement. This means you cannot use `BEGIN ... END` blocks, declare variables, or traditionally use conditional logic. However, you can still express quite a bit of logic using a CASE statement or expressions within the `SELECT`.

Scalar functions

Let's look at an example in which we define a function that calculates a discount based on the input sales amount. If the amount exceeds $1,000, we return a 5% discount; otherwise, we return zero:

```
CREATE FUNCTION fn_CalculateDiscount (@SalesAmount DECIMAL(10,2))
RETURNS TABLE
AS
RETURN
    SELECT
        CASE
            WHEN @SalesAmount > 1000 THEN @SalesAmount * 0.05
            ELSE 0
        END AS Discount;
```

After we run the query, we can see a new function in the Functions folder of our warehouse (see Figure 3-2).

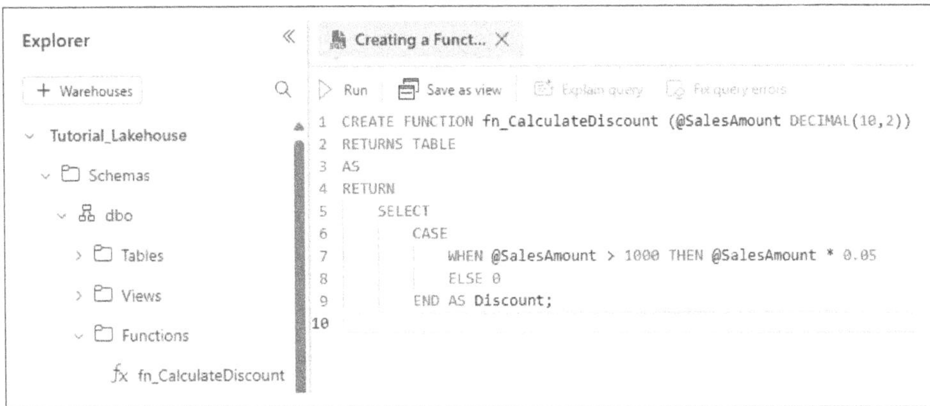

Figure 3-2. Query to define a function to create a discount of 5% when the sales amount is higher than $1,000

Once you've created this function, you can use it in a SELECT statement by passing a value as the parameter:

```
SELECT Discount
FROM fn_CalculateDiscount(1500)

SELECT Discount
FROM fn_CalculateDiscount(999)
```

The result for the top statement is 75, which is 5% of 1,500, while the number returned for the second statement is 0. Since 999 is below the 1,000 threshold, no discount applies. You can then use the value returned by this function in other SQL queries or views, for example, to calculate the total discount per customer or add discount logic to a sales report.

Table-valued functions

Now, let's now look at an example of a table-valued function, which returns multiple rows from a table based on input parameters. Table-valued functions are especially useful when you want to return a filtered or calculated subset of data that's based on one or more values you provide. Imagine you often need to retrieve high-value sales, meaning those where the sales amount exceeds a certain threshold. Rather than repeating the same filtering logic in every query, you can create a reusable function for that logic.

Here's an example of a table-valued function that accepts a minimum sales amount as input and returns all rows from the `fact_sale` table in which the total meets or exceeds the minimum amount. This example is based on the sales demo data provided in the Microsoft Fabric Lakehouse:

```
CREATE FUNCTION fn_GetHighValueSales (@MinAmount DECIMAL(10,2))
RETURNS TABLE
AS
RETURN
    SELECT
        SaleKey,
        CustomerKey,
        Profit,
        TotalExcludingTax,
        InvoiceDateKey
    FROM fact_sale
    WHERE TotalExcludingTax >= @MinAmount
```

This function accepts a single parameter: `@MinAmount`. It returns a table that contains all sales records in which `TotalExcludingTax` is greater than or equal to the amount passed in. The returned table includes selected columns such as the sale key, customer key, profit, and invoice date that may be relevant when you're analyzing high-value transactions.

After creating the function, you can use it in a query like you would any other table or view:

```
SELECT *
FROM fn_GetHighValueSales(500)
```

This query will return all sales with a total of $500 or more. The primary benefit of this is that the filtering logic is stored in one place (within the function), which makes it easy to reuse and maintain. If you ever want to change the threshold logic or add more filters, you only need to update the function once, instead of editing every individual query where this logic appears.

Stored Procedures

While views and functions are great for encapsulating reusable logic, *stored procedures* are ideal when you need to perform a series of steps or actions in a defined order. A stored procedure is a saved block of SQL statements that you can execute as a single unit. Unlike views and functions, which are primarily used to return data, stored procedures are typically used to perform actions, such as inserting data, updating tables, cleaning up staging data, and calling other procedures or functions.

Stored procedures are especially useful when you're automating a repetitive data preparation process or when you want to package logic that's too complex for a single `SELECT` statement.

Let's say you have a table with new sales records that you need to process and insert into your main `fact_sale` table. In traditional relational databases, this type of logic, which involves inserting data and optionally logging or validating it, is stored in a stored procedure. Here's an example of what a stored procedure might look like in a Fabric warehouse:

```
CREATE PROCEDURE sp_LoadSalesData
AS
BEGIN
    INSERT INTO fact_sale (SaleKey, CustomerKey, Profit, TotalExcludingTax)
    SELECT SaleKey, CustomerKey, Profit, TotalExcludingTax
    FROM stg_sale;
END
```

It's worth noting that Fabric lakehouses do support stored procedures, but with limited functionality. You can use them to run a fixed set of SQL commands, such as inserting data from one table into another. However, they don't support control-flow logic, such as IF statements, `WHILE` loops, and variable usage. Additionally, you can't call stored procedures in a lakehouse from notebooks or pipelines at this time. In practice, this means a stored procedure in a lakehouse acts more like a simple wrapper around a static SQL script. While this can be useful for organizing basic operations, it's not as flexible or dynamic as a stored procedure in a Fabric warehouse.

In Microsoft Fabric, views, functions, and stored procedures help you structure and reuse logic efficiently. Views are virtual tables based on SQL queries. They don't store data, but they simplify complex queries and control data access. Views are great when you want to simplify data access, abstract business logic, or control what information is shown to different users. Functions allow you to define reusable logic. Scalar functions return a single value, while table-valued functions return a full table. Functions are useful when you need consistent calculations or filtering logic across different queries or reports. Stored procedures group multiple SQL steps into a single unit, and they're ideal for tasks like inserting data, cleaning up staging tables, and running data workflows. In warehouses, stored procedures are flexible and support T-SQL features. In lakehouses, stored procedures are supported but limited, and you can only run simple SQL scripts without logic, variables, or parameters. You also can't call lakehouse-stored procedures from notebooks or pipelines. Table 3-1 provides an overview of all of this.

Table 3-1. Comparison of views, functions, and stored procedures

	Views	Functions	Stored procedures
What it is	A virtual table	Reusable logic	A group of steps
Stores data?	No	No	No
Returns	A table	One value or a table	Nothing (runs the steps)
Use cases	Simplifying queries and controlling data access	Repeating the same calculation	Running workflows
Used in	Reports and queries	Reports and queries	Pipelines and workflows
Supported in Fabric?	Yes	Yes	Fully in warehouses and limited in lakehouses

Enriching Data

Often, the tables containing data we receive from source systems are not exactly what we're looking for. Therefore, we need to understand how we can enrich our data by adding new columns or tables. In Fabric, we can enrich data both at the data engineering level in the lakehouse and warehouse and at the modeling level by adding columns and tables inside the Power BI data model.

Enriching Data in the Fabric Warehouse with SQL

The Fabric warehouse environment is built on a SQL engine similar to Azure SQL or SQL Server. Here, tables are relational and stored in a structured format that's optimized for fast queries. You enrich your data by creating new tables or modifying existing ones using Data Definition Language (DDL) SQL commands such as `CREATE TABLE` and `ALTER TABLE`.

For example, say you have a sales fact table that contains basic columns like `OrderID`, `ProductID`, and `SalesAmount`. If you realize that you need another column like `DiscountAmount`, you could create it by writing a SQL statement to change (alter) the existing table:

```
ALTER TABLE fact_sales
ADD DiscountAmount DECIMAL(10, 2);
```

Additionally, you could create new tables, such as a `dim_product` table with columns for product keys, names, categories, and prices:

```
CREATE TABLE dim_product (
    ProductKey INT NOT NULL,
    ProductName VARCHAR,
    Category VARCHAR,
    Price DECIMAL(10, 2)
);
```

The Fabric warehouse supports a wide variety of schema modifications. You're not limited to just adding new columns; you can also rename existing columns, change data types, and even remove columns when they are no longer needed.

Enriching Data in the Fabric Lakehouse with Notebooks

The Fabric lakehouse stores data in *Delta tables*, which are files saved in a special format (Parquet) that also supports transformation. These tables live in OneLake and are well suited to handling large, analytical datasets. You enrich your data in a Fabric lakehouse by adding new columns or creating new tables, just like in a Fabric warehouse. However, some things work a bit differently.

The most common way to enrich data is by using a notebook with Spark SQL, but other methods exist, such as dataflows and Hive queries. We'll focus on Spark SQL, but it is good to know that alternatives are available.

Let's say you have a table called `customer_data` that was created by loading a CSV file. It includes columns such as `Timestamp` and `CustomerName`. Later, you decide to enrich this data by adding a new column to classify each customer based on their region.

In a Microsoft Fabric notebook, you can use Spark SQL to do this. If you don't have a sample table you can work with, go ahead and create one by pasting this code into a Fabric lakehouse notebook:

```
%%sql
CREATE TABLE customer_data (
    CustomerID STRING,
    CustomerName STRING,
    Timestamp TIMESTAMP
);
```

Now, to add a new column called `Region` based on a condition (e.g., classifying customers by name), you can create a temporary view in a new notebook section:

```
%%sql
CREATE OR REPLACE TEMP VIEW customer_data_view AS
SELECT *,
       CASE
           WHEN CustomerName LIKE 'A%' THEN 'North'
           WHEN CustomerName LIKE 'B%' THEN 'South'
           ELSE 'Unknown'
       END AS Region
FROM customer_data;
```

Then, you can create a third notebook cell and overwrite the existing table with this enriched data using PySpark:

```
df = spark.sql("SELECT * FROM customer_data_view")
df.write.mode("overwrite").format("delta").saveAsTable("customer_data")
```

This workflow allows you to enrich your Delta table with new columns and logic while working within the lakehouse environment using notebooks and PySpark.

Enriching Data in the Fabric Lakehouse with Dataflow Gen2

If you're not comfortable enriching data by using notebooks and PySpark, you can employ the user-friendly interface of Dataflow Gen2. It offers a visual, no-code environment that you can use to transform and enrich your data in the Fabric lakehouse. This interface is easier for beginners or those who prefer a more guided approach to work with. This approach is also similar to the one we use when we transform our data in Power BI using Power Query.

You can also use Dataflow Gen2 with a Fabric warehouse, but the examples in this chapter focus on the Fabric lakehouse.

To use this approach, open your lakehouse and click on Get Data and New Dataflow Gen2 (see Figure 3-3).

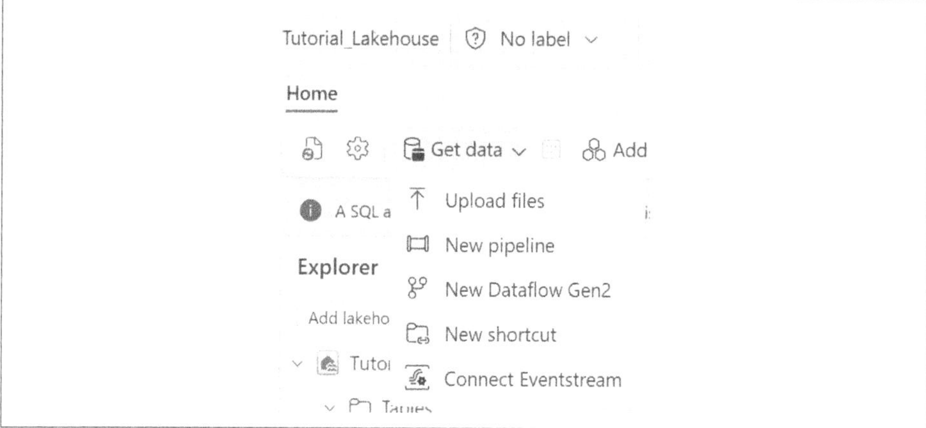

Figure 3-3. Creating a new Dataflow Gen2 in a Fabric lakehouse

After creating a new dataflow, you can connect it to your data source (for example, an existing `dimension_customer` table in your Fabric lakehouse). When you select the table you want to enrich or transform, it will bring up the query editor, at the top of which you'll find a Transform tab that offers a variety of options such as grouping, renaming, and splitting columns. Right next to it is the Add Column tab, where you can add new columns to your data.

For instance, you can add a conditional column that classifies customers based on existing fields like Customer. This functionality is very similar to writing a CASE statement in SQL or PySpark, but it uses an easy, visual interface, and no coding is required. See Figure 3-4 for an example of this interface.

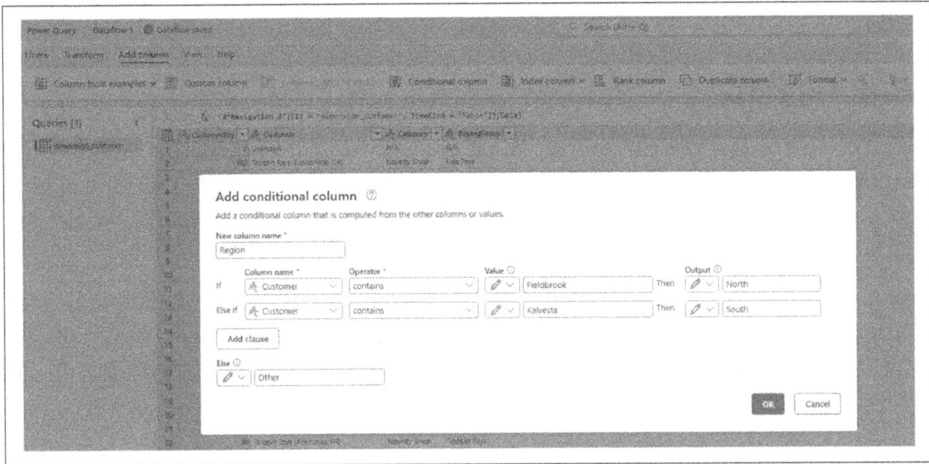

Figure 3-4. Creating a conditional column in Dataflow Gen2 in a Fabric lakehouse

Before publishing the table, you can check the bottom right to determine whether the data destination is correctly configured. Then, after you've made all the transformations you want to make, you can publish the table by clicking the Publish button (see Figure 3-5).

Figure 3-5. Choosing a destination and publishing transformations in Dataflow Gen2

The dataflow will apply the transformations and write the updated dataset back into OneLake as a Delta table. Using Dataflow Gen2, you can perform this transformation entirely without coding, through a visual interface.

Whether you work in the Fabric warehouse or the lakehouse, adding new columns or tables to your data helps you keep pace with changing business needs. By enriching your data, you can store new information, add useful categories, and enhance your analysis, making it clearer and more meaningful. For instance, creating tables allows you to filter and group your data easily, while adding columns prepares your data for more advanced calculations using SQL or DAX. Microsoft Fabric gives you the flexibility to enrich your data in ways that suit your skills and the project, whether by writing simple SQL commands, using notebooks with Spark SQL and PySpark, or working visually with Dataflow Gen2's no-code interface.

Learning these enrichment techniques is an important step in building data models and reports that evolve with your business and provide better and more meaningful insights.

Refining Data

Now that we've learned how to get data into Fabric and enrich it by adding new columns or tables, the next step is to refine it even further. Often, the information you need is spread across multiple tables or files. To get the whole picture, we need to combine that data.

Besides combining data, you often need to summarize it, filter it, and make sure each column has the correct data type. These are essential steps in preparing your data for reporting or analysis. There are different ways to do these things, depending on the choices you make for your data source and your personal preferences.

Let's start by exploring joins and merges for combining multiple tables.

Joins for Combining Data

Let's imagine we have two tables, one with orders (in `Order ID`, `Invoice Date`, and `Order Date` columns) and a shipment table (with `Shipment ID`, `Order ID`, and `Shipped Date` columns). These tables are related by the `Order ID` column, which appears in both. When we want to bring the data together (for example, to see when each order was shipped), we use a *join*. The `Order ID` column is referred to as a *key*, and we use it to match the rows.

Before we look at how to join data in Microsoft Fabric, let's look at the most common types of joins:

INNER JOIN

An INNER JOIN only keeps rows where a match is found in both tables. In our example, the following apply:

- If an order has a shipment, it will be included.
- If an order has no shipment (or a shipment has no matching order), it will be excluded.

This is useful when we only want to work with complete data (for example, only orders that have already shipped). Figure 3-6 shows you visually what an INNER JOIN looks like.

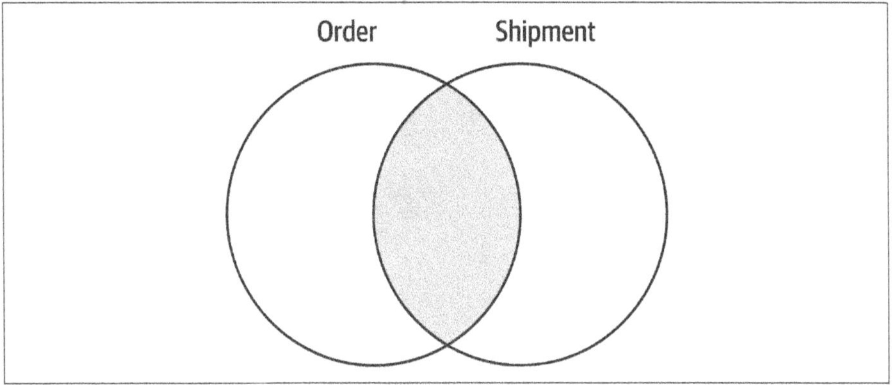

Figure 3-6. INNER JOIN of the order and shipment table, with only rows found in both tables kept

LEFT OUTER JOIN

A LEFT OUTER JOIN keeps all the rows from the first (left) table, even if no match is found in the second (right) table. In our example, the following apply:

- All orders are included.
- If a shipment is available, the shipped date is shown.
- If not, the shipment fields will be empty (NULL).

This is useful when you want to see all orders, including the ones that haven't shipped yet. Figure 3-7 shows you visually what a LEFT OUTER JOIN looks like.

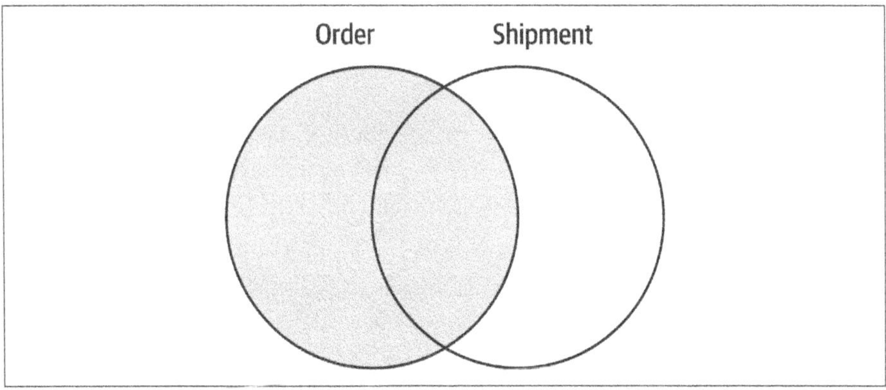

Figure 3-7. LEFT OUTER JOIN of the order and shipment table, with all rows from the left table and matching rows from the right table kept

RIGHT OUTER JOIN

A RIGHT OUTER JOIN is the opposite of a LEFT OUTER JOIN. It keeps all rows from the second (right) table, even if there's no match in the first (left) table. In our example, the following apply:

- All shipments are included.
- If there's a matching order, its details are shown.
- If not, the order fields will be empty (`NULL`).

This is less common but is sometimes used when the second table is the main focus.

Figure 3-8 shows you visually what a RIGHT OUTER JOIN looks like.

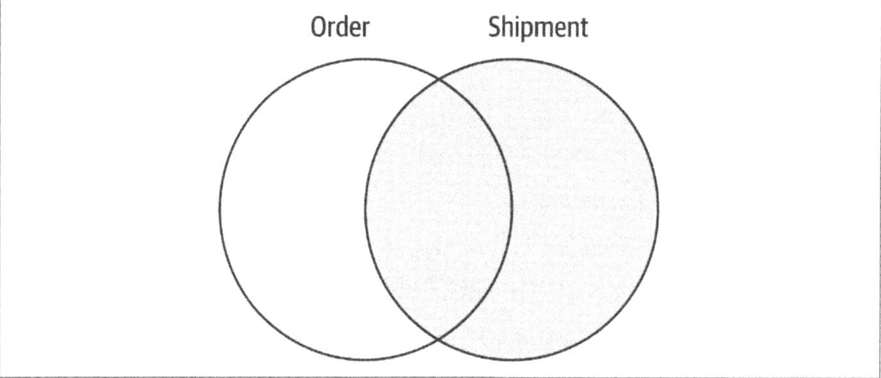

Figure 3-8. RIGHT OUTER JOIN of the order and shipment table, with all rows from the right table and matching rows from the left table kept

FULL OUTER JOIN

A FULL OUTER JOIN keeps all rows from both tables. Where there's a match, the data is combined, and if there's no match, the missing values are shown as empty. In our example, you get every order and every shipment.

Orders without shipments and shipments without orders are both shown, with empty fields where data is missing. This is useful in audits and quality checks to identify mismatches. Figure 3-9 shows you visually what a FULL OUTER JOIN looks like.

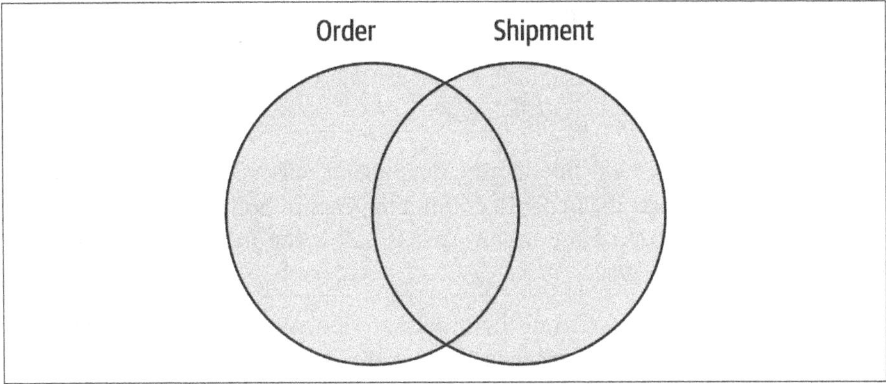

Figure 3-9. FULL OUTER JOIN of the order and shipment table, with all rows kept

Joins in a Fabric Warehouse

In a Fabric warehouse, you work with structured tables using T-SQL. Let's use our example again, in which we have an order table and a shipment table. Suppose you want to list all orders and show their shipment date if available. You'll use a `LEFT JOIN` for this:

```
SELECT
    o.OrderID,
    o.OrderDate,
    o.InvoiceDate,
    s.ShippedDate
FROM
    orders o
LEFT JOIN
    shipments s
ON
    o.OrderID = s.OrderID;
```

If you're new to SQL, the code might look a bit confusing at first, so let's break it down:

```
FROM
    orders o
```

This means we're starting with the orders table (the left table in Figure 3-9). The `o` is an alias that we assign to the table; it makes the rest of the query easier to read, especially if we have many columns or joins. Whenever we refer to the orders table, we can just write o, instead of the full name:

```
LEFT OUTER JOIN
    shipments s
```

This means we want to join the shipment table, with the alias s, and the join we want to perform is a LEFT JOIN:

```
ON
    o.OrderID = s.OrderID
```

This is the most important line in any join since it tells SQL how the two tables are connected. In this case, the OrderID column appears in both tables, and it represents the same thing: the ID of the order. This is called the *join condition*, and it must always be written after ON.

In our SQL query, all rows from the orders are included. If there's a shipment with the same OrderID, the ShippedDate is shown; if not, the ShippedDate column will be empty (NULL). This is a very common join in business scenarios (for example, to show all orders and whether they've been shipped yet).

Joins in a Fabric Lakehouse Using Notebooks

In the previous section, we used SQL in the Fabric warehouse to join two tables. But if we work with a lakehouse, we can use notebooks to perform the same operation. Let's continue with our example of orders and shipments. We want to join them using a LEFT JOIN, so that we keep all orders, even if no shipment has been registered yet.

First, we define a temporary view using Spark SQL, and then, we use PySpark to query the result:

```
%%sql
CREATE OR REPLACE TEMP VIEW order_shipments AS
SELECT o.OrderID,
       o.OrderDate,
       o.TotalAmount,
       s.ShippedDate,
       s.Carrier
FROM orders o
LEFT JOIN shipments s
  ON o.OrderID = s.OrderID;
```

This query creates a temporary view that combines both tables. For each order, we want to add the shipment information; however, if there is no shipment yet, those fields will be NULL. After creating the view, we can query it by using PySpark:

```
df = spark.sql("SELECT * FROM order_shipments")
display(df)
```

The df = spark.sql("SELECT * FROM order_shipments") line runs a SQL query inside the Fabric notebook using the Spark engine. It selects all the data from the temporary order_shipments view, which was previously created. The result of this query is stored in a variable named df, which is a Spark DataFrame. Once the data is loaded into this DataFrame, the next line, `display(df)`, shows the contents of that DataFrame directly in the notebook.

Alternatively, you can perform the join directly in PySpark without creating a SQL view:

```
df_orders = spark.table("orders")
df_shipments = spark.table("shipments")

df_joined = df_orders.join(df_shipments, df_orders.OrderID ==
    df_shipments.OrderID, "left")
display(df_joined)
```

The `df_joined = df_orders.join(...)` line runs a join operation entirely in PySpark, returning a Spark DataFrame. This shows the same result as the SQL approach, but it provides more flexibility if you want to apply further transformations programmatically.

In a Fabric lakehouse, using notebooks is a powerful way to work with large datasets. You can join tables using Spark SQL or PySpark, making it easy to combine data, enrich it, and prepare it for analysis or further transformation.

Joins in a Fabric Lakehouse Using Dataflow Gen2

A more visual and code-free way to join data is available through Dataflow Gen2. Within the lakehouse, we can create a new Dataflow Gen2 by selecting one of our tables and then use the Merge queries option on the home tab (see Figure 3-10).

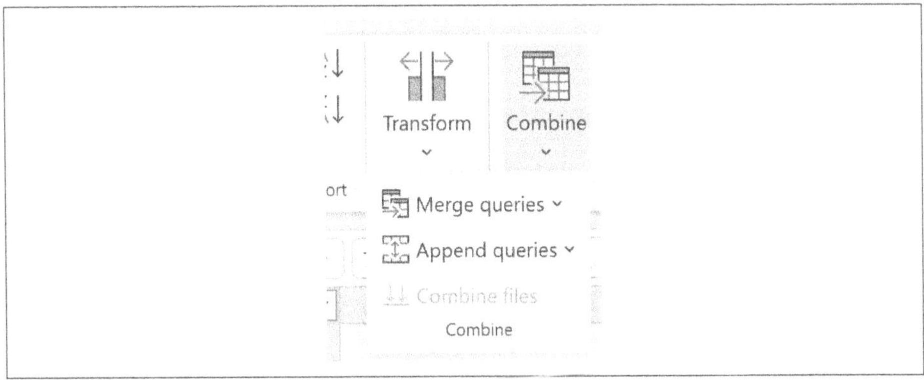

Figure 3-10. Merging queries, either in the current table or as a new table

Once you click Merge queries, you'll be asked to provide the second table (the right table) and then indicate the matching key by clicking on the columns, as shown in Figure 3-11. You can indicate multiple columns by holding down the Ctrl key on your keyboard while clicking on the columns.

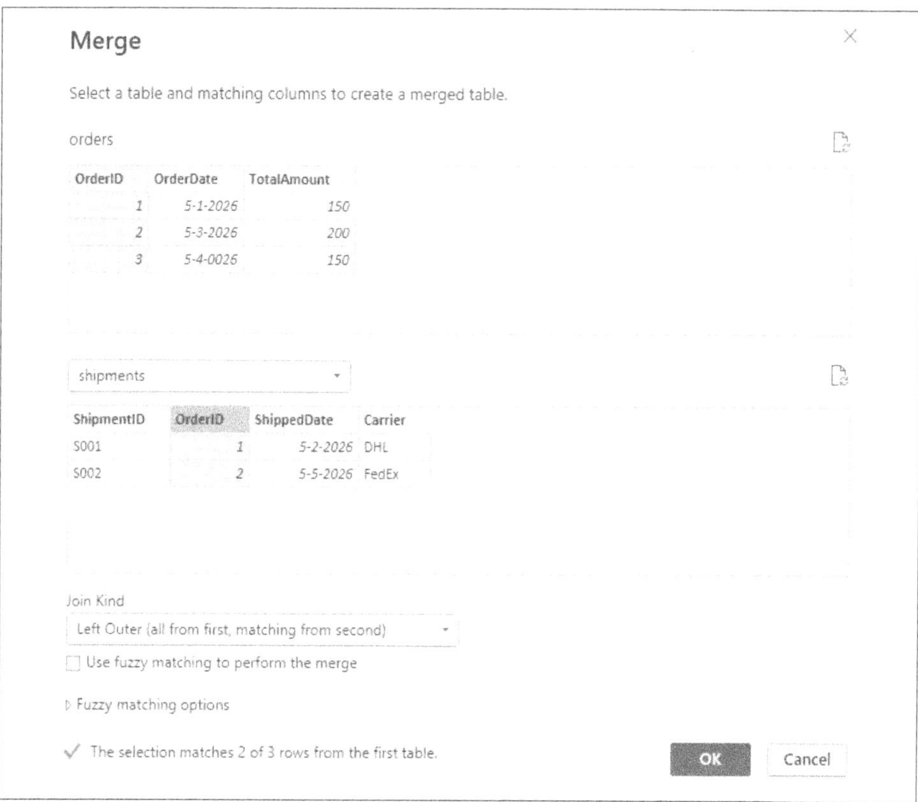

Figure 3-11. Selecting the second table in a pop-up and indicating the column where the merge should happen

After you choose the tables to join and specify the type of join, you'll see at the bottom of the pop-up window how many rows match between the tables. In our example, two out of three rows match. When you confirm the merge and expand the related columns, such as ShippedDate, the row without a match will show a NULL value for ShippedDate (see Figure 3-12).

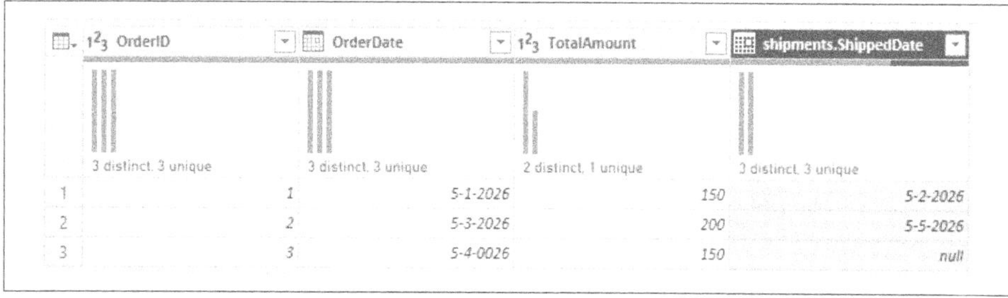

OrderID
OrderDate
TotalAmount
shipments.ShippedDate
3 distinct, 3 unique
3 distinct, 3 unique
2 distinct, 1 unique
3 distinct, 3 unique
1 1 5-1-2026 150 5-2-2026
2 2 5-3-2026 200 5-5-2026
3 3 5-4-0026 150 null

Figure 3-12. Results of a LEFT OUTER JOIN with one value not available in the second table

The result is a combined table that is ready for reporting or further transformation. Thanks to the intuitive visual interface, you don't need to write any code to perform these joins. This makes working with related data accessible for beginners and those who are less familiar with SQL or Spark. You may also notice join types called LEFT ANTI and RIGHT ANTI in the merge options (refer back to Figure 3-11). These join types are useful when you want to find rows in one table that do not have a corresponding match in the other table; this helps you quickly identify unmatched or missing data.

Whether you use SQL in the Fabric warehouse or notebooks and Dataflow Gen2 in the Fabric Lakehouse, you need to understand joins and merges. It helps you to bring together related data from different sources and create tables that support clear and insightful reporting and analysis.

Summarizing Data

After you combine your data by using joins, the next important step is to summarize it.

Aggregations to Summarize Data

Aggregations help you group your data and calculate meaningful totals, averages, and counts, and they can help you find minimum and maximum values. Common aggregation functions are as follows:

`SUM`
: This adds up all values in a group.

`COUNT`
: This counts the number of rows or non-NULL values.

`AVG`
: This calculates the average value.

`MIN`
: This finds the smallest value.

`MAX`
: This finds the largest value.

Let's look at two practical examples, total sales by product and number of customers by region, and how we can aggregate them in a Fabric warehouse by using SQL and a Fabric lakehouse with notebooks and Dataflow Gen2.

Aggregation in a Fabric Warehouse with SQL

Using SQL, we group and aggregate data with the `GROUP BY` clause. That clause tells SQL which column(s) to group the rows by, while the aggregation functions like `SUM` and `COUNT` operate on the grouped rows to calculate the summary value. For example, if we want to see total sales per product, we group the data by the `ProductName` column. The `SUM(SalesAmount)` part calculates the total sales within each group:

```
SELECT
    ProductName,
    SUM(SalesAmount) AS TotalSales
FROM
    sales
GROUP BY
    ProductName;
```

This query groups the sales data by product (`ProductName`) and calculates the total sales amount for each product using `SUM`. The result is a table that shows each product with its total sales.

Similarly, to count customers by region, we group by the `Region` column and use the `COUNT` function in the `CustomerID` column to find the number of customers in each region:

```
SELECT
    Region,
    COUNT(CustomerID) AS NumberOfCustomers
FROM
    customers
GROUP BY
    Region;
```

Here, the query groups rows by `Region` and counts the number of customer IDs in each group.

These SQL aggregation queries also work in a Fabric lakehouse using Spark SQL. In this chapter, we focus on the warehouse examples for clarity, but the same operations are possible in both environments.

Aggregation in a Fabric Lakehouse with Notebooks

In a notebook in a Fabric lakehouse, we use PySpark and work with DataFrames. To perform aggregations, we use the `.groupBy()` method to define the column(s) to group by, followed by an aggregation function like `.sum()`, `.count()`, or `.agg()`. Let's say we want to calculate total sales per product. Here's how we do it in PySpark:

```
sales_df.groupBy("ProductName").sum("SalesAmount").show()
```

The .groupBy("ProductName") method groups the data by the product name, .sum("SalesAmount") calculates the total sales per group, and .show() displays the result in the notebook. The results show each product with the corresponding sum of sales (see Figure 3-13).

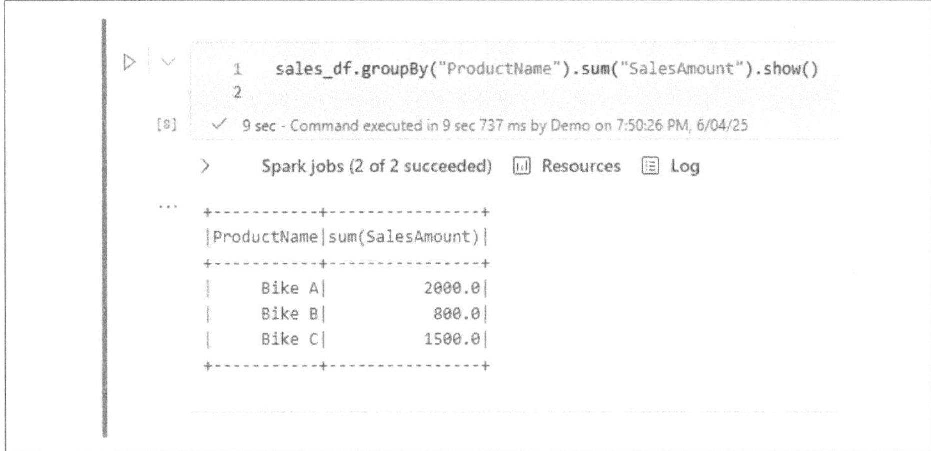

Figure 3-13. Grouping sales by product in a notebook

To count the number of customers by region, we can do something similar:

```
customers_df.groupBy("Region").count().show()
```

In this example, .count() counts how many rows (customers) are in each region. Since we're using .count() directly after .groupBy(), it returns the total number of rows in each group—which in this case is each region.

Aggregation in a Fabric Lakehouse with Dataflow Gen2

In Dataflow Gen2, aggregations are done visually through transformations in the Power Query editor. In our lakehouse, we can create a new Dataflow Gen2 and load our tables, and once we have the tables, we can click on Transform to reveal the Group by button (see Figure 3-14).

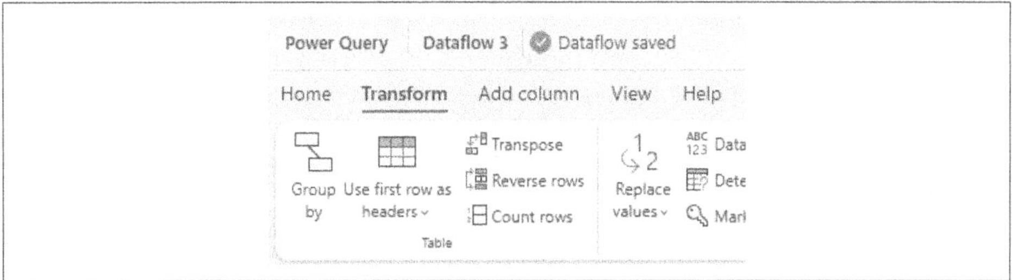

Figure 3-14. Clicking on Transform reveals the Group by button

Then, we can click on "Group by" to define how we want to group. For example, we can group by ProductName and then say what should happen, like summarizing the SalesAmount (see Figure 3-15).

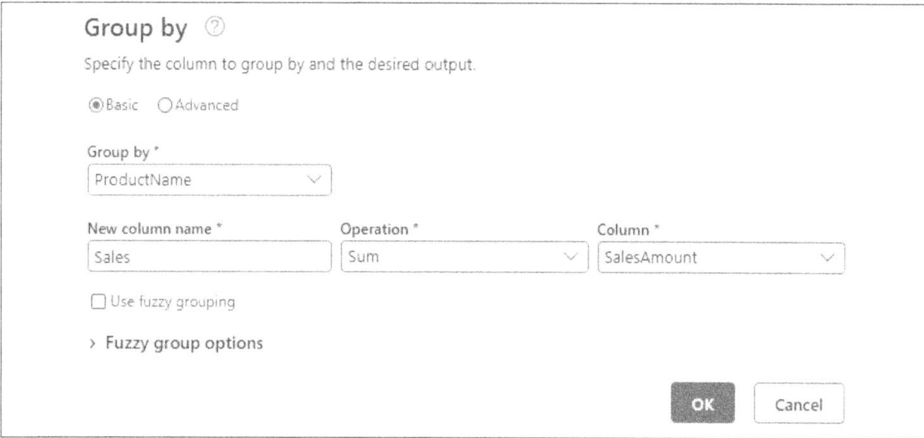

Figure 3-15. Summarizing the sales amount by product name

The result will be the Product in one column and the SalesAmount in the other.

After combining data using joins, *aggregation* is the next crucial step in transforming detailed data into meaningful summaries. Aggregations allow you to group rows by one or more columns and apply functions like `SUM`, `COUNT`, `AVG`, `MIN`, and `MAX` to calculate totals, averages, counts, or extremes within each group. In the Fabric warehouse, SQL's `GROUP BY` clause groups data while aggregation functions calculate summary values per group. In the Fabric lakehouse, notebooks utilize the `.groupBy()` method with aggregation functions such as `.sum()` and `.count()` to achieve the same result. Dataflow Gen2 enables visual grouping and aggregation via the Power Query "Group by" transformation, making summarizing accessible without code.

Whether you work in the Fabric warehouse or the lakehouse, adding new columns or tables to your data helps you keep pace with changing business needs.

Filters and Focusing on Relevant Data

Another important step when working with data is filtering it to make it as narrow and relevant as possible. We filter our tables to include only rows that meet certain criteria, because it enhances performance and makes analysis more straightforward. Depending on where we handle our data, we can use different filtering approaches:

- The `WHERE` clause in SQL, which specifies conditions rows must meet to be included

- Filtering rows in notebooks, using Spark/PySpark DataFrames with conditional expressions
- Visual filters in Dataflow Gen2, using Power Query transformations

Filtering Data

Let's have a look at how to apply filters in a Fabric warehouse using SQL, in a Fabric lakehouse using notebooks, and visually in Dataflow Gen2.

Filtering in a Fabric Warehouse with SQL

In SQL, you perform filtering with the `WHERE` clause, which allows you to specify conditions for rows to be selected. For example, if you only want to look at sales orders from the last 30 days, you can filter based on the order date:

```
SELECT *
FROM sales
WHERE
OrderDate >= DATEADD(day, -30, CURRENT_DATE);
```

This query returns all rows where the `OrderDate` is within the 30 days prior to today. To filter sales where the amount is greater than $100, the query would be as follows:

```
SELECT *
FROM sales
WHERE SalesAmount > 100;
```

The `WHERE` clause tells SQL to include only rows where the condition is true.

Filtering in a Fabric Lakehouse with Notebooks

In PySpark notebooks, you perform filtering by applying conditional expressions on DataFrames using the `.filter()` or `.where()` method. Both `.filter()` and `.where()` work the same way, and you can chain them with other transformations. For example, to filter orders from the last 30 days, do the following:

```
from pyspark.sql.functions import current_date, date_sub

recent_sales_df = sales_df.where(sales_df.OrderDate >=
date_sub(current_date(), 30))
recent_sales_df.show()
```

Here, `.filter()` keeps only rows where the `OrderDate` is within the last 30 days.

In Microsoft Fabric notebooks, you can use both SparkSQL and PySpark to filter and transform data. While SparkSQL uses SQL-like syntax and PySpark uses Python-based DataFrame operations, the two are interchangeable for most tasks. Throughout this chapter, we'll show examples using PySpark.

Filtering in a Fabric Lakehouse with Dataflow Gen2

In Dataflow Gen2, we perform filtering visually in the Power Query editor. When we select a column that we want to filter, we can click on the arrow next to the column name and select the action. For example, in a date column, we can choose Date filters (see Figure 3-16).

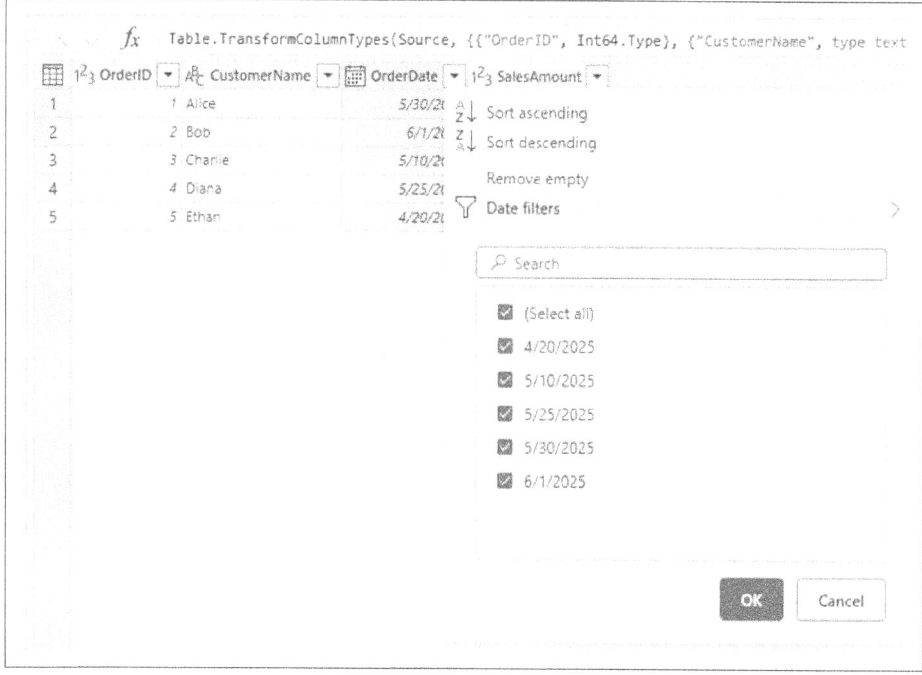

Figure 3-16. Filter options in Power Query for a date column

Here we can choose "is in the previous," which will open a new window where we can define what we mean by *previous*, like the previous 30 days (see Figure 3-17).

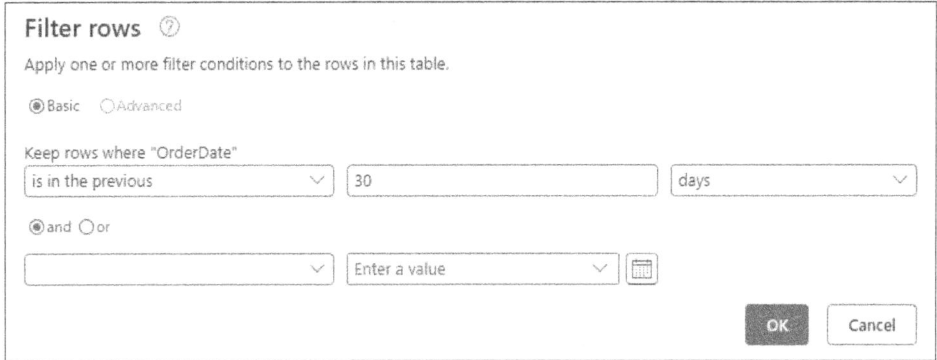

Figure 3-17. Filtering rows that are in the previous 30 days

Depending on the data type the column has, we have different options for filtering. For example, we could filter on a SalesAmount column with currency as the data type (see Figure 3-18).

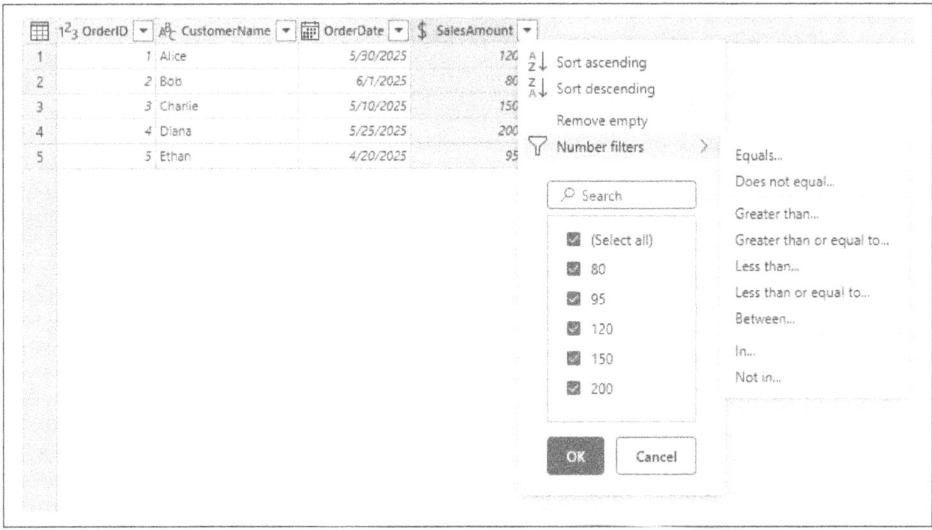

Figure 3-18. Filter options for a SalesAmount column

Previously, we could filter on dates, and now, we can filter on numbers. We can also filter on specific numbers with "Equals" and "Does not equal" or provide a range like "Greater than."

Filtering is an important technique for narrowing down our data to only what's relevant for our analysis. In SQL, we do this using the `WHERE` clause, which allows us to specify conditions. In notebooks, we use the `.filter()` or `.where()` method on DataFrames to apply similar conditional logic. In Dataflow Gen2, we do filtering visually through the Power Query editor, where we can set conditions on columns to include only the rows we want. Applying filters not only reduces the data volume we work with but also helps improve query performance, thus ensuring that our insights are focused on the most important data.

Data Types

Data types define the type of data stored in each column, such as integers, strings, decimals, or date and time values. We need to understand data types because they determine the operations that we can perform on the data. For example, we can't sum a text column, and trying to do so will cause errors or unexpected results. Common data types include integers (int), decimal numbers, strings (text), and dates and timestamps. Sometimes, data is stored in the wrong type (e.g., numbers may be saved as text), and that can lead to issues when aggregating or filtering data. Also, storing dates as strings can prevent correct sorting or date calculations.

To avoid these problems, we need to ensure that each column has the appropriate data type. There are three different ways to manage data types, depending on whether we're doing it in SQL, notebooks, or Dataflow Gen2:

In SQL
: We can change a column's data type by using the `CAST` function. For example, if a column is stored as text but contains numbers, we can convert it to an integer with `CAST(column AS INT)` to perform mathematical operations.

In PySpark notebooks
: We can manage data types by using the `.cast()` method. We create a new `DataFrame` column with the desired type by applying `.withColumn("column", df["column"].cast("int"))`, which converts the column to integers so numeric calculations can be done correctly. Have a look at Figure 3-19 to see how a SalesAmount column, which was a text data type, is transformed to an integer.

  At the bottom of the figure, you'll see that we can now also make calculations with this column.

```
total_sales = df_casted.groupBy().sum("SalesAmount").collect()[0][0]
print(f"Total sales: {total_sales}")

[1] ✓ 17 sec - Session ready in 12 sec 1 ms. Command executed in 5 sec 466 ms by Demo on 9:05:05 PM, 6/04/25

> Spark jobs (8 of 8 succeeded)  Resources

... Original schema:
root
 |-- ProductName: string (nullable = true)
 |-- SalesAmount: string (nullable = true)

+-----------+-----------+
|ProductName|SalesAmount|
+-----------+-----------+
|   ProductA|        100|
|   ProductB|        200|
|   ProductC|        150|
+-----------+-----------+

Schema after casting SalesAmount to int:
root
 |-- ProductName: string (nullable = true)
 |-- SalesAmount: integer (nullable = true)

+-----------+-----------+
|ProductName|SalesAmount|
+-----------+-----------+
|   ProductA|        100|
|   ProductB|        200|
|   ProductC|        150|
+-----------+-----------+

Total sales: 450
```

Figure 3-19. The SalesAmount column was a text data type and is transformed to an integer data type

In Dataflow Gen2

We can manage data types visually by selecting a column and choosing the correct type from the Data Type drop-down menu to the left of the column name in the Power Query editor (see Figure 3-20).

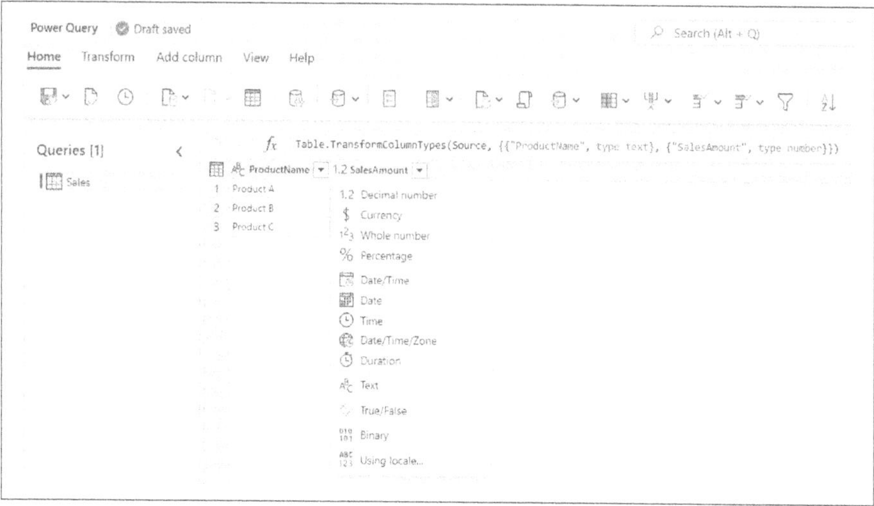

Figure 3-20. Changing the data type in a Dataflow Gen2 by clicking on the column and choosing a data type

In summary, we need to correctly understand and manage data types to ensure accurate data processing and analysis. Ensuring each column has the appropriate type prevents errors, improves performance, and enables meaningful calculations and filtering. Whether they're using SQL, notebooks, or Dataflow Gen2, mastering data type conversions is an essential skill for any data analyst working with Fabric.

By learning how to join tables, summarize values, apply filters, and manage data types, you're taking the key steps toward transforming raw data into meaningful, structured datasets. These operations form the backbone of data preparation. Whether you're writing SQL queries, analyzing data in notebooks, or designing dataflows, you can employ these skills to ensure that your data is reliable, relevant, and ready for analysis.

Handling and Resolving Duplicate, Missing, and NULL Values

Real-world data is hardly ever perfect when we load it into our data source. Regardless of whether we're preparing data in a warehouse or a lakehouse, we frequently encounter missing fields, duplicate rows, and unexpected NULL values. We need to address these issues before delivering the data to the person who'll be working with it, to ensure that the end user can trust the data and easily work with it without having to perform numerous transformations themselves.

Deduplication: Removing Duplicate Data

Duplicate data can appear in tables for many reasons. Data may be loaded multiple times, a join may not be performing as it should, or there may simply be an error in the source system. If we don't remove duplicate table rows, they can harm our data analysis. For example, sales numbers may be too high, and that can lead to a lack of trust in the data.

We have different options for deduplicating our data, depending on the transformation method we choose. Let's have a look at the table shown in Figure 3-21, where we see order data with duplicate rows.

	123 OrderID	ABC CustomerID	OrderDate	1.2 TotalAmount
1	1	C001	2024-06-01	100.00
2	2	C002	2024-06-01	200.00
3	3	C001	2024-06-02	150.00
4	3	C001	2024-06-02	150.00
5	4	C003	2024-06-03	*NULL*
6	5	C004	*NULL*	300.00
7	6	*NULL*	2024-06-04	120.00
8	6	*NULL*	2024-06-04	120.00

Figure 3-21. Table with OrderIDs 3 and 6 loaded twice, resulting in duplicates

Deduplication in a Fabric Warehouse with SQL

In a Fabric warehouse, we can use SQL to select only the rows that are unique by using the `DISTINCT` statement:

```
SELECT DISTINCT CustomerID
FROM orders_with_issues;
```

Figure 3-22 shows the results this statement produces.

We can also choose to remove duplicates based on specific columns:

```
SELECT DISTINCT OrderID, CustomerID, OrderDate
FROM orders_with_issues;
```

Messages Results

	OrderID	CustomerID
1	1	C001
2	2	C002
3	3	C001
4	4	C003
5	5	C004
6	6	*NULL*

Figure 3-22. Table containing only unique rows due to the `DISTINCT` statement in the SQL query

This table is quite straightforward, but often, we'll deal with much larger tables in which it's much harder to spot duplicates in the data. To find out if there are any duplicates, we can write another query that counts, for example, every row where a specific column appears more than once:

```
SELECT OrderID, COUNT(*) AS Count
FROM orders_with_issues
GROUP BY OrderID
HAVING COUNT(*) > 1;
```

This SQL query helps identify duplicates in the `orders_with_issues` table. It groups all rows by the `OrderID` column and counts the number of times each `OrderID` appears. If an `OrderID` appears more than once, it's considered a duplicate. The `HAVING COUNT(*) > 1` code filters the results so that only the duplicates are shown. The result is a list of `OrderIDs` that occur multiple times, along with the frequency of their appearance. Figure 3-23 shows the results of this query for our example.

Messages Results

	OrderID	Count
1	3	2
2	6	2

Figure 3-23. Query results showing two duplicate table rows that were identified with the `HAVING` statement

Deduplication in a Fabric Lakehouse with Notebooks

We can also handle and resolve duplicates with notebooks, by writing PySpark code in a notebook linked to our lakehouse. Just as in SQL, we can state that we want to remove duplicates in general or based on a column like `OrderID`. We do this by using the `.dropDuplicates` statement, which we can do in the following ways:

`orders_df.dropDuplicates().show()`
: This removes duplicates.

`orders_df.dropDuplicates(["OrderID"]).show()`
: This removes duplicates based on OrderID.

This allows us to either fully remove identical rows or simply deduplicate based on a specific key, such as `OrderID`. This way, we can remove duplicates easily using a notebook (see Figure 3-24).

```
Table with duplicates
+-------+----------+----------+-----------+
|OrderID| OrderDate|CustomerID|TotalAmount|
+-------+----------+----------+-----------+
|   A001|2024-06-01|      C001|      100.0|
|   A004|2024-06-04|      C004|      200.0|
|   A002|2024-06-02|      C002|       NULL|
|   A003|2024-06-03|      NULL|      150.0|
+-------+----------+----------+-----------+

Table after removing duplicates)
+-------+----------+----------+-----------+
|OrderID| OrderDate|CustomerID|TotalAmount|
+-------+----------+----------+-----------+
|   A001|2024-06-01|      C001|      100.0|
|   A002|2024-06-02|      C002|       NULL|
|   A003|2024-06-03|      NULL|      150.0|
|   A004|2024-06-04|      C004|      200.0|
+-------+----------+----------+-----------+
```

Figure 3-24. Table in a notebook before and after application of `dropDuplicates` statement

Deduplication in a Fabric Lakehouse with Dataflow Gen2

In Fabric Dataflow Gen2, we can handle duplicates and NULL values by using visual transformations without writing code. We do this by applying filters and transformations in the Power Query editor. After we open our dataflow, we can click on "Remove rows" and then "Remove duplicates" in the navigation pane (see Figure 3-25).

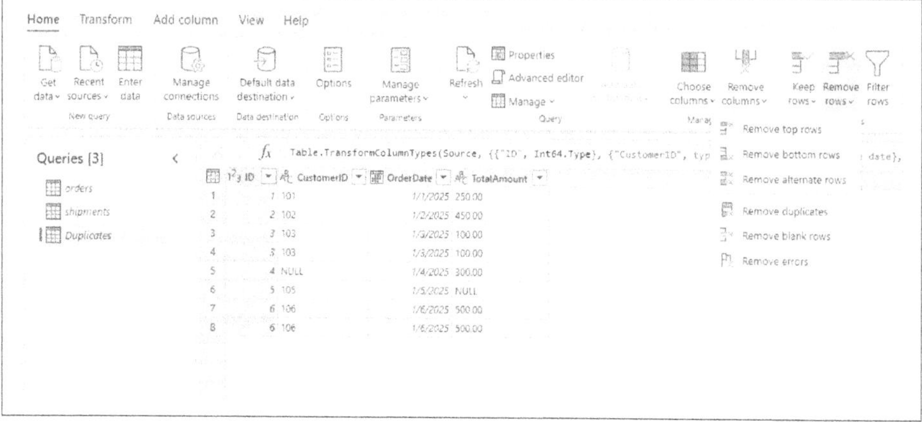

Figure 3-25. Removing duplicates in Dataflow Gen2

If we want to see exactly which rows are duplicates, we can click on "Keep rows" and "Keep duplicates" (see Figure 3-26).

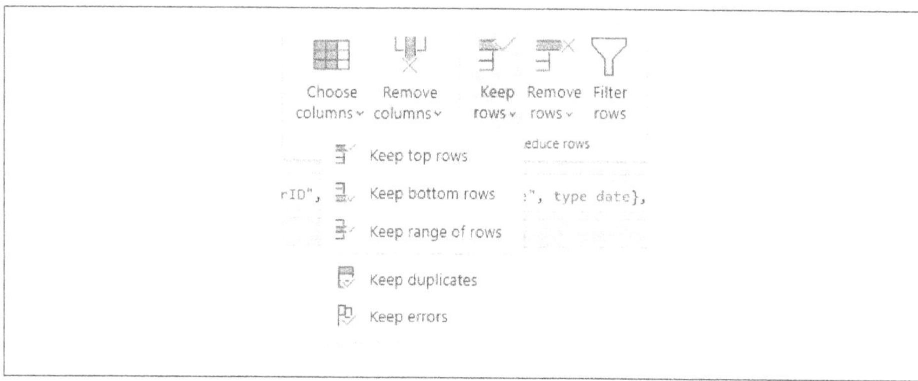

Figure 3-26. Viewing duplicates

Keeping all the duplicates can be very handy when you want to analyze the cause of the duplicates and how many rows are impacted.

Handling NULLs and Missing Values

A NULL represents unknown or missing data. While common, NULLs can cause problems if you don't handle them properly. For example, trying to sum or compare NULLs can return unexpected results. However, a NULL is not simply an empty value or zero; it means unknown or missing information, which means that we can't simply replace it with a zero value. Also, a NULL value is not equal to anything, not even another NULL value, which means that it's treated as false in filtering or joining data. For example, if we write a query and put `NULL = NULL` in the `WHERE` statement, we'll get no results.

Before you take any action to handle a NULL, such as replacing or dropping it, you need to understand why a value is missing. Is it missing because of late-arriving data, is there a technical issue (such as a failed load), or is the field optional and the NULL completely valid? Understanding the cause of a NULL helps you choose the right strategy for dealing with it. Replacing a `NULL` with a default value like `0` or `" "` (an empty string) might seem harmless, but it could lead to incorrect interpretations of the data and business decisions based on wrong data. In addition to understanding the technical aspects, you need to discuss these kinds of issues with, for example, the data owner/architect, the business stakeholders who understand the process behind the data, or other team members involved in the development process.

Handling NULLs in a Fabric Warehouse with SQL

When writing SQL in a Fabric warehouse, we need to understand how to handle missing values correctly. We know that missing values are shown as NULL, and when we write a query, we can use `IS NULL` or `IS NOT NULL` to detect missing values. For example, if we want to find out which `CustomerID` in our example is `NULL`, we can write the following query, which returns only rows where the `CustomerID` is `NULL`:

```
SELECT *
FROM orders_with_issues
WHERE CustomerID IS NULL;
```

Figure 3-27 shows the results.

Messages Results

	123 OrderID	ABC CustomerID	OrderDate	1.2 TotalAmount
1	6	*NULL*	2024-06-04	120.00

Figure 3-27. Results of a SQL query to find all rows where the `CustomerID` column is `NULL`

Sometimes, you'll want to replace NULL with a default value (for example, to make totals easier to aggregate or display in a report). But be careful! Replacing NULL with 0 or an empty string can lead to a misinterpretation of the data. For instance, a NULL in `TotalAmount` might indicate that the order is not yet finalized, while a `0` might suggest that the order is free or has been cancelled:

```
SELECT OrderID, COALESCE(TotalAmount, 0) AS TotalAmount
FROM orders_with_issues;
```

Figure 3-28 shows the results of a query that replaces NULL with 0.

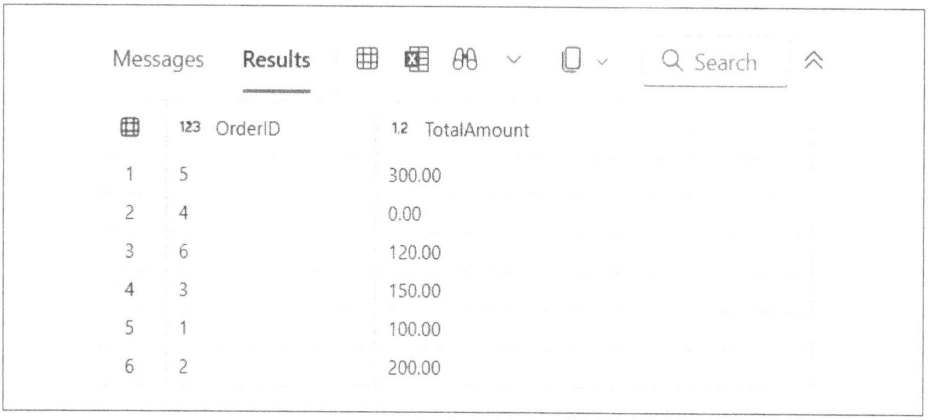

Messages Results Search

	OrderID	TotalAmount
1	5	300.00
2	4	0.00
3	6	120.00
4	3	150.00
5	1	100.00
6	2	200.00

Figure 3-28. Results of replacing a NULL with a 0

You should only apply this when you're sure that a default value reflects the intended meaning of the missing data. Replacing NULL changes the meaning of the data, and unless you're confident about the business logic behind it, it's not a good idea to replace NULLs with zeros.

In some cases, it's best to exclude rows with missing values. We can filter them out with this code:

```
SELECT *
FROM orders_with_issues
WHERE CustomerID IS NOT NULL;
```

This removes rows where the CustomerID is unknown, and it ensures that your dataset includes only valid references.

Handling NULLs in a Fabric Lakehouse with Notebooks

In Microsoft Fabric notebooks, `NULL`s are handled like they are in SQL. They represent missing or unknown data, and operations like comparisons or aggregations behave differently when `NULL`s are present. Using PySpark, we can choose several statements to transform `NULL` values. The most common ones are as follows:

`.Na.drop()`
: This function removes entire rows if one or more columns contain `NULL` values. While this can help clean up incomplete records, it also comes with risks because dropping rows may lead to unintended data loss. So, before you use `.na.drop()`, you need to determine whether the affected rows contain valuable data that should be retained and whether the missing value truly makes the entire row unusable.

`.fillna()`
: With `.fillna()`, you replace `NULL` with a specific default, so you should only use `.fillna()` when you're confident that the default value reflects the intended meaning. For example, using `0` might be misleading if the actual reason for the `NULL` was a processing delay or a missing entry from another system.

`.replace()`
: While `.fillna()` specifically targets `NULL` (which indicates missing values), `.replace()` is a more general function that's used to replace any specified value with another. This is useful for standardizing or cleaning data beyond just handling `NULL`s (for example, replacing placeholder strings like `"N/A"` or correcting inconsistent spellings). It can replace values regardless of whether they are `NULL` or not.

Figure 3-29 shows us the effect each of these commands has on our data.

```
Original data with NULLs:
+-------+----------+----------+-----------+
|OrderID| OrderDate|CustomerID|TotalAmount|
+-------+----------+----------+-----------+
|   A001|2024-06-01|      C001|      100.0|
|   A002|2024-06-02|      C002|       NULL|
|   A003|2024-06-03|      NULL|      150.0|
|   A004|2024-06-04|      C004|      200.0|
|   A005|2024-06-05|      NULL|       NULL|
+-------+----------+----------+-----------+

Drop rows with NULL CustomerID:
+-------+----------+----------+-----------+
|OrderID| OrderDate|CustomerID|TotalAmount|
+-------+----------+----------+-----------+
|   A001|2024-06-01|      C001|      100.0|
|   A002|2024-06-02|      C002|       NULL|
|   A004|2024-06-04|      C004|      200.0|
+-------+----------+----------+-----------+

Fill NULL TotalAmount with 0:
+-------+----------+----------+-----------+
|OrderID| OrderDate|CustomerID|TotalAmount|
+-------+----------+----------+-----------+
|   A001|2024-06-01|      C001|      100.0|
|   A002|2024-06-02|      C002|        0.0|
|   A003|2024-06-03|      NULL|      150.0|
|   A004|2024-06-04|      C004|      200.0|
|   A005|2024-06-05|      NULL|        0.0|
+-------+----------+----------+-----------+

Replace NULL CustomerID with 'Unknown':
+-------+----------+----------+-----------+
|OrderID| OrderDate|CustomerID|TotalAmount|
+-------+----------+----------+-----------+
|   A001|2024-06-01|      C001|      100.0|
|   A002|2024-06-02|      C002|       NULL|
|   A003|2024-06-03|   Unknown|      150.0|
|   A004|2024-06-04|      C004|      200.0|
|   A005|2024-06-05|   Unknown|       NULL|
+-------+----------+----------+-----------+
```

Figure 3-29. The original table, a table where `NULLs` are removed, a table where `NULLs` for `TotalAmount` are replaced with 0, and a table where `NULLs` for `CustomerID` are replaced with `UNKNOWN`

While the examples in the following section use PySpark, SparkSQL is also a valid option. It handles NULLs slightly more predictably in some cases, especially in comparisons.

Handling NULLs in a Fabric Lakehouse with Dataflow Gen2

In Dataflow Gen 2, we handle `NULL` or missing values through visual transformations, which makes it intuitive to detect, replace, or filter out `NULL`s without writing code.

You can replace `NULL`s or any specific value in a selected column by applying the "Replace values" transformation. This is useful for substituting `NULL`s with a default value like `UNKNOWN` or 0, but only when such a value accurately reflects the data context. You can find the "Replace values" option in the navigation pane (see Figure 3-30) or by right-clicking on a column name (see Figure 3-31).

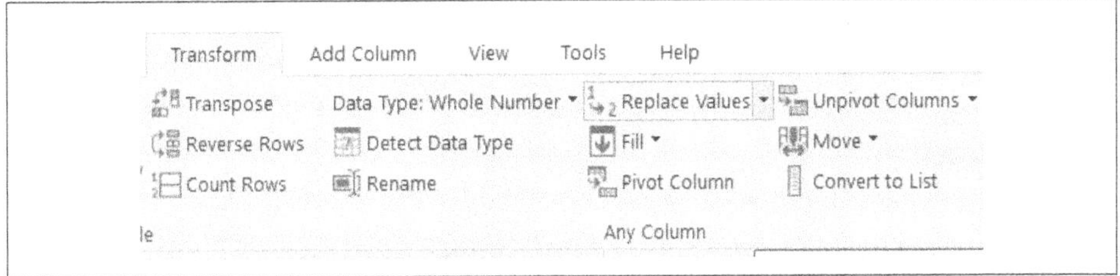

Figure 3-30. Replacing values in the selected column with any specified value by clicking the "Replace values" button

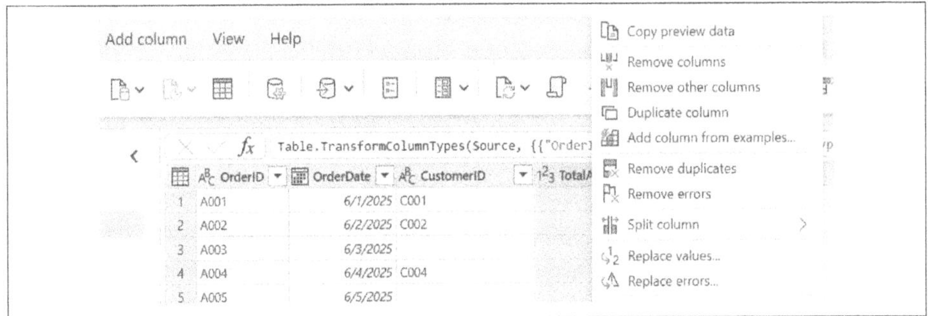

Figure 3-31. Replacing values by right-clicking on a column name and then clicking on "Replace values"

We can also filter the rows that contain `NULL`s by clicking on "Filter rows" in the navigation pane (see Figure 3-32). That opens another window, where we can also choose whether to filter a single column or multiple columns (see Figure 3-33).

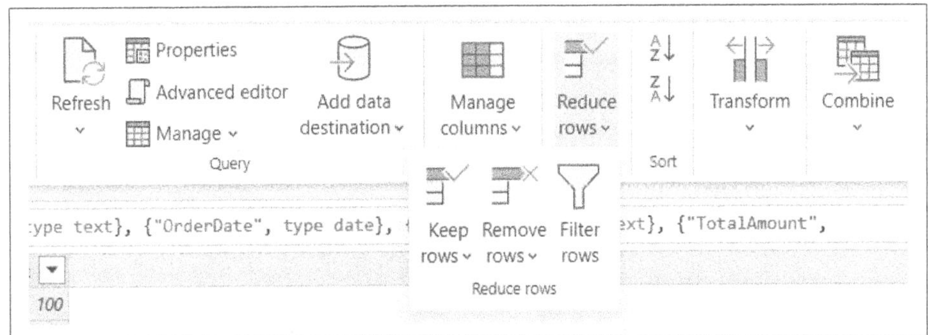

Figure 3-32. Filtering rows in a table by clicking "Filter rows" and specifying a filter action

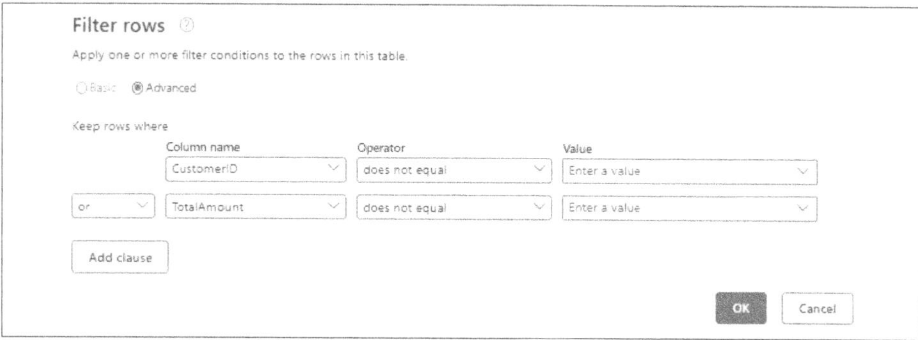

Figure 3-33. Filtering multiple rows that do not contain NULLs

As you can see, you can also filter on other conditions by using the "Filter rows" transformation.

Handling duplicates, NULLs, and missing data is a fundamental part of preparing data for analysis and reporting. Duplicates can inflate counts or totals, leading to misleading insights. NULLs and missing data represent unknown or incomplete information that requires attention, and simply replacing them without understanding the context can negatively impact your data's meaning.

In practice, it's important to identify why data is missing or duplicated before taking action. This involves working closely with data owners, source system experts, or business users to gain a thorough understanding of the data.

Star Schema for Fabric Lakehouse and Warehouse

After preparing and cleaning our data, removing duplicates, handling NULLs, enriching the data with new columns, and shaping it through joins and aggregations, the next step is to organize this data for efficient analysis and reporting. This is where the *star schema* comes in. The star schema is a widely used approach for modeling data. Ralph Kimball introduced it in 1996, and it has remained a best practice ever since, due to its simplicity, performance, and flexibility. While it's not exclusive to Microsoft Fabric, the star schema remains highly relevant to building efficient data models on modern platforms.

In a star schema, data is divided into two main types of tables: fact tables and dimension tables. *Fact tables* store actual events or numeric values (such as sales amounts or quantities), while *dimension tables* describe the context of those values (such as products, customers, time, or locations).

This design offers several advantages. It helps users navigate the data more intuitively, and queries perform better because the structure minimizes the number of joins.

Additionally, the model is easier to maintain and adapt when the business changes (for example, if a customer moves or a product is rebranded).

In summary, we choose a star schema because it lets us create fast, scalable, and easy-to-understand data models for a wide array of users. For instance, we can import a star schema developed within a Fabric lakehouse or warehouse into Power BI.

Due to the design of the star schema, Power BI developers can easily establish relationships, resulting in a data model that is both clear and reliable.

Figure 3-34 shows an example of a star schema.

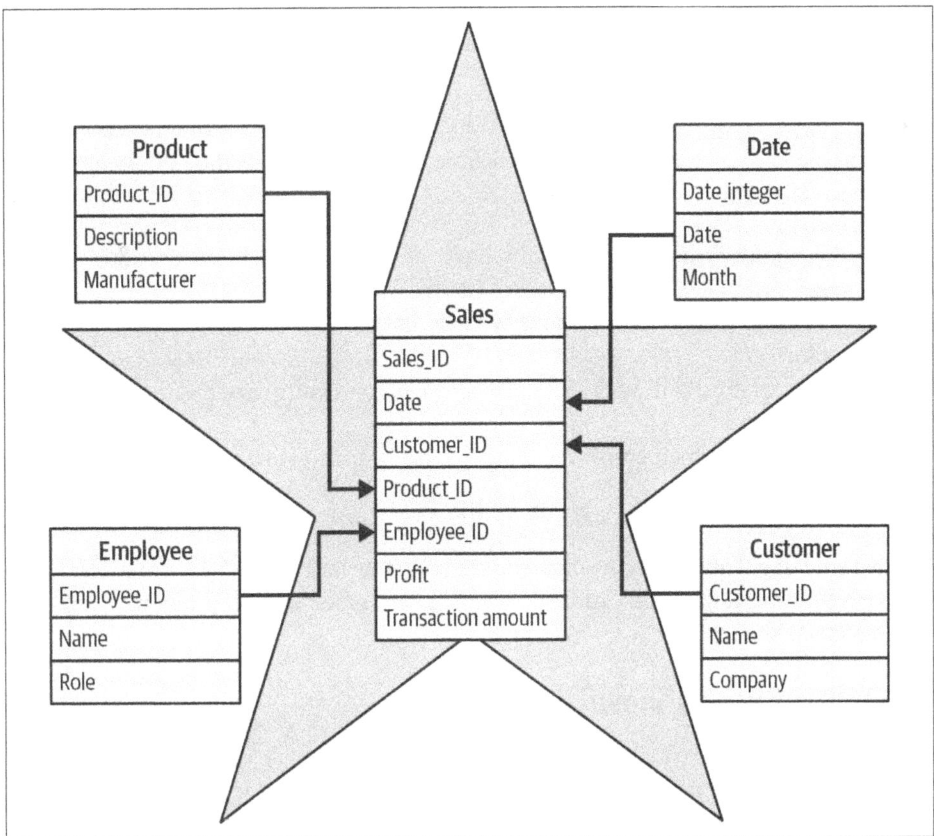

Figure 3-34. A star schema with one fact table and four dimension tables connected to it

So now, you might be wondering, what does a star schema look like and how can I create one? Let's start with the basics. As shown in Figure 3-34, a star schema typically features one central fact table (in this case, Sales) with a number of dimension tables that refer to it. Let's dive into the details of each kind of table:

Fact table

The fact table measures events and contains numerical values. In our example, it contains numerical data about sales transactions, but it could also contain values like sales amounts, profits, discounts, and various measurable metrics. The fact table is at the center of the star, and it connects to each dimension table.

Each row in a fact table represents an event (e.g., sales) and links to the corresponding dimension keys. This enhances query efficiency and enables users to interact with the data more easily in tools like Power BI, as a well-structured model with reliable relationships allows the Power BI developer to concentrate on creating insights from the data instead of remodeling it within Power BI.

Dimension tables

The dimension tables contain descriptive information (called *dimensions*) that help users answer questions like "Who, what, where, why, and when?" In the example in Figure 3-31, these dimensions and the questions they can help answer are as follows:

Customer: who made the purchase, and what is their name, address, and age?
Product: what was sold, and what is its product name, category, size, and color?
Date: when did the sale take place, in what year or quarter and on which day of the week?
Employee: which employee handled the sale, and what's their name, address, and role?

But before we get into how to create a star schema in a Fabric lakehouse or warehouse, we want to address another well-known schema and show why the star schema is our schema of choice for use in Fabric.

Star Schema versus Snowflake Schema

You may have also heard about the *snowflake schema*, which is a variation in which dimension tables are normalized into subdimensions. For example, a Product dimension table might be divided into Product and Product detail tables (see Figure 3-35).

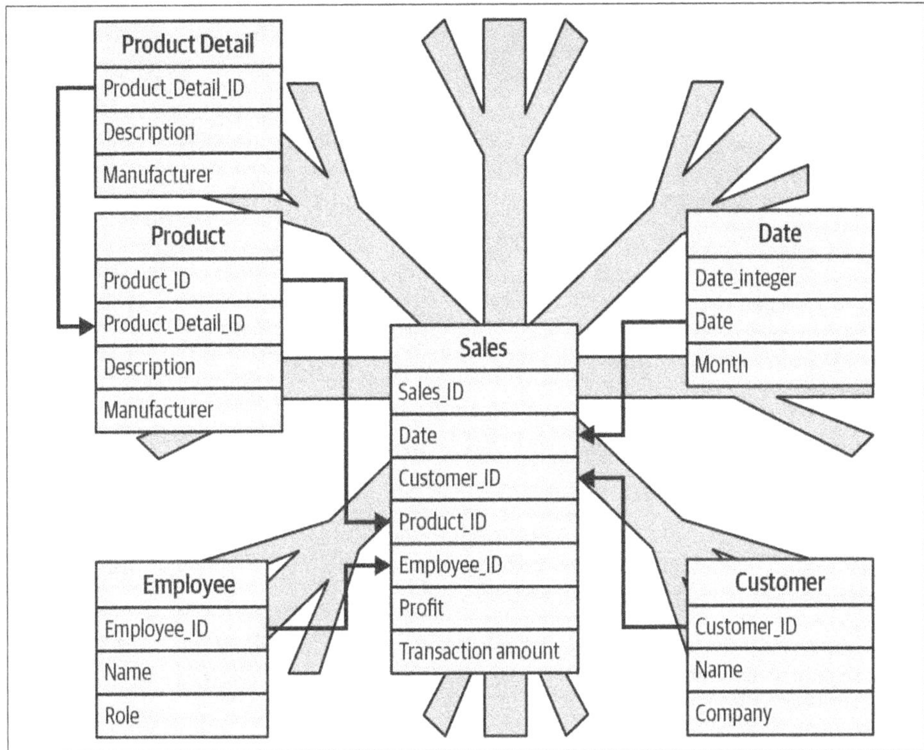

Figure 3-35. A snowflake schema

This approach reduces data redundancy, which can be helpful in certain transactional or storage-optimized systems. However, in analytics scenarios, such as those built in Power BI or Fabric, this normalization usually causes more problems than it solves. It increases the number of relationships and joins in your model, which can make queries slower and the model harder to navigate and filter. That's why the star schema is almost always preferred. It simplifies the data structure, improves query performance, and makes the model more intuitive for end users.

While the star and snowflake schemas are the most commonly used ones for analytics, other modeling approaches exist and are typically used for other purposes, such as staging and operational systems.

Implementing a Star Schema in a Fabric Lakehouse

Now that we've explored the definitions and basics, let's have a look at what we need to do to implement a star schema in a Fabric lakehouse (we'll cover implementation in a warehouse later, since it's a slightly different process). After you create a lakehouse in Fabric and load some data, such as one of the sample datasets provided by Microsoft, you can begin transforming it with either of the following methods, depending on your expertise and preferences:

Notebooks (PySpark)
: This is ideal for large-scale or complex transformations, especially on semi-structured data.

Dataflows Gen2
: This is suitable for low-code users (as is Power Query in Power BI).

Both methods are suitable for creating a star schema; they use different approaches to achieve the same goal of organizing and transforming your data. Regardless of the approach you choose, you will need to create a fact table (e.g., Sales) and dimension tables (e.g., Customer, Product, Date, and Store).

Each dimension should have a unique key, known as the *primary key*, and the fact table should store foreign keys that reference those dimensions. In Figure 3-36, you can see a fact table in a lakehouse.

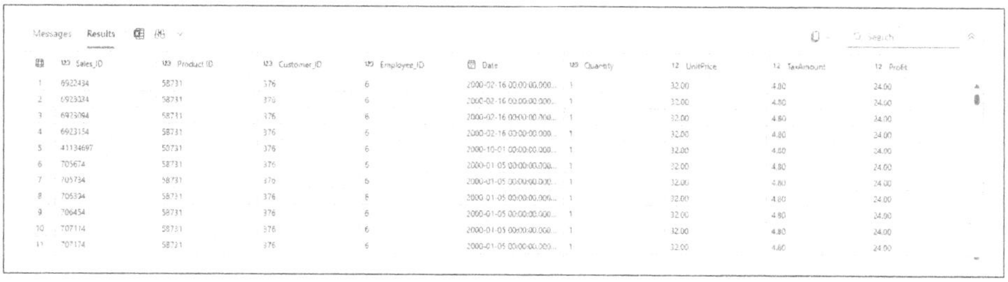

Messages Results

	Sales_ID	Product ID	Customer_ID	Employee_ID	Date	Quantity	UnitPrice	TaxAmount	Profit
1	6922434	58731	376	6	2000-02-16 00:00:00.000...	1	32.00	4.80	24.00
2	6923034	58731	376	6	2000-02-16 00:00:00.000...	1	32.00	4.80	24.00
3	6923094	58731	376	6	2000-02-16 00:00:00.000...	1	32.00	4.80	24.00
4	6923154	58731	376	6	2000-02-16 00:00:00.000...	1	32.00	4.80	24.00
5	41134697	50731	376	6	2000-10-01 00:00:00.000...	1	32.00	4.80	24.00
6	705674	58731	376	6	2000-01-05 00:00:00.000...	1	32.00	4.80	24.00
7	705734	58731	376	6	2000-01-05 00:00:00.000...	1	32.00	4.80	24.00
8	706334	58731	376	6	2000-01-05 00:00:00.000...	1	32.00	4.80	24.00
9	706454	58731	376	6	2000-01-05 00:00:00.000...	1	32.00	4.80	24.00
10	707114	58731	376	6	2000-01-05 00:00:00.000...	1	32.00	4.80	24.00
11	707174	58731	376	6	2000-01-05 00:00:00.000...	1	32.00	4.80	24.00

Figure 3-36. A fact table in a Fabric lakehouse, containing all the foreign keys related to the primary keys in the dimension table

The fact table displays all the foreign keys related to the primary keys in the dimension tables. For example, Customer_ID 376 corresponds to the record in Figure 3-37 in the Customer dimension table.

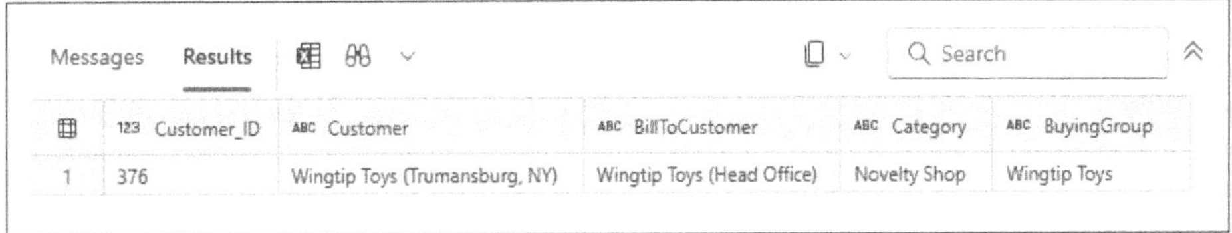

	Customer_ID	Customer	BillToCustomer	Category	BuyingGroup
1	376	Wingtip Toys (Trumansburg, NY)	Wingtip Toys (Head Office)	Novelty Shop	Wingtip Toys

Figure 3-37. Record in the Customer dimension table that's related to the fact table in Figure 3-36

You'll often need to create these tables yourself, since most data sources don't deliver data structured like this. For each dimension table, you need to define a primary key, and for the fact table, you need to include foreign keys that reference the keys in the dimension tables. By creating the different tables and providing the keys, you create the base for a star schema in your lakehouse that Power BI can consume.

Implementing with PySpark notebooks

To create tables via a PySpark notebook, you go to your lakehouse in Fabric and click on Open notebook > New notebook (see Figure 3-38). This lets you start a new Spark notebook that's attached to the lakehouse.

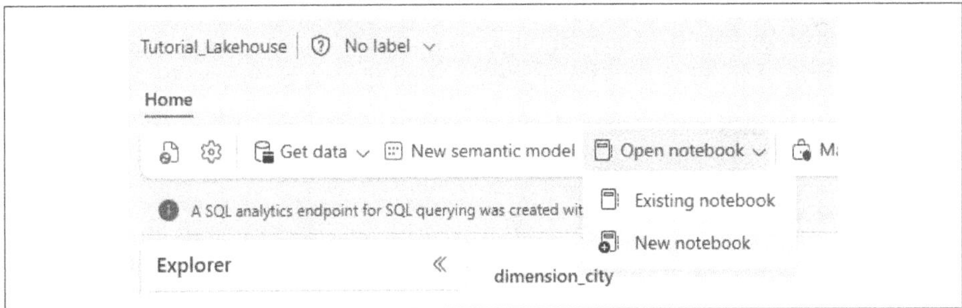

Figure 3-38. Opening a new notebook in the lakehouse

Once you've opened the notebook, you can write the Python code to create the dimension and fact tables. We've provided some example code in Figure 3-39.

```
# Welcome to your new notebook
# Type here in the cell editor to add code!

Dimension_Customer = spark.read.table("Tutorial_Lakehouse.dimension_customer")
Dimension_Customer = Dimension_Customer.select("CustomerKey", "Customer", "Category", "BuyingGroup").dropDuplicates(["CustomerKey"])
Dimension_Customer.write.mode("overwrite").saveAsTable("Dimension_Customer")
```

3 sec - Running   PySpark (Python)

Figure 3-39. Notebook with Python code for creating a customer table

With the Python code, you can create a table for the Customer dimension with a primary key that will be linked to the fact table. The Customer dimension table will include the customer's name, category, and buying group (see Figure 3-40).

Data preview - dimension_customer Showing 1000 rows

	CustomerKey	Customer	Category	BuyingGroup
1	0	Unknown	N/A	N/A
2	1	Tailspin Toys (Head Office)	Novelty Shop	Tailspin Toys
3	2	Tailspin Toys (Sylvanite, ...	Novelty Shop	Tailspin Toys
4	3	Tailspin Toys (Peeples Va...	Novelty Shop	Tailspin Toys
5	4	Tailspin Toys (Medicine L...	Novelty Shop	Tailspin Toys
6	5	Tailspin Toys (Gasport, N...	Novelty Shop	Tailspin Toys

Figure 3-40. Customer dimension table in a Fabric lakehouse

Implementing with Dataflow Gen2

You can also perform the same implementation with Dataflow Gen2. This can be very convenient for developers (especially those with experience in transforming data in Power BI) who are looking for a low-code/no-code approach.

To transform the data using Dataflow Gen2, go to your Fabric lakehouse, click on Get Data, and then select New Dataflow Gen2 (see Figure 3-41).

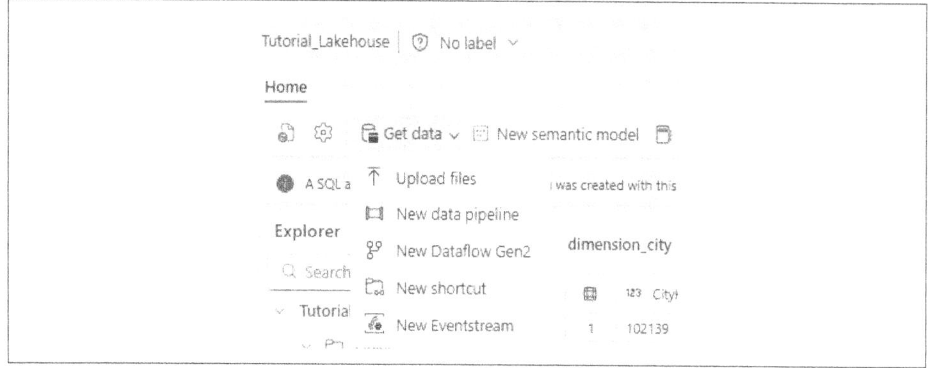

Figure 3-41. Creating a New Dataflow Gen2 in a Fabric lakehouse

That will open a Power Query Editor, where you can connect to the existing tables in the lakehouse, transform them, or create new tables to build the dimension and fact tables you want. The entire experience is similar to what we have in Power BI, so no coding experience is required. After making all the changes to your tables, you can publish the dataflow to the lakehouse.

Whether you choose Notebooks or Dataflows Gen2, your goal remains the same: shape your data into dimension and fact tables with clearly defined relationships. This structure allows for efficient querying and reporting in Power BI. The two methods produce identical types of tables that will be stored in the lakehouse and ready for use in a star schema model. Which method you should choose depends on your level of expertise and whether you prefer to write code or work with a graphical interface.

Next, we'll explore how to implement a star schema in a Fabric warehouse, which follows a slightly different process.

Implementing a Star Schema in a Fabric Warehouse with SQL

Just like in a lakehouse, you can build a star schema in a Fabric warehouse by creating dimension and fact tables. The main difference is that a warehouse supports T-SQL and works with structured tables by default. This approach is well-suited to users who prefer writing SQL or want to work in a more classic data warehouse environment. You can load your own data or sample data into the warehouse, and you can use T-SQL to shape and structure the data into dimension and fact tables.

Just as in a lakehouse, each dimension table in a warehouse should have a primary key and the fact table stores foreign keys that reference those dimensions. The primary advantage here is that warehouses support schema definitions, data types, constraints, and indexing, making them ideal for structured reporting workloads.

When you open your Fabric warehouse, you can write queries yourself to create the tables or use the SQL templates provided (see Figure 3-42).

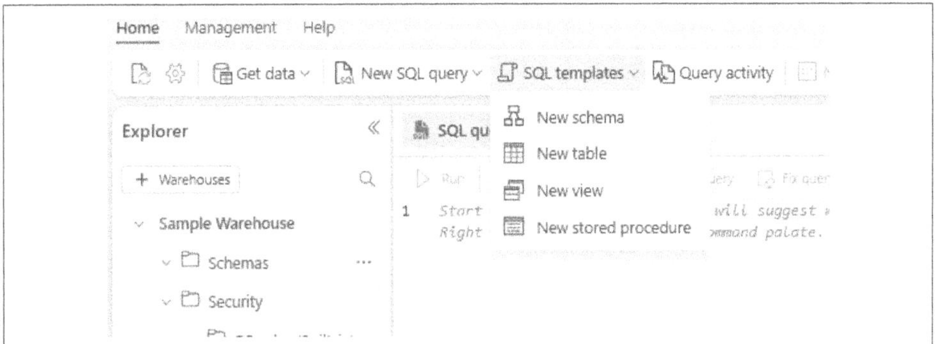

Figure 3-42. SQL templates in a Fabric Warehouse

Starting from a SQL template can make it easier for you to create the fact table and dimension tables.

General Principles of Dimensional Modeling

Whether you're working in a lakehouse (which is more flexible and suited to big data and semi-structured sources) or a warehouse (which has strict schema and is ideal for structured, relational data), the principles of dimensional modeling remain the same:

- Use fact tables to measure business events.
- Use dimension tables to describe your business and those events.
- Keep it simple for both technical and business users.

The structure you create forms the foundation for Power BI data models and reports. A well-designed star schema enables faster performance, better usability, and a reliable starting point for analysis.

Denormalization of Data

In the previous section, we explored how a star schema provides structure and clarity to our data. It separates business concepts (dimensions) from measurable events (facts) to create a clean and comprehensible model. We also briefly explained the snowflake schema, where sales data was connected to a Product table that was linked to a Product detail table (see Figure 3-43).

This setup is technically correct and follows the rules of *normalization*, which involves splitting your data into smaller, related tables to avoid repetition. However, it can also make your model more difficult to use in Power BI. Why? It's because Power BI needs to follow the relationships between these tables every time a user interacts with a visual or applies a filter, which can lead to slower performance and more complex DAX calculations. It also makes it more difficult for report users to explore the data themselves, especially if they don't understand the underlying structure.

That's where denormalization comes in. Let's say you have these tables in your model:

- Fact: Sales
- Dimension: Product
- Dimension: Product detail

To denormalize, we want to combine the information in the Product and Product detail tables so that we end up working with just one table, which will make our model a star schema instead of a snowflake schema.

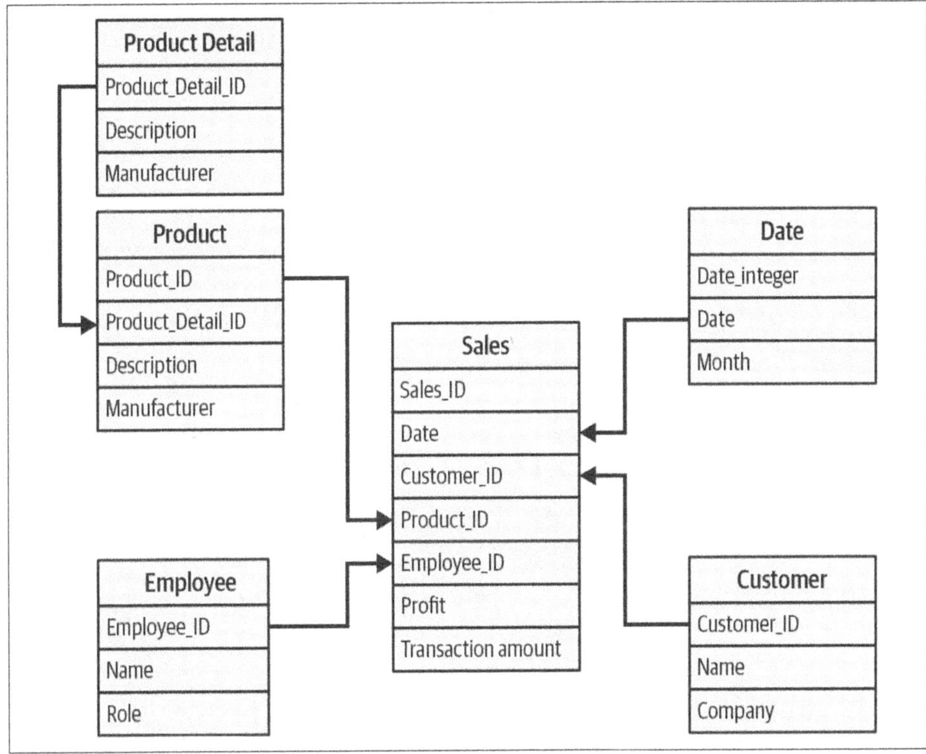

Figure 3-43. A snowflake schema with a Product table and a Product detail table

Denormalizing Tables with Power Query

Let's say you are working in Power BI and connected to the tables in your Fabric lakehouse or warehouse that you created earlier. Now, you have a Product table and a Product detail table (see Figures 3-44 and 3-45).

Product_ID	ProductName	ProductCategory	ProductSubCategory
1	Running Shoes	Footwear	Sports
2	Basketball Shoes	Footwear	Sports
3	Leather Boots	Footwear	Casual
4	T-Shirt	Apparel	Casual
5	Sweatshirt	Apparel	Sportswear
6	Baseball Cap	Accessories	Headwear
7	Sunglasses	Accessories	Eyewear
8	Sports Watch	Electronics	Wearable
9	Laptop Backpack	Accessories	Bags
10	Yoga Pants	Apparel	Sportswear

Figure 3-44. Product table with a `Product_ID` column

Product_Detail_ID	Product_ID	Color	Size	Material
101	1	Blue	42	Mesh
102	1	Black	44	Mesh
103	2	Red	43	Synthetic
104	3	Brown	44	Leather
105	4	White	M	Cotton
106	5	Gray	L	Fleece
107	6	Navy Blue	One Size	Polyester
108	7	Black	One Size	Plastic Frames
109	8	Black	N/A	Silicon/Rubber
110	9	Black	N/A	Nylon

Figure 3-45. Product detail table with a `Product_ID` column

As you can see in Figure 3-46, the Product detail table has a relationship to the Product table through the `Product_Detail_ID` column that's in both tables.

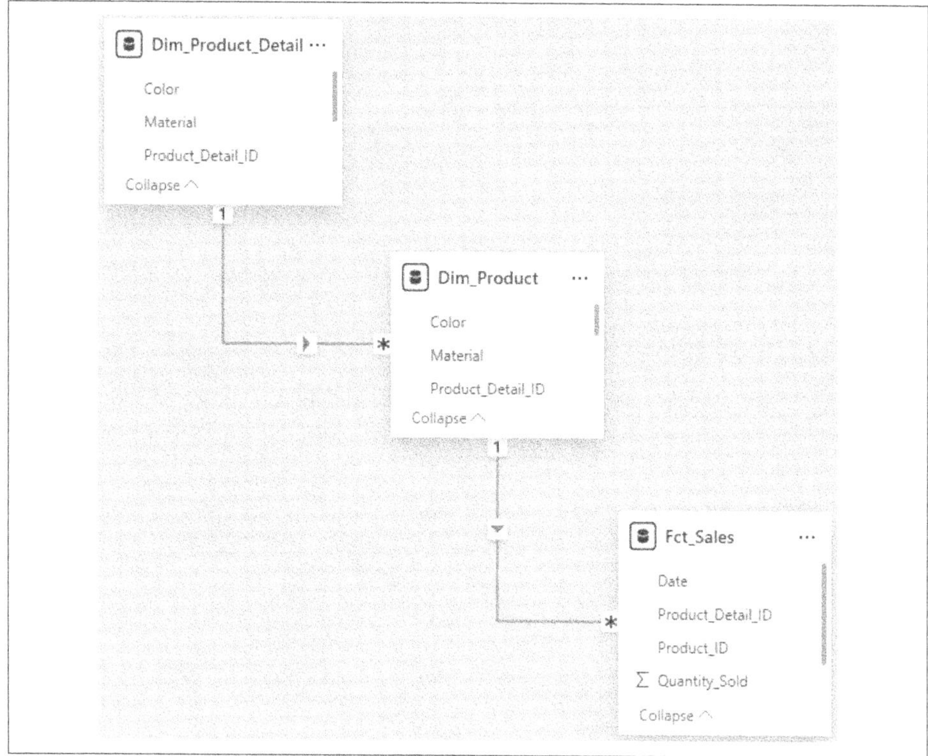

Figure 3-46. The Product and Product detail tables have a relationship to each other

You can denormalize directly in Power BI, specifically in Power Query. By following the steps in this section, you can merge the Product detail table with the Product table to create a single table that lets you maintain a star schema when connecting the Product table to the fact table while keeping all the necessary data available.

To accomplish this, start by loading all the tables into Power BI and going to the Power Query Editor by clicking Transform data. Then, select the Product table and click on Merge Queries in the ribbon. That will open a pop-up window where you can choose the Product detail table as the table you want to merge (see Figure 3-47).

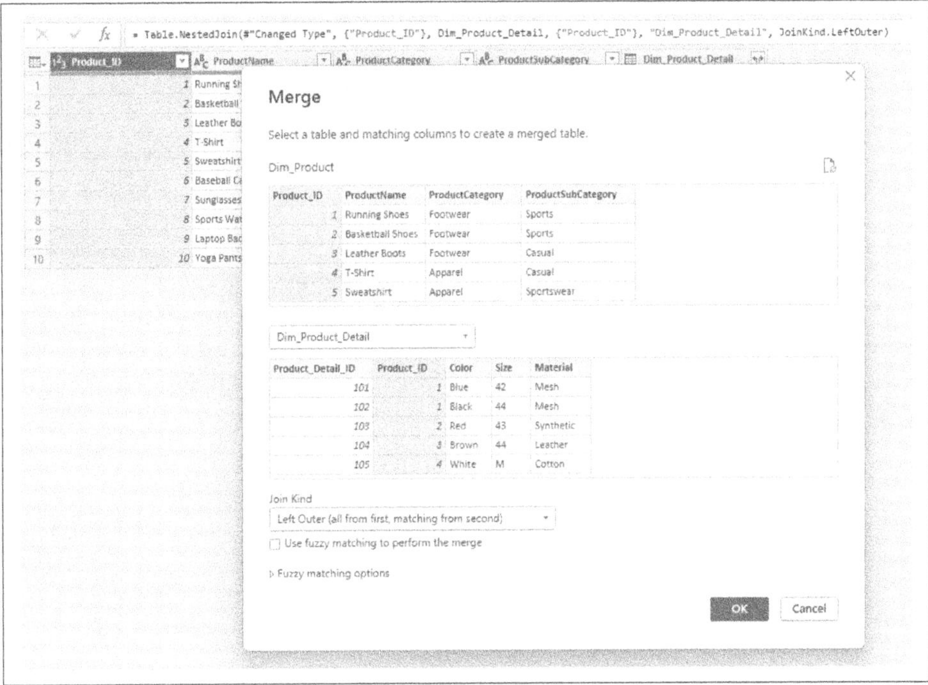

Figure 3-47. Merging the two related tables in the Power Query Editor

In the Power Query Editor, you'll be prompted to select the columns to merge the two tables. In our example, the `Product_ID` column serves as a common identifier because it contains the same information in both tables. You want to choose a LEFT OUTER JOIN to retain all product IDs from the Product table and add the matching ones from the Product detail table. Next, you need to expand the merged columns to include all relevant Product detail fields, such as Color, Size, and Material (see Figure 3-48).

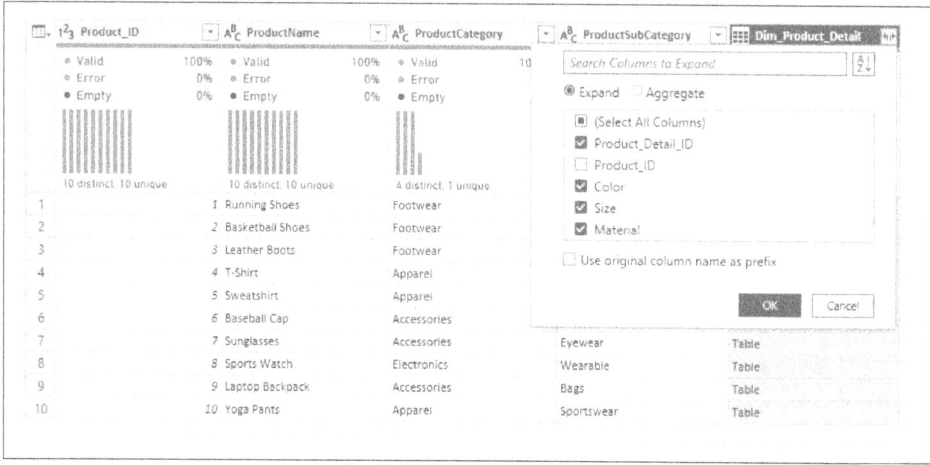

Figure 3-48. Expanding the relevant columns from the merged table

Before you load the tables, you want to ensure that the Product detail table is no longer visible in your Power BI data model. It's also important to note that you can't simply remove the table, as your merge would then fail. What you need to do is go to the Product detail table in Power Query, right-click on it, and select "Disable load." Once you do that, the menu will look like Figure 3-49. You'll still be able to use the table in your merge, but it won't be shown in the data model.

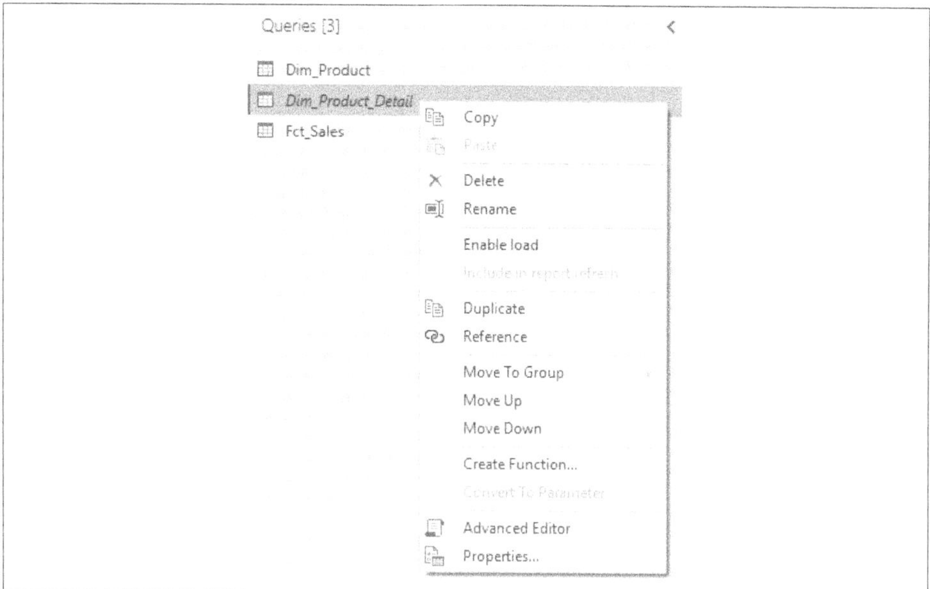

Figure 3-49. Product detail table with load disabled

Once you click on Close and Apply in the Power Query Editor, the new table structure will be available in the Power BI model view. You'll have the Product dimension table and the fact table, and the Product dimension table will contain all the necessary information from the Product detail table (see Figure 3-50).

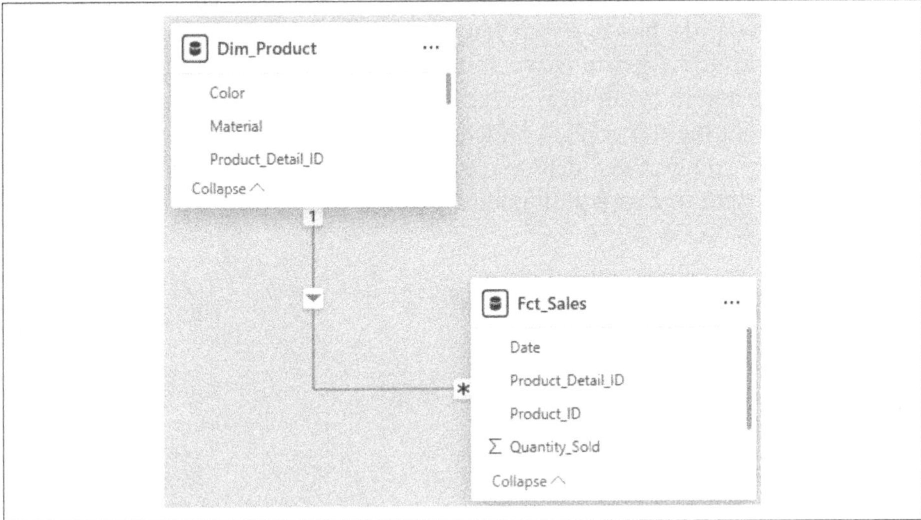

Figure 3-50. Our data model after denormalizing

Denormalization is a great technique for simplifying your data model and enhancing performance in Power BI, particularly when you're working with snowflake schemas that contain multiple related dimension tables. By merging related tables, such as Product and Product detail, into a single dimension table, you create a cleaner star schema. This approach reduces the number of relationships that Power BI needs to manage, making the model easier to understand and use for report consumers.

However, you should be careful when applying denormalization. While it's effective for dimension tables with manageable data sizes, we don't recommend denormalization for fact tables. That's because fact tables often contain a large volume of detailed transactional data, and denormalizing them can lead to data duplication, increase model size, and slow down refresh and query performance. Keeping fact tables narrow and focused on measurable events helps maintain efficient query performance, simplifies maintenance, and enhances scalability. So, before deciding to normalize, you should always weigh the advantages of a simpler model against potential downsides like data redundancy and negative impacts on performance.

Summary

In this chapter, you learned how to prepare data for analysis by cleaning, enriching, and transforming it in Fabric. You practiced creating views, functions, and stored procedures to reuse logic and make data preparation easier. You added new columns and connected related tables to enrich your data, and you worked with joins, aggregations, filters, and data types to shape your data so it matches your business needs. You handled common issues like duplicates, missing values, and `NULL`s, and you also learned about the star schema, which helps organize data for faster and clearer analysis. Finally, you explored denormalization, which combines related tables into one to improve performance and simplify reporting.

CHAPTER 4

Querying and Analyzing Data

In Chapters 1 through 3, we explained how to get data from various sources by using the Power BI Desktop application and the web-based experiences found in Microsoft Fabric. We also showed you how to transform the data that's ingested in the entire data platform.

In this chapter, we'll cover the topic of querying and analyzing data using the visual query editor, the T-SQL language, and the KQL script language.

First, we'll dive into the visual query editor and show you how to use the web-based tool to alter the structure of data and analyze it from the Fabric environment. Next, we'll jump into the T-SQL world of Fabric and show you how to leverage the well-known script language of SQL to analyze data. And finally, we'll introduce you to the KQL language that's used in the Real-Time Intelligence part of Microsoft Fabric.

The Visual Query Editor

The *visual query editor* is a tool that helps you design queries using a visual representation of the steps you take to query and analyze your data.

As the name might imply, the visual query editor is not limited to mouse interactions. Although the main purpose of this tool is to ease the creation of queries using an interactive approach, you can still use your known T-SQL skills to do what you need to do when using the tool. However, there are some caveats when using T-SQL, and we'll go into those later in this chapter.

The visual query editor is available in both the warehouse and the lakehouse items of Microsoft Fabric. You can find it in the top menu ribbon when you open the warehouse item from your workspace or the OneLake catalog experience, as we described in Chapter 1 (see Figure 4-1). In the lakehouse experience, you will only find the visual query editor when you're working with the SQL analytics endpoint in Microsoft Fabric.

One limitation of the visual query editor is that you can only create `SELECT` statements that can manipulate the output based on existing data. You cannot `UPDATE` or `DELETE` data using this approach.

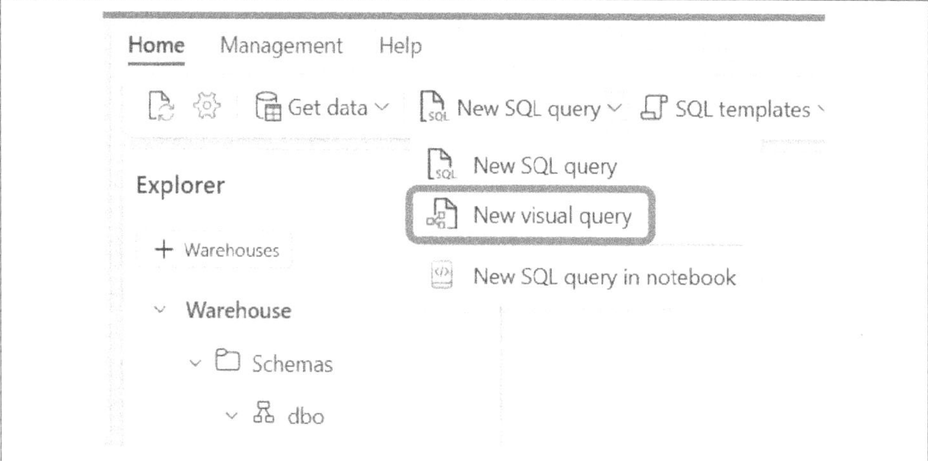

Figure 4-1. Creating a new visual query in which you'll use the visual query editor

When you create your visual query, a blank canvas will appear, and you'll need to add your first table to the query canvas. You do this by using the drag-and-drop method from your tables in the warehouse or lakehouse to the canvas.

In Figure 4-2, you can see that the first table has been added to the canvas. At this point, we're ready to begin manipulating our data.

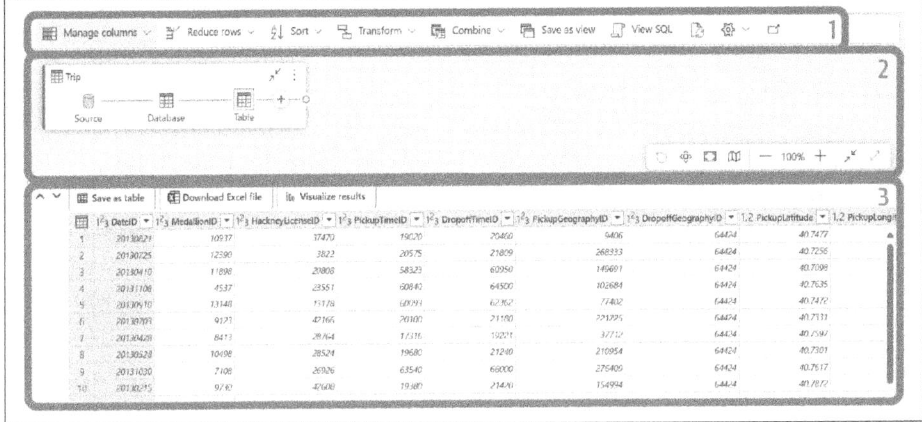

Figure 4-2. Visual query canvas with the first table added

Next, we'll guide you through the canvas and show you what it consists of. We've highlighted some important areas (numbered 1–3):

Top bar (area 1)
: This is where you'll find the main actions options for manipulating your data. Here, you can use different tools to transform, filter, change columns, combine tables, etc.

  You'll also see a configuration gear near the far right of the screen. This option gives you access to the experience from the Power Query in Power BI, which shows column statistics for each column in the results set (see Figure 4-3).

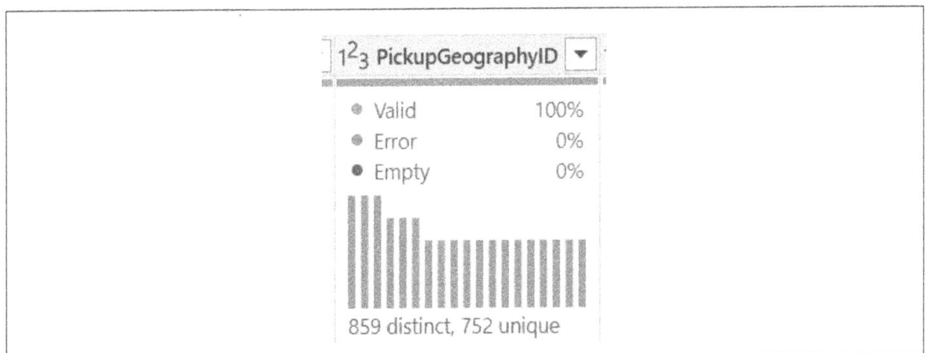

Figure 4-3. Column statistics enabled in the visual query editor

Canvas (area 2)
: This is the visual representation of the data manipulation that you're performing, and each data element is represented by its own box of information that contains

the source, database, and table. At the bottom of the canvas, you'll also find the zoom functions and a minimap of your visual query, for your convenience.

Results area (area 3)
: This is the bottom part of the screen, where you can see the results set of the current query you're working with. Here, you'll also find the "Save as table," "Download Excel file," and "Visualize results" buttons. The "Save as table" button saves the result from the query to a new table in either the lakehouse or the warehouse. The "Download Excel file" button saves the current results set as an Excel file on your local computer. The "Visualize results" button helps you do an analysis of the results set in a visual manner.

When you click the "Visualize results" button, it takes you to the Power BI online experience for building reports. See Figure 2-26, also repeated here for reference:

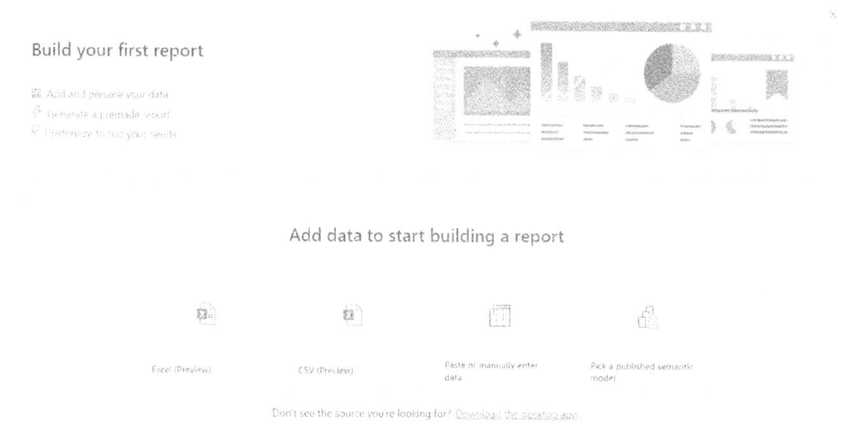

Directly from this, you can save the output as a report and share the dataset in that way. But that's not the main intention of the visual query editor, so let's jump back to the canvas and begin to work with and manipulate the data.

You have different options for working with individual tables in the visual query editor. One option is to use the top menu bar, as mentioned earlier. Another is to view the full option list by clicking the three-dot-menu in the top right corner of a table. Lastly, you can click the plus sign on the right side of a table and view a list of all the actions that are available for that table (see Figure 4-4). There's also a search bar at the top of the list if you can't find what you're looking for.

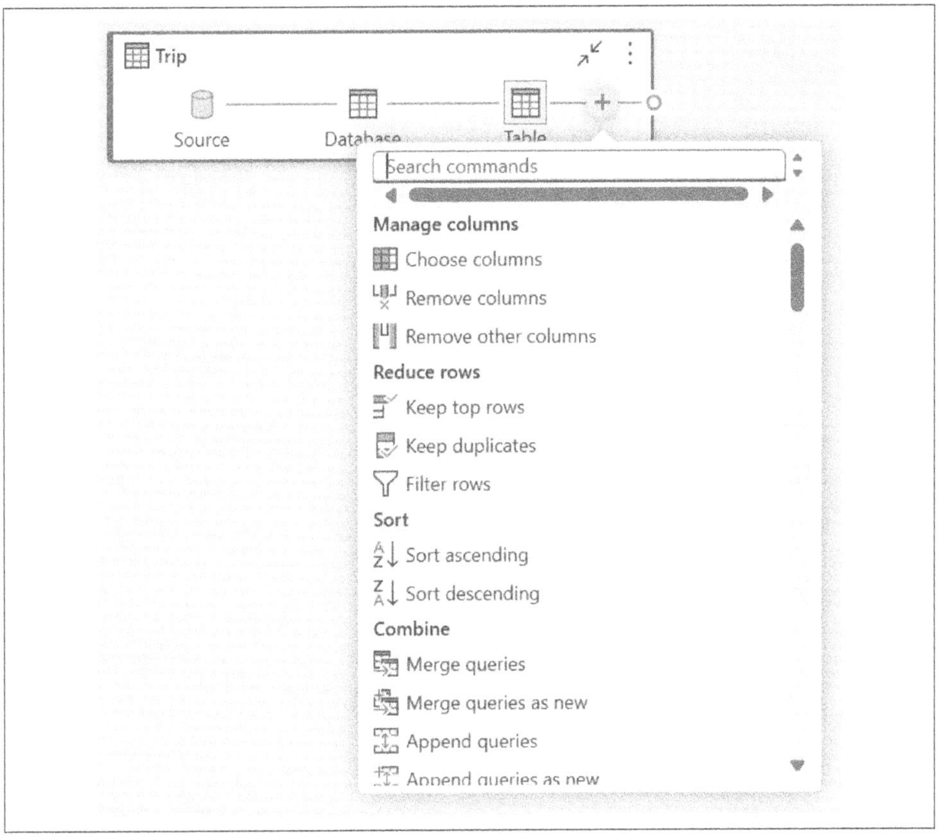

Figure 4-4. List of actions available by clicking the plus sign on a table

You may recognize the list of actions here because some items are the same ones you can find in Power Query. The list here includes T-SQL capabilities to do calculations and arithmetic on numbers, plus text manipulation.

The introduction in this book to the visual query editor has only been around a single table, but this service lets you handle more tables and perform joins and other operations on the data.

Working with Tables Using the Visual Query Editor

In the visual query editor, you can perform nearly all of the same operations on and manipulations of data that you can with T-SQL script, including joins and merges. Figure 4-5 shows the available actions on the drop-down list you can bring up by clicking the plus sign in any table.

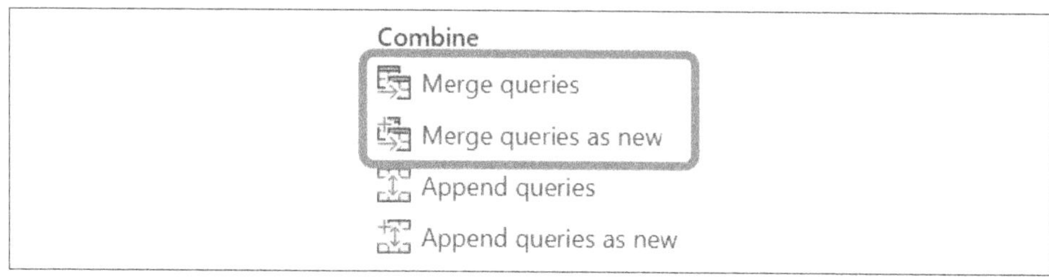

Figure 4-5. Available operations in the visual query editor

Joins

When using T-SQL, we would normally call the join operator to join two or more tables in the query. In the visual query editor, this operation is called a *merge*. You can merge two tables by either using the left table or the right table in the join. As we mentioned in Chapter 3, there are different methods of joining data.

When you choose the Merge option from the screen shown in Figure 4-5, you'll be presented with two options: "Merge queries" and "Merge queries as new." These are the same options you'd get from the Power Query experience. Both of them add a new column to the existing table, with the result being an embedded table in that column, which you can expand to give you as many columns as you need.

However, choosing between the two options can be quite challenging. The rule of thumb here is that if you need all the columns from both the tables in the join, then you should choose the "Merge queries as new" option as this will add all the columns from the two joins to the new column. If not, choose the "Merge queries" option and expand to select only the columns you need.

There is no performance implementation when choosing either of the options. This means that whichever option you choose, the performance of the task will be the same and the query will have the same execution time.

Figure 4-6 shows how the two different options appear onscreen.

When we're creating a merge of two tables in this service, we also get some help on the merge operation from the visual query editor, both in the visual representation of the data and on what columns to perform the merge. Figure 4-7 demonstrates this and will help guide you through the merge experience.

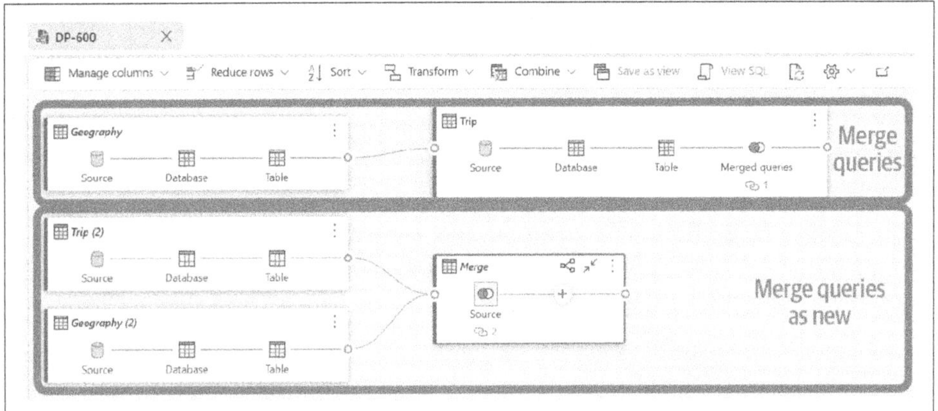

Figure 4-6. How the "Merge queries" and "Merge queries as new" options appear onscreen

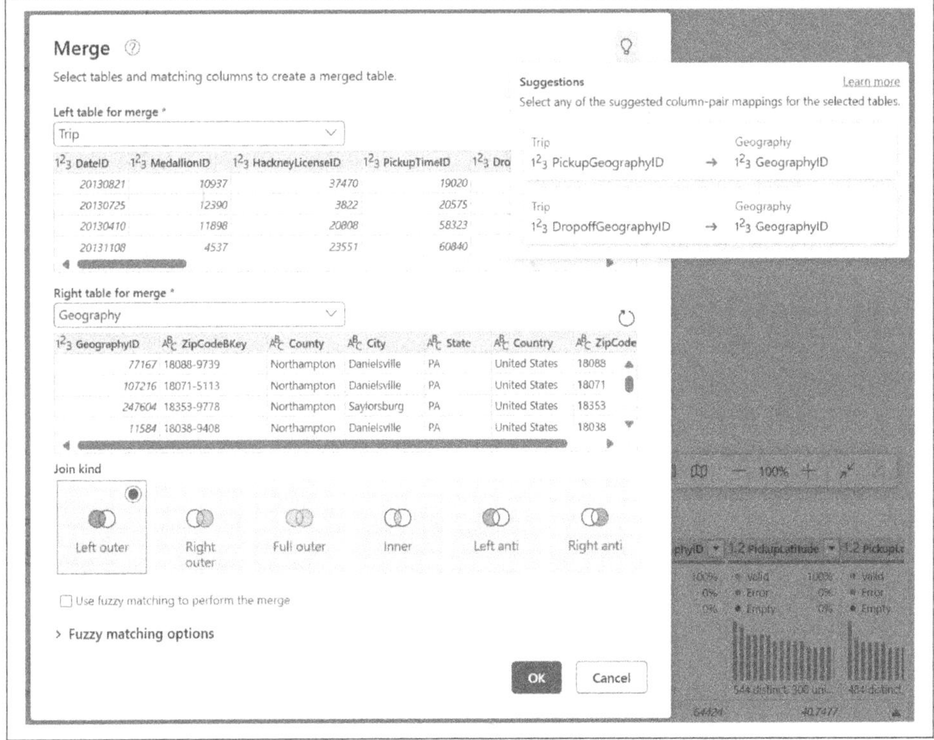

Figure 4-7. Merge experience in the visual query editor

In the figure, you can see that we're trying to merge two tables: Trip as the left table and Geography as the right table in the join.

When you're selecting two tables to merge, the engine tries to help you select the columns in which to do the join. If you click on the light bulb in the top right corner, you'll see options to select the columns in which the engine has assumed the join would work. In the example in Figure 4-7, you have the following options: either the `PickUpGeographyID` column or the `DropOffGeograhpyID` column from the Trip table, and only the GeographyID column from the Geography table.

If the engine's autoselection of a column is not correct (e.g., if you have a different naming scheme or other business rules to implement), you can always click on the column you need from either of the tables and create the join that way.

Also note the "Join kind" menu at the bottom of the screen. There, you can use the knowledge you gained from Chapter 3 to select the right type of join in this operation.

But sometimes, the ordinary join types aren't enough. For instance, if humans type in the columns by hand, we'll sometimes see errors or typos in the values. This is where fuzzy joins come to play.

Fuzzy joins

Fuzzy joins involve creating joins in columns that have a matching algorithm. Figure 4-8 shows the options that will appear when you check the "Use fuzzy matching to perform the merge" box at the bottom of the "Join kind" menu in Figure 4-7.

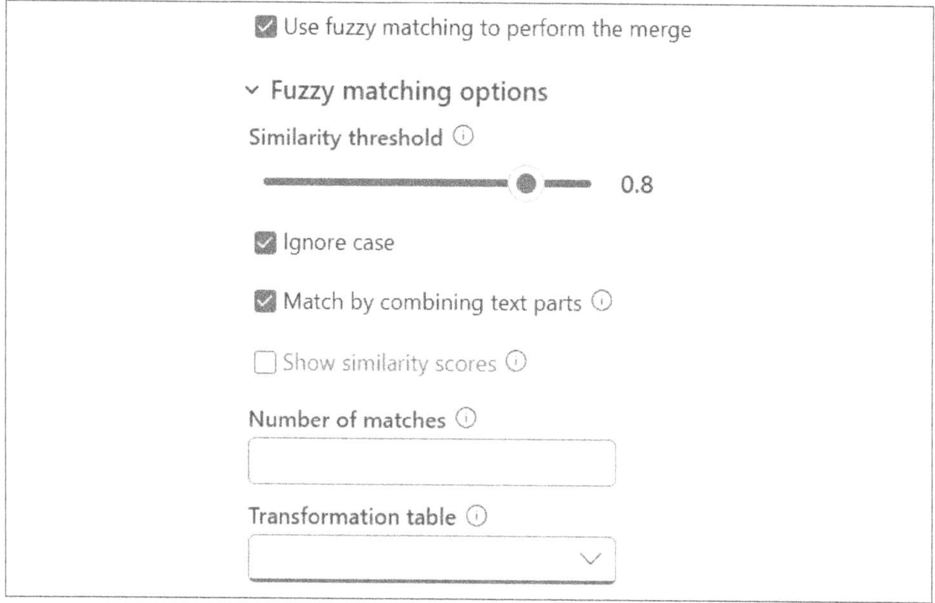

Figure 4-8. Fuzzy matching options in visual query editor

The fuzzy join function from the visual query editor gives us more options for making a match between two tables when working with lower-quality data from either side of the join.

By *lower-quality data,* we mean any data that might include typos, incorrect capitalization, or other errors that could cause data inputs to not be 100% accurate. Note that this is a very basic explanation of data quality, it's a topic that could fill an entire book all by itself, so we won't dive into the details of it in this book.

Let's go over each of the fuzzy matching options:

Similarity threshold

From the UI, we get this description when we hover our cursor over the circled *i*:

- This option indicates how similar two values need to be in order to match. The minimum value of 0 will cause all values with any level of similarity to match each other, and the maximum value of 1 will only allow exact matches. (Note that a fuzzy "exact match" might ignore differences like casing, word order, and punctuation.) The default is 0.8.

The *matching level* is a percentage that represents how much the corresponding value matches the lookup value from the main table. Therefore, the text "4ppl4s" matches the text "Apples" at a level of around 87%, while "I really like 4ppl4s" only matches "Apples" at a level of around 57%. This calculation is done behind the scenes by a clustering function.

Ignore case

This box is checked by default, and it makes the fuzzy algorithm not take into account the differences between capital letters and small letters. This means the fuzzy algorithm is case insensitive by default, so you can make it case sensitive by unchecking the box.

Match by combining text parts

From the UI, we get this description when we hover our cursor over the circled *i*:

- Try combining text parts (such as "Micro" and "soft" into "Microsoft") in order to find matches.

When this box is checked, the algorithm tries to group words and find similarities (e.g., grouping *Micro* and *soft* to create *Microsoft*). It does this not only on adjacent words but also on words throughout the entire value field.

Show similarity scores

Checking this box adds a new column to the dataset that includes the scoring of the similarity match done by the engine. The score and the number in the column will have the same possible values as the ones you can configure in the "Similarity threshold" mentioned previously.

Number of matches

From the UI, we get this description when we hover our cursor over the circled *i*:

- This option controls the maximum number of matching rows that will be returned for each input row. For example, if you only want to find one matching row for each input row, specify a value of 1.

This almost says it all. If you want to control the output of matching rows within the threshold of the setting, you can set this value to a different number. Note, though, that if this value is higher than 1, the resulting row will be copied for each match and we'll have to do the selection ourselves.

Transformation table

From the UI, we get this description when we hover our cursor over the circled *i*:

- Select a transformation table that will be used to map values (such as "MSFT" to "Microsoft") during the matching process. The table should contain a "From" column and a "To" column.

When doing fuzzy joins, it can be a good idea to help the algorithm with a transformation table to map different known values to new values. For example, this can include mapping *MSFT* (the stock market abbreviation for Microsoft) *Microsoft* (the company's full name).

Switching from Visual Query Editor to T-SQL Statements

If you want to follow along with script development from a T-SQL perspective, you can click View SQL in the top menu bar found in Figure 4-2.

In Figure 4-9, you'll see an example taken from the query merge in Figure 4-6, with all columns expanded from the join.

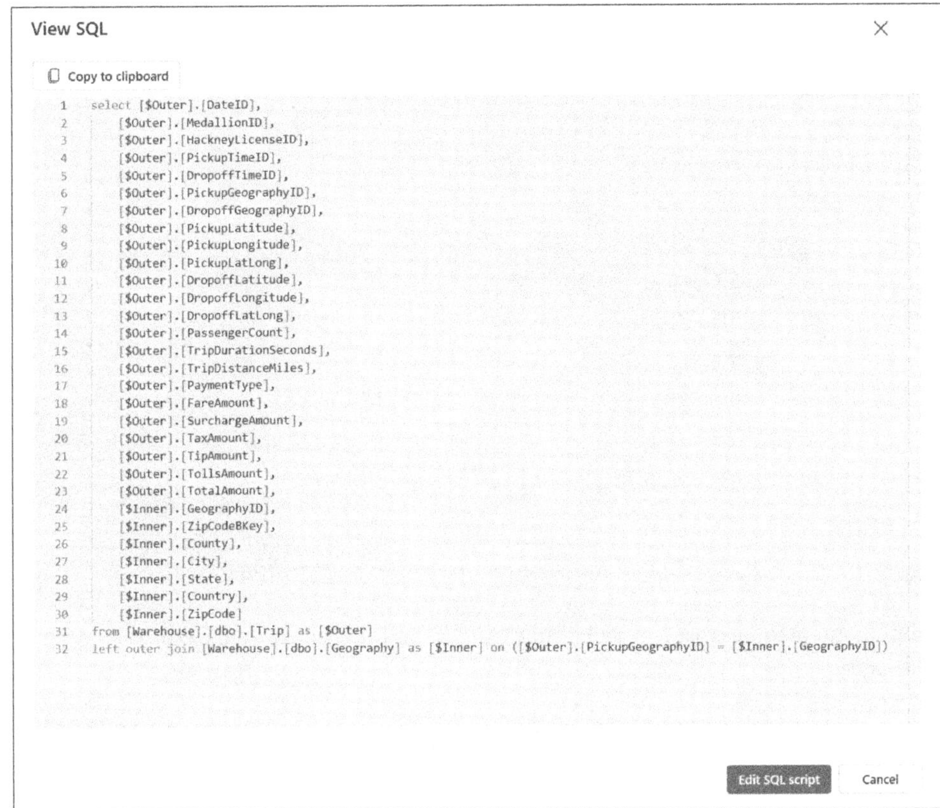
View SQL
Copy to clipboard
select [$Outer].[DateID],
[$Outer].[MedallionID],
[$Outer].[HackneyLicenseID],
[$Outer].[PickupTimeID],
[$Outer].[DropoffTimeID],
[$Outer].[PickupGeographyID],
[$Outer].[DropoffGeographyID],
[$Outer].[PickupLatitude],
[$Outer].[PickupLongitude],
[$Outer].[PickupLatLong],
[$Outer].[DropoffLatitude],
[$Outer].[DropoffLongitude],
[$Outer].[DropoffLatLong],
[$Outer].[PassengerCount],
[$Outer].[TripDurationSeconds],
[$Outer].[TripDistanceMiles],
[$Outer].[PaymentType],
[$Outer].[FareAmount],
[$Outer].[SurchargeAmount],
[$Outer].[TaxAmount],
[$Outer].[TipAmount],
[$Outer].[TollsAmount],
[$Outer].[TotalAmount],
[$Inner].[GeographyID],
[$Inner].[ZipCodeBKey],
[$Inner].[County],
[$Inner].[City],
[$Inner].[State],
[$Inner].[Country],
[$Inner].[ZipCode]
from [Warehouse].[dbo].[Trip] as [$Outer]
left outer join [Warehouse].[dbo].[Geography] as [$Inner] on ([$Outer].[PickupGeographyID] = [$Inner].[GeographyID])
Edit SQL script
Cancel

Figure 4-9. T-SQL statement from the visual query editor

This is a T-SQL statement from the visual query editor, and you can clearly see that the two table names are automatically renamed to [$Inner] and [$Outer], based on the merge operation we did earlier.

There are also two buttons at the bottom of the new window: "Edit SQL script" and "Cancel."

Clicking the "Edit SQL script" button doesn't directly open an edit mode for the provided T-SQL script for the visual query editor. Instead, it opens a new query in the warehouse or lakehouse, based on the shown T-SQL script. From there, you can then modify or change the script to fit your needs.

Figure 4-10 shows an example of this new query.

Figure 4-10. T-SQL script in edit mode from the visual query editor

There is no standard way of switching from T-SQL to visual query editor in Microsoft Fabric.

Cross-Lakehouse and Cross-Warehouse Queries

This feature is based on the cross-database query (*https://oreil.ly/lK5SL*) capability from Microsoft Fabric. Cross-database queries and analytics are heavily implemented in Microsoft Fabric and continue to be developed.

The visual query editor also supports the use of tables and views from databases in other warehouses and lakehouses. You can do this by adding a warehouse or lakehouse in the Explorer area on the left side of the visual query editor window. Click the + Warehouses button to open a new window, where you can add reference to a different warehouse. Thereafter, you can work with that warehouse just like any other object.

Saving a Query or a Query's Output

When you're done manipulating data to fit your needs, you have two options:

- Save the query as a view
- Save the output of the query to a table

Saving a query as a view

To save a query as a view, you start by selecting the "Save as view" option from the top menu bar. That will bring up the pop-up window shown in Figure 4-11.

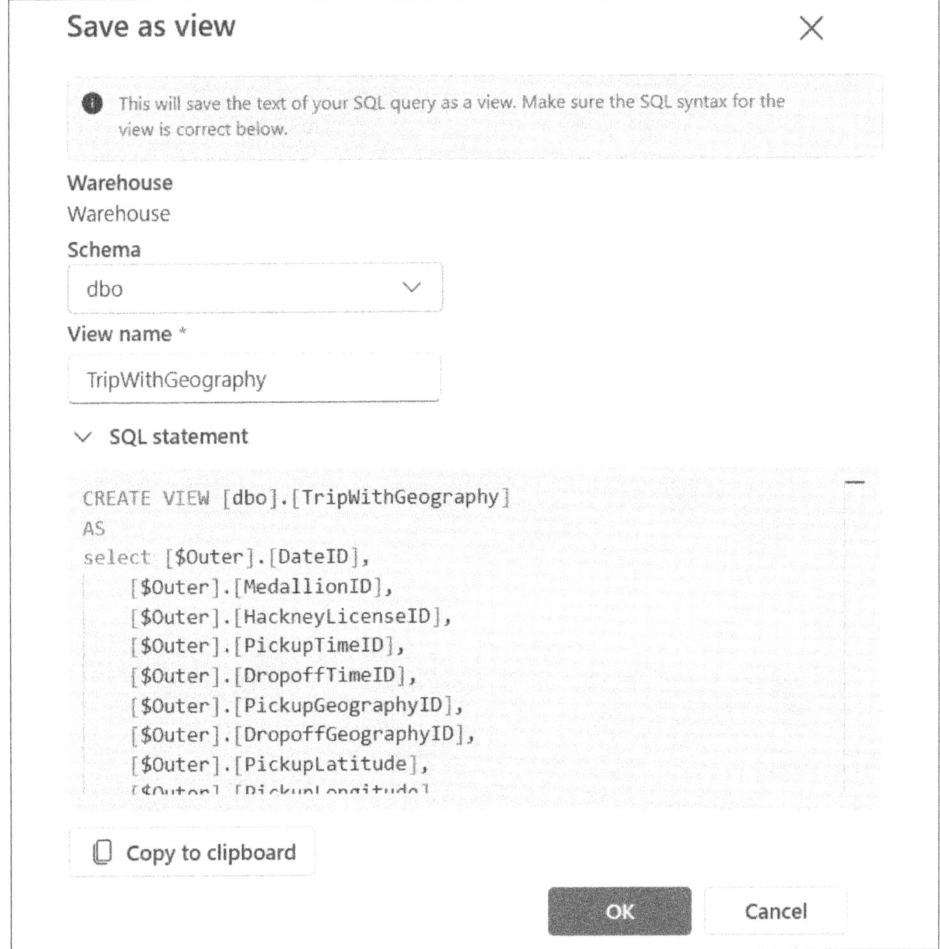
Save as view
This will save the text of your SQL query as a view. Make sure the SQL syntax for the view is correct below.
Warehouse
Warehouse
Schema
dbo
View name *
TripWithGeography
SQL statement
CREATE VIEW [dbo].[TripWithGeography]
AS
select [$Outer].[DateID],
[$Outer].[MedallionID],
[$Outer].[HackneyLicenseID],
[$Outer].[PickupTimeID],
[$Outer].[DropoffTimeID],
[$Outer].[PickupGeographyID],
[$Outer].[DropoffGeographyID],
[$Outer].[PickupLatitude],
Copy to clipboard
OK
Cancel

Figure 4-11. "Save as view" pop-up window from the visual query editor

Then, fill in the "View name" field (in our example, we've filled it in with the name TripWithGeography).

Schemas are used to separate logical layers, business areas, and other groupings, based on the technical aspects and implementation rules you may have in your organization. You can select a different schema if you need to (for example, if you have an implemented naming convention in your lakehouse or warehouse).

From this window, you also have the option to copy the view statement to the clipboard and paste it to a new query window and continue your work. Click the "Copy to clipboard" button to do so.

When you're done, click the OK button and your new view will be populated and ready to use.

Saving the output of a query to a table

You also have the option to save the output of your visual query to a new table in your warehouse. To do so, click the "Save as table" button at the top of the results area and give your table a new name and schema in the pop-up window that appears (see Figure 4-12).

Notice the change in the SQL statement. In Figure 4-11, the SQL statement begins with `CREATE VIEW...AS`, but in Figure 4-12, it begins with `CREATE TABLE...AS`.

Also note that the same "Copy to clipboard" button is available here as in "Save as view" pop-up window.

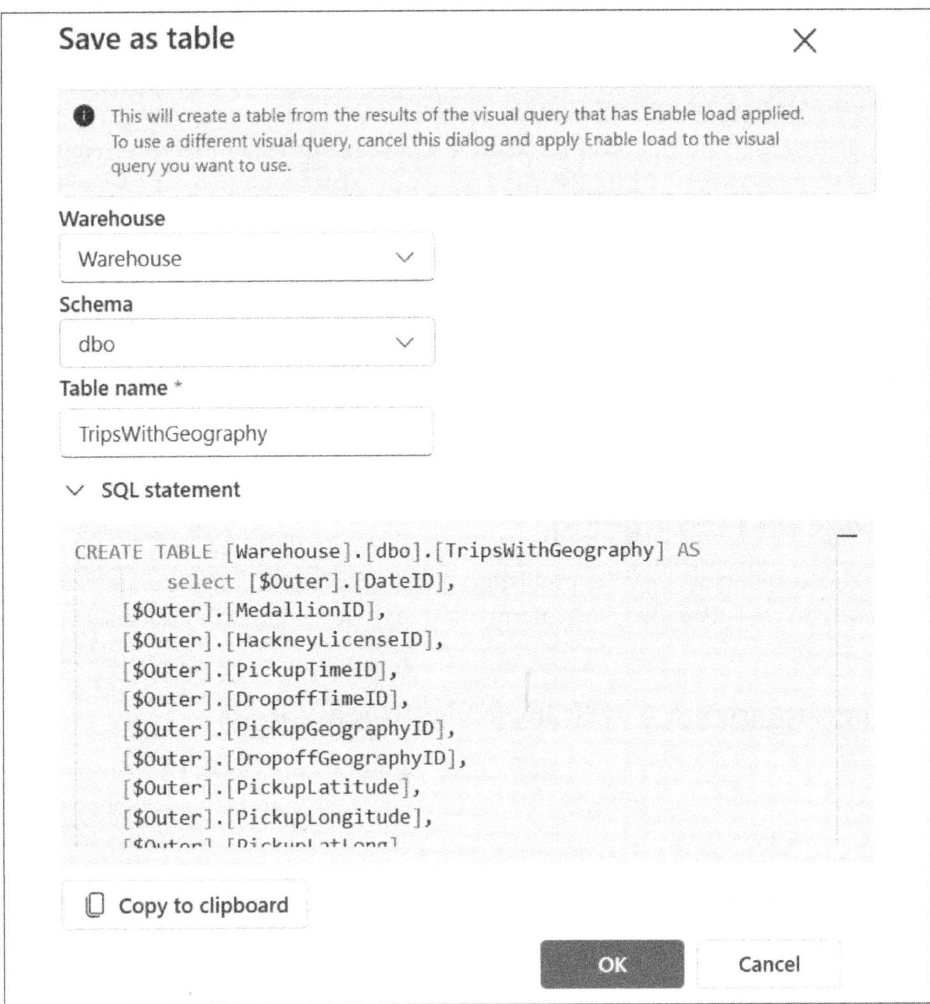
Save as table
This will create a table from the results of the visual query that has Enable load applied. To use a different visual query, cancel this dialog and apply Enable load to the visual query you want to use.
Warehouse
Warehouse
Schema
dbo
Table name *
TripsWithGeography
SQL statement
CREATE TABLE [Warehouse].[dbo].[TripsWithGeography] AS
select [$Outer].[DateID],
[$Outer].[MedallionID],
[$Outer].[HackneyLicenseID],
[$Outer].[PickupTimeID],
[$Outer].[DropoffTimeID],
[$Outer].[PickupGeographyID],
[$Outer].[DropoffGeographyID],
[$Outer].[PickupLatitude],
[$Outer].[PickupLongitude],
Copy to clipboard
OK
Cancel

Figure 4-12. "Save as table" pop-up window from the visual query editor

Limitations

When working with the visual query editor, you can only create data query language (DQL) scripts from the T-SQL package of options. This means that you can't do data manipulation (insertions, updates, and deletes) on existing tables in the database with the visual query editor. Also, you can only create data definition language (DDL) scripts by using the "Save as table" options from the results area of the visual query editor.

There are some functions and features of the visual query editor that are only available in the visual query editor experience and can't be translated into T-SQL. Though they're outside the scope of the DP-600 exam, you might find it interesting to read more about these functions (*https://oreil.ly/y0OyR*).

Lineage and Debugging

If you encounter errors or other problems when working with the visual query editor, you have several options for determining what may have gone wrong each step of the way.

Clicking on Each Box with Steps to View Query Results

When you click each main box of steps (which is also named in the UI as a query) in the visual query editor, the results pane changes to show you the results set from the last step in that query.

Clicking on Each Step in Each Query to View Results of That Step

You can click on each step inside the queries to see that step's specific results set.

Viewing the Data Source Query

You can right-click on each of the steps within a query to view the data source query. For example, Figure 4-13 shows the results of the `TripWithGeography` visual query's last step.

Data source query

```
select [$Outer].[DateID],
    [$Outer].[MedallionID],
    [$Outer].[HackneyLicenseID],
    [$Outer].[PickupTimeID],
    [$Outer].[DropoffTimeID],
    [$Outer].[PickupGeographyID],
    [$Outer].[DropoffGeographyID],
    [$Outer].[PickupLatitude],
    [$Outer].[PickupLongitude],
    [$Outer].[PickupLatLong],
    [$Outer].[DropoffLatitude],
    [$Outer].[DropoffLongitude],
    [$Outer].[DropoffLatLong],
    [$Outer].[PassengerCount],
    [$Outer].[TripDurationSeconds],
    [$Outer].[TripDistanceMiles],
    [$Outer].[PaymentType],
    [$Outer].[FareAmount],
    [$Outer].[SurchargeAmount],
    [$Outer].[TaxAmount],
    [$Outer].[TipAmount],
    [$Outer].[TollsAmount],
    [$Outer].[TotalAmount],
    [$Inner].[GeographyID],
    [$Inner].[ZipCodeBKey],
    [$Inner].[County],
    [$Inner].[City],
    [$Inner].[State],
    [$Inner].[Country],
    [$Inner].[ZipCode]
from [Warehouse].[dbo].[Trip] as [$Outer]
left outer join [Warehouse].[dbo].[Geography] as [$Inner] on ([$Outer].[PickupGeographyID] =
[$Inner].[GeographyID])
```

OK

Figure 4-13. View of data source query

Viewing the Query Plan

You can right-click a specific step within a query box to view that step's query plan (see Figure 4-14).

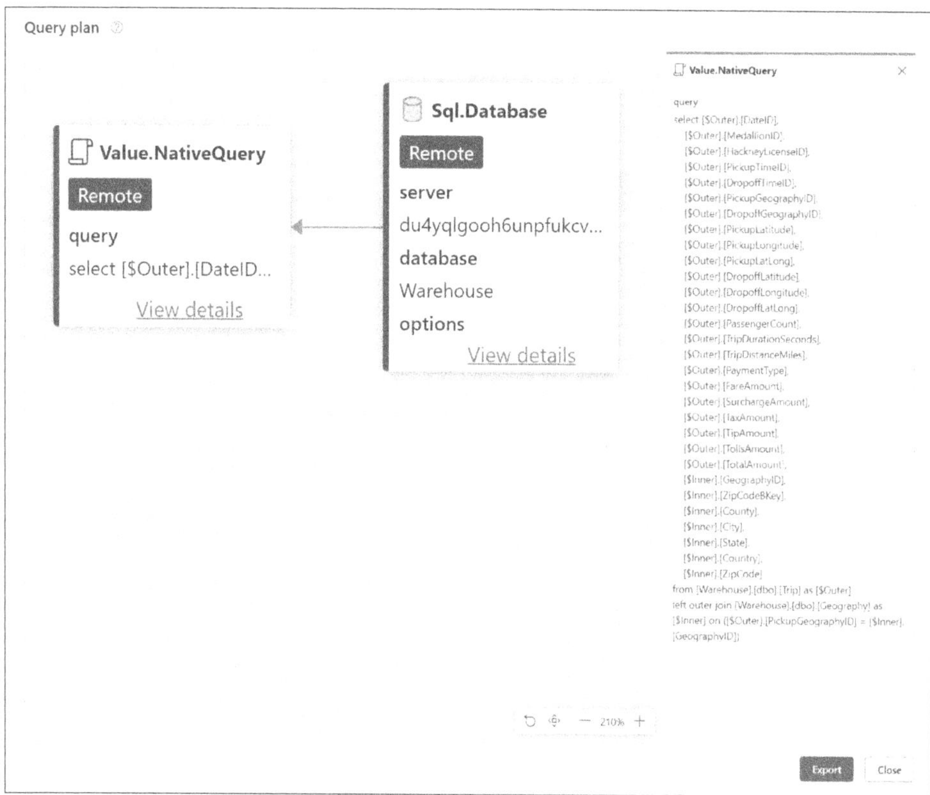
Query plan
Value.NativeQuery
Remote
query
select [$Outer].[DateID...
View details
Sql.Database
Remote
server
du4yqlgooh6unpfukcv...
database
Warehouse
options
View details
Value.NativeQuery
query
select [$Outer].[DateID],
[$Outer].[MedallionID],
[$Outer].[HackneyLicenseID],
[$Outer].[PickupTimeID],
[$Outer].[DropoffTimeID],
[$Outer].[PickupGeographyID],
[$Outer].[DropoffGeographyID],
[$Outer].[PickupLatitude],
[$Outer].[PickupLongitude],
[$Outer].[PickupLatLong],
[$Outer].[DropoffLatitude],
[$Outer].[DropoffLongitude],
[$Outer].[DropoffLatLong],
[$Outer].[PassengerCount],
[$Outer].[TripDurationSeconds],
[$Outer].[TripDistanceMiles],
[$Outer].[PaymentType],
[$Outer].[FareAmount],
[$Outer].[SurchargeAmount],
[$Outer].[TaxAmount],
[$Outer].[TipAmount],
[$Outer].[TollsAmount],
[$Outer].[TotalAmount],
[$Inner].[GeographyID],
[$Inner].[ZipCodeBKey],
[$Inner].[County],
[$Inner].[City],
[$Inner].[State],
[$Inner].[Country],
[$Inner].[ZipCode]
from [Warehouse].[dbo].[Trip] as [$Outer]
left outer join [Warehouse].[dbo].[Geography] as
[$Inner] on ([$Outer].[PickupGeographyID] = [$Inner].
[GeographyID])
210%
Export
Close

Figure 4-14. View of query plan from visual query editor

In this query plan view, we can now begin to see the flow of data from the SQL database (on the right) to the native query (on the left). When you click "View details" in `Value.NativeQuery`, it will bring up the `Value.NativeQuery` statement on the right-hand side of the screen. When you click "View details" in `Sql.Database`, it will bring up the server name, the database name, and the options configuration of the connection (see Figure 4-15).

You can export this entire query plan to a JSON object by using this option to view the query plan. Click the Export button at the bottom of the screen shown in Figure 4-14 to download the JSON definition of the visual query editor.

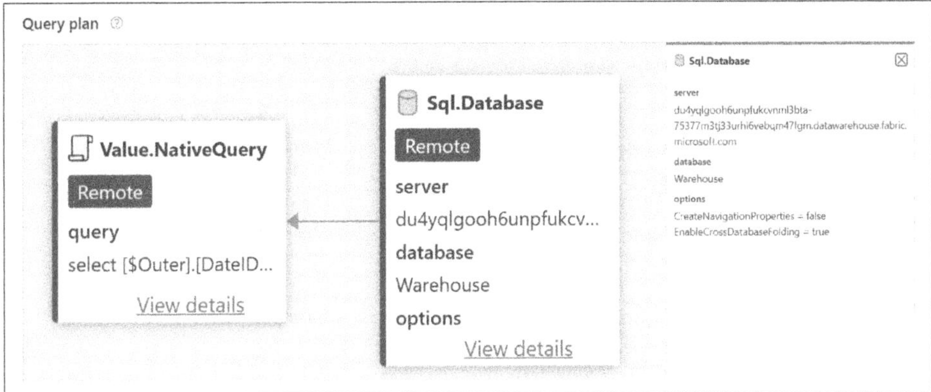

Figure 4-15. Details of Sql.Database from the query plan view in the visual query editor

An example of this JSON follows, and it's formatted and truncated to be more readable.

The original exported JSON has escape characters where needed and a different line break structure than shown here:

```
{
    "queryName": "Merge",
    "stepName": "Expanded Geography",
    "diagnostics": [
        {
            "queryName": "Trip",
            "queryPlan": {
                "nodes": [
                    {
                        "kind": "Invocation",
                        ...
                        ...
                        "argumentsByName": {}
                    }
                ],
                "removedStructuredColumns": false
            },
            "queryPlanAsSteps": "
let
#"Sql.Database" = Sql.Database("<server address>", <database>,
[ CreateNavigationProperties = false,
EnableCrossDatabaseFolding = true ]),
#"Value.NativeQuery" = Value.NativeQuery(#"Sql.Database",
select [$Table].[DateID] as [DateID],
...
...
as [TotalAmount]
from [<database>].[dbo].[Trip] as [$Table])
in
```

```
    #"Value.NativeQuery"",
            "queryPlanStatus": "Succeeded",
            "queryScript": "
let
Source = Sql.Databases("<server address>",
[CreateNavigationProperties=false,
EnableCrossDatabaseFolding=true]),
Database = Source{[Name = "<database>"]}[Data],
Table = Database{[Schema = "dbo", Item = "Trip"]}[Data]
In
Table
        },
        {
            "queryName": "Geography",
            "queryPlan": {
                "nodes":
...
```

You may recognize the language used in this JSON object: Power Query. The `let` and `in` operators are the giveaways. This example shows the well-known Power Query engine making its way to the end user as the underlying query engine for this visual query editor. And if you want to, you can copy the Power Query statement, paste it to Dataflow Gen2, and continue your work there.

> ### CI/CD
>
> At the time of writing this book, the queries from the visual query editor are not parts of the CI/CD process provided by Fabric.
>
> One of the important things to know when working with Fabric is what items (lakehouses, warehouses, dataflows, etc.) are supported by the built-in CI/CD capabilities. It's also important to dig one level deeper and know what subitems (queries, visual queries, etc.) are supported by the CI/CD process.
>
> This will give you as the developer a very good baseline to work with Fabric from a development governance point of view (though that's not currently within the scope of the DP-600 exam).

As you can see, the visual query editor is a comprehensive service, and the features and power of the Power Query language and the ability to translate it to T-SQL and work with later have their benefits. First, you don't need deep T-SQL skills to get moving with your data manipulation needs, and second, you can learn new skills, like using T-SQL and Power Query at the same time.

That said, there is also an option to use the T-SQL language directly. In the next section, we'll help you on your way to understanding the T-SQL landscape of Microsoft Fabric and how to use it to manipulate data.

Manipulating Data with SQL

In Microsoft Fabric, you have the option to use the T-SQL language to manipulate and transform your data to fit your needs. In this section, we provide a guide to the SQL language, where to use it, and the current limitations on it.

It's also worth noting that notebooks are using the *SparkSQL* version of the SQL scripting language. Spark SQL is a module of Apache Spark, and it's a powerful distributed computing engine that's designed for big data processing. It's based on the American National Standards Institute Structured Query Language (ANSI SQL), and it's engineered for analytical workloads across massive, distributed datasets. It leverages Spark's ability to scale, so it's ideal for large-scale ETL pipelines, real-time stream processing, and advanced analytics like machine learning (via integration with Spark MLlib). Spark SQL is optimized for reading data from various distributed sources (like Parquet, JSON, and Delta Lake) and performing complex, iterative transformations in which processing speed and throughput are prioritized over strict transactional control.

Where to Find the SQL Language

Before we dive in and show you how to use the SQL language, we want to show you where to find it. Here, we've provided a list of the areas where you'll find the options to use the SparkSQL language:

In notebooks

In the PySpark notebook item in Microsoft Fabric, you can use the SQL language by using one of two main options. You can either use the cell magic of `%%sql` or mark the cell as a SQL cell. Both options are shown in Figure 4-16.

In the second option, you use the following Spark function:

```
spark.sql(<your sql statement>)"
```

In the space with the *<your sql statement>* placeholder, you can write your SQL code to read data to a DataFrame or manipulate data in an existing database or table.

The notebook approach is a data engineering task, so the details of it are outside the scope of this book. All you need to know is that you have the option to use it here.

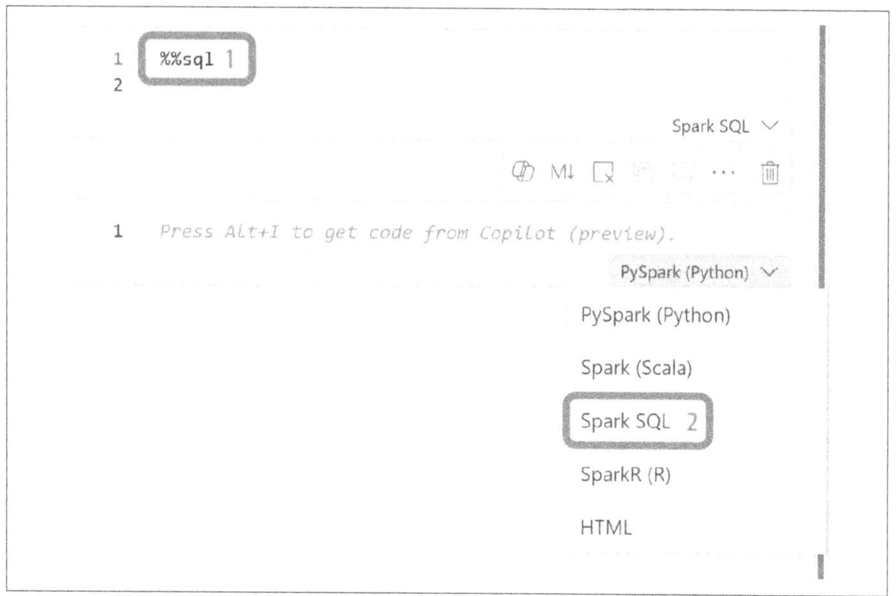

Figure 4-16. The SQL options in a PySpark notebook

In a warehouse

As you've learned from previous chapters, the warehouse approach in Microsoft Fabric is mainly based on the SQL method of data storage and manipulation. The warehouse exposes the so-called *T-SQL surface area*. This special implementation of the T-SQL language is the default language for working with the warehouse, but it also comes with a functionality that's limited, compared to the full SQL server experience. We'll cover these limitations in the section called "The T-SQL Surface Area."

In a SQL database

The native SQL database item in Microsoft Fabric brings the entire SQL language to you as the developer, and it will have almost all the features you need to manipulate the data. You'll have access to the same SQL statements and functions as you can find in the serverless Azure SQL database. The details of the differences in T-SQL between the native SQL database in Fabric and the serverless Azure SQL database are outside the scope of this exam, but you can find detailed explanations of them at the following Microsoft Learn sites:

T-SQL differences between SQL Server and Azure SQL Database (*https://oreil.ly/oSgeH*)

Limitations in SQL database in Microsoft Fabric (*https://oreil.ly/TQlSL*)

In a lakehouse
: When using the lakehouse item in Microsoft Fabric, you also have access to a SQL analytics endpoint, from which you can do data manipulation using the T-SQL language. As with the warehouse item, there are some limitations, which we'll describe in the next section.

The T-SQL Surface Area

The special implementation of the T-SQL language capabilities in Microsoft Fabric is called the *T-SQL surface area* and is used in the SQL Analytics endpoints and the warehouse item.

This implementation has some limitations that are natural consequences of the delta parquet storage format and the underlying compute engine behind Microsoft Fabric. The following is a detailed list of these limitations and differences in the T-SQL surface area between the Warehouse and the SQL Analytics endpoint:

- Creating, altering, and dropping tables, and inserting, updating, and deleting are only supported in warehouses in Microsoft Fabric, not in the SQL analytics endpoint of the lakehouse.
- You can create your own T-SQL views, functions, and procedures on top of the tables that reference your Delta Lake data in the SQL analytics endpoint of the lakehouse.
- You can create tables in the warehouse in two ways: with the `CREATE TABLE` or `CREATE TABLE AS SELECT` statements.
- You can create temp tables (the ones with the # before the name) as explicit commands like this:

  ```
  CREATE TABLE #table_name (
     Col1 data_type1,
     Col2 data_type2
   );
  ```

- Global temp tables (the ones with ## before the name) are currently not supported.
- Fabric warehouse and SQL analytics endpoints both support standard, sequential, and nested common table expressions (CTEs). CTEs are generally available in Microsoft Fabric.
- `TRUNCATE TABLE` is supported in the warehouse in Microsoft Fabric.
- To change the name of the column in a user table in a warehouse, use the `sp_rename` stored procedure.
- A subset of query and join hints is supported.

- Session-scoped distributed #temp tables are supported in the warehouse in Microsoft Fabric.

The following is a list of functions that are not currently supported by the T-SQL surface area in Microsoft Fabric:

- `ALTER TABLE ADD` and `ALTER`
  Currently, only the following subset of ALTER TABLE operations in the warehouse in Microsoft Fabric is supported:
  - `ADD` nullable columns of supported column data types.
  - `DROP COLUMN`.
  - `ADD` or `DROP PRIMARY KEY`, `UNIQUE`, and `FOREIGN_KEY` column constraints, but only if the `NOT ENFORCED` option has been specified. All other `ALTER TABLE` operations are blocked.
- `BULK LOAD`
- `CREATE USER`
- `FOR JSON` must be the last operator in the query, so it's not allowed inside subqueries.
- `IDENTITY` columns
- Manually created multi-column stats
- Materialized views
- `MERGE`
- `PREDICT`
- Queries targeting system and user tables
- Recursive queries
- Result set caching
- / and \

  Schema and table names can't contain these.
- `SELECT - FOR XML`
- `SET ROWCOUNT`
- `SET TRANSACTION ISOLATION LEVEL`
- `sp_showspaceused`
- Triggers

In these two tables and the introductions to the warehouse, lakehouse and SQL Analytics endpoints, we've helped you understand the limitations and the implementation of the T-SQL surface area. This will help you find the T-SQL capabilities you need to manipulate data in these services.

However, this book is not meant to be a T-SQL training guide, so we'll leave it to you to learn more about the T-SQL language if you need to. Here are some useful links to get you started:

- Microsoft Learn's official free course on getting started with querying (*https://oreil.ly/EwVTh*) using the T-SQL script language
- Microsoft Learn's official free course on getting well acquainted (*https://oreil.ly/70jXT*) with the T-SQL language
- Learning SQL, 3rd Edition (O'Reilly) (*https://oreil.ly/Nj5VO*)
- Advanced SQL (*https://oreil.ly/VZd_5*)

These links to both free online courses and books for purchase will give you all you need to handle data with the T-SQL language.

With all of that said, using T-SQL is just one way to handle and manipulate data in Microsoft Fabric. Another one is KQL, which we'll cover next.

Manipulating Data with KQL

The *Kusto Query Language* (KQL) is the main scripting language used in the Real-Time Intelligence suite of services in Microsoft Fabric. This suite contains services like eventstreams, eventhouses, the KQL database, KQL querysets, the Real-Time dashboard, and the Activator items.

All these services are mainly based on the same underlying compute and storage engine: the Kusto database. This database has many special features, and one of them is the fact that it is built from the ground up by Microsoft to support the storage and manipulation of streaming data. Data from IoT devices, log events, and telemetry data are just a few examples of this kind of data. The common denominator of this data is that it is always emitting statuses and/or events and is time based. The database handles everything, including indexes, files, compression, and table optimization, so you can focus on data manipulation.

When manipulating data from the Kusto database, you get the best experience if you use KQL. Yes, you could use the T-SQL language, and we'll go into that in the next section, but the full experience and feature set comes from using the KQL script language.

Before we dive into where to find the KQL statements, you must know how to get started. The list of Microsoft Fabric Real-Time Intelligence items we included at the beginning of this section includes KQL querysets. These are special items that hold

KQL queries and scripts to be reused or used as a form of documentation for future developers to read and understand.

You can create a KQL queryset in two different ways: through autocreation and by creating a standalone queryset.

Auto-Creating a KQL Queryset While Creating an Eventhouse

In the first option, when you create the eventhouse item in Microsoft Fabric, you get two default items along with it: a KQL database with the same name as the eventhouse and a KQL queryset with the prefix of the eventhouse name (see Figure 4-17).

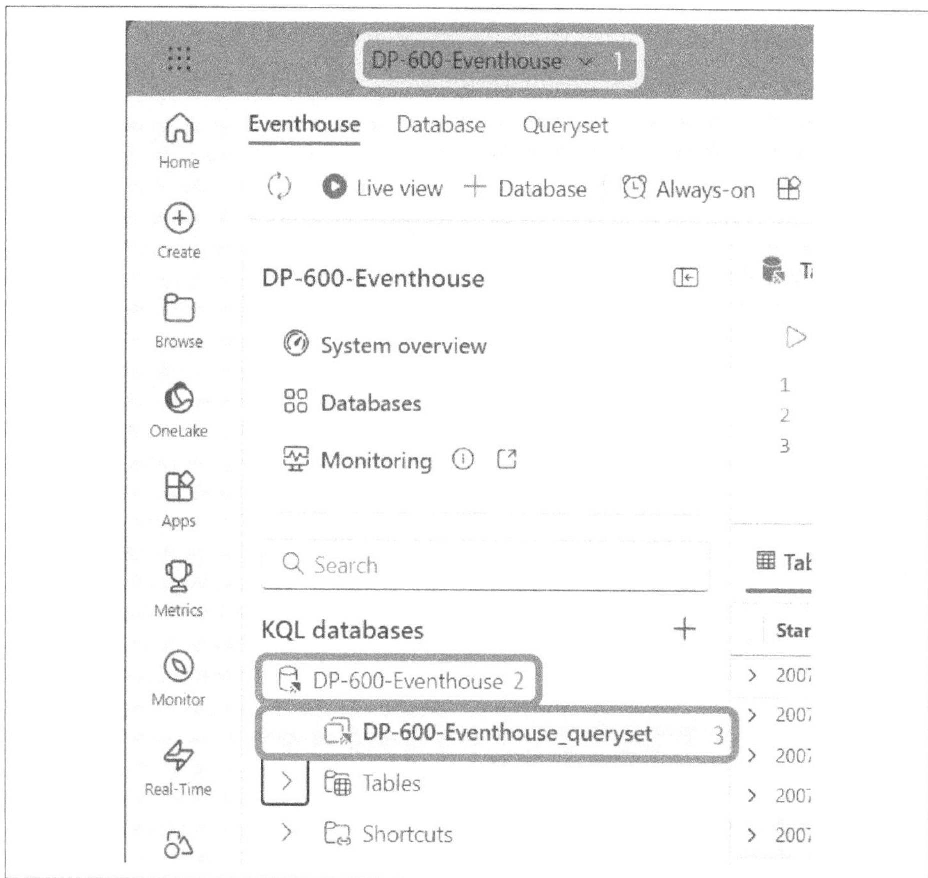

Figure 4-17. The three items in an eventhouse

We've highlighted some items in Figure 4-17 (numbered 1–3):

DP-600-Eventhouse (item 1)
: This is the eventhouse's name.

DP-600-Eventhouse (item 2)
: This is the KQL database's name.

DP-600-Eventhouse_queryset (item 3)
: This is the KQL queryset.

As you can see, the item names are reused across the eventhouse and the first KQL database, which is created in the same step in which you create the eventhouse. Also, if you wish, you can create a new KQL database in the eventhouse and delete the default one so you can have a different name for the KQL database. The eventhouse acts as a form of server for your KQL databases.

The KQL database name can contain alphanumeric characters, underscores, periods, and hyphens. Special characters aren't supported.

Along with the autocreation of a KQL database comes the autocreation of a KQL queryset within each database (item 3 in Figure 4-17).

Creating a Standalone KQL Queryset

The second option is to create a KQL queryset as a standalone item in your Fabric workspace. If you click the "+ New item" button in the workspace menu, you'll find KQL Queryset as a new item on the list (see Figure 4-18).

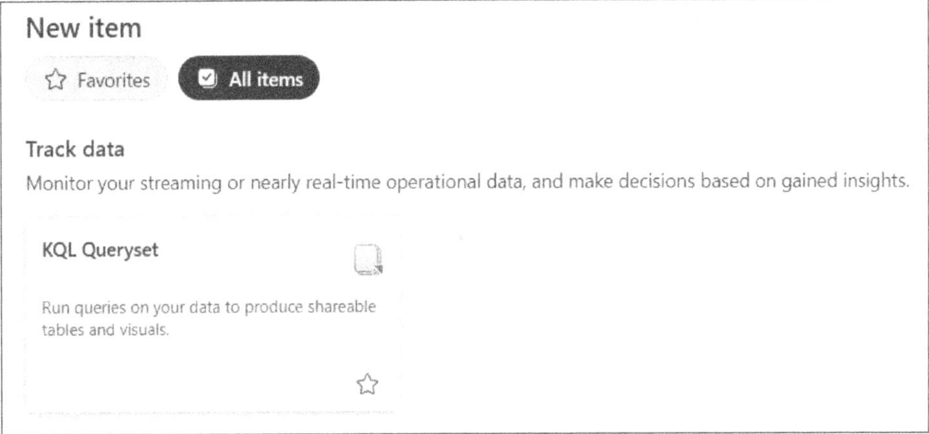

Figure 4-18. Standalone KQL queryset in Microsoft Fabric

No matter how you wish to utilize the KQL Queryset, you need one to get started writing your first KQL statement.

In the next sections, we'll cover the option of using T-SQL and then ease into how to learn the KQL script language and go to the next levels of learning. Even though this book is not a KQL training book, we'll walk you through some good examples of usage options for the language, show you what it can do, and give you information on where to learn more.

We can't train you on the entire KQL language, as that would take a book (or two) all by itself.

Using T-SQL in the Kusto Database

As previously mentioned, you can use the T-SQL language to some extent in the Kusto database. This is because the Kusto database by default can handle most of the T-SQL script base, but only for `SELECT` statements. You can't use T-SQL to create tables, update data, or execute Data Definition Language (DDL) or Data Manipulation Language (DML) statements in other ways.

Using T-SQL in the Kusto database is as simple as writing your T-SQL command as you would in any other T-SQL–based database. Here's an example with a table named `Weather`:

```
select top 10 * from Weather
```

In Figure 4-19, you can find the query executed in a KQL queryset along with the results set below it. (Note: not all columns are shown in the figure.)

```
select top 10 * from Weather
```

StartTime	EndTime	EpisodeId	EventId	State	EventType	InjuriesDirect	InjuriesIndirect	DeathsDirect
2007-01-01 00:00:00.0000000	2007-01-01 00:00:00.0000000	2,592	13,208	NORTH CAROLINA	Thunderstorm Wind	0	0	0
2007-01-01 00:00:00.0000000	2007-01-01 05:00:00.0000000	4,171	23,358	WISCONSIN	Winter Storm	0	0	0
2007-01-01 00:00:00.0000000	2007-01-01 05:00:00.0000000	4,171	23,357	WISCONSIN	Winter Storm	0	0	0
2007-01-01 00:00:00.0000000	2007-01-01 06:00:00.0000000	1,930	9,494	NEW YORK	Winter Weather	0	0	0
2007-01-01 00:00:00.0000000	2007-01-01 06:00:00.0000000	1,930	9,488	NEW YORK	Winter Weather	0	0	0
2007-01-01 00:00:00.0000000	2007-01-01 06:00:00.0000000	1,930	9,487	NEW YORK	Winter Weather	0	0	0
2007-01-01 00:00:00.0000000	2007-01-01 06:00:00.0000000	1,930	9,485	NEW YORK	Winter Weather	0	0	0
2007-01-01 00:00:00.0000000	2007-01-01 06:00:00.0000000	1,930	9,486	NEW YORK	Winter Weather	0	0	0
2007-01-01 00:00:00.0000000	2007-01-01 06:00:00.0000000	1,930	9,493	NEW YORK	Winter Weather	0	0	0
2007-01-01 00:00:00.0000000	2007-01-01 06:00:00.0000000	1,930	9,489	NEW YORK	Winter Weather	0	0	0

Figure 4-19. Using T-SQL in a KQL queryset

You can also add the following to the preceding T-SQL script: a `WHERE` clause, aggregations and row-based calculations, and joins and rename columns (as you would any other `SELECT` statement in a T-SQL based database).

There are also limitations on using the T-SQL language in the Kusto database. For example, you can't use CTE or subqueries.

To read the full documentation of the usage of T-SQL in the Kusto world, go to Microsoft Learn (*https://oreil.ly/P2psG*).

When you are done developing your T-SQL script, you can do one of two things:

Execute the statement
: Either click the Run button in the top menu bar or press SHIFT and ENTER to execute the script.

Translate from T-SQL to KQL
: The Kusto engine comes with a very supportive feature that helps you understand the KQL language and move from T-SQL to KQL. The engine can translate your written T-SQL script directly into KQL with the `EXPLAIN` operator.

Let's go back to the T-SQL statement we started earlier in this section:

```
select top 10 * from Weather
```

Now, add these two lines:

```
--
explain
```

Before the actual T-SQL script, you'll get a different output. The results set will be gone, and instead, you'll get a translation of your T-SQL script into KQL (see Figure 4-20).

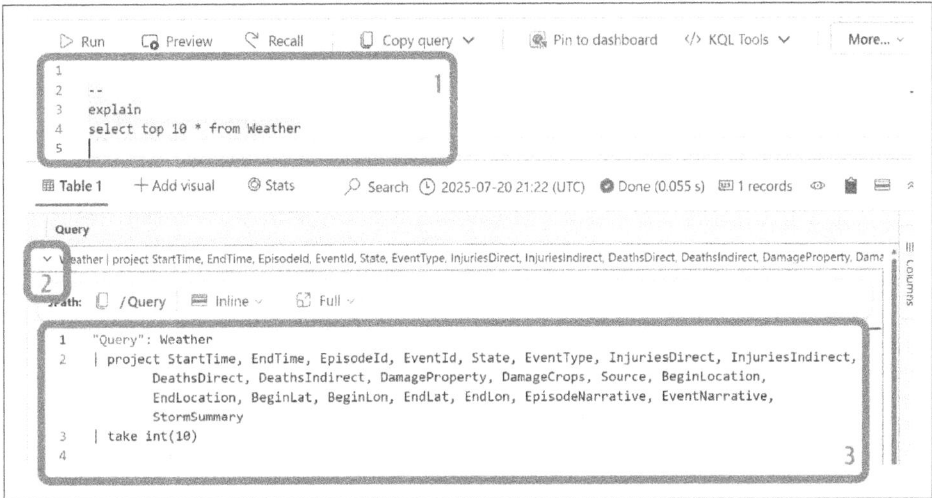

Figure 4-20. Results set translated from T-SQL into KQL

In the figure, we've a few areas (numbered 1–3):

The T-SQL statement with the newly added `explain` *operator (area 1)*
: The newly added operator is just above the T-SQL statement. The two dashes (--) on the line above it are optional and will remove red underlines in your code. Without the two dashes, you'll still get the newly translated results set, but the command will have red squiggly lines indicating any syntax errors.

The "open result set" button (area 2)
: Here, you can "open" the results set to view the newly translated KQL statement in a more readable format than the single-line results set you get by default.

The newly translated KQL script (area 3)
: This is the new translation of the T-SQL statement into a KQL statement written in the KQL queryset.

In the figure, you can also see that the engine tries to give you some nudges towards a best-practice approach for writing KQL script. (We'll touch more on that in section 3). You can see the `project` operator, which is the equivalent of "Select these columns." Using any T-SQL statement with the wildcard (*) is not a best practice because we want to help the engine use only the needed columns. Neither is the KQL statement with all the columns, unless you really need all the columns. If you only need a subset of the columns, you can use the `project` operator and list only the columns you need for the query.

The last line of the KQL script selects only the first 10 rows of data by using the `take` operator with the number of rows after it. The explicit `int(10)`script casts the `10` string to an integer. This is not a requirement, but again, the engine nudges you to use a best practice, as you should avoid any implicit data type conventions in your code when writing your KQL statements.

Translating your T-SQL statements into KQL by using the `explain` operator is fine when you're just getting started with learning the KQL language, but it won't give you all the benefits of working with your streaming data from the Kusto database. To get all those benefits, you need to learn the KQL syntax, operators, and functions.

Now that you've translated your first statements from T-SQL into KQL, you're ready to move on and start writing your first KQL statements directly in the KQL queryset window.

Structure of a KQL Statement

The syntax of a KQL statement is very much like the language you'd use to tell your colleague how to build a query. It could sound something like this:

> From the Weather table, take the data only from the last 100 days and only the first 200 rows. Aggregate these rows by <*aggregation type*> on <*column*> and group the results by <*columns*>.

Directly translated, this requirement will look like this in KQL:

```
Weather
| where StartTime >= ago(100d)
| take 200
| summarize
   sum(DamageCrops)
   by State
```

From this KQL statement, you can see that the narrative fits the syntax of the query structure. Start with the table name (`Weather`) and filter (with `where`) on the `StartTime` column and only the last 100 days. From this, `take` the `200` rows and `summarize` the `sum` of `DamageCrops by State`.

As you can see, the KQL language is a script language that works and sounds very much like how you would describe your needs to the developer. But you still need to understand how to write in this language, and that's what this section will teach you.

Starting a New Line of Code

You must start every new line of code with a pipe (`|`) to tell the Kusto engine that you're writing a new task in the statement. This also means that you can begin to structure your script with line breaks and indentation, as seen in the last line of code in the previous script. This feature can be very useful to the next developer when you're structuring your script, as it makes it easier to read and understand the script at first glance.

Funneling Data with KQL Statements

You can also think of any given KQL statement as a funnel into which you pour data. At the top of the funnel is all the data, and as you read the statement, it filters, aggregates, and manipulates the data in other ways to make it fit the requirements of the output (see Figure 4-21).

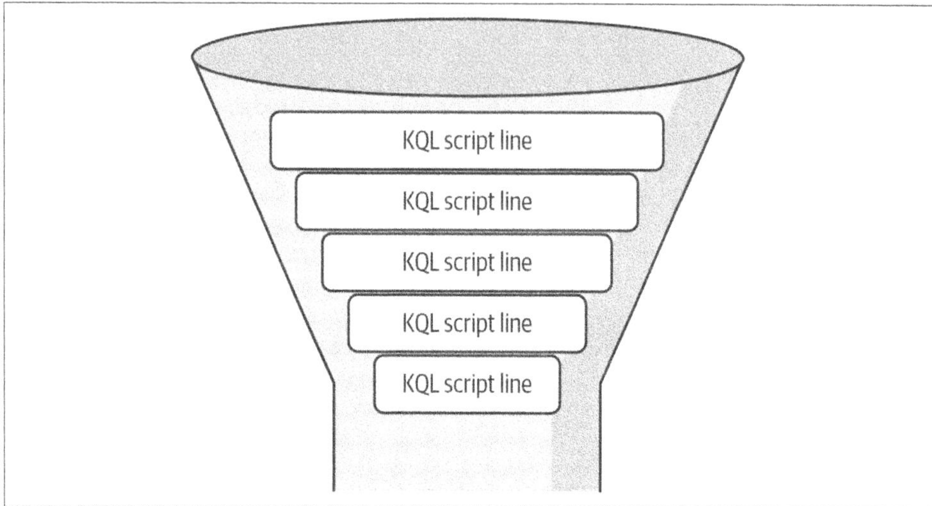

Figure 4-21. KQL statement depicted as a funnel for data

In the figure, the data is narrowed down as you follow the script lines of the KQL statement and get deeper into the funnel. This general illustration is a good way to think of your KQL statement.

If we define a new line beginning with the pipe (`|`) character, any given line of code in a KQL statement has its own results set. In other words, you can execute every specific new line of code, with all the preceding lines, and get a result. The reason we want you to know this is that the faster you can limit the result set, the faster your KQL statement will return the result to you. So to use a visual example, you can make the funnel in Figure 4-21 filter faster by changing the angle of its sides so they're closer to horizontal.

To make the funnel filter faster, you can move your where operator up in the lines and put it as early in the script as possible. Sometimes, a `where` clause cannot be put in line 2, right after the table declaration, but remember to try to place it as early as possible to help the Kusto engine limit the dataset for the next row(s) in the complete KQL statement.

The Simplest KQL Statement

To get started writing your own KQL statements, you write the simplest statement of all: a statement in which you tell the engine to give you all the data from the table. You do that by simply writing the table name in the KQL queryset window and executing that line. Using an example from our `Weather` table, you would write this:

```
Weather
```

Then, execute this script to start the Kusto engine, which will give you all the rows in the table.

But there's a catch. As the Microsoft Fabric service is web based, it's highly dependent on your browser's capability to show data. If your table has more than 64 MB of data, the error message in Figure 4-22 will appear in the results pane.

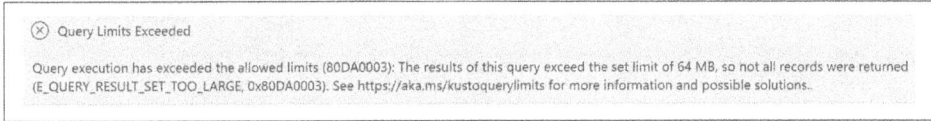

Query Limits Exceeded

Query execution has exceeded the allowed limits (80DA0003): The results of this query exceed the set limit of 64 MB, so not all records were returned (E_QUERY_RESULT_SET_TOO_LARGE, 0x80DA0003). See https://aka.ms/kustoquerylimits for more information and possible solutions.

Figure 4-22. Error message when the results set exceeds a browser's internal limits

The error message states that the default limit on the rows in the results set was exceeded when the engine tried to render them in the browser. You can choose to bypass this limit, but we strongly recommend that you don't. If you allow the browser to try to render the rest of the rows, it will often become unresponsive due to its internal memory limitations. This also means you should try to limit your data as soon as possible.

Now that you know the simplest and most basic KQL statement you can execute, we will introduce you to more common KQL operators every Fabric analyst must know.

An important difference between the T-SQL language and the KQL language is that in KQL, you can have as many of the same operators as you need in your statement. For instance, you can have more than one where operator, and you can place it wherever you need in the complete KQL statement.

Common KQL Operators

The operators you must know perform the following functions:

Because this book is focused on the DP-600 exam and not on providing all the details of the Real-Time Intelligence suite of services, we'll only give you the following list of 10 common operators.

- Counting rows
- Getting a subset of rows of data and the first *n* rows
- Getting a column subset of data
- Getting a list of unique values
- Filtering a results set
- Sorting a results set
- Performing row-based calculations

- Performing aggregations
- Creating joins
- Creating visualizations

In this section, we'll introduce you to each of these KQL operators in detail.

Unless we say otherwise, the example KQL scripts in this section are based on the Weather demo table script we started earlier in this chapter.

Counting Rows

To count the number of rows in a results set, you can use the `count` operator as shown here:

```
Weather
| count
```

This script will give you the results set (see Figure 4-23).

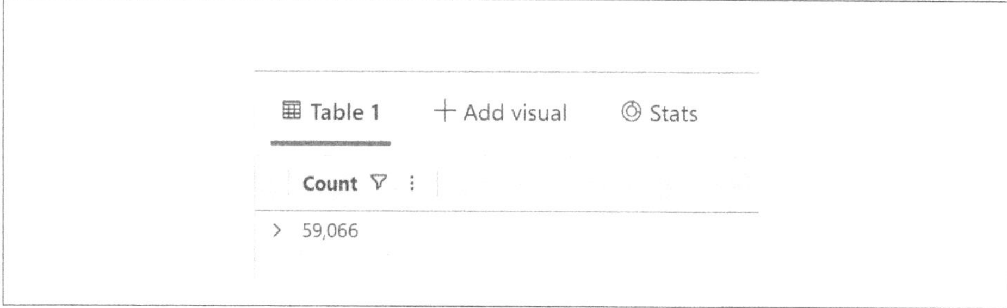

Figure 4-23. Results set from the `count` operator in KQL

Getting a Subset of Rows of Data and the First *n* Rows

You can take an arbitrary subset of data from a results set by using the `take` operator. This gives you the first *n* rows of data that the Kusto engine reads from the database. Here's an example of how you can use the `take` operator:

```
Weather
| take 5
```

This script will give you something like the results set shown in Figure 4-24. You may not get the same results set because your data may be physically structured in a different way on the disk in the database.

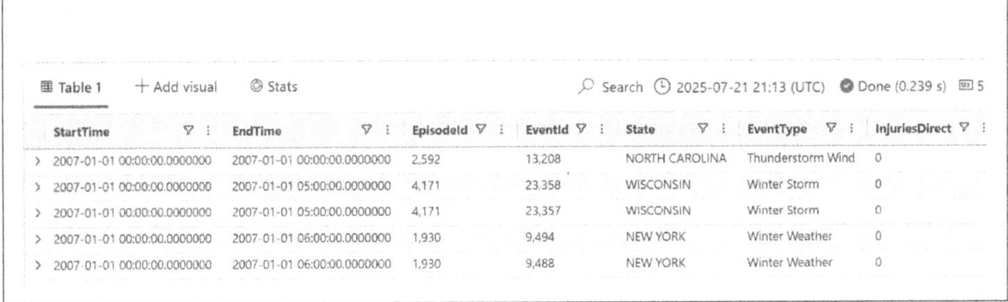

Table 1 | + Add visual | Stats | Search | 2025-07-21 21:13 (UTC) | Done (0.239 s) | 5

StartTime	EndTime	EpisodeId	EventId	State	EventType	InjuriesDirect
2007-01-01 00:00:00.0000000	2007-01-01 00:00:00.0000000	2,592	13,208	NORTH CAROLINA	Thunderstorm Wind	0
2007-01-01 00:00:00.0000000	2007-01-01 05:00:00.0000000	4,171	23,358	WISCONSIN	Winter Storm	0
2007-01-01 00:00:00.0000000	2007-01-01 05:00:00.0000000	4,171	23,357	WISCONSIN	Winter Storm	0
2007-01-01 00:00:00.0000000	2007-01-01 06:00:00.0000000	1,930	9,494	NEW YORK	Winter Weather	0
2007-01-01 00:00:00.0000000	2007-01-01 06:00:00.0000000	1,930	9,488	NEW YORK	Winter Weather	0

Figure 4-24. Results set from the `take` *operator in KQL*

In KQL, the take operator has a synonym called `limit` that works in the exact same way.

If you want a specific *n* number of rows, based on column sorting, you can add *by <columnname> <optional sort type (desc or asc)>* to your script as shown here:

```
Weather
| take 5 by EpisodeId
```

This gives you the results set shown in Figure 4-25.

Table 1 | + Add visual | Stats | Search | 2025-07-21 21:17 (UTC) | Done (0.072 s)

StartTime	EndTime	EpisodeId	EventId	State	EventType	InjuriesDirect
2007-09-06 13:00:00.0000000	2007-09-09 19:00:00.0000000	77,492	467,538	FLORIDA	High Surf	0
2007-11-02 07:00:00.0000000	2007-11-06 19:00:00.0000000	77,491	467,536	FLORIDA	Rip Current	0
2007-06-16 07:00:00.0000000	2007-06-18 19:00:00.0000000	75,596	456,342	FLORIDA	Rip Current	0
2007-05-22 07:00:00.0000000	2007-05-30 19:00:00.0000000	75,595	456,341	FLORIDA	Rip Current	0
2007-11-13 06:28:00.0000000	2007-11-13 07:28:00.0000000	13,564	75,740	PUERTO RICO	Heavy Rain	0

Figure 4-25. Results set from the take operator with added column sorting in KQL

Notice that the `EpisodeId` column is now sorted in the default descending (`desc`) order. To change that, add `asc` to the end of the line.

Getting a Column Subset of Data

To select a column subset of the data, you have two functions to choose from:

- project
- project-away

The project function actively selects the columns you want in your results set. Here's an example of how you can use it:

```
Weather
| project StartTime, EpisodeId, EventType
```

This example script returns only the listed columns: StartTime, EpisodeId, and EventType. Figure 4-26 shows a subset of the results.

StartTime	EpisodeId	EventType
2007-01-01 00:00:00.000	2,592	Thunderstorm Wind
2007-01-01 00:00:00.000	4,171	Winter Storm
2007-01-01 00:00:00.000	4,171	Winter Storm
2007-01-01 00:00:00.000	1,930	Winter Weather
2007-01-01 00:00:00.000	1,930	Winter Weather
2007-01-01 00:00:00.000	1,930	Winter Weather
2007-01-01 00:00:00.000	1,930	Winter Weather
2007-01-01 00:00:00.000	1,930	Winter Weather
2007-01-01 00:00:00.000	1,930	Winter Weather
2007-01-01 00:00:00.000	1,930	Winter Weather
2007-01-01 00:00:00.000	1,930	Winter Weather
2007-01-01 00:00:00.000	1,930	Winter Weather
2007-01-01 00:00:00.000	765	Blizzard
2007-01-01 00:00:00.000	1,979	Heavy Rain

Figure 4-26. Using the project function to actively select the columns you need

On the other hand, with the project-away function, you can remove the columns you don't need from your results set. Here's how you use it:

```
Weather
| project-away StartTime, EpisodeId, EventType, StormSummary,
  EventNarrative, EpisodeNarrative, EndLon, EndLat, BeginLat, BeginLon
```

This query returns the results set in Figure 4-27.

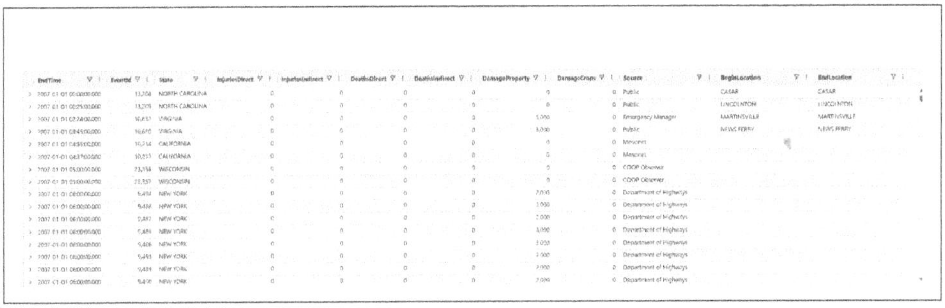

Figure 4-27. Using the `project-away` function to remove columns from the results set

Getting a List of Unique Values

To get a list of unique values from the results set, we can use the `distinct` function. This works across multiple columns. First, you input the `distinct` function, and then, you list the columns you need, as in this example:

```
Weather
| distinct State, Source
```

This query returns the results shown in Figure 4-28.

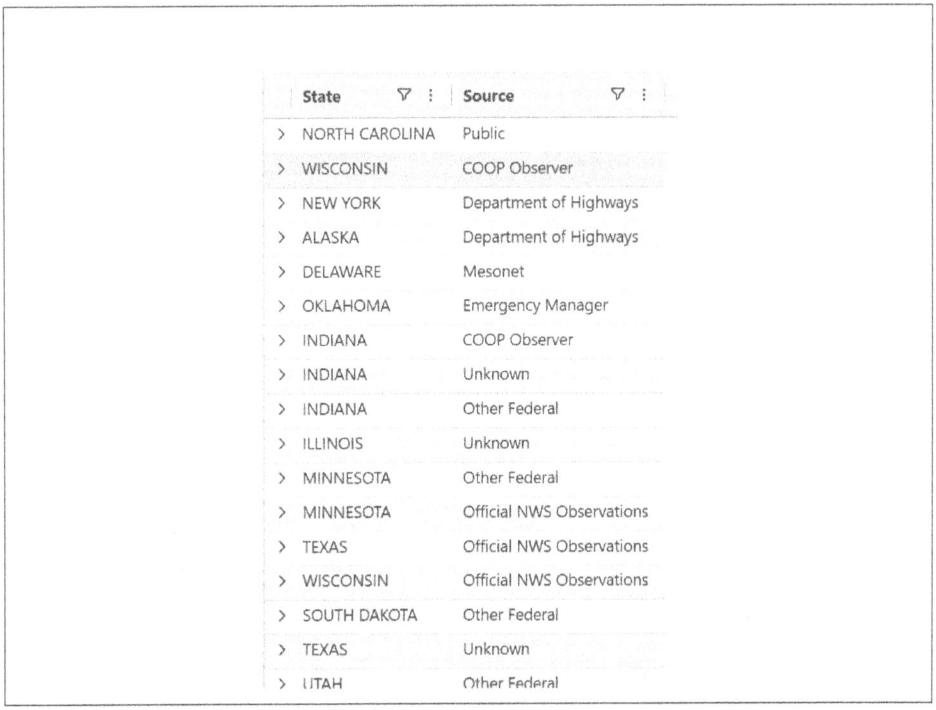

State	Source
NORTH CAROLINA	Public
WISCONSIN	COOP Observer
NEW YORK	Department of Highways
ALASKA	Department of Highways
DELAWARE	Mesonet
OKLAHOMA	Emergency Manager
INDIANA	COOP Observer
INDIANA	Unknown
INDIANA	Other Federal
ILLINOIS	Unknown
MINNESOTA	Other Federal
MINNESOTA	Official NWS Observations
TEXAS	Official NWS Observations
WISCONSIN	Official NWS Observations
SOUTH DAKOTA	Other Federal
TEXAS	Unknown
UTAH	Other Federal

Figure 4-28. Using the `distinct` function to retrieve multiple columns

Also note that you can use the `aggregate` function to get distinct values, but then, you need a column across which to do the aggregation. But with the `distinct` function, you don't need an aggregation column to get unique values.

Filtering a Results Set

To filter your result set based on column values, you can use the `where` operator in your KQL statement, like this:

```
Weather
| where State == "FLORIDA"
```

This script filters the `Weather` table on the `State` column and only returns the rows that match the "`FLORIDA`" value (see Figure 4-29). (Note that the results in the figure are truncated.)

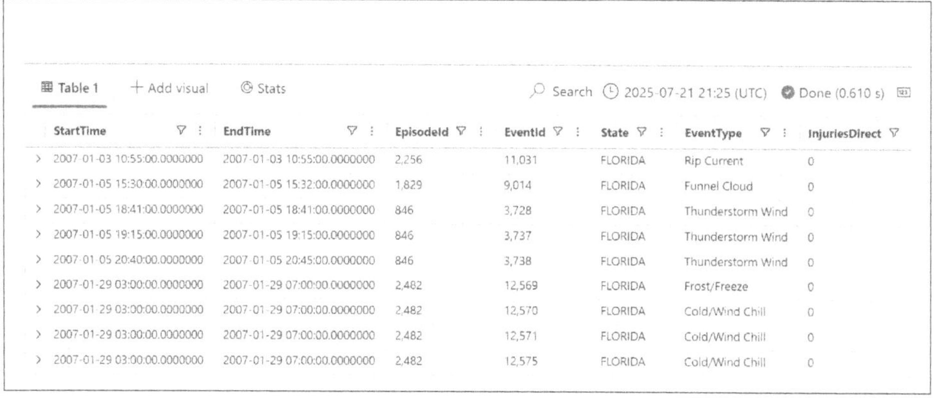

Table 1 + Add visual Stats Search 2025-07-21 21:25 (UTC) Done (0.610 s)

StartTime	EndTime	EpisodeId	EventId	State	EventType	InjuriesDirect
2007-01-03 10:55:00.0000000	2007-01-03 10:55:00.0000000	2,256	11,031	FLORIDA	Rip Current	0
2007-01-05 15:30:00.0000000	2007-01-05 15:32:00.0000000	1,829	9,014	FLORIDA	Funnel Cloud	0
2007-01-05 18:41:00.0000000	2007-01-05 18:41:00.0000000	846	3,728	FLORIDA	Thunderstorm Wind	0
2007-01-05 19:15:00.0000000	2007-01-05 19:15:00.0000000	846	3,737	FLORIDA	Thunderstorm Wind	0
2007-01-05 20:40:00.0000000	2007-01-05 20:45:00.0000000	846	3,738	FLORIDA	Thunderstorm Wind	0
2007-01-29 03:00:00.0000000	2007-01-29 07:00:00.0000000	2,482	12,569	FLORIDA	Frost/Freeze	0
2007-01-29 03:00:00.0000000	2007-01-29 07:00:00.0000000	2,482	12,570	FLORIDA	Cold/Wind Chill	0
2007-01-29 03:00:00.0000000	2007-01-29 07:00:00.0000000	2,482	12,571	FLORIDA	Cold/Wind Chill	0
2007-01-29 03:00:00.0000000	2007-01-29 07:00:00.0000000	2,482	12,575	FLORIDA	Cold/Wind Chill	0

Figure 4-29. Results set from filtering in KQL

In this figure, you can see that the results set now only contains rows with `FLORIDA` in the State column.

If you need more filters, you have two options. You can add an `and` or an `or` clause to the existing line, or you can add a new line with a new `where` clause and further filter your result set. Here are examples of both:

```
Weather
| where State == "FLORIDA" and EventType == "Frost/Freeze"

Weather
| where State == "FLORIDA"
| where EventType == "Frost/Freeze"
```

Both of these scripts return the same results set. If you want to add an `or` to your statement, you must write it in one line of code in your KQL statement.

Sorting a Results Set

You can sort your results set by any given column, both from the table itself or from a calculated column. (See more later on how to create a new column.)

The following example script sorts the results set by the `EndTime` column in ascending order:

```
Weather
| sort by EndTime asc
```

This will give you the results set shown in Figure 4-30 (which is truncated here).

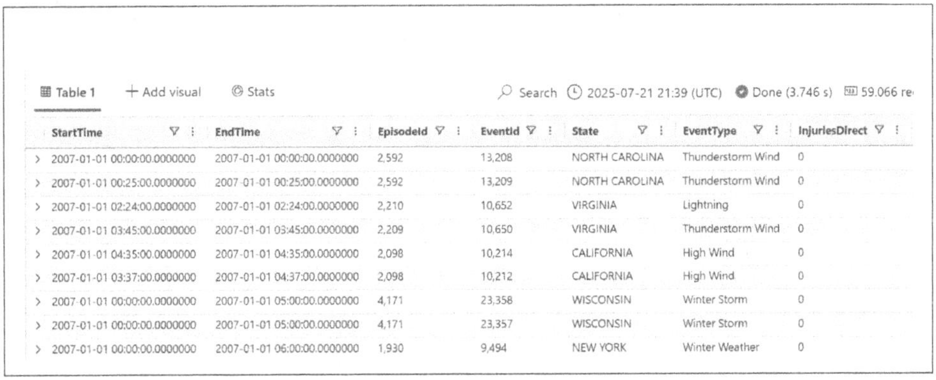

Table 1   + Add visual   Stats   Search   2025-07-21 21:39 (UTC)   Done (3.746 s)   59.066 re

StartTime	EndTime	EpisodeId	EventId	State	EventType	InjuriesDirect
2007-01-01 00:00:00.0000000	2007-01-01 00:00:00.0000000	2,592	13,208	NORTH CAROLINA	Thunderstorm Wind	0
2007-01-01 00:25:00.0000000	2007-01-01 00:25:00.0000000	2,592	13,209	NORTH CAROLINA	Thunderstorm Wind	0
2007-01-01 02:24:00.0000000	2007-01-01 02:24:00.0000000	2,210	10,652	VIRGINIA	Lightning	0
2007-01-01 03:45:00.0000000	2007-01-01 03:45:00.0000000	2,209	10,650	VIRGINIA	Thunderstorm Wind	0
2007-01-01 04:35:00.0000000	2007-01-01 04:35:00.0000000	2,098	10,214	CALIFORNIA	High Wind	0
2007-01-01 03:37:00.0000000	2007-01-01 04:37:00.0000000	2,098	10,212	CALIFORNIA	High Wind	0
2007-01-01 00:00:00.0000000	2007-01-01 05:00:00.0000000	4,171	23,358	WISCONSIN	Winter Storm	0
2007-01-01 00:00:00.0000000	2007-01-01 05:00:00.0000000	4,171	23,357	WISCONSIN	Winter Storm	0
2007-01-01 00:00:00.0000000	2007-01-01 06:00:00.0000000	1,930	9,494	NEW YORK	Winter Weather	0

Figure 4-30. Sorting the results set in KQL

You can add more sorting by other columns by using a comma (`,`) and typing in the names of the columns you need. You can also type **`asc`** to put them in ascending order or leave them in descending order (`desc`), which is the default.

Row-Based Calculations

When implementing the requirements for row-based calculations, the KQL script language is very similar to the T-SQL language.

For example, in the `Weather` table, you can add the `DamageCrop` and `DamageProperty` columns by using the `extend` operator. This operator adds a new column to the existing results set. Here's an example script:

```
Weather
| extend TotalDamage = DamageCrop + DamageProperty
```

This script gives you the results set shown in Figure 4-31. Look at the column on the far right.

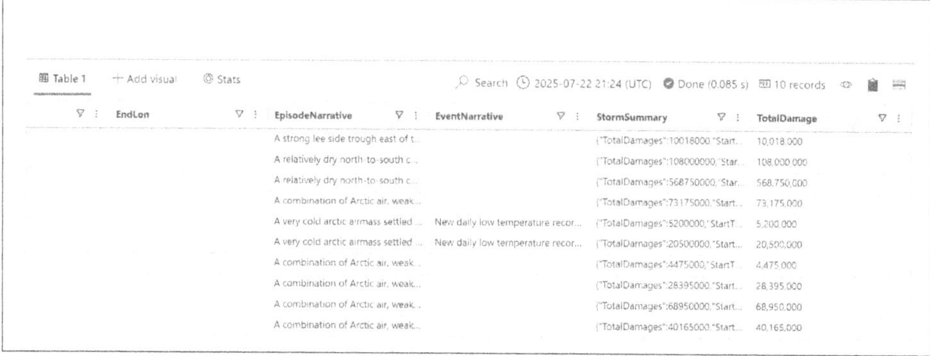

EndLon	EpisodeNarrative	EventNarrative	StormSummary	TotalDamage
	A strong lee side trough east of t...		{"TotalDamages":10018000,"Start...	10,018,000
	A relatively dry north-to-south c...		{"TotalDamages":108000000,"Star...	108,000,000
	A relatively dry north-to-south c...		{"TotalDamages":568750000,"Star...	568,750,000
	A combination of Arctic air, weak...		{"TotalDamages":73175000,"Start...	73,175,000
	A very cold arctic airmass settled ...	New daily low temperature recor...	{"TotalDamages":5200000,"StartT...	5,200,000
	A very cold arctic airmass settled ...	New daily low temperature recor...	{"TotalDamages":20500000,"Start...	20,500,000
	A combination of Arctic air, weak...		{"TotalDamages":4475000,"StartT...	4,475,000
	A combination of Arctic air, weak...		{"TotalDamages":28395000,"Start...	28,395,000
	A combination of Arctic air, weak...		{"TotalDamages":68950000,"Start...	68,950,000
	A combination of Arctic air, weak...		{"TotalDamages":40165000,"Start...	40,165,000

Figure 4-31. Adding a new column by using the extend operator in KQL

In the previous example script, we made a very simple addition of two columns. Of course, we can do more advanced column manipulation. For example, we can use the `extend` operator to replace an existing column. To do this, we simply give the new column the same name as an existing one.

This example script replaces the `State` column in the results set:

```
Weather
| extend State = "Demo state"
```

Figure 4-32 shows the output from this script.

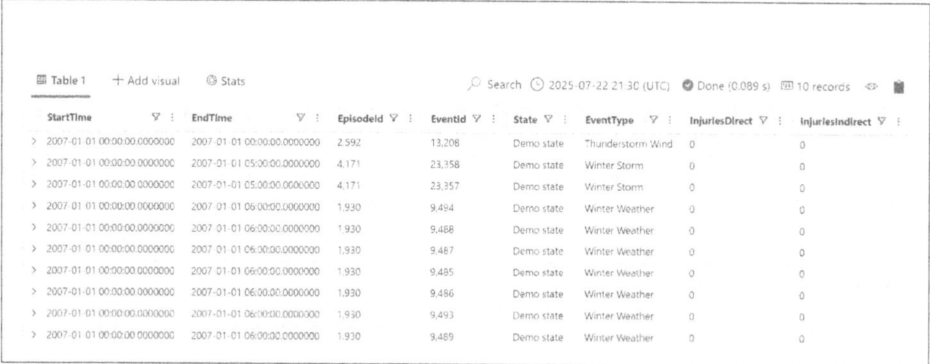

StartTime	EndTime	EpisodeId	EventId	State	EventType	InjuriesDirect	InjuriesIndirect
2007-01-01 00:00:00.0000000	2007-01-01 00:00:00.0000000	2,592	13,208	Demo state	Thunderstorm Wind	0	0
2007-01-01 00:00:00.0000000	2007-01-01 05:00:00.0000000	4,171	23,358	Demo state	Winter Storm	0	0
2007-01-01 00:00:00.0000000	2007-01-01 05:00:00.0000000	4,171	23,357	Demo state	Winter Storm	0	0
2007-01-01 00:00:00.0000000	2007-01-01 06:00:00.0000000	1,930	9,494	Demo state	Winter Weather	0	0
2007-01-01 00:00:00.0000000	2007-01-01 06:00:00.0000000	1,930	9,488	Demo state	Winter Weather	0	0
2007-01-01 00:00:00.0000000	2007-01-01 06:00:00.0000000	1,930	9,487	Demo state	Winter Weather	0	0
2007-01-01 00:00:00.0000000	2007-01-01 06:00:00.0000000	1,930	9,485	Demo state	Winter Weather	0	0
2007-01-01 00:00:00.0000000	2007-01-01 06:00:00.0000000	1,930	9,486	Demo state	Winter Weather	0	0
2007-01-01 00:00:00.0000000	2007-01-01 06:00:00.0000000	1,930	9,493	Demo state	Winter Weather	0	0
2007-01-01 00:00:00.0000000	2007-01-01 06:00:00.0000000	1,930	9,489	Demo state	Winter Weather	0	0

Figure 4-32. Replacing an existing column by using the `extend` operator in KQL

Performing Aggregations

One of the many strengths of the Kusto engine is its ability to perform aggregations on huge datasets extremely fast. The `summarize` operator is the key to getting started with this. It gives you the ability to create aggregations in one line of code, which is much easier than in the T-SQL world, where you must remember to add `GROUP BY` and all the columns that are not in an aggregation function.

In KQL, you simply start your new line with **`summarize`**, type in the aggregation function you need, type **by**, and then type in the names of the columns you need to use as group-by columns. Here's an example of that, in which the `Weather` table is aggregating the sum of `DamageCrops` by `State`:

```
Weather
| summarize sum(DamageCrops) by State
```

Figure 4-33 shows the output of this script.

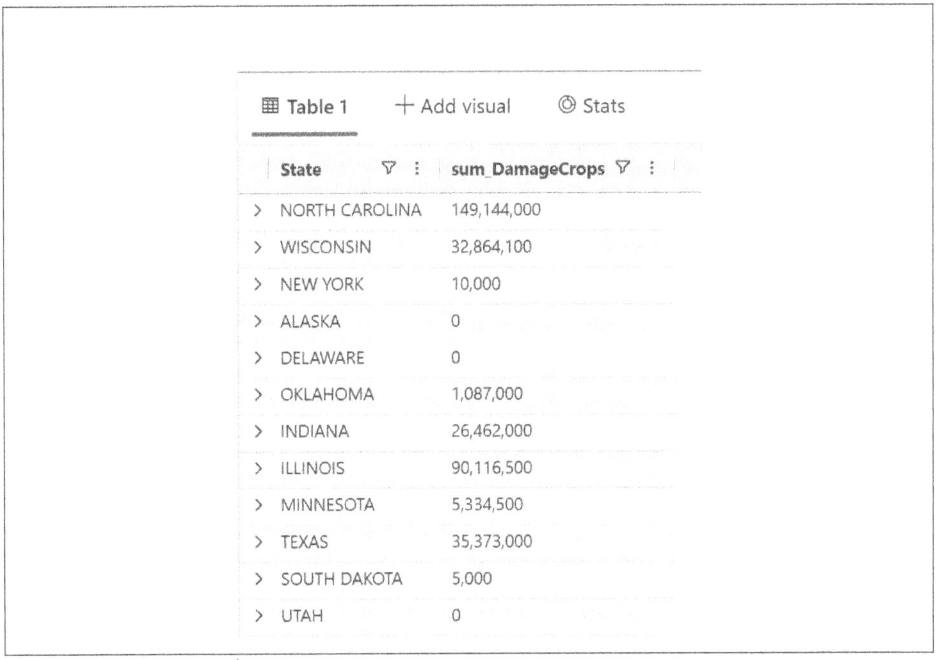

Table 1 + Add visual Stats

State	sum_DamageCrops
NORTH CAROLINA	149,144,000
WISCONSIN	32,864,100
NEW YORK	10,000
ALASKA	0
DELAWARE	0
OKLAHOMA	1,087,000
INDIANA	26,462,000
ILLINOIS	90,116,500
MINNESOTA	5,334,500
TEXAS	35,373,000
SOUTH DAKOTA	5,000
UTAH	0

Figure 4-33. Results of using the `summarize` operator in KQL

You will also notice that the new column name is autogenerated, based on the aggregation function, an underscore (_), and the table name. You can specify the new column name by typing in the name you want before the aggregation function, as in this example:

```
Weather
| summarize SumOfDamageCrops = sum(DamageCrops) by State
```

You can see the new column name in Figure 4-34.

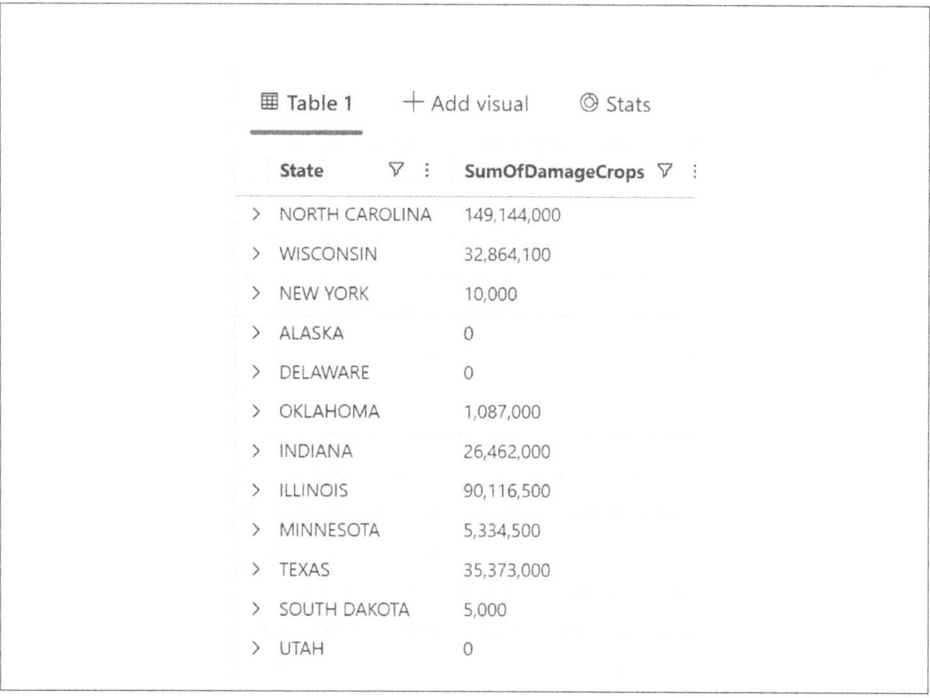

State	SumOfDamageCrops
NORTH CAROLINA	149,144,000
WISCONSIN	32,864,100
NEW YORK	10,000
ALASKA	0
DELAWARE	0
OKLAHOMA	1,087,000
INDIANA	26,462,000
ILLINOIS	90,116,500
MINNESOTA	5,334,500
TEXAS	35,373,000
SOUTH DAKOTA	5,000
UTAH	0

Figure 4-34. Specifying a new column name in aggregation functions in KQL

One of the benefits of using KQL is the ability to add more than one aggregation function to the same line of code. If you want to find both the `sum` and the `max` of the `DamageCrops` column, you can use the script in the following example:

```
Weather
| summarize
    SumOfDamageCrops = sum(DamageCrops),
    MaxOfDamageCrop = max(DamageCrops)
    by State
```

Figure 4-35 shows the results of this script.

State	SumOfDamageCrops	MaxOfDamageCrop
NORTH CAROLINA	149,144,000	10,000,000
WISCONSIN	32,864,100	10,000,000
NEW YORK	10,000	10,000
ALASKA	0	0
DELAWARE	0	0
OKLAHOMA	1,087,000	500,000
INDIANA	26,462,000	3,030,000
ILLINOIS	90,116,500	3,450,000
MINNESOTA	5,334,500	750,000
TEXAS	35,373,000	13,000,000
SOUTH DAKOTA	5,000	5,000
UTAH	0	0
COLORADO	320,000	100,000

Figure 4-35. Implementing several aggregation functions in the same line using KQL

Creating Joins

The process of creating joins in KQL is the same one we covered in Chapter 3 when explaining the theory of joins and Venn diagrams. However, there are three additional types of joins in KQL: the ANTI JOIN, the INNERUNIQUE JOIN, and the SEMI JOIN.

First, we'll introduce you to the three new join types, and then, we'll walk you through the ways of writing and executing joins in KQL:

ANTI JOIN
: This is the same as a combination of a LEFT JOIN from Chapter 3 and a filter that takes only the rows in the right table that are blank because they do not match any rows from the left table. In KQL, you can do this in one command with the ANTI JOIN. Figure 4-36 is a Venn diagram of this join.

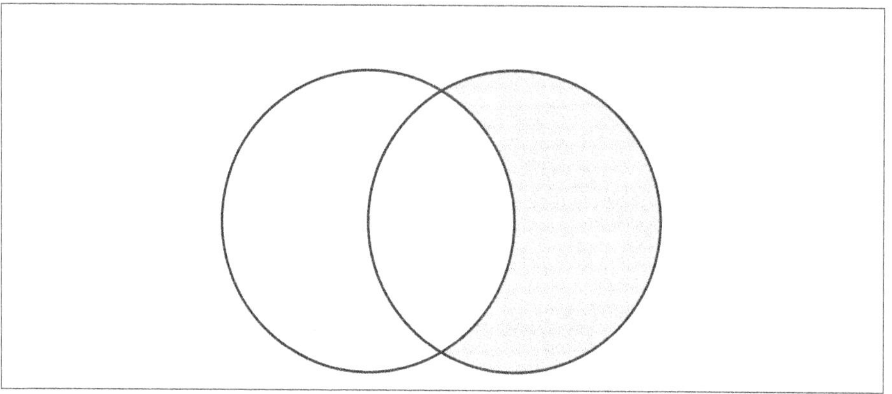

Figure 4-36. The ANTI JOIN in KQL

INNERUNIQUE JOIN

This is the default join type in KQL if nothing else is declared. (See later in this chapter for default joins and declarations.) This join removes duplicate keys from the left table and only returns the rows from both tables where there is a match.

Figure 4-37 illustrates this.

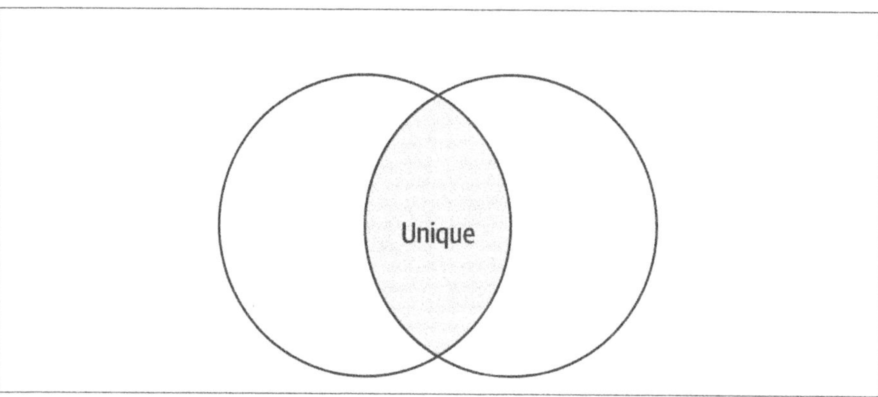

Figure 4-37. The INNERUNIQUE JOIN in KQL

`SEMI JOIN`

This is a bit like a normal INNER JOIN, but the difference is that the engine automatically only returns columns from the right table. This can be useful for filtering data in the right table on rows from the left table, but the left table is only a reference table and does not play any other role in the dataset.

Figure 4-38 illustrates this.

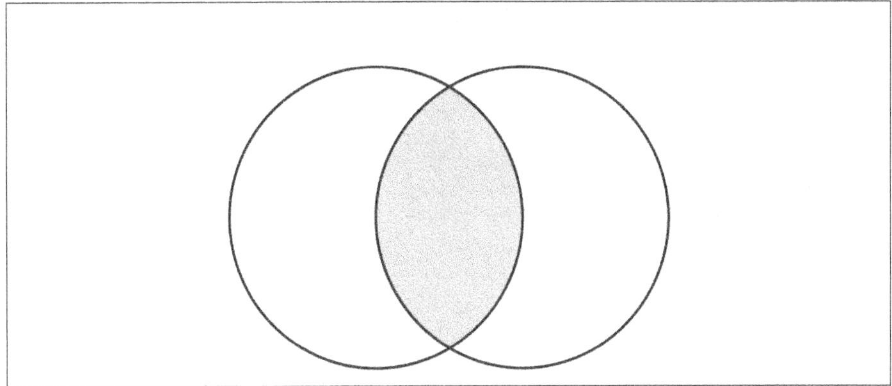

Figure 4-38. The `SEMI JOIN` in KQL

You can also combine join types in KQL to create extra join types. For instance, LEFTANTISEMI is a left ANTI JOIN that only returns columns from the right table. You can see a full list of available join types later in this section.

Join approaches

Now that we've introduced you to the new join types in KQL, we can give you a general introduction to the syntax of writing and using the different join operators in your scripts.

First, you can perform the join operation in KQL with two different approaches: `join` and `lookup`. You'll choose between the two approaches based on the characteristics of the tables in the join, and we'll look at each approach separately.

The join approach. You should use this approach when the right table is significantly longer (in row count) than the left table. For example, say you have a table that logs data from millions of events and you need to add columns to it from a reference table with data from hundreds of thousands of devices. You should use the `join` approach because the tables are not significantly different in length.

To use the `join` approach, you need to specify the join type (just like in the T-SQL approach), but you must use one of the join types listed here:

- innerunique
- inner
- leftouter
- rightouter
- fullouter
- leftsemi
- leftanti, anti, or leftantisemi
- rightsemi
- rightanti or rightantisemi

When writing the join type in the syntax, you have one of two syntaxes to choose from.

- If the column names on both sides of the join are the same, you can use this syntax:

  ```
  <LeftTableName>
  | join kind=<jointype> <RightTableName> on <ColumnName>
  ```

  Here's an example:

  ```
  Weather
  | join kind=innerjoin Locations on LocationId
  ```

- If the column names on both sides of the join are not the same, you need to use this syntax:

  ```
  <LeftTableName>
  | join kind=<jointype> <RightTableName>
    on $left.<ColumnNameLeftTable> = $right.<ColumnNameRightTable>
  ```

  Here's an example:

  ```
  Weather
  | join kind=innerjoin Locations on $left.LocationId = $right.LocationKey
  ```

  Note that the `$left` and $right table references must *always* be in this order: `$left` first and `$right` second. You'll get an execution error if you make `$right` the first reference.

The lookup approach. You should use this approach when the right table is significantly shorter (in row count) than the left table. For example, say you have a fact-based table that contains data (like temperature and humidity) from streaming-emitting devices citywide and that you need to add columns to it from a list of devices in your own office building. Since the device list from your office building is significantly shorter than the fact table, you should use the `lookup` approach.

To use the `lookup` approach, you must have the same column names in both tables because you don't have the option to explicitly declare the join columns.

The syntax for the `lookup` is as follows:

```
<LeftTableName>
| lookup <RightTableName> on <ColumnName>
```

Here's an example:

```
Weather
| lookup Locations on LocationId
```

Now that we've covered the join approaches in KQL, you're ready to begin creating and finalizing your own KQL queries.

Creating Visualizations

One really amazing feature of the KQL script language is the capability to create visualizations directly from the script without performing any extra steps or using special visualization applications. The KQL language brings built-in features for visualizing data directly from within the KQL code. This approach is not as extensive and customizable as you see in Power BI, and that's because the KQL engine is built for speed on huge amounts of data and the visuals must be fast enough to render based on the results sets from the query.

And now, without going any further into the differences between Power BI and visualizations in KQL, let's dive right into how to create visuals based on the KQL language.

This is where the `render` query operator comes to play. This operator is the key to visualizing data from a results set directly in the KQL script.

This example script renders a bar chart based on the query:

```
Weather
| summarize SumDamageProperty = sum(DamageProperty) by State
| take 10
| order by SumDamageProperty desc
| render barchart
```

In Figure 4-39, you can see the results of this query.

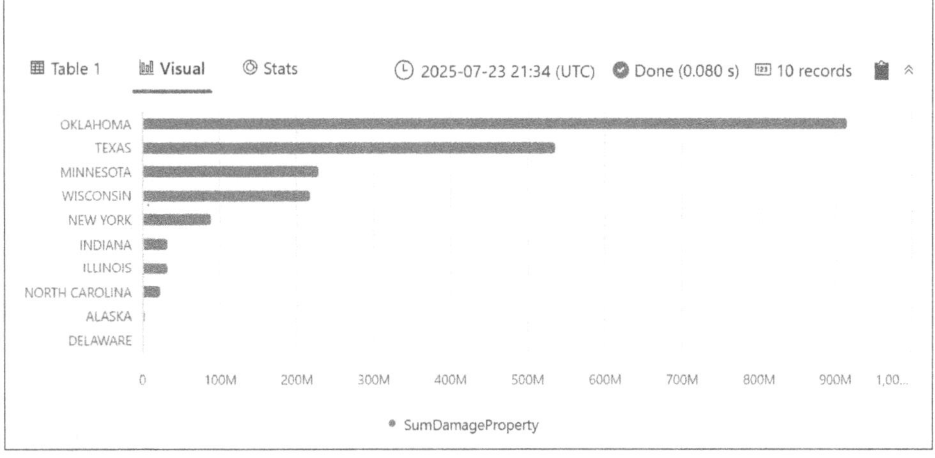

Figure 4-39. Rendering of a bar chart in KQL

The `render` operator in the last line of the example script tells the Kusto engine to render a specific chart based on the results set from the preceding lines of code in the script.

The `render` operator (and the KQL engine) also comes with a standard set of visuals:

- Table
- Bar chart
- Column chart
- Area chart
- Line chart
- Stat/multi-stat chart
- Pie chart
- Scatter chart/map
- Time chart
- Anomaly chart
- Funnel chart
- Heatmap
- Plotly

As you can see from this list, the options to render visuals in KQL are somewhat limited, compared to those in Microsoft Power BI.

The Plotly visual is the Python library for creating custom visuals. It's outside of the scope of the exam, but if you want to read more about it, this link is a good starting point: *https://oreil.ly/LnvIy*.

The different rendering possibilities come with their own options for customizing the visualizations. We won't go through them here because they're not part of the exam for this certification.

Summary

In this chapter, you've learned how to query and manipulate data with the visual query editor, the special T-SQL implementation, and the KQL language approach. You've learned about the limitations and capabilities of all three options when using them in Microsoft Fabric. You've learned how to switch from the visual query editor to SQL, how to change to SQL in a notebook, and how to work with T-SQL in a lakehouse and a warehouse. You've also learned how to write your first KQL statement, both via the translation option from SQL to KQL on the Kusto database and by typing in the code yourself.

In addition, you've learned how to help the Kusto engine optimize a query by moving the different operators around in the execution order of the query. You've practiced different ways of writing the KQL language by using the basic operators like `count`, `where`, `take`, etc. You've also learned how to do aggregations with the `summarize` operator and how to join data between two tables with either the `join` option or the `lookup` option, choosing between them based on characteristics of the two tables. Lastly, you've learned how to render the results directly in the KQL queryset for visual analysis of the results.

PART II

Implementing and Managing Semantic Models

In the next two chapters, we'll learn how to design and optimize semantic models in Power BI and Microsoft Fabric.

In Chapter 5, we'll guide you through building efficient, well-structured models using best practices like star schemas, relationships, field parameters, and calculation groups. We'll also have a look at what we can do when we get very large semantic models by using large storage models, and we'll explore how composite models can help us when we have different data sources with different import settings.

In Chapter 6, we'll focus on making our semantic models perform well at scale. This chapter covers essential techniques for speeding up queries and visuals, optimizing your Data Analysis Expression (DAX) code, and configuring advanced features like incremental refresh.

Together, these two chapters provide the foundation for building scalable, maintainable, and high-performing semantic models that can support real-world business needs. Reading these chapters will help you understand not just how to build semantic models but also how to make them efficient and reliable in enterprise environments.

CHAPTER 5

Designing and Building Semantic Models

When working with Power BI, it's easy to start with a simple data setup and let things grow over time, adding more tables to the model, more visuals to the report, more fields, and more measures. But at some point, maintaining performance and clarity can become a challenge. This chapter focuses on several ways to keep your model manageable, even as it grows.

We'll start with the basics: choosing the right storage mode in Power BI. After that, we have a look at how to build relationships between tables and how to create a star schema. Relationships between tables are essential for creating a semantic model that performs well and behaves predictably when our users slice and filter the report.

Then, we'll look at how to reduce the number of repetitive DAX measures by using calculation groups, and we'll show you how we can use field parameters to give our report users control over what fields or measures are shown in the Power BI report.

Finally, we'll look at two more advanced topics that are especially relevant in large enterprise models: the large semantic model storage format and building composite models.

Choosing a Storage Mode

When we begin developing a semantic model in Power BI, we need to select the storage mode that best suits our needs. Making the right choice is important because each mode has its own advantages and limitations that directly affect performance, flexibility, and how up-to-date our data is. Power BI has four storage mode options: Import, DirectQuery, Direct Lake, and Dual. Let's look at each storage mode and delve into its strengths and weaknesses.

When you store your data in DirectQuery mode, you can choose to switch to Import mode later. This change is permanent, and you can't switch it back to DirectQuery afterward. Therefore, you need to be sure about the change before making it.

Import Mode

Import mode should always be our first choice if the semantic model allows it. In Import mode, we load the data directly into Power BI and store it there. This usually provides the best trade-off between performance and flexibility, as Power BI doesn't need to reach out to the source every time we interact with the report. However, the data is only as current as the last scheduled or manual refresh, so it's not real-time.

Strengths

The strength of Import mode lies in the fact that it lets our report respond very quickly, even with large amounts of data. This is because Power BI already stores all the data in memory and doesn't need to continuously send queries to the original data source.

Weaknesses

The weakness of Import mode is that our data only reflects what was loaded during the last refresh. If the data has changed in the source since then, the report won't show those updates. Also, refreshing very large datasets can take a lot of time or fail if a dataset exceeds the available capacity.

DirectQuery Mode

DirectQuery mode keeps the data in the source and queries it live whenever a user interacts with the report. This is useful for very large datasets or when we need near-real-time results. However, it often has slower performance than Import mode.

Strengths

The strength of DirectQuery mode is that we can always see the most up-to-date information without waiting for a refresh, which is important when working with data that changes frequently.

Weaknesses

A weakness of DirectQuery mode is that reports can feel slower and less responsive, especially when the data source is under heavy load or when there are many visuals and filters, as Power BI needs to send a new query every time the report is interacted with. DirectQuery mode depends on the speed of the data source, and that limits some modeling features (like calculated tables or certain complex measures).

Direct Lake Mode

Direct Lake mode lets us query data directly from a Microsoft Fabric lakehouse or warehouse, without storing it in the semantic model. It's optimized to quickly load data into memory from large Delta tables stored in Microsoft Fabric, and queries are processed by the VertiPaq engine, just as in Import mode. Also, unlike DirectQuery, Direct Lake doesn't require a separate compute engine to serve queries. Instead, it loads only the necessary columns into memory on demand, making it efficient for large-scale models when properly optimized.

However, this mode requires a lakehouse or warehouse setup and may require tuning for optimal performance. In specific scenarios, such as when memory pressure prevents column loading or when we're using unsupported features like SQL views, Direct Lake can fall back to DirectQuery mode, which may impact performance.

Strengths

Direct Lake mode provides us with quick access to large amounts of data, thus eliminating the need to import it into Power BI. This is particularly helpful when we aim to avoid loading times or storage limits.

Weaknesses

The weakness of Direct Lake mode is that it only works with Microsoft Fabric lakehouses or warehouses, which means we must set up and maintain such an environment. Also, if the Delta tables in our lakehouse are not well-optimized, we may still experience slow performance.

Dual Mode

Dual mode allows us to mix Import mode and DirectQuery mode in a single model or combine multiple DirectQuery data sources. This provides flexibility for using both real-time and imported data, and it supports many-to-many relationships without requiring bridge tables. However, it comes with complexity and potential performance issues, especially when combining data from multiple sources.

Strengths

The strength of dual mode is that we can get the best of both worlds: the fast performance of Import mode for some tables and real-time data updates through DirectQuery for others. That helps us balance performance and up-to-date information.

Weaknesses

The weakness of dual mode is that imported tables still need to be refreshed regularly, and combining data from different sources can slow down the report or cause issues with how relationships work, which can make troubleshooting and maintenance harder.

Table 5-1 summarizes the storage modes and their strengths and weaknesses.

Table 5-1. Comparison of different storage modes in Power BI

Storage modes	Descriptions	Strengths	Weaknesses
Import	It loads and stores data in Power BI.	It provides fast performance, and all data is in memory.	Data is only as fresh as the last refresh, and large refreshes can be slow or fail.
DirectQuery	It queries data live, from the source.	It's always up-to-date.	It gives slower performance, has limited modeling features, and depends on source speed.
Direct Lake	It queries data directly from a Fabric lakehouse or warehouse.	It provides fast access to large datasets, and no full import is needed.	It requires a Fabric environment, and its performance depends on table optimization.
Dual	It's a hybrid of Import and DirectQuery in a single model.	It provides a balance of performance and real-time data, and it's flexible.	It adds complexity, imported tables still need refreshing, and combining sources may slow reports.

Star Schemas for Semantic Models

In the "Star Schema for Fabric Lakehouse and Warehouse" section of Chapter 3, we explained what a star schema is and how to implement one in a Fabric lakehouse or warehouse. If you haven't read that section yet and you're not already well versed in star schemas, we recommend that you read it now. You'll need to have a grasp of the basic information we provide there (the fundamentals of star schemas, the differences between star and snowflake schemas, and why star schemas are preferred for analytics scenarios) to fully understand what we present in this section.

The same star schema principles that apply to a Fabric lakehouse or Fabric warehouse, such as having several dimension tables that connect to a fact table, also apply when implementing a semantic model in Power BI. Figure 5-1 shows the same star schema we discussed in Chapter 3.

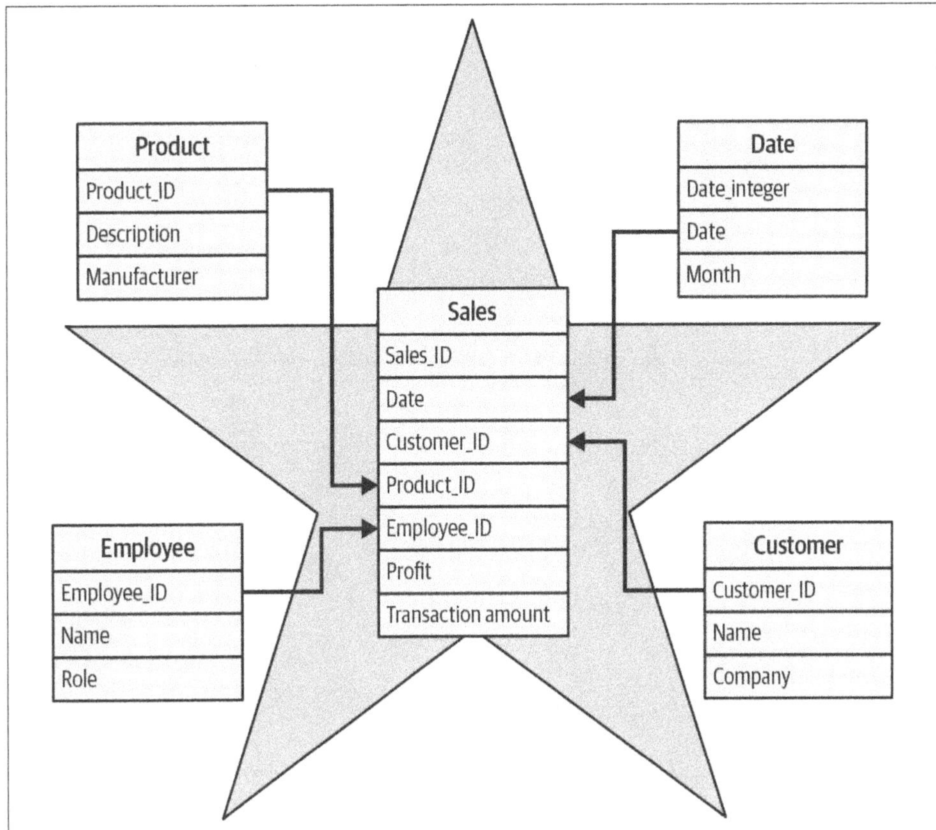

Figure 5-1. Typical star schema with one fact table and several dimension tables

To quickly review, a star schema consists of a fact table and several dimension tables. A fact table stores measurements, metrics, and transactional data (e.g., sales, orders), and it typically contains numeric columns and foreign keys that link to dimension tables. Dimension tables store descriptive attributes related to business entities (e.g., customer information, product information). The information from the dimension tables is often used for filtering data in reports.

Once you import your fact and dimension tables (for example, from Fabric or another data source), you need to create relationships between these tables to form a star schema in your Power BI dataset. This enables efficient filtering, aggregation, and intuitive analysis. You can see what this looks like in Figure 5-2, and we'll discuss how to create these relationships in the next section.

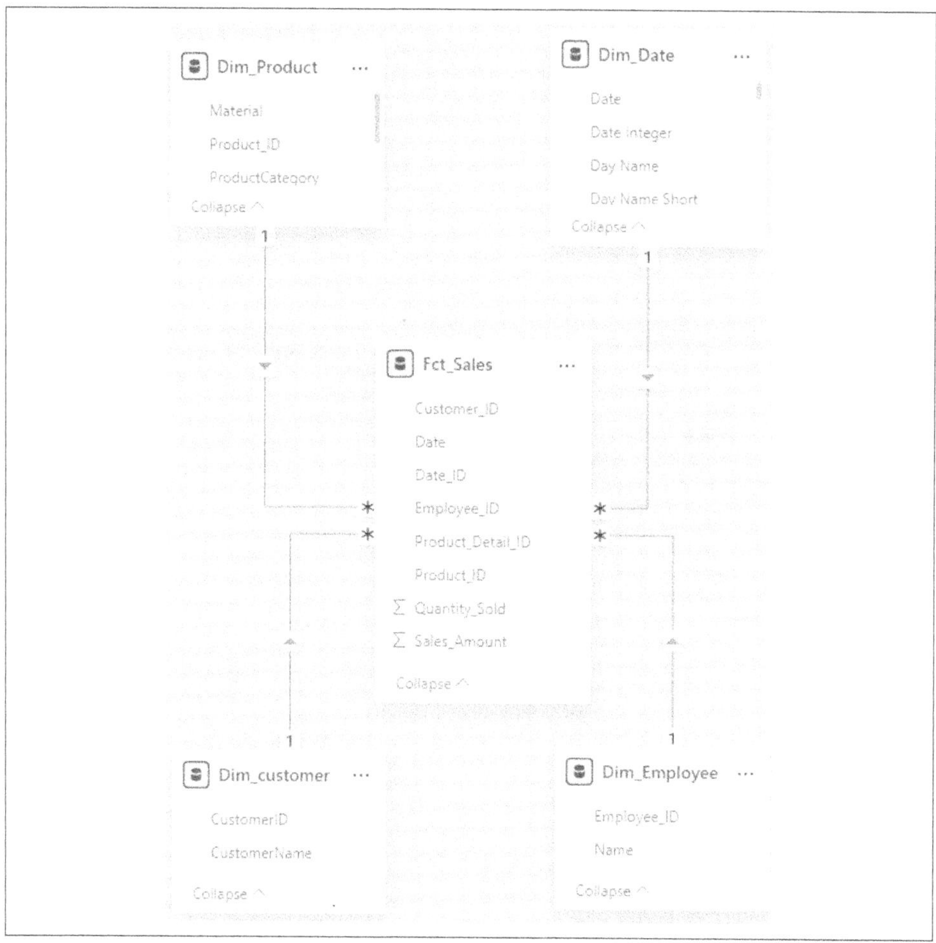

Figure 5-2. Star model created in Power BI with one fact table and several dimension tables

Creating Relationships in a Semantic Model

After loading our tables into Power BI, we need to create relationships among them so they can work together effectively. Without relationships, the tables remain standalone: you can still see the data, but if you want to combine information (such as by using different dimension tables to filter or analyze data in your fact table), you can only do it if correct relationships exist.

Figure 5-3 presents a data model with several tables. We can see that the `Fct_Sales` table and the `Dim_Employee` table currently have no connection between them.

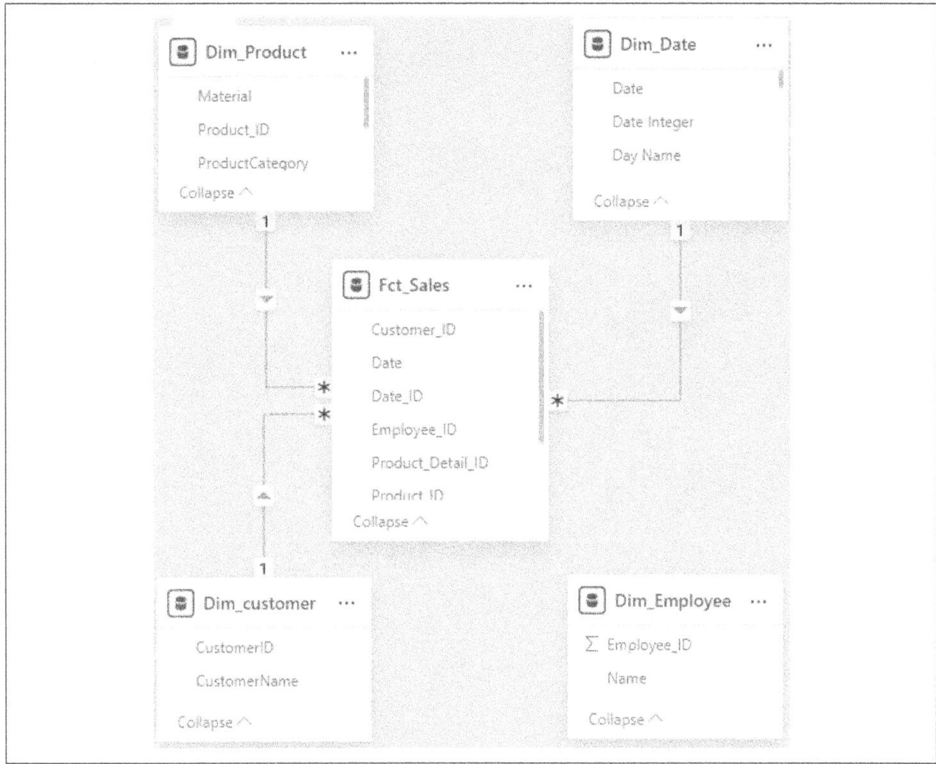

Figure 5-3. Tables in the Model View in Power BI, showing that one dimension table has no relationship to the fact table

In this situation, if we add the employee name from the `Dim_Employee` table as a slicer in a report, it won't affect any visuals based on the `Fct_Sales` table. The slicer will only filter visuals that use data directly from the `Dim_Employee` table, and that happens because there's no relationship between the tables to connect employee information with sales data. Therefore, we need to create a relationship between the tables to enable them to interact correctly.

Creating relationships in Power BI is easy. You can simply click on a column, such as the `Employee_ID` column in the `Dim_Employee` table, and drag it into the corresponding column in the `Fct_Sales` table. Then, Power BI will automatically open a window where you can define the relationship in more detail. In this window, you can configure the tables and columns involved in the relationship, set the cardinality (such as One to many), and specify the cross-filter direction. Figure 5-4 shows an example of this relationship settings window.

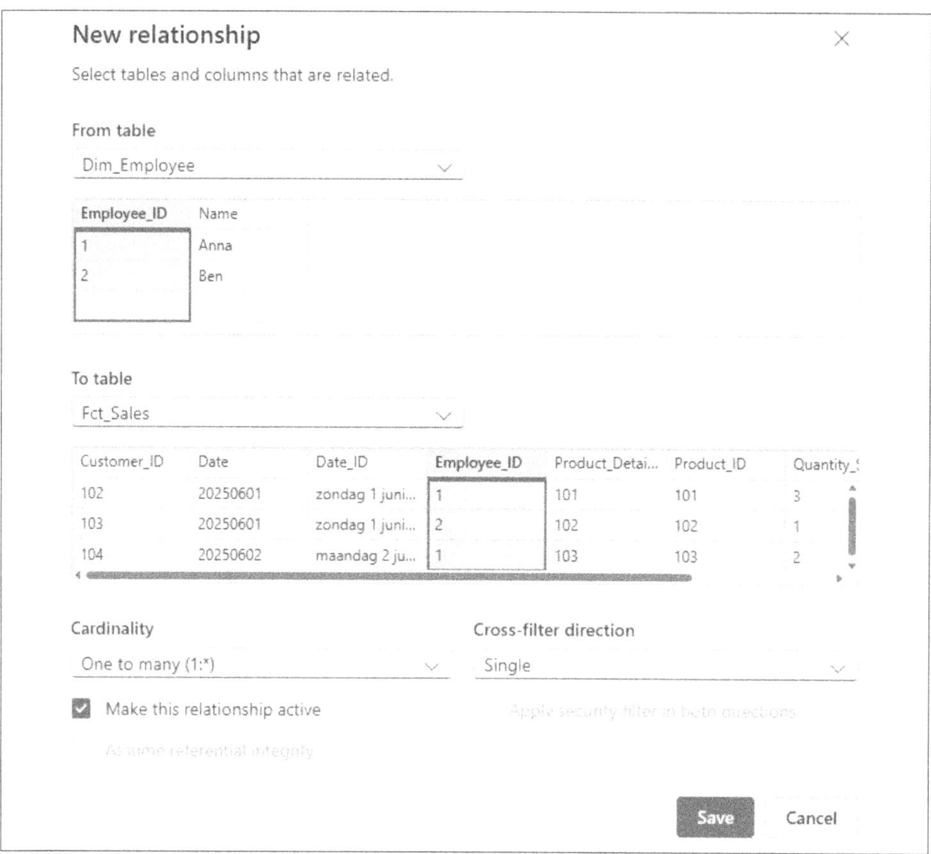

Figure 5-4. Creating a new relationship in Power BI by defining the tables, cardinality, and cross-filter direction

The first step is to choose the two tables you want to connect. When you drag and drop columns from one table into another, Power BI automatically selects these tables in the relationship editor. However, you may accidentally drop the column in the wrong place or realize you actually need to connect a different table. In these cases, you can manually adjust your selection. In the relationship window, you can click on the column in each table that represents the relationship. Also make sure to select the columns with the correct keys: a primary key in the dimension table and a corresponding foreign key in the fact table.

Once we select the tables we want to connect, we need to look at the *cardinality*, which defines the type of relationship between the two tables based on how rows in one table relate to rows in the other. It tells Power BI whether each value in one table matches one or many values in the other. Figure 5-5 shows the various cardinality options.

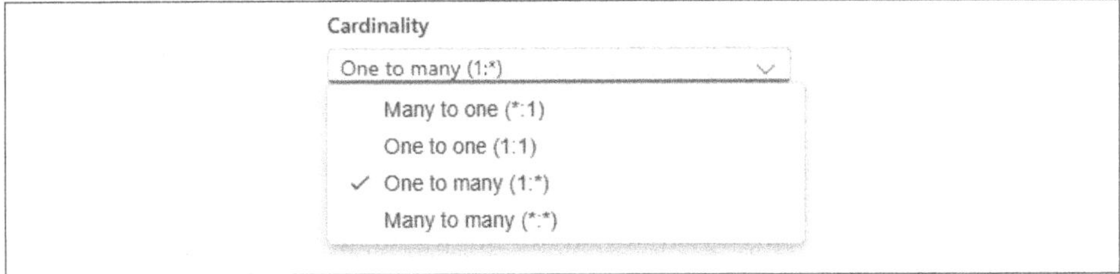

Figure 5-5. Different cardinality options in Power BI

Selecting the correct option is very important for ensuring your report's functionality. Having the right cardinality ensures that filters and aggregations work as expected. On the other hand, if you choose the wrong cardinality, the results shown in your report might be incorrect and may lead users to make mistakes or reach false conclusions. Correct cardinality also helps performance because Power BI doesn't have to guess how tables are related to one another. When a relationship is clearly defined, Power BI can generate more efficient queries.

Cardinality: Different Types of Relationships

Let's have a closer look at the different cardinality options:

Many to one (`*:1`) *or One to many* (`1:*`)

This is the most common type of relationship in a star schema: multiple rows in the fact table correspond to a single value in the dimension table. For example, consider the `Fct_Sales` and `Dim_Employee` tables: each employee (with a unique Employee_ID) can appear multiple times in the sales data for each sale they make. However, each employee should have only one unique key in the dimension table referencing them.

Whether you should choose Many to one (`*:1`) or One to many (`1:*`) depends on the order in which you select your tables when creating the relationship. If you choose your dimension table first, it becomes the "one" side and the fact table will be the "many" side, so you should choose the One to many (`1:*`) cardinality. On the other hand, if you choose your fact table first, you should choose the Many to one (`*:1`) cardinality because the fact table contains many records related to one dimension value.

One to one (`1:1`)

With this cardinality, each row in one table matches exactly one row in the other table. This is uncommon and usually indicates that the two tables contain similar or overlapping data that could be merged into a single table, resulting in a simpler model. One to one (`1:1`) relationships can happen, for example, when tables are split in the data source but actually could be one table in the semantic model. Always consider merging these tables together for a simplified semantic model.

Many to many (:*)*
: This relationship happens when both tables have repeating values in the columns you're using to create the relationship. This usually occurs when there's no unique key in either table. For example, suppose you have the following:

  - A sales target dimension table that lists region names multiple times, because there are targets for each month in each region.
  - A sales fact table that also lists region names multiple times, because there are many sales per region.

  If you try to create a relationship between these two tables by using the region name column, both tables will have duplicates of the region value. As a consequence, Power BI won't be able to determine a single, clear relationship between the rows, so there's a Many to many (*:*) relationship between the tables. This can lead to incorrect totals, double-counting, and confusing filters, so you need to be very sure that this is the relationship you want.

Cross-Filter Direction

In addition to the relationship cardinality, we need to select the cross-filter direction when we create a relationship between two tables. We have two options to choose from: Single and Both (see Figure 5-6).

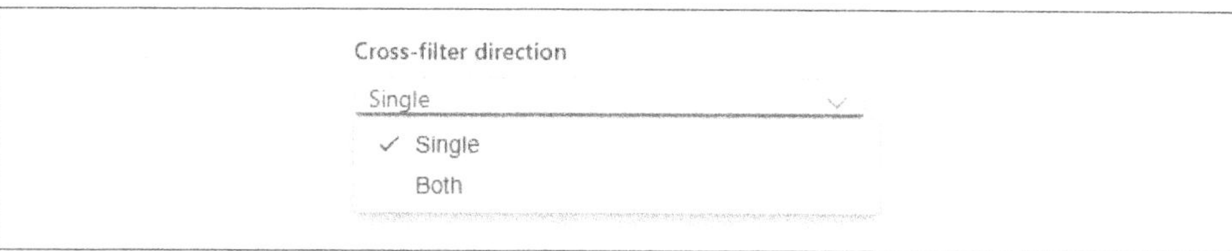

Figure 5-6. Cross-filter direction options in Power BI

Single

In a star schema, the filter direction is typically set to Single, which makes it flow from dimension tables to fact tables. This means that when you select or filter something in a dimension table (like a product category), the engine automatically filters the related records in your fact table (like sales data for that category). This is the recommended and most common setting because it keeps your model simple, avoids unexpected results, and ensures faster query performance. With single-direction filtering, Power BI only needs to calculate filters in one way, which is quicker and easier to understand.

Both

Both-direction filtering allows filters to move both ways between two tables, which means that selecting something in either table can affect the other. While this can sometimes be useful (for example, if you want slicers or visuals from both tables to interact with each other), it can also make your model harder to follow and cause confusing results if filters get applied in ways you don't expect. It can also slow down performance, especially when several tables are connected with bi-directional filters.

Active and Inactive Relationships

Sometimes, a semantic model needs more than one relationship between two tables but only one of them can be active at a time. For example, imagine our `Fct_Sales` table has both an `Order Date` column and a `Shipment Date` column, which should have a relationship with the `Date` column in the `Dim_Date` table. We need two relationships because we want to analyze sales data by order date in some visuals and by shipment date in others. Since Power BI only allows one active relationship between two tables, we can create a second relationship that will be shown as an inactive relationship.

Figure 5-7 shows two tables with an active and an inactive relationship.

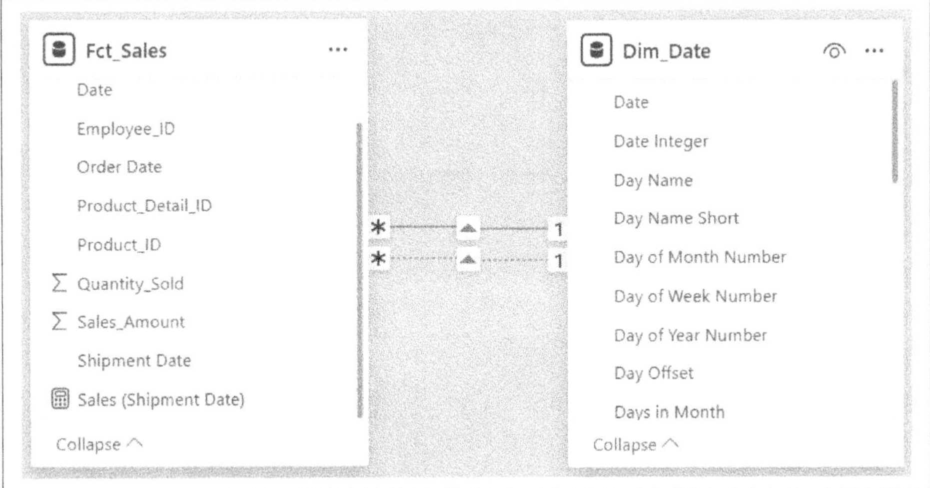

Figure 5-7. Two tables with an active and an inactive relationship

When we try to create a new relationship between two tables that already have an existing relationship, Power BI sets the new relationship as inactive. You'll also see an error message if you attempt to make both relationships active (see Figure 5-8).

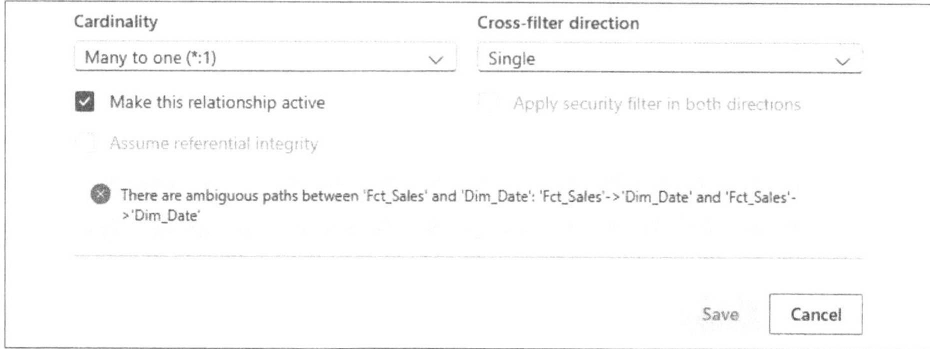

Figure 5-8. Error message when we attempt to create a second active relationship

To use an inactive relationship in Power BI, you need to activate it explicitly in your DAX measure. You do this by using the `USERELATIONSHIP()` function in your DAX formula. For example, consider an `FCT_Sales` table with `Order Date` and `Shipment Date` columns that have a relationship with the `Dim_Date` table. The `Order Date` has the active relationship, but if you want to use the `Shipment Date`, you can create the DAX shown in Figure 5-9.

```
Sales (Shipment Date) =
CALCULATE (
    SUM ( Fct_Sales[Sales_Amount] ),
    USERELATIONSHIP ( Dim_Date[Date], Fct_Sales[Shipment Date] )
    )
```

Figure 5-9. Using the `USERELATIONSHIP()` function in DAX to activate an inactive relationship

So, although Power BI allows only one active relationship between two tables, we can create multiple inactive relationships and switch between them dynamically by using `USERELATIONSHIP()` in our DAX measure.

Disconnected Tables

Not every table in our data model needs to be directly connected to other tables. In some cases, we actually don't want a relationship at all, and that's where *disconnected tables* come in. Disconnected tables are often used as input tables because they provide report users with a way to interact with measures without altering the underlying data relationships.

For example, imagine we want users to set a target to perform a what-if analysis. We'll create a small table with fixed options like 0.8, 1, 1.2, and 1.5, representing different target scenarios. This disconnected table is not related to any of our other tables in the semantic model. We could add this target as a slicer and then use the following DAX to create a measure that corresponds to these targets:

```
Adjusted Target Sales =
    [Total Sales] * Target
```

This works because the disconnected table provides us with the targets, the slicer lets us select these values, and the DAX measure then dynamically changes the values in the visuals based on the input. It doesn't matter that the table is disconnected, because you're not trying to filter other tables directly. Instead, you're just capturing the user's selection and using it inside your DAX measures. This makes using disconnected tables a powerful way to add flexible, interactive features to your reports without adding unnecessary complexity or relationships to your model.

Implementing Calculation Groups, Field Parameters, and Dynamic Format Strings

Now, let's have a look into two Power BI features that help you build more flexible reports: calculation groups and field parameters. They let us reuse logic across multiple measures, and they allow users to switch between fields or visuals. When we know how to implement these options, we can not only increase the performance of our reports but also make them easier to understand and less complex, due to the reusable logic.

Let's start with calculation groups.

Calculation Groups

Using calculation groups is a great way to reduce the number of DAX measures in your reports. Instead of repeating similar logic for each measure, you can group that logic into a calculation group and reuse it. A common use case is time intelligence calculations, such as year-to-date (YTD), month-to-date (MTD), and last-year-to-date calculations. If you have multiple base measures like sales, quantity, and profit, you'd normally create separate YTD, MTD, and last-year-to-date versions for each one. But with a calculation group, you can apply those calculations across all relevant measures without duplicating the logic.

Before we get into how to create calculation groups, let's look at where to find them. In Power BI Desktop, go to the Model view (where you can see your tables and relationships). At the top, you'll see an icon for adding a calculation group (see Figure 5-10).

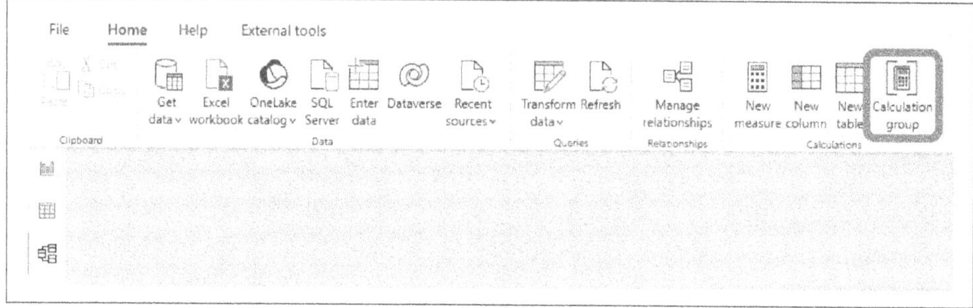

Figure 5-10. Calculation group button in the Model view in Power BI

Once we create a calculation group, it appears as a table with one column. This column represents the calculation item(s) that we can apply to our existing measures, like sales or quantity. Figure 5-11 shows how a calculation group is displayed in the report view.

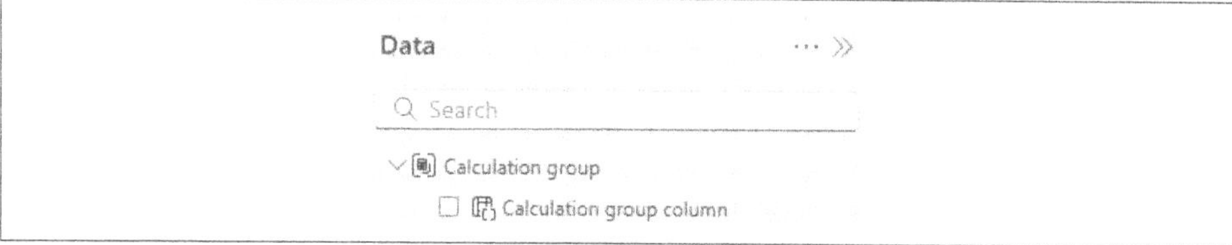

Figure 5-11. Calculation group displayed as a table with one column in the report view

In our example, the calculation group includes three items: month-to-date, year-to-date, and last-year-to-date. While we can't directly see the content of these items in the report view, we can apply them in a table visual by dragging the calculation group field and one of our measures, like Sales. Figure 5-12 shows the results.

Calculation group column	Sales
Month To Date	19.286.681,49
Year To Date	147.798.883,48
Last Year To Date	146.056.128,67

Figure 5-12. Table with the calculation group and one measure showing three time intelligence measures

As we can see here, the three calculation group items are automatically applied to the measure we select in our report. If we select another DAX measure like total quantity, the same calculations will be created for that measure.

Implicit and Explicit Measures

When you create a calculation group, Power BI will display a warning that calculation groups only work with explicit measures. Figure 5-13 shows this warning.

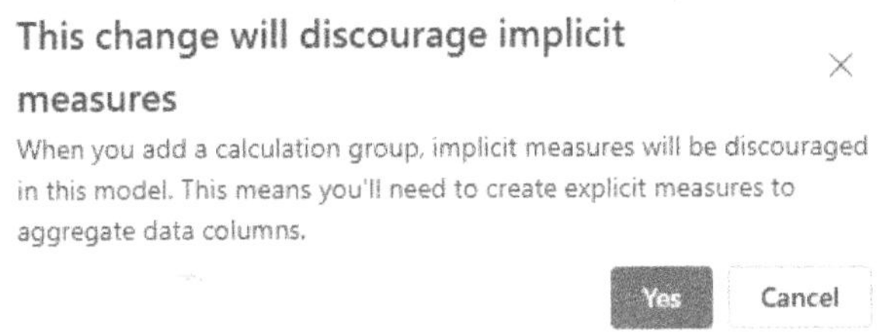

This change will discourage implicit measures
When you add a calculation group, implicit measures will be discouraged in this model. This means you'll need to create explicit measures to aggregate data columns.
Yes
Cancel

Figure 5-13. Warning that calculation groups only work with explicit measures

So, what's the difference between implicit and explicit measures? *Implicit measures* are created automatically when you drag a field into a visual, where Power BI will (most of the time) sum or count the field for you. *Explicit measures* are the ones you write yourself using DAX measures. Calculation groups require explicit measures, and if you try to use an implicit one, Power BI will remind you that it's not possible.

Creating a calculation group

When you bring up the Model view and click on the calculation group button, two things happen: a DAX formula bar appears at the top, and a pane opens on the right. A new calculation item is created by default:

```
Calculation item = SELECTEDMEASURE()
```

This simply returns the current value of the selected measure, which is often used as a "base" or "current" item (though you can keep it or change it). Figure 5-14 shows what the pane looks like when there's one calculation group and four calculation items.

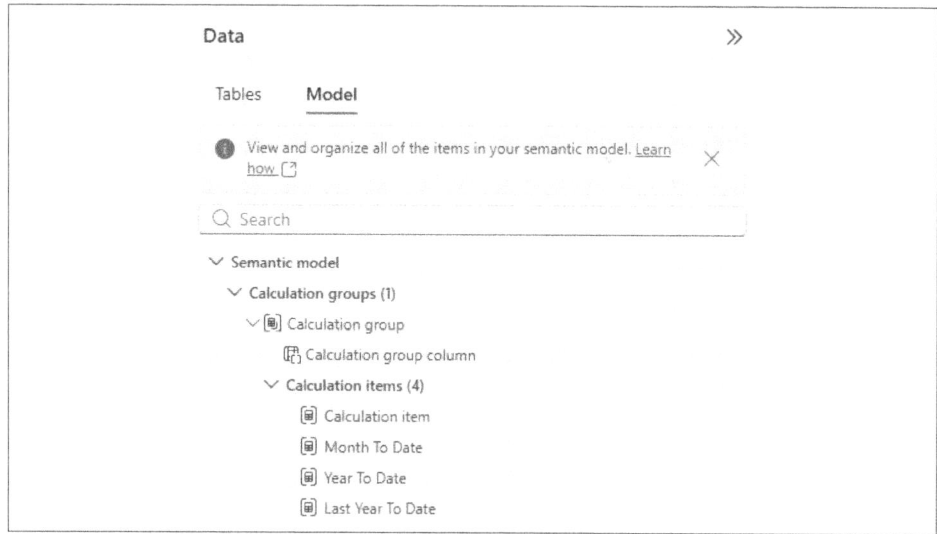

Figure 5-14. Calculation group view in Power BI in the model view

You can create additional calculation items by right-clicking on "Calculation items" and then choosing "New calculation item" (see Figure 5-15).

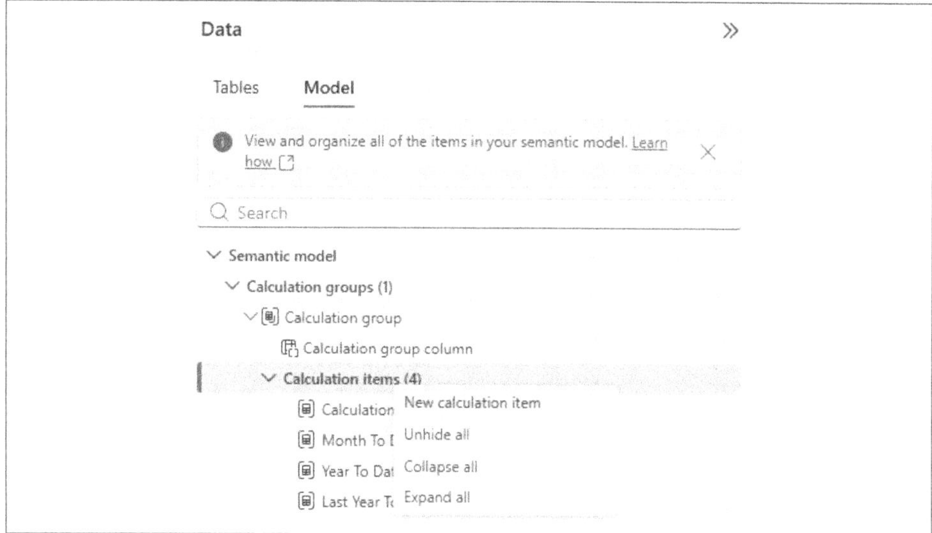

Figure 5-15. Right-click on "Calculation items" to create a new item

Each calculation item has its own name and DAX expression. Some examples for time-intelligence are as follows:

Month to Date

```
MTD = CALCULATE(SELECTEDMEASURE(), DATESMTD(DimDate[Date]))
```

Year to Date

```
YTD = CALCULATE(SELECTEDMEASURE(), DATESYTD(DimDate[Date]))
```

Last Year to Date

```
LYTD = CALCULATE(
    SELECTEDMEASURE(),
    SAMEPERIODLASTYEAR(DimDate[Date]),
    'Time Intelligence'[Time Calculation] = "YTD"
)
```

If you want to change the order in which the calculation items appear (for example, to show YTD before Last Year to Date), open the Properties pane, click on the calculation group, and drag the items to reorder them (see Figure 5-16).

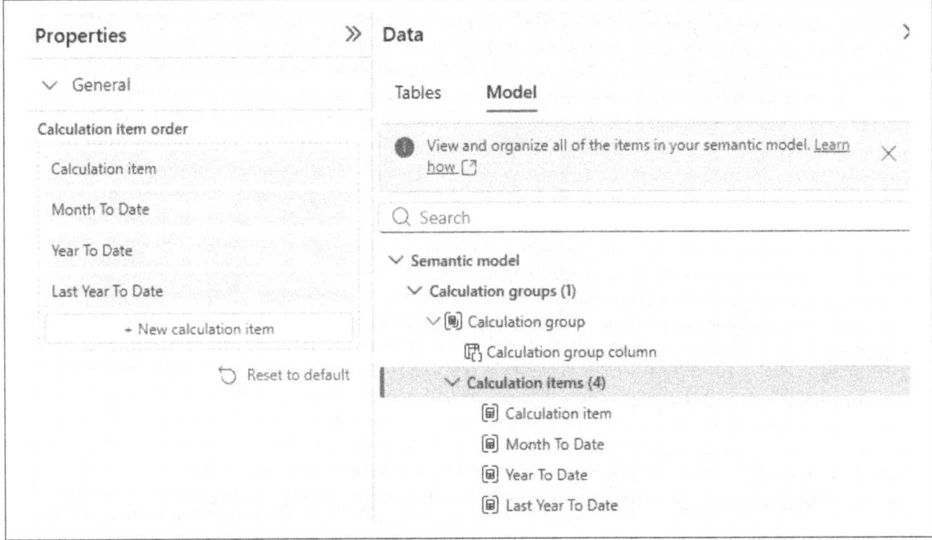

Figure 5-16. Reordering the calculation items in the properties pane of the model view

Dynamic format strings for calculation Items

By default, calculation items use the formatting of the underlying measure. However, you can override this with a dynamic format string. For example, you can click on your Year to Date item, enable dynamic formatting in the Properties pane, and then simply fill in the format string you want to use. An example of this is "`$#,##0`", which will show the value with a $ sign preceding it. Figure 5-17 is a screenshot of the pane with YTD as an example.

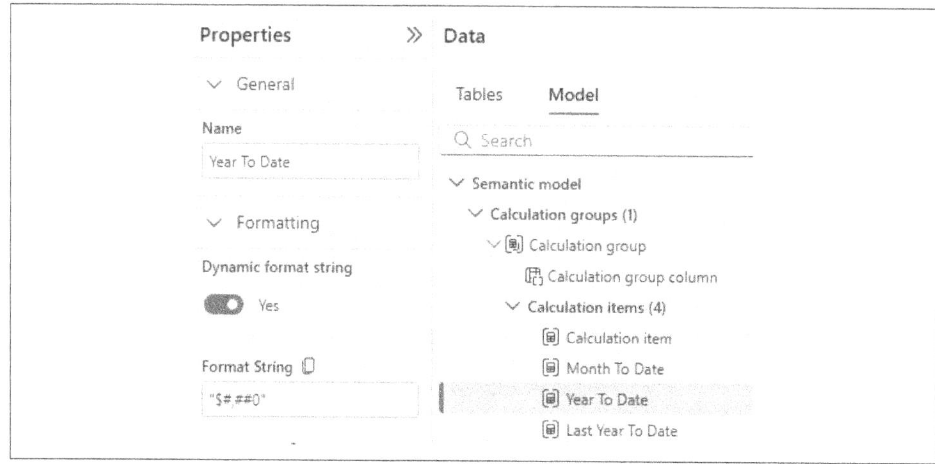

Figure 5-17. Choosing a different format string for the YTD calculation item in the Properties pane

Figure 5-18 shows how this format is applied in the visual. It makes the YTD value stand out because it's the only one with a dollar sign and formatting.

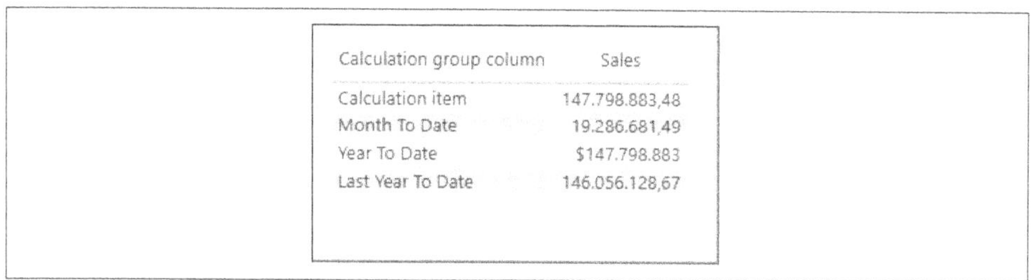

Calculation group column	Sales
Calculation item	147.798.883,48
Month To Date	19.286.681,49
Year To Date	$147.798.883
Last Year To Date	146.056.128,67

Figure 5-18. The YTD calculation item has a dynamic format string configured and therefore does not use the underlying formatting

Calculation groups allow you to simplify your model by applying shared logic like time intelligence across multiple measures. They help reduce redundancy and keep your model clean and efficient. However, there are a few limitations:

- Calculation groups don't work with implicit measures, only explicit ones.
- Row-level security (RLS) and object-level security (OLS) aren't supported.
- Dynamic format strings won't work when using a live connection to a model.

Make sure to keep these things in mind when deciding on whether to use calculation groups in your Power BI model.

Field Parameters

While calculation groups help reduce the number of DAX measures by applying shared logic across multiple measures, field parameters give you control over what fields are shown in a visual. With field parameters, users can switch between different measures or dimensions (for example, using a slicer to choose among product, category, and country). It's a simple way to make your reports more interactive without cluttering the page.

Imagine we have a report showing sales by product, category, and country. One option is to create a separate visual for each (see Figure 5-19).

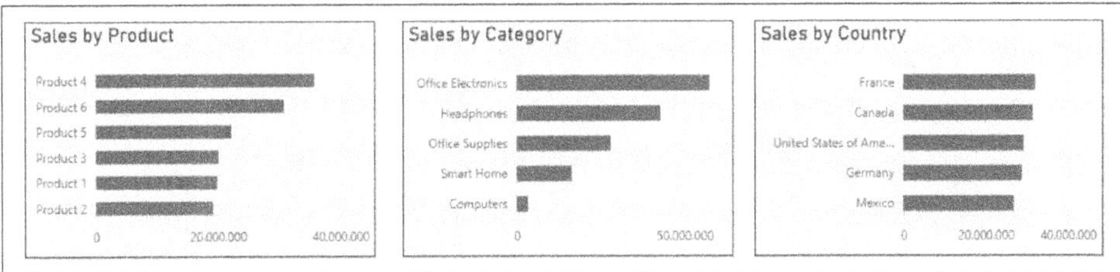

Figure 5-19. Three bar charts showing sales by product, category, and country

This works, but it takes up space and isn't always necessary. Often, different users want to use different views—for example, the product manager may want to use the product view, the category manager may want the category view, and leadership may want the country view. But they don't all need to see everything at once, and field parameters help us resolve this issue. Instead of showing all three visuals, we let the user choose what they want to see. This keeps the report clean while still offering flexibility.

Let's walk through how to set up two types of field parameters: one that switches dimensions and one that switches measures.

Creating field parameters

We need to create a field parameter before we can use it in our report. In the report view in Power BI, we go to Modeling, click on the "New parameter" icon, and choose Fields (see Figure 5-20).

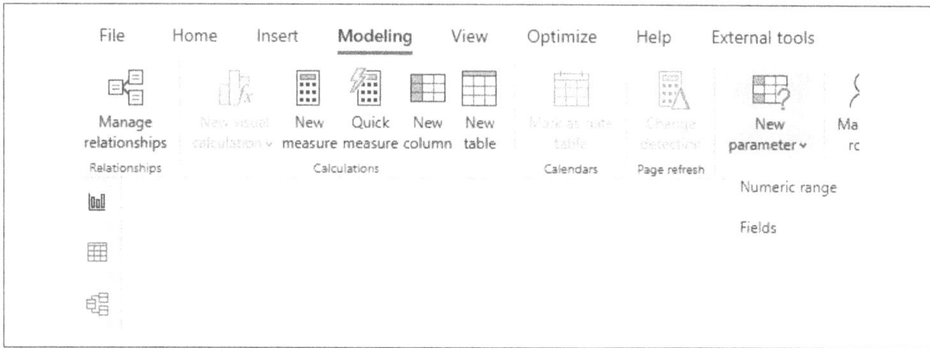

Figure 5-20. Creating a field parameter in Power BI by clicking Modeling and then "New parameter"

Then, a pop-up called Parameters will appear. This is where we set things up. First, Power BI asks what we want to create a parameter for. In our case, we want to switch fields, so the default selection is fine. Then, we give our parameter a name, and below that, we select the fields we want to include. At the bottom, there's an option to automatically add a slicer to the page. This is selected by default, and we keep it that way because we use this slicer to navigate among the different dimensions in the final visual. Figure 5-21 shows what the pop-up looks like with three dimensions added: Product, Category, and Country.

Then, we click on Create to create the field parameter. It is shown in the Data pane as a table, together with the tables of our model. To use the parameter, we can simply create a bar chart like the one we created before, with the sales on the x-axis and the parameter on the y-axis (see Figure 5-22).

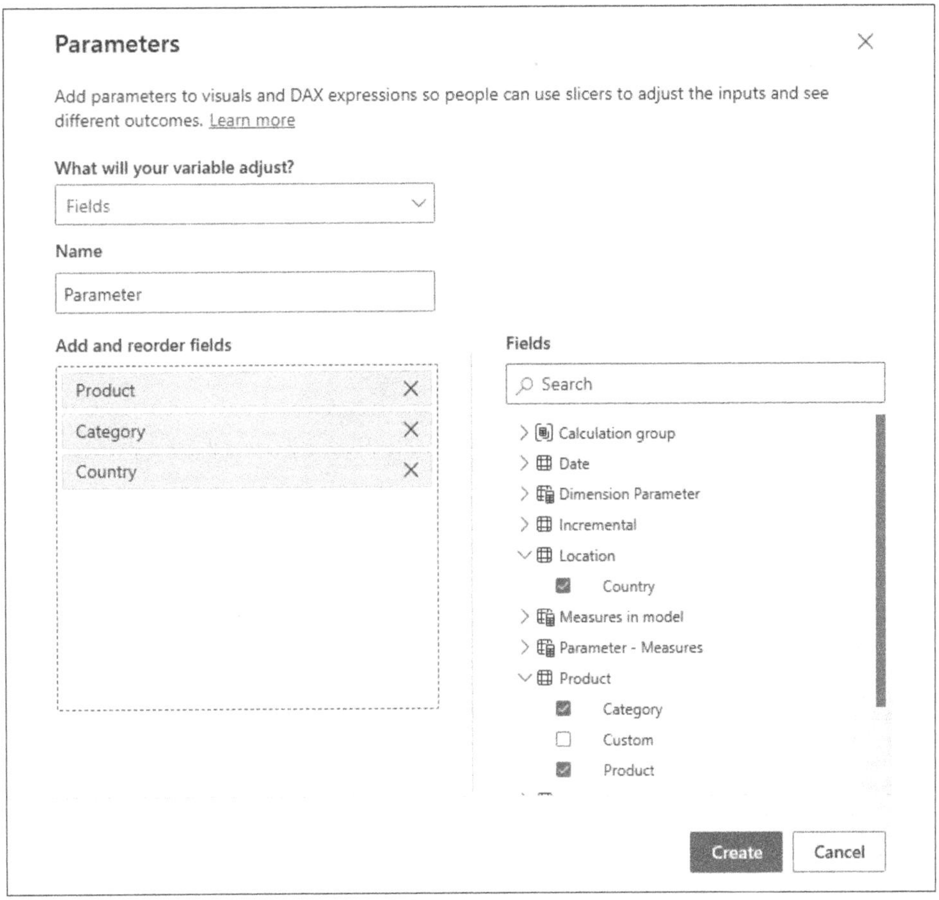

Figure 5-21. Pop-up we use to set up our parameters

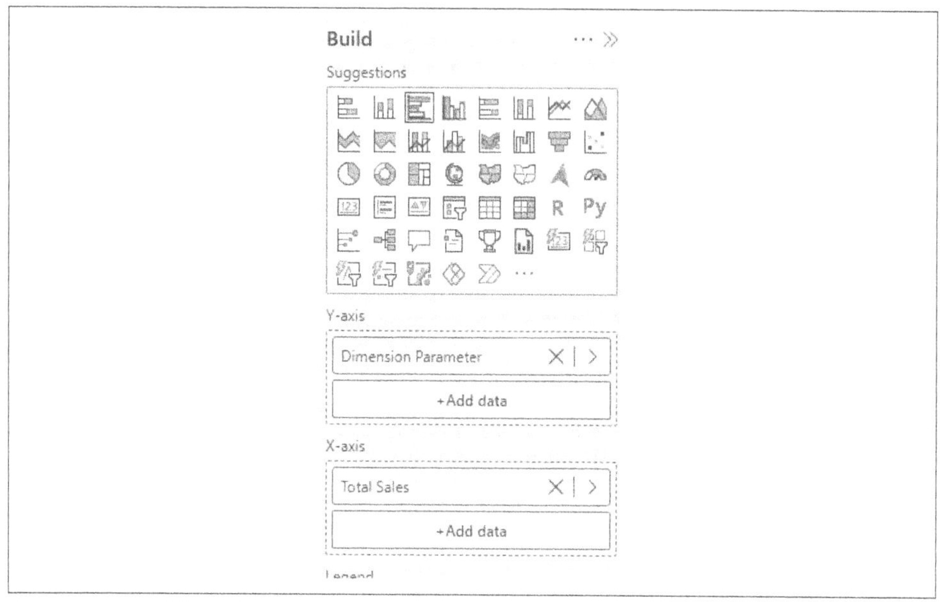

Figure 5-22. Adding the parameter in our visual, just like we added a normal dimension before

When we were creating the parameter, we had "Create slicer" selected, so a slicer visual with the parameter values is added automatically to our report page. If we hadn't done that, we could have always selected a slicer visual and added the parameter to it. But now, we have a slicer and a visual (see Figure 5-23).

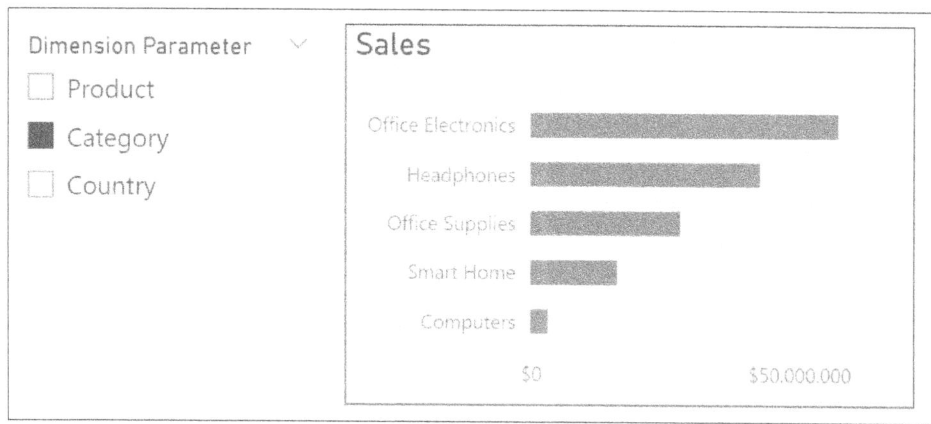

Figure 5-23. A visual with a field parameter on the y-axis that we control with the slicer

We can now switch among the three different dimensions with a click on the slicer, and the visual will automatically switch among the dimensions. This is super handy when a large audience looks at your reports and you want to provide your user with the option to quickly change between views and provide everyone with the information that is most valuable to them.

Modifying field parameters

Now you might wonder, what if I want to make a change to the field parameter, like adding a dimension or changing the sorting order? You can't get back to the pop-up window that you used previously, but when you click on your parameter in the data overview, the DAX pane will open and you'll see the configuration of your field parameter (see Figure 5-24).

```
Dimension Parameter = {
    ("Product", NAMEOF('Product'[Product]), 0),
    ("Category", NAMEOF('Product'[Category]), 1),
    ("Country", NAMEOF('Location'[Country]), 2)
}
```

Figure 5-24. Configuration of your field parameter, viewed in the DAX pane

So, when we want to add a category, we can simply add a row to the DAX measure. Each row represents a dimension. It starts with the name, then defines the dimension it refers to, and then shows the sorting order. If we want the Country to show first in the slicer, we can simply switch Product and Country in the sorting order.

In addition to using field parameters for dimensions, we can use them for measures (for example, when we want to switch in a visual between Sales and Quantity). The setup is the same: we click on the Fields parameter icon, and instead of adding the dimensions, we add the measures we want to see in the parameter (see Figure 5-25).

After we create the measures for the field parameter, we can add it to the bar chart we created before, on the x-axis. Then, by clicking on the slicer with the two parameter options, we can dynamically switch between the two measures (see Figures 5-26 and 5-27).

Parameters

Add parameters to visuals and DAX expressions so people can use slicers to adjust the inputs and see different outcomes. Learn more

What will your variable adjust?

Fields

Name

Parameter - Measures

Add and reorder fields

Total Sales

Total Units Sold

Add slicer to this page

Fields

Search

SalesID

Segment

Sheet

Sheet1_1

Total Sales

Total Units Sold

Total Units Sold LY

Units Sold

Units Sold YoY Growth %

Units Sold YoY Growth % variable

Window No partition

Window Running Sum by Year

Create

Cancel

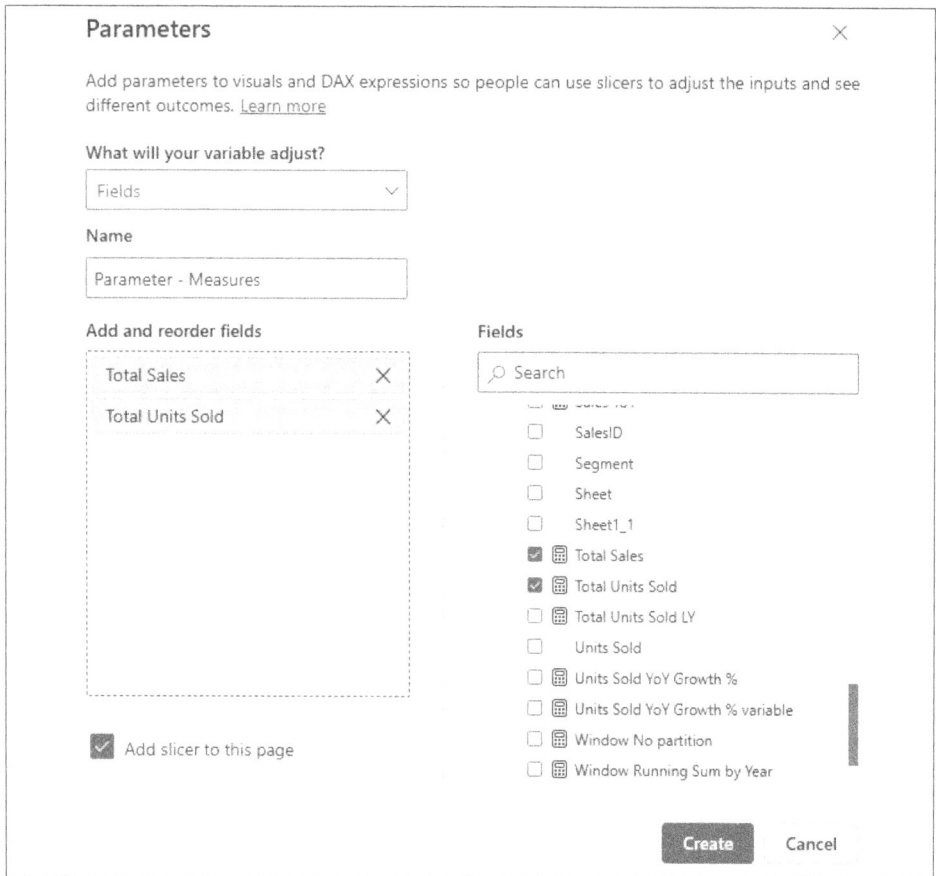

Figure 5-25. Adding two measures to a field parameter

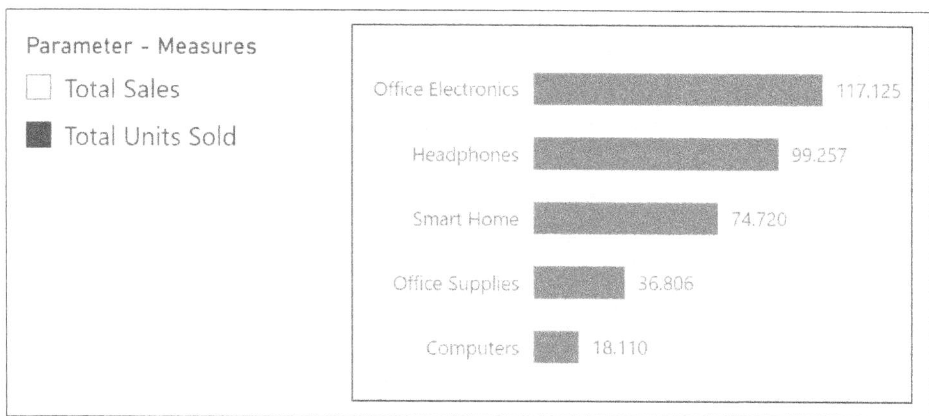

Figure 5-26. Bar chart with two field parameter options for measures, with Total Units Sold selected

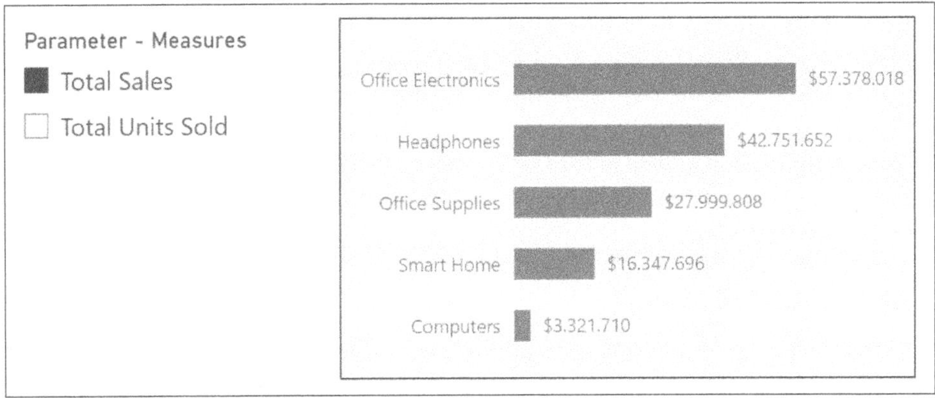

Figure 5-27. Bar chart with two field parameter options for measures, with Total Sales selected

We can also use two field parameters together. For example, we can use the field parameter we created first, with the three dimensions and the field parameter we created last for the measures. To do that, we put them both in a visual and make sure both have a slicer visual, to provide the user with the option to select what they want to see in the visual (see Figure 5-28).

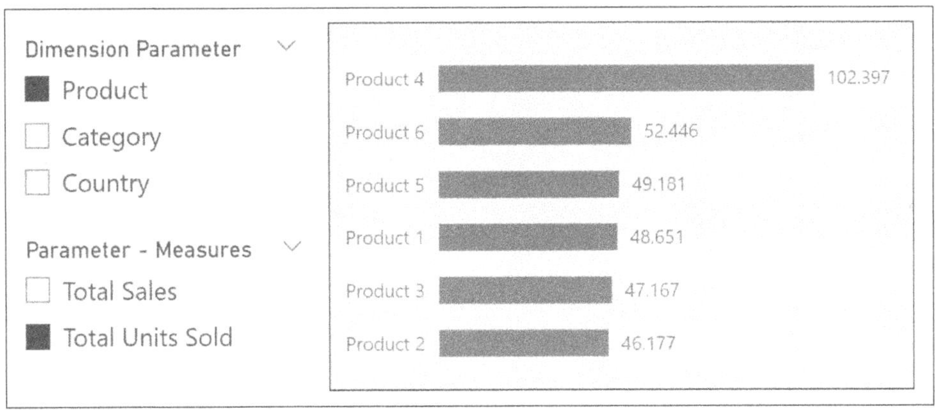

Figure 5-28. Visual with two field parameters: one for the dimensions and another for the measures

Using field parameters is a simple but powerful way to make your reports more flexible. Instead of showing everything at once, you can give users control over what they want to see. Whether it's switching between dimensions or measures, field parameters help you keep your reports clean, focused, and easier to use.

Limitations

There are a few limitations on field parameters that we need to keep in mind. We need to use a slicer to switch between the dimensions and measures, and when nothing is selected, everything is shown. This means we need to keep in mind that we need to activate "Force selection" for the slicer. Also, field parameters don't work with a live connection, so the model needs to be in Import mode. They also only work with explicit measures.

Dynamic Format Strings

Dynamic format strings let us control how a measure is displayed in a visual based on conditions or rules, without changing the underlying value. We've already showed you how this works with calculation groups, but you can also apply dynamic format strings directly to individual measures. This provides more flexibility and avoids duplicating measures with different formatting.

Creating dynamic format strings

To create a dynamic format string, you first need to enable it for a measure by clicking on it in the data pane in Power BI. Then, you can change the format to Dynamic in the "Measure tools" tab (see Figure 5-29).

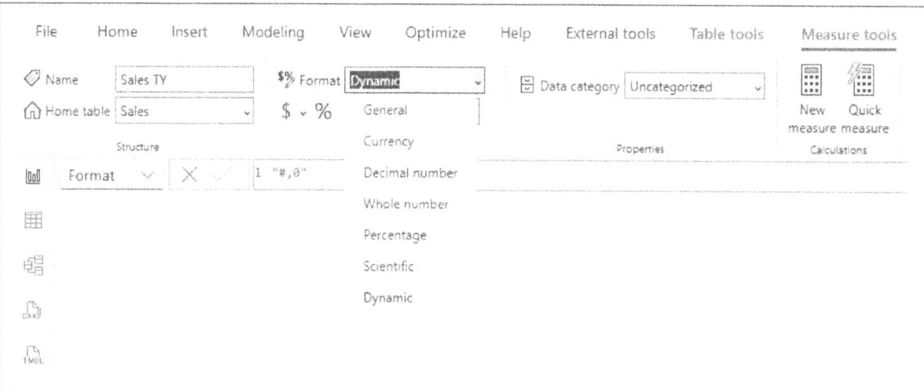

Figure 5-29. Clicking on a measure and changing its format to Dynamic

After you enable dynamic formatting, the listbox in the "Measure tools" tab will show the Format view, indicating that you are now viewing format settings. You can also click the listbox to switch back to the Measure view (see Figure 5-30).

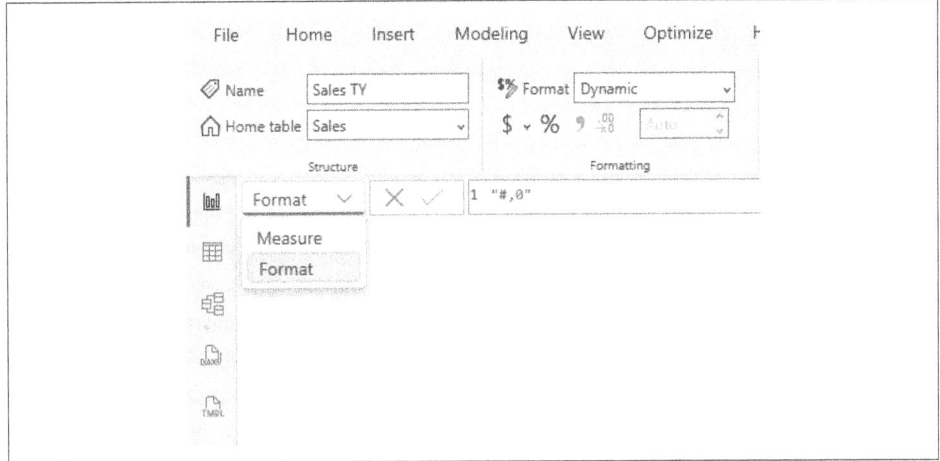

Figure 5-30. Switching between Format and Measure views by clicking on the listbox

Let's assume we have a table with countries, currencies, and the format we want to use. Each country can have a different currency and format (see Figure 5-31).

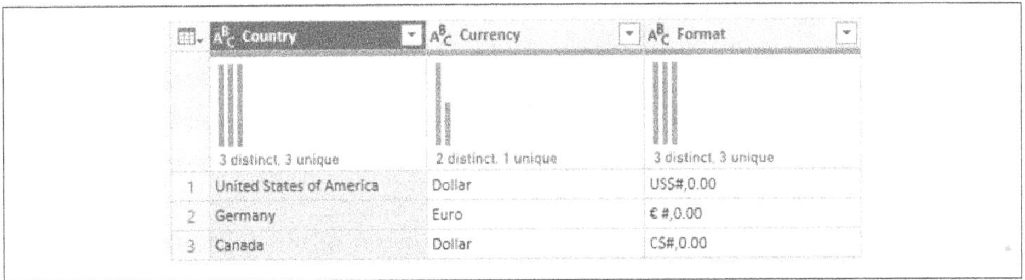

	Country	Currency	Format
	3 distinct, 3 unique	2 distinct, 1 unique	3 distinct, 3 unique
1	United States of America	Dollar	US$#,0.00
2	Germany	Euro	€ #,0.00
3	Canada	Dollar	C$#,0.00

Figure 5-31. Table with countries, currencies, and corresponding format strings

Now, we can go to our Sales measure and change the format to Dynamic. In the format listbox, we set the string to a DAX expression that returns the correct format string based on the selected country. Here's an example:

```
SELECTEDVALUE('Country Currency Format Strings'[Format],
    "\$#,0.00;(\$#,0.00);\$#,0.00")
```

This expression looks up the format string from the table. If no selection is made, it uses the default format: `"$#,0.00;($#,0.00);$#,0.00"`. This default format displays positive numbers with a dollar sign and two decimal places (e.g., $1,234.50), negative numbers in parentheses (e.g., ($1,234.50)), and zero values as $0.00. Essentially, it dynamically applies the correct formatting to the measure depending on the context or filter. See Figure 5-32 for the results of the dynamic format string.

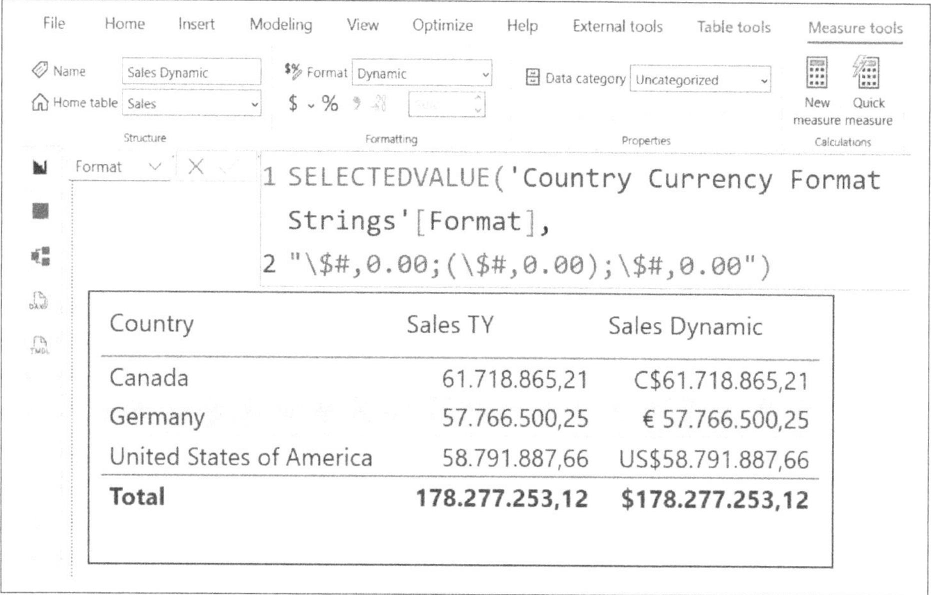

Figure 5-32. Assigning a dynamic format string to a measure by using a lookup table

Once the measure has a dynamic format string, the visuals will automatically display the correct formatting (see Figure 5-33). For example, a line chart will show the correct currency on the y-axis when the user filters by country.

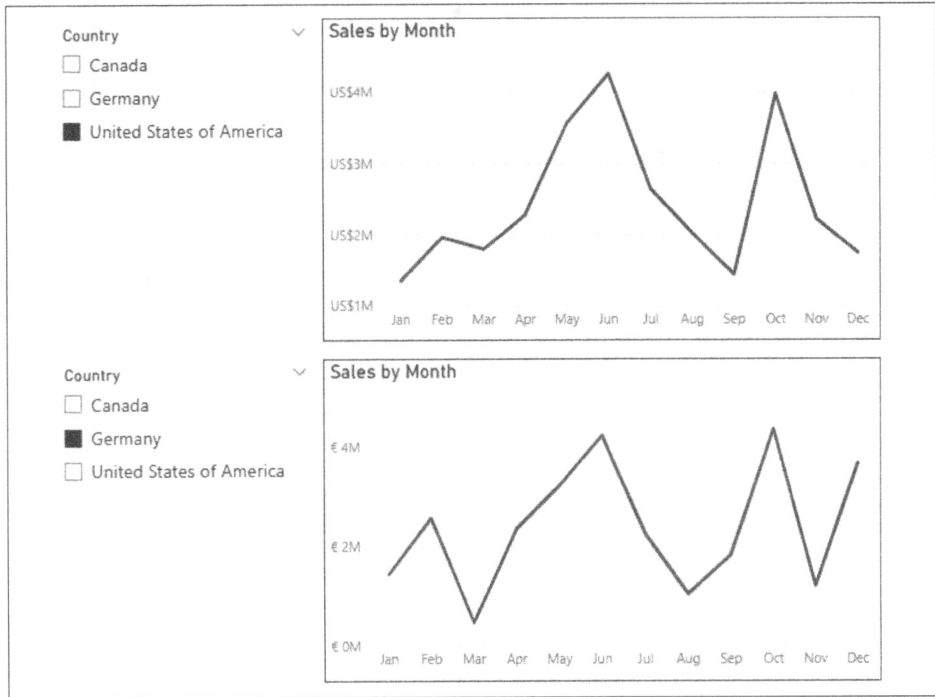

Figure 5-33. Visual where the y-axis automatically updates to the correct currency, based on selection

Benefits and limitations

Dynamic format strings can make reports easier to read and automatically adjust to the context in which data is shown. They help users interpret values correctly by displaying them in the right format, such as currency or percentages, without creating multiple versions of the same measure. This makes reports more user-friendly and reduces maintenance effort.

However, you need to be aware that dynamic format strings only work with explicit measures and are not supported in DirectQuery mode for live connections. Nevertheless, they provide a practical way to make reports more dynamic and readable, without adding unnecessary complexity to the model.

Large Semantic Model Storage Format

Sometimes, especially when we work with a lot of data, even if we optimize our data model by implementing a star schema, creating calculation groups and field parameters can make our dataset grow so large that it reaches its limit for import mode in Power BI. By default, Power BI datasets are limited to 1 GB when using Import mode with a Power BI Pro license. However, if you're working in a premium workspace, you can switch to the *large semantic model storage* format, which allows your dataset to grow beyond 10 GB. This format is designed for enterprise-scale models, and it enables more flexibility when working with large volumes of data.

The limit of the large model storage mode is defined by the limit of the Fabric capacity. Table 5-2 provides an overview of such limits.

Table 5-2. Large model storage mode limits

Capacity	Limit1
F2	1 GB
F4	2 GB
F8/EM1/A1	3 GB
F16/EM2/A2	5 GB
F32/EM3/A3	6 GB
F64/P1/A4	10 GB
F128/P2/A5	10 GB
F256/P3/A6	10 GB
F512/P4/A7	10 GB
F1024/P5/A8	10 GB
F2048	10 GB

The limits in this table correspond to the compressed size of the dataset in Power BI. The actual amount of data in the source tables can be much larger. Power BI uses highly efficient columnar compression, and typical compression ratios range from 5x to 10x. That means a 5 GB dataset in Power BI could represent 25–50 GB of raw source data.

To enable the large semantic model storage format, we need to go to the Power BI service, which is the online Power BI environment. There, we can either create a new workspace with the large storage format or change an existing one.

To create a new workspace, we select "New workspace," go to the workspace settings, and select "Large semantic model storage format" (see Figure 5-34).

Create a workspace
License mode
Pro
Select Pro to use basic Power BI features and collaborate on reports, dashboards, and scorecards. To access a Pro workspace, users need Pro per-user licenses. Learn more
Premium per-user
Select Premium per-user to collaborate using Power BI Premium features, including advanced dataflows, and datamarts. To collaborate and share content in a Premium per-user workspace, users need Premium per-user licenses. Learn more
Premium capacity
Embedded
Fabric capacity
Select Fabric capacity if the workspace will be hosted in a Microsoft Fabric capacity. With Fabric capacities, users can create Microsoft Fabric items and collaborate with others using Fabric features and experiences. Explore new capabilities in Power BI, Data Factory, Data Engineering, and Real-Time Intelligence, among others. Learn more
Trial
Select Trial to assign this workspace to a Fabric trial capacity. A Microsoft Fabric trial
Apply
Cancel

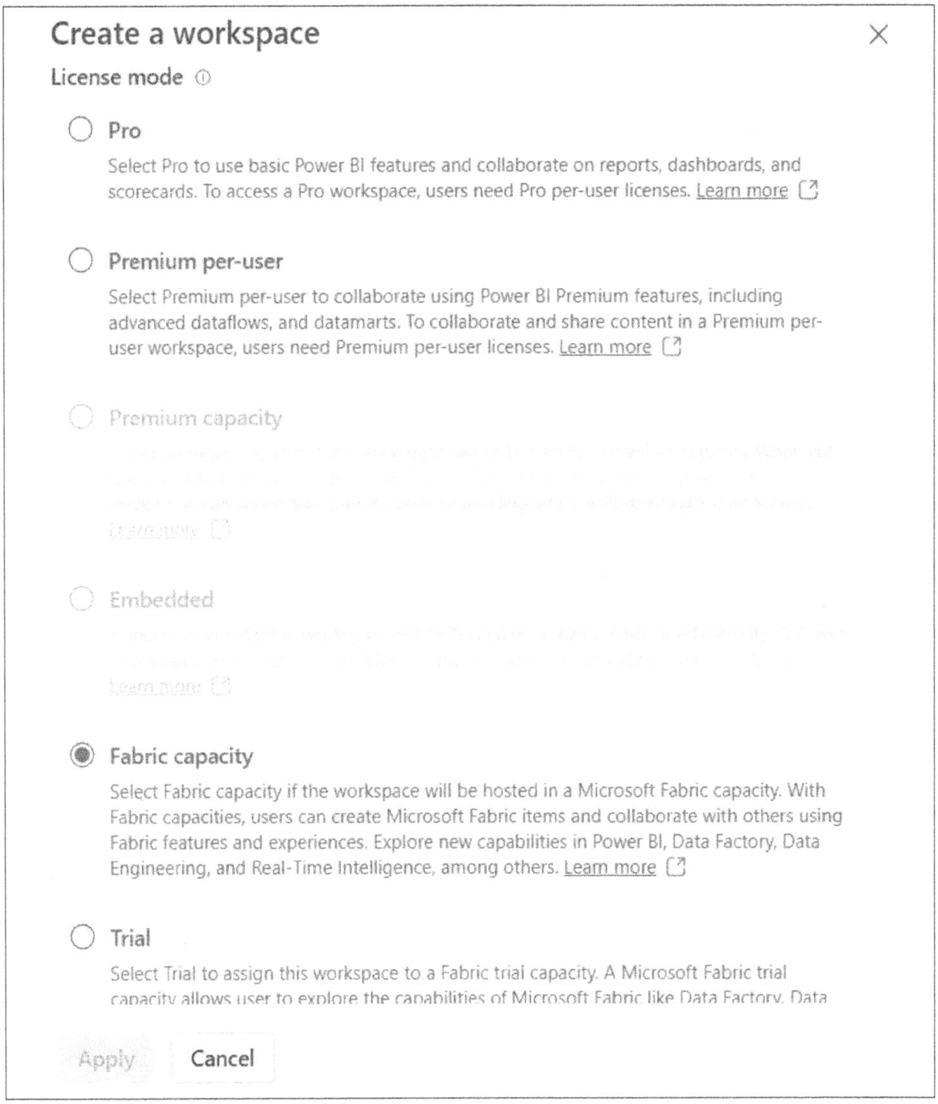

Figure 5-34. Choosing a storage mode when creating a new workspace

If we already have a workspace and want to change the storage model, we can go to the settings of the semantic model that we want to change, scroll down to the "Large semantic model storage format" section, and enable the option for an existing semantic model (see Figure 5-35).

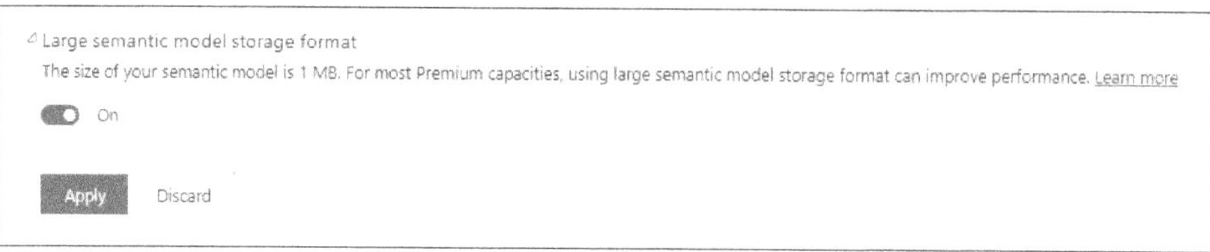

Figure 5-35. Changing the storage mode of a semantic model in the semantic model settings

When working with large datasets in Power BI, switching to the large semantic model storage format allows you to go beyond the default size limits. This option is easy to enable in the Power BI Service, and it depends on your Fabric capacity. It's also especially useful for enterprise-grade models that need more room to grow while maintaining performance and flexibility.

Designing and Building Composite Models

When you're working with enterprise-sized models, you'll often have data from multiple sources. Some data may be stored in Import mode, while other data may require a live connection using DirectQuery. A data model that combines different storage modes like this is called a *composite model*.

Composite models allow us to combine data from multiple sources in a single report. We can mix Import mode with one or more DirectQuery connections or even combine multiple DirectQuery data sources. This gives us flexibility when we're working with data sources that have different refresh schedules or when we need real-time access. For example, we may import updated sales data once a day while using a live connection for real-time inventory data.

A composite model allows a dataset to have two or more connections from different source groups. These can be as follows:

- One or more DirectQuery connections combined with Import mode
- Multiple DirectQuery connections from different data sources
- Any other combination of supported sources

Creating a Composite Model

It only takes a few steps to create a composite model in Power BI. Let's imagine that we have an Import mode semantic model in Power BI. We realize that we need one table from one of our Fabric eventhouses and that we need a live connection to the data. We can load this data into Power BI, and once we do that, we'll see a message from Power BI asking us how we want the data to connect: via Import mode or via DirectQuery. In this case, because we want to have a live connection to the data, we choose DirectQuery. Power BI will then add the new table, and you'll recognize it by the fact that its top bar will be bolded and in a different color (see the Tutorial table in Figure 5-36).

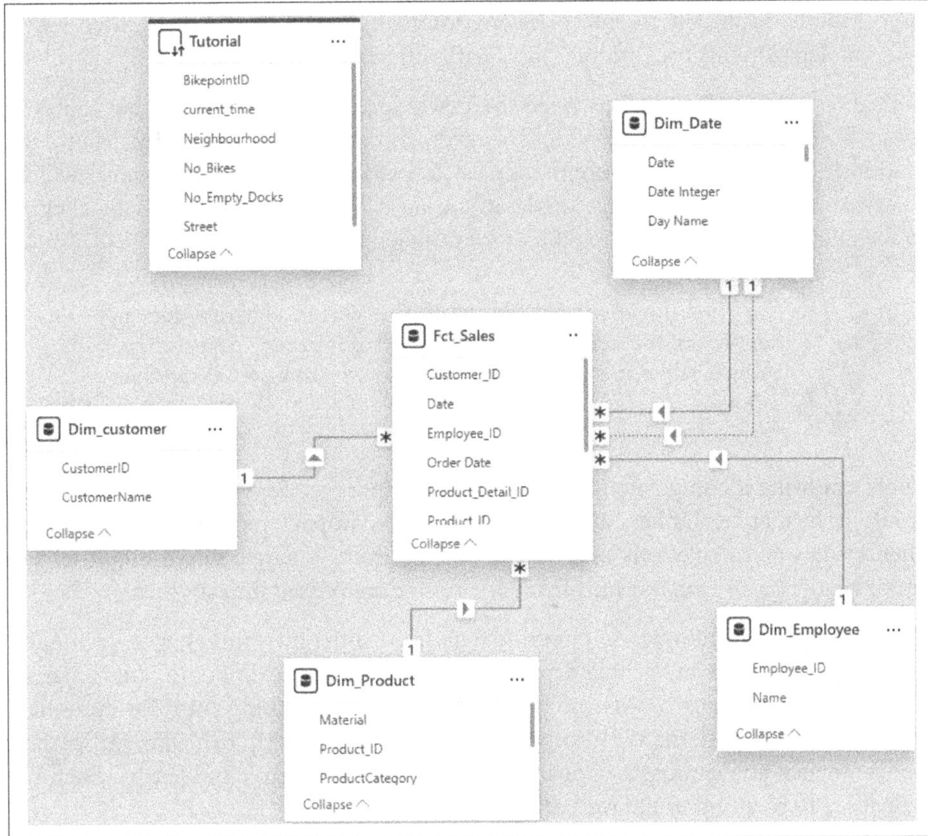

Figure 5-36. Composite model with one direct query table next to import mode tables

Once we have a composite model in Power BI, then in the bottom right corner, we'll see the message in Figure 5-37.

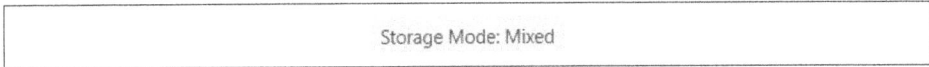

Storage Mode: Mixed

Figure 5-37. Message indicating a composite model

Benefits and Limitations

Using composite models makes a lot of sense when you want to combine data from multiple data sources where some data needs to be live and other data can be in Import mode. Especially in enterprise environments, you'll see this very often where different departments use different tools with different data storage.

You can create relationships between the newly loaded table and the other tables in Power BI, just like you normally do. However, you need to know that by default, the relationship between two different sources (Import mode and DirectQuery) will be many-to-many. You can change this, but you need to do this proactively by clicking on the relationship and changing it to, for example, one-to-many.

In Dual mode composite models, this default behavior does not apply, as the relationship is handled differently, depending on which tables are in Import mode and which are in DirectQuery mode.

Before choosing a composite model instead of Import mode, you also need to think about performance. Using composite models can impact performance, especially when visuals or calculations rely on multiple sources. A single visual might trigger multiple queries, in which results from one source are passed into another.

Composite models allow us to combine data from different sources, storage modes, and refresh strategies in a single dataset. They provide the flexibility to build smarter, more responsive reports, without the need to force everything into the same data source or refresh pattern. With some awareness of relationship behavior and performance impact, you can use composite models to build semantic models in which the data needs to be at different levels of "freshness."

Summary

This chapter covered the key concepts for building well-structured semantic models in Power BI.

We started by covering how to choose a storage mode. Then, we went over relationships and the importance of designing a star schema. Next, we looked at calculation groups, which allow us to apply shared logic (such as Year to Date and Last Year to Date) across multiple measures without duplicating DAX. We also discussed dynamic formatting, which lets you change number formats for different calculation items. Then, we moved on to field parameters, a feature that makes reports more interactive by letting users select the fields or measures they want to see in a visual. This reduces the number of visuals on a page and tailors the experience to different users. Next, we had a look into what large semantic models are and how we can configure them ourselves. Finally, we went over composite models, which are semantic models that use different kinds of storage modes for their data sources.

Each of these aspects is an important part of designing and building semantic models in Power BI. Knowing this should make it easier for you to create semantic models that scale over time while maintaining performance.

CHAPTER 6

Optimizing Enterprise-Scale Semantic Models

As your semantic model increases in size, its performance may become an issue. For smaller models, workarounds might work, but as your models grow, you'll discover that optimization is not only nice to have—it's crucial. A sluggish model can impact all the things you produce, including your Power BI reports, which must have quick-loading visuals and efficient refreshes so that end users will view them as workable. Over time, these performance challenges can create significant headaches for both the people working with the data and the end users.

This chapter will focus on helping you optimize performance by making smarter decisions on how to query, store, and refresh data. We'll begin by identifying performance issues with DAX `INFO.VIEW` functions and the Power BI performance analyzer. Next, we'll look at practical techniques for improving DAX performance, such as refining your measures. Then, we'll look into Direct Lake, which is a storage mode that's especially suitable for large semantic models, including those in enterprise-scale operations. Lastly, we'll cover incremental refresh, which allows you to update only newly added data rather than reloading all data repeatedly. This becomes essential when you're dealing with large semantic models with large amounts of frequently added data.

Understanding Performance Metrics in DAX Queries and Report Visuals

Slow performance can frustrate users and hurt adoption when building Power BI reports. To improve performance, you need to understand where delays come from—guessing won't get you far. You need visibility into what's happening behind the scenes, and you need to start by measuring and analyzing performance.

In this section, we'll look at how to gain insights into the performance of your report visuals and DAX queries. First, we'll introduce `INFO.VIEW` functions, which let you query metadata about your semantic model (such as measures, tables, columns, and relationships) directly in Power BI, with no external tools required. This metadata helps you identify potential bottlenecks like excessive calculated columns, and it's also useful for documenting what's happening in your model.

Next, we'll explore the performance analyzer in Power BI Desktop. This built-in tool helps you understand how long each visual takes to load. More importantly, it breaks down how that time is spent on things like rendering the visual, preparing the DAX query, and waiting for the data source to respond. It shows exactly how Power BI interacts with your model behind the scenes, and it also lets you export the results, which makes it easier to review them later or share findings with your team. Using the performance analyzer is a practical way to identify what's slowing down your reports and where to focus your optimization efforts.

DAX INFO.VIEW Functions

When working with Power BI, understanding your data is important for visualization. However, grasping the semantic model, including its structure and performance, is equally important. Gaining these insights will help you produce better documentation and achieve simpler maintenance and smarter performance optimization.

Here are a few questions that may come to mind when working with a Power BI report:

- What DAX measures exist in the model?
- What are the DAX expressions in the measures?
- Are there hidden tables or columns that need review?
- What are the relationships among the different tables?

You could answer the first question (What DAX measures exist in the model?) by manually clicking through each DAX measure and looking at the syntax. But that quickly becomes tedious, especially in larger models. A much faster and more scalable option is to use the `INFO.VIEW` functions in Power BI, which return the semantic model's metadata in a tabular format. This approach is useful for documentation and governance, but it's also great for spotting optimization opportunities, such as unused columns and overly complex measures.

Let's take a look at some examples of how to retrieve information about the measures, columns, tables, and relationships we use. First, we'll look into retrieving this data using the DAX query view, and after that, we'll look into retrieving the information and visualizing it in a Power BI report.

Before we get into the queries, we need to make you aware of a few limitations. The `INFO.VIEW` functions require write access to the semantic model, and users with only read access can't run these queries because they expose metadata like measures, columns, and relationships. This also means you can't use `INFO.VIEW` functions when you're live connected to a published dataset. In that case, you'll need to work directly in a local or editable model.

DAX Query View Examples

Let's start with the DAX query view. If you haven't worked with this before, you can find it in the left-hand pane of Power BI Desktop (see Figure 6-1).

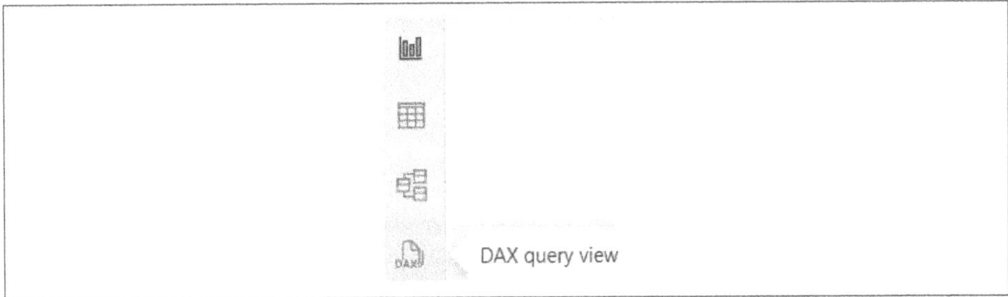

Figure 6-1. DAX query view in the left-hand pane of Power BI Desktop

You can run queries directly against your semantic model by using an `EVALUATE` statement in the DAX query view. For example, to get an overview of all tables in your model, you can use this code:

```
EVALUATE INFO.VIEW.TABLES()
```

It returns a table with metadata for each table in your model, including the table name, whether it's hidden, the storage mode, and whether it was created with a DAX expression.

Performing this overview is a great way to quickly assess your model's structure. It can help you spot hidden tables that are no longer needed and tables that are built with calculated expressions that you can optimize. It also helps with cleanup, performance tuning, and even governance. Figure 6-2 shows the results of such a query.

▷ Run | Update model with changes (0)

```
EVALUATE INFO.VIEW.TABLES()
```

Results | Result 1 of 1 | Copy

	[ID]	[Name]	[Model]	[DataCategory]	[Des...	[IsHidden]	[StorageMode]
1	14	Sales	e952ec70...	Regular		False	Import
2	17	Date	e952ec70...	Time		False	Import
3	20	Location	e952ec70...	Regular		False	Import
4	23	Product	e952ec70...	Regular		False	Import

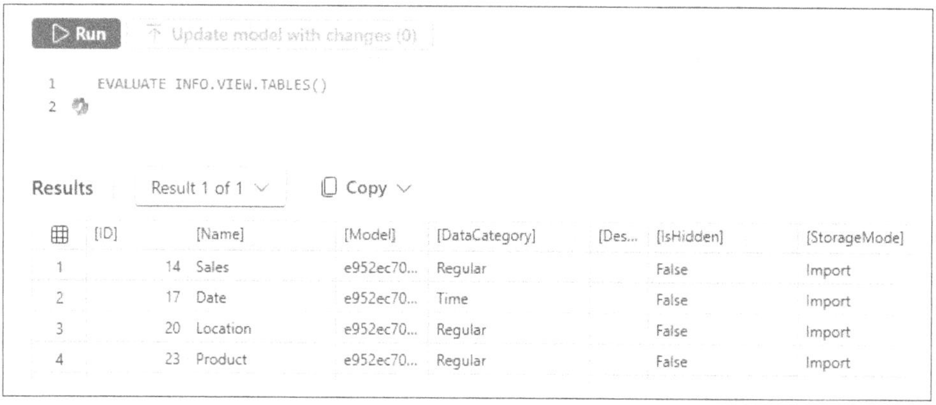

Figure 6-2. Results of an `INFO.VIEW.TABLES()` query in DAX query view

You can also retrieve information about the columns in our model with this code:

```
EVALUATE INFO.VIEW.COLUMNS()
```

This gives you an overview of all columns in your model, and it returns metadata like the column name, data type, and whether a column is hidden or not. This will help you review which columns are actually used, spot unnecessary columns still lingering in the model, and check consistency in naming and data types. Also, if your model is getting big, this kind of overview can save you a lot of clicking around.

Now, something everyone looks for after they've worked with Power BI for some time is the DAX measures in the model. You can get this information with this query:

```
EVALUATE INFO.VIEW.MEASURES()
```

This gives you a full list of all measures in the model, including their names, DAX expressions, and format strings. This is a great way to check whether your measures are consistently named, any logic can be reused or simplified, or certain measures are missing documentation. When working in teams or on long-term projects, you should also keep an eye on visibility since hidden measures might not be intended to stay hidden forever.

Here's another handy query that can help you inspect the relationships between tables in your model:

```
EVALUATE INFO.VIEW.RELATIONSHIPS()
```

It returns the `from` and `to` columns, the relationship type, cross-filter direction, and whether a relationship is active. This metadata can give you a clear picture of what's happening without you having to scan the semantic model diagram visually. Figure 6-3 shows the results of such a query.

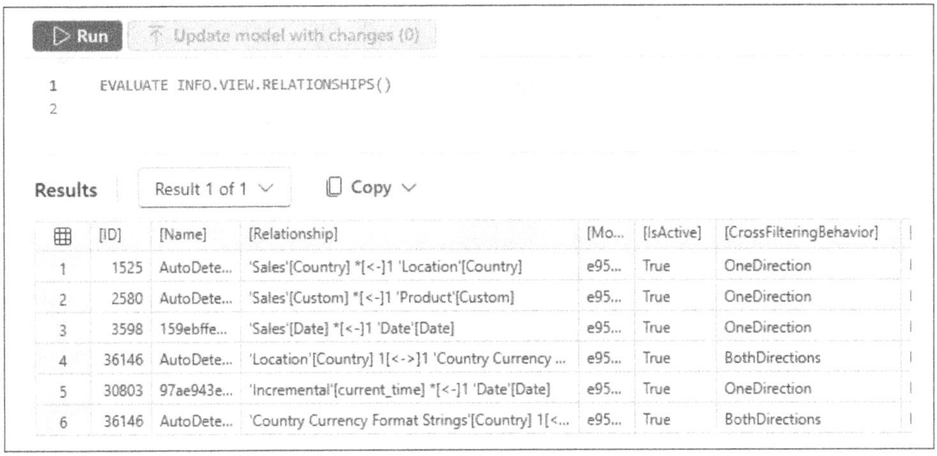

▷ Run | Update model with changes (0)

```
EVALUATE INFO.VIEW.RELATIONSHIPS()
```

Results | Result 1 of 1 | Copy

	[ID]	[Name]	[Relationship]	[Mo...	[IsActive]	[CrossFilteringBehavior]
1	1525	AutoDete...	'Sales'[Country] *[<-]1 'Location'[Country]	e95...	True	OneDirection
2	2580	AutoDete...	'Sales'[Custom] *[<-]1 'Product'[Custom]	e95...	True	OneDirection
3	3598	159ebffe...	'Sales'[Date] *[<-]1 'Date'[Date]	e95...	True	OneDirection
4	36146	AutoDete...	'Location'[Country] 1[<->]1 'Country Currency ...	e95...	True	BothDirections
5	30803	97ae943e...	'Incremental'[current_time] *[<-]1 'Date'[Date]	e95...	True	OneDirection
6	36146	AutoDete...	'Country Currency Format Strings'[Country] 1[<...	e95...	True	BothDirections

Figure 6-3. Relationships listed in the DAX query view

Now that we've viewed the results of these queries in the DAX query view, it's important to mention that you're not limited to using these functions in queries. You can also use them in calculated tables or measures to bring metadata directly into your model. This means you can visualize these results in a Power BI report, which can greatly help you with model documentation, governance, and general clean-up. For example, you can create DAX measures that provide a quick overview of your semantic model by counting the number of measures, columns, tables, and relationships (see Figure 6-4). This will help you monitor model complexity and identify unexpected changes after development.

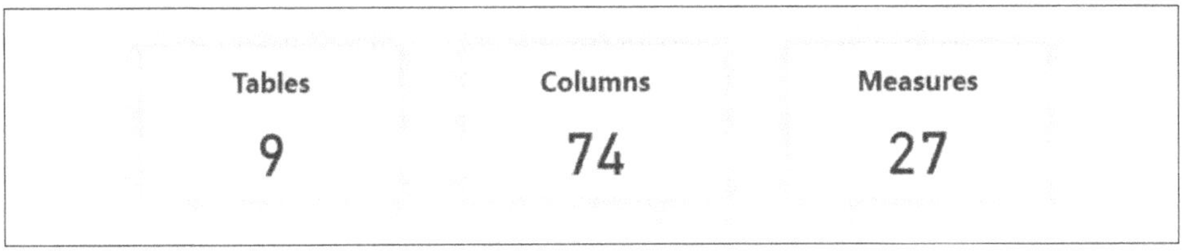

Tables	Columns	Measures
9	74	27

Figure 6-4. Overview of the model's tables, columns, and measures in a Power BI report

You can achieve this with simple `COUNTROWS` statements like the following:

```
Number of measures =
    COUNTROWS( INFO.VIEW.MEASURES() )
Number of columns =
    COUNTROWS( INFO.VIEW.COLUMNS() )
Number of tables =
    COUNTROWS( INFO.VIEW.TABLES() )
Number of relationships =
    COUNTROWS( INFO.VIEW.RELATIONSHIPS() )
```

In addition to using these measures in card visuals in Power BI, you can create a calculated table with detailed information about all the measures used in the model. Figure 6-5 shows an example of a query you can use to do this.

```
Measures in model =
SELECTCOLUMNS(
    INFO.VIEW.MEASURES(),
    "Table", [Table],
    "Measure Name", [Name],
    "DAX formula", [Expression],
    "Is Hidden", [IsHidden]
)
```

Figure 6-5. DAX query for a calculated table, showing all measures and DAX formulas associated with it

This creates a table with useful metadata about your measures, such as where they're located, their names, the actual DAX formula, and whether they're hidden or not. In this example, we're only selecting four columns, but you can easily include more by referencing additional fields from `INFO.VIEW.MEASURES()`. Figure 6-6 is an example of a Power BI table visual with the columns from the calculated table.

INFO.VIEW.MEASURES()

Table	Measure Name	DAX formula	Is Hidden
Sales	Total Sales	SUM(Sales[Sales])	False
Sales	Total Units Sold	SUM(Sales[Units Sold])	False
Sales	Total Units Sold LY	CALCULATE([Total Units Sold],SAMEPERIODLASTYEAR('Date'[Date]))	False
Sales	Units Sold YoY Growth %	DIVIDE([Total Units Sold] - CALCULATE([Total Units Sold], SAMEPERIODLASTYEAR('Date'[Date])), CALCULATE([Total Units Sold], SAMEPERIODLASTYEAR('Date'[Date])))	False
Sales	Units Sold YoY Growth % variable	VAR PrevUnitSales = CALCULATE([Total Units Sold], SAMEPERIODLASTYEAR('Date'[Date])) RETURN DIVIDE(	False

Figure 6-6. Table visual with the columns from the calculated table

Performance Testing in Power BI: Performance Analyzer

When building reports in Power BI, you might wonder why certain pages or visuals feel slow. Is it because of a specific visual, a heavy DAX query, or something else happening in the background? The performance analyzer in Power BI Desktop can help answer these questions. It measures how long different parts of your report take to load or respond when a user interacts with them.

You can find the performance analyzer by going to the Optimize tab in the top ribbon and selecting "Performance analyzer" (see Figure 6-7).

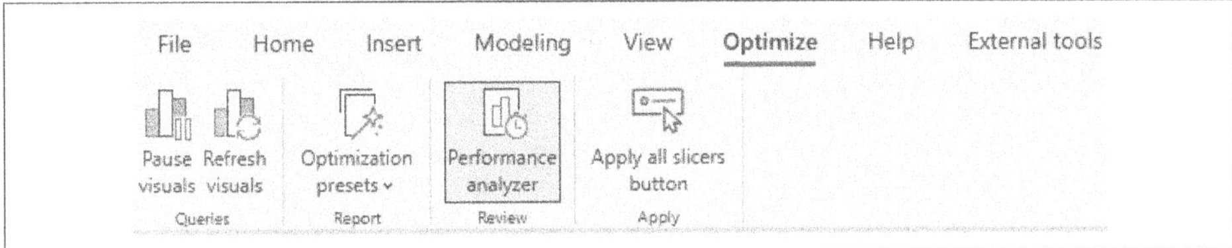

Figure 6-7. Performance analyzer icon

This opens the performance analyzer pane on the right side of your Power BI Desktop screen (see Figure 6-8).

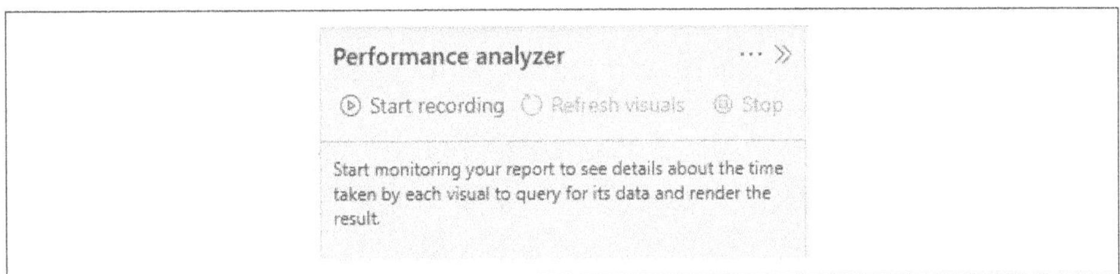

Figure 6-8. Performance analyzer pane

How the Performance Analyzer in Power BI Works

You'll see a "Start recording" button in the performance analyzer pane. The "Stop" and "Refresh visuals" options will be grayed out until recording begins. When you click "Start recording," Power BI starts tracking the performance of your interactions. Whether you use a slicer, filter a table, or change a visual, Power BI will log all your interactions in the order in which they occur.

This helps you identify which visuals are slow, what causes the delays (DAX, rendering, or something else), and whether any changes you make improve performance. You can either test everything all at once by clicking "Refresh visuals" or manually interact with the report to track the impact of individual actions in real time. Figure 6-9 is a screenshot of the options.

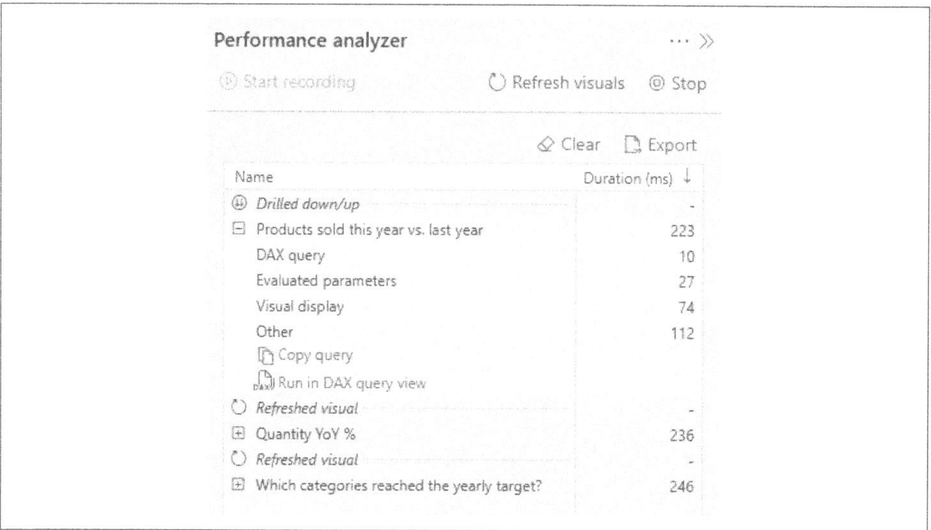

Figure 6-9. Performance analyzer after refreshing some visuals

When you expand the log entry for a visual by clicking the + icon, you'll see the following four types of performance metrics:

DAX query
: This is the time it takes Power BI to run the DAX query generated by the visual. It measures the interval between when you send the query and when you receive the results from the data model. Long intervals here often indicate complex or inefficient DAX calculations or relationships in your model.

Evaluated parameters (preview)
: If you're using field parameters (for dynamic field selection), this indicates how long it takes to evaluate those parameters. This helps you understand the impact of dynamic visuals on performance.

Visual display
: This is the time it takes for the visual to actually appear on the screen.

Other
: This covers any remaining time not included in the preceding sections, including time spent preparing queries, waiting for other visuals to finish, or running background processes.

Instead of refreshing all visuals, you can also test one visual at a time by clicking the "Analyze this visual" icon (which is highlighted in Figure 6-10). This will refresh only that visual and display its performance metrics, which is helpful when you're trying to identify a single visual that's slowing down a page.

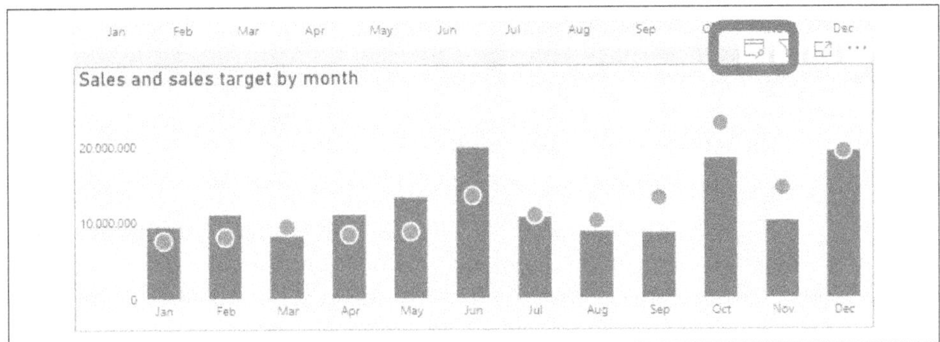

Figure 6-10. Refreshing a single visual and analyzing the performance by clicking on the highlighted icon

When you're done testing, click Export to save the results as a *.json* file. This can be useful for documentation, sharing insights with your team, and comparing performance over time as you improve your report. To start fresh, click Clear in the performance analyzer pane to remove all previous logs and then click "Start recording" again to run a new test.

Implementing Improvements in Performance for DAX

The moment you start working with more than a clean demo dataset in Power BI, you'll realize that Power BI reports can quickly become complex and that both performance and the user experience can worsen just as rapidly as the dataset grows. While we want reports to load smoothly and quickly for our end users, they often become slower over time.

Inefficiently written DAX can cause long refresh times, slow down visuals, and even lead to inaccurate results. To prevent this, we can implement different strategies to improve the efficiency and clarity of our DAX expressions.

In this section, we'll examine how to write better-performing DAX and how these changes can make it easier to understand and eventually maintain DAX. We'll cover how variables can simplify your DAX formulas by reducing repeated calculations and, at the same time, improving readability. You'll also learn why blank values and error handling matter, and you'll learn how to manage them to avoid performance pitfalls.

We'll also compare different DAX approaches, such as using the `DIVIDE` function instead of the `divide` operator, to help you understand their impact on performance and error prevention.

Using Variables to Improve DAX Formulas

So, what exactly is a *variable* in DAX? It's a value or expression you store using the VAR keyword, and you refer to it later in the formula with RETURN. It helps you avoid repeating yourself and keep your measure more structured.

Using variables in Power BI helps you to structure your DAX logic clearly and improves performance at the same time. When you're working on improving the DAX in your Power BI report, it's easy to focus only on fine-tuning formulas and adjusting functions to get the correct result. But writing DAX is not just about getting the outcome right; it's also about writing efficient, readable code.

Using variables in your DAX measure helps in two important ways. First, it can improve performance. By calculating a value once and reusing it, Power BI avoids having to repeat the same calculation several times. Second, using variables makes your measure easier to read and maintain. A formula may make perfect sense to you when you're writing it, but when you revisit it six months later, especially if it's a bit complex, it might take you a while to figure it out.

Let's look at two examples of DAX measures: one using a variable and the other without.

Imagine you're working with sales data and want to calculate the year-over-year growth percentage, which shows how many more (or fewer) units were sold this year compared to last year. A DAX measure without a variable could look like this:

```
Units Sold YoY Growth % =
DIVIDE (
    [Total Units Sold]
        - CALCULATE (
            [Total Units Sold],
            SAMEPERIODLASTYEAR ( 'Date'[Date] )
        ),
    CALCULATE (
        [Total Units Sold],
        SAMEPERIODLASTYEAR ( 'Date'[Date] )
    )
)
```

The result of this DAX measure will provide the answer you're looking for, but when you review it, you'll see that you're repeating one part of the measure twice:

```
CALCULATE([Total Units Sold], SAMEPERIODLASTYEAR('Date'[Date])
```

Not only is repeating inefficient, but it also makes the measure appear far more complex than it is, making it harder to read. We can simplify this by using a variable. Here's what this DAX formula looks like after we add a variable:

```
Units Sold YoY Growth % variable =
VAR PrevUnitSales =
    CALCULATE([Total Units Sold], SAMEPERIODLASTYEAR('Date'[Date]))
RETURN
    DIVIDE(
        [Total Units Sold] - PrevUnitSales,
        PrevUnitSales
    )
```

In this example, we store the previous year's sales in a variable called `PrevUnitSales` and then use it in the `RETURN` section of the DAX without repeating the same calculation. This approach makes the formula simpler, easier to maintain, and more efficient. You can also define multiple variables and use them all in the `RETURN` statement, which is the part of the DAX measure where you tell Power BI what the final result should be. It's where you place the logic that uses the previously defined variables.

Think of it this way: first, you prepare everything you need, and those are your variables. Then, you write the part that returns the final value, and that's the `RETURN`.

In summary, using variables in DAX has several benefits. It improves performance by calculating values only once, makes your formulas easier to read, helps you debug faster, and reduces complexity in your code. As your DAX formulas grow more complex, using variables will make your work much more manageable.

Counting Table Rows: COUNTROWS versus COUNT

When working with data in Power BI, there are instances when we need to count something, such as the number of rows in a specific table. In DAX, we have two functions that can assist with this: `COUNT` and `COUNTROWS`. Although they sound similar, they function differently and can yield different results depending on your data. You need to understand the distinction between them to avoid making mistakes in your report measures.

Here's the key difference:

`COUNT`
: It counts the number of non-blank values in a single column you specify:

```
DAX
COUNT(<column>)
```

`COUNTROWS`
: It counts the total number of rows in a table, regardless of what's in the columns:

```
DAX
COUNTROWS([<table>])
```

Let's say you have a Sales table with three hundred rows. Each row represents a single sales transaction, and you want to create a measure that counts the number of sales orders made. You could write that measure in two ways (see Figure 6-11).

Figure 6-11. `COUNT` and `COUNTROWS` showing the same result

Both measures return the same value: 300. At first glance, this seems logical; every sales order has a date. Therefore, whether you count the rows or the number of dates, you arrive at the same result.

But now, imagine there's an issue with your data. Perhaps two rows don't have a date filled in. They still represent sales, but the date field was left blank for some reason, such as an import error, a manual entry error, or missing data.

In this case, the result of the measures would be different:

`COUNT(Sales[Date])`
: Returns 298 because it skips over the two blanks.

`COUNTROWS(Sales)`
: Still returns 300 because it doesn't care what's in the row; it counts every one of them.

Figure 6-12 shows the results.

Figure 6-12. Difference between `COUNT` and `COUNTROWS` due to empty values

There are some important details to remember. It makes sense to use `COUNT` when you specifically want to check the number of entries a column contains, like the number of orders with a shipping date filled in. However, to count the number of records in the table, you should always use `COUNTROWS`.

Imagine building a Power BI report that tracks order volume over time. If you use `COUNT(Sales[Date])` and some dates are missing, your numbers will be incorrect. That could affect decisions and forecasting or even lead someone to think the data is incomplete when the data is there, just not in the column you're counting.

Here's a good rule of thumb to avoid this kind of issue: use `COUNTROWS` if you want to count the rows in a table and use `COUNT` if you want to count values in a specific column (excluding blank ones).

Converting NULL to 0

Sometimes, when you're working with real-world datasets, you may encounter NULL values. They can appear when, for example, data is missing, data has not been loaded yet, or data quality is low. You may wonder whether you should leave these values empty or replace them with, for example, a 0. Say you have a table showing total sales by country and one of the rows, for Germany, shows no sales value on a given day. You'll likely be tempted to replace that empty value with a 0, and you may even be asked to do it to make it look cleaner. Have a look at Figure 6-13 to see what a table with an empty value looks like.

Bike Sales

Date	Country	Sales
1-6-25	Germany	
1-6-25	Mexico	6.305,76
1-6-25	France	7.247,10
1-6-25	Canada	7.388,85

Figure 6-13. Table with an empty value in the Sales column

A DAX measure to replace the NULL (blank) value could be something like this:

```
Sales blank to 0 =
IF(
    ISBLANK([Total Sales]),
    0,
    [Total Sales]
)
```

The results of this DAX measure would include a 0 instead of the NULL value (see Figure 6-14).

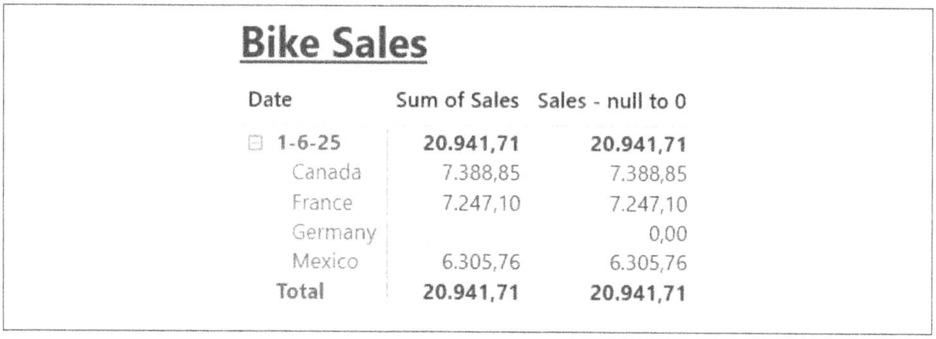

Bike Sales

Date	Sum of Sales	Sales - null to 0
⊟ **1-6-25**	**20.941,71**	**20.941,71**
Canada	7.388,85	7.388,85
France	7.247,10	7.247,10
Germany		0,00
Mexico	6.305,76	6.305,76
Total	**20.941,71**	**20.941,71**

Figure 6-14. Replacing 0 with NULL in the last column

Visually, this might be more intuitive, but will it impact your calculations? In many cases, Power BI handles this surprisingly well. Say you use your "blank to 0" version in a `DIVIDE()` measure like this:

```
Profit Margin Bike Sales = Divide([Profit Bikes],Sales[Sales - null to 0])
```

It will still give the expected result (see Figure 6-15).

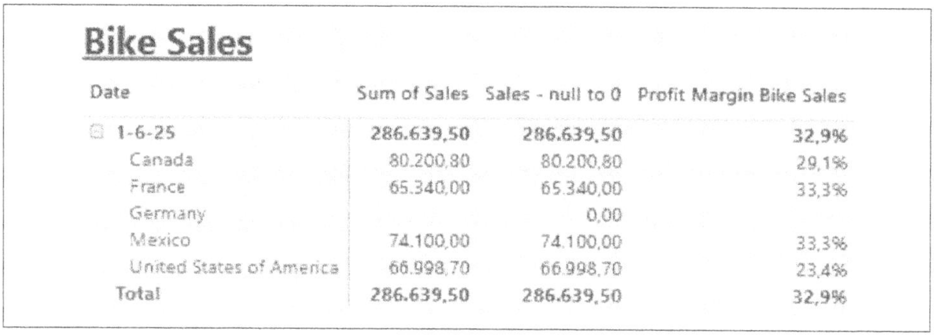

Bike Sales

Date	Sum of Sales	Sales - null to 0	Profit Margin Bike Sales
⊟ **1-6-25**	**286.639,50**	**286.639,50**	**32,9%**
Canada	80.200,80	80.200,80	29,1%
France	65.340,00	65.340,00	33,3%
Germany		0,00	
Mexico	74.100,00	74.100,00	33,3%
United States of America	66.998,70	66.998,70	23,4%
Total	**286.639,50**	**286.639,50**	**32,9%**

Figure 6-15. The result of a `DIVIDE` measure

If `[Profit Bikes]` is also blank when `[Total Sales]` is blank (which is usually the case), then the whole expression stays blank. Even if it's not blank, users often understand that dividing by 0 gives either a blank or "infinity."

So, you may think, why does it matter whether or not you use a 0 value? The answer is that using a 0 value doesn't always go smoothly. It can influence your results and show incorrect findings. For example, let's look at these two `AVERAGEX` calculations:

```
AverageX Bike Sales = AVERAGEX(Sales,[Total Sales])

AverageX Bike Sales - 0 value = AVERAGEX(Sales,[Sales - null to 0])
```

The difference between them is in how they treat blanks:

`AVERAGEX(Sales, [Total Sales])`
: This skips blanks and ignores Germany.

`AVERAGEX(Sales, [Sales - null to 0])`
: This includes Germany as 0.

If you replace a blank with 0, then suddenly, you're calculating something completely different. This can seriously mess up key performance indicators (KPIs), dashboards, and anything else in which precision matters (as shown in Figure 6-16).

Bike Sales

Date	Sum of Sales	Sales - null to 0	AverageX Bike Sales	AverageX Bike Sales - 0 value
⊟ 1-6-25				
Canada	80.200,80	80.200,80	40.100,40	40.100,40
France	65.340,00	65.340,00	32.670,00	32.670,00
Germany		0,00		0,00
Mexico	74.100,00	74.100,00	37.050,00	37.050,00
United States of America	66.998,70	66.998,70	33.499,35	33.499,35
Total	**286.639,50**	**286.639,50**	**35.829,94**	**28.663,95**

Figure 6-16. Table showing how blanks and 0 are treated in a measure

Showing a 0 might seem cleaner, but a blank and a 0 don't mean the same thing:

A blank
: This means no data—maybe nothing was sold, the product doesn't exist, or the data hasn't been collected yet.

0
: This means a real value of zero.

Replacing blank values with 0 might seem like a harmless change that enhances your report's appearance. However, once you begin using these 0 values in calculations, problems can quickly arise. `AVERAGEX`, for instance, treats blanks and zeros very differently. While it ignores blanks in the calculation, it counts zeroes and thus pulls down your average and potentially misrepresents your data. This can impact how users interpret KPIs.

There's also a performance aspect to consider. Using an expression like `IF(ISBLANK(), 0)`introduces additional logic that the Power BI engine must evaluate for each row. Especially within iterator functions like `AVERAGEX` and `SUMX`, Power BI evaluates that branching repeatedly, row by row. While this may not matter in a small model, it becomes significant in real-world datasets with millions of rows, as it can slow down performance.

Using DIVIDE Instead of the / Operator

When report creators start using Power BI and DAX, they often use the slash (/) operator to divide one value by another. It feels intuitive, and Power BI allows it without complaint.

However, there's also the DIVIDE function, which offers important benefits over the / operator. It not only optimizes for better performance, but it also handles blank values efficiently (see Figure 6-17).

Bike Sales

Date	Country	Sales	Profit	/ Operator	DIVIDE Blank	DIVIDE -
1-6-25	Canada	80.200,80	23.320,80	29,1%	29,1%	29,1%
1-6-25	France	65.340,00	21.780,00	33,3%	33,3%	33,3%
1-6-25	Germany		8.880,00	Infinity		-
1-6-25	Mexico	74.100,00	24.700,00	33,3%	33,3%	33,3%
1-6-25	United States of America	66.998,70	15.658,70	23,4%	23,4%	23,4%
Total		**286.639,50**	**94.339,50**	**32,9%**	**32,9%**	**32,9%**

Figure 6-17. Using DIVIDE instead of / to handle blank values efficiently

Also, DIVIDE has an optional third argument that enables you to define an alternative result when the division can't be performed (for instance, when the denominator is a NULL value):

```
DIVIDE(<numerator>, <denominator> [,<alternateresult>])
```

Without DIVIDE, you'd need to write additional IF logic to manage such cases, and that requires more writing effort from you and more time for Power BI to evaluate.

Let's look at our bike sales table in Figure 6-18 again. Note that it has a NULL value in the Sales column:

Bike Sales

Date	Country	Sales	Profit
1-6-25	Canada	80.200,80	23.320,80
1-6-25	France	65.340,00	21.780,00
1-6-25	Germany		8.880,00
1-6-25	Mexico	74.100,00	24.700,00
1-6-25	United States of America	66.998,70	15.658,70
Total		**286.639,50**	**94.339,50**

Figure 6-18. Table with a NULL value

Our sales dataset has data by date and country, showing both sales and profit. To calculate the profit margin, we divide profit by total sales, and there are two ways to do this in DAX: use the standard slash (/) operator or use the `DIVIDE` function. The `DIVIDE` function is more robust, especially when we're dealing with missing or zero values, as in our example.

We've created two DAX measures to show the effect of dividing the profit (the numerator) by the sales (the denominator). In this initial example, we don't provide an alternative result for the `DIVIDE` function to show you how NULL values are handled:

```
Margin / Operator = [Profit Bikes]/Sales[Total Sales]
```

```
Margin DIVIDE = Divide([Profit Bikes],Sales[Total Sales])
```

When we compare the two approaches, the difference between them becomes clear. Using the slash operator results in "infinity" when total sales are blank, because Power BI can't properly handle that scenario. With the `DIVIDE` function, however, Power BI returns a blank value as expected, because no alternate result was provided. This makes the `DIVIDE` function the safer and more predictable option for handling division in your DAX measures (see Figure 6-19).

Bike Sales

Date	Country	Sales	Profit	Margin / Operator	Margin DIVIDE
1-6-25	Canada	80.200,80	23.320,80	29,1%	29,1%
1-6-25	France	65.340,00	21.780,00	33,3%	33,3%
1-6-25	Germany		8.880,00	Infinity	
1-6-25	Mexico	74.100,00	24.700,00	33,3%	33,3%
1-6-25	United States of America	66.998,70	15.658,70	23,4%	23,4%
Total		**286.639,50**	**94.339,50**	**32,9%**	**32,9%**

Figure 6-19. Preventing "infinity" by using a DIVIDE statement

Of course, you can also provide an alternate result for cases in which the division isn't possible. This result can be any value you want, such as 0, a dash ("–"), or even custom text. You add it as the third argument in the `DIVIDE` function, like this:

```
Margin DIVIDE - = Divide([Profit Bikes],Sales[Total Sales],"-")
```

This way, instead of returning a blank when the denominator is 0 or absent, Power BI will display your chosen value in the result (see Figure 6-20).

Bike Sales

Date	Country	Sales	Profit	Margin / Operator	Margin DIVIDE
1-6-25	Canada	80.200,80	23.320,80	29,1%	29,1%
1-6-25	France	65.340,00	21.780,00	33,3%	33,3%
1-6-25	Germany		8.880,00	Infinity	-
1-6-25	Mexico	74.100,00	24.700,00	33,3%	33,3%
1-6-25	United States of America	66.998,70	15.658,70	23,4%	23,4%
Total		286.639,50	94.339,50	32,9%	32,9%

Figure 6-20. Displaying a chosen value instead of a blank

Using the `DIVIDE` function is better than using the / operator in DAX. While both calculate the same result, `DIVIDE` is more reliable; it handles division by zero or blank values without returning "infinity" as a result, and you can even choose what should be returned in such cases. Moreover, it improves performance by avoiding the need for extra `IF` statements to manage exceptions. Additionally, `DIVIDE` makes your DAX code easier to read and maintain, especially when you're working with more complex measures.

Are IFERROR and ISERROR as Helpful as They Look?

If you're experienced with Excel, you're probably familiar with `IFERROR` and `ISERROR`. They seem like handy tools: they catch errors, return a fallback value, and are done. However, in Power BI, these functions can slow things down, especially in larger models or more complex reports.

The DAX for the two tools look like this:

```
ISERROR = ISERROR(<value>)
IFERROR = IFERROR(value, value_if_error)
```

The difference between them is that `ISERROR` returns either `TRUE` (there's an error) or `FALSE` (if there's no error), while `IFERROR` evaluates whether there's an error and then provides an alternative value for that error. While all of that sounds helpful, the issue is that, even when there is no error, the whole logic is executed to check for any error, and that adds performance time.

Also, while the function may seem helpful sometimes, we may have other logic that works better. Let's look at this example based on our bike sales margin, where one column returns a NULL value:

```
ISERROR = ISERROR([Margin / Operator])
IFERROR = IFERROR([Margin / Operator], BLANK())
```

The `ISERROR` statement will return a `TRUE` value when we have a NULL value, and the `IFERROR` measure will return a blank value when we find the NULL value. But if you revisit the previous section on the `DIVIDE` function, you may realize that `DIVIDE` would be a great option for this, too, because it automatically returns a blank value when no value can be returned:

```
Margin DIVIDE = DIVIDE([Profit Bikes], Sales[Total Sales])
```

Figure 6-21 shows the difference between handling a blank value with `ISERROR` and doing it with `IFERROR`.

Bike Sales

Date	Country	Sales	Profit	/ Operator	ISERROR	IFERROR	DIVIDE
1-6-25	Canada	$80.201	$23.321	29,1%	False	29,1%	29,1%
1-6-25	France	$65.340	$21.780	33,3%	False	33,3%	33,3%
1-6-25	Germany		$8.880	Infinity	True		
1-6-25	Mexico	$74.100	$24.700	33,3%	False	33,3%	33,3%
1-6-25	United States of America	$66.999	$15.659	23,4%	False	23,4%	23,4%
Total		**$286.640**	**$94.340**	**32,9%**	**False**	**32,9%**	**32,9%**

Figure 6-21. Difference between handling a blank value with `ISERROR` and doing it with `IFERROR`

But then, you may ask, how much of a difference will it make in my reporting? We placed both measures in a simple card visual and used the performance analyzer to test them. The results were the same, but `IFERROR` took longer to execute. The resulting time difference is small in a simple report, but it increases quickly when scaled up to complex DAX logic or larger datasets.

When addressing data quality issues or potential errors, the best approach is to resolve the problem as far upstream as possible so errors don't enter the model at all. Ideally, you should do this at the source. If that's not feasible, then you should critically assess whether functions like `IFERROR` and `ISERROR` genuinely add value or if there are alternative functions that address the problem with less impact on Power BI performance.

Special DAX Functions: ORDERBY, PARTITIONBY, and MATCHBY

You may be familiar with ordering and partitioning when working with data. In Power BI, we have three special DAX functions—`ORDERBY`, `PARTITIONBY`, and `MATCHBY`—which are used with window functions (such as `INDEX`, `OFFSET`, `WINDOW`, `RANK`, and `ROWNUMBER`).

These special functions help you organize your data before making calculations, so that you can define how to group, sort, and match rows in a window function. Each function serves a unique purpose in making your calculations more efficient and accurate. Table 6-1 lists how they work.

Table 6-1. Special DAX functions and their effects

Function	Effect
`ORDERBY`	Defines the sort order
`PARTITIONBY`	Defines the grouping or partition
`MATCHBY`	Defines how to match and find the current row

You can't use these functions independently; they only work inside a window function. You can think of them as helpers that tell DAX how to organize the data before calculating.

Let's look at each of these functions in detail.

ORDERBY

This function defines the sort order of the data inside a window function. It tells DAX, "This is the order I want you to use when calculating." Without a clear `ORDERBY`, DAX doesn't know which row is first, second, third, etc.

Let's look at the example in Figure 6-22, in which we want to calculate the running sum of our sales by year and order it by segment.

Running Sum Sales by Year

Year Category	Sales	2025 Running Sum Order by Segment
⊟ Computers		
1	28.855,56	$28.855,56
2	645.300,00	$674.155,56
3	25.932,00	$700.087,56
4	79.794,24	$779.881,8
5		$779.881,8
6	1.378.669,56	$2.158.551,36
7	20.344,98	$2.178.896,34
8	25.692,00	$2.204.588,34
9	71.561,16	$2.276.149,5
10	32.751,60	$2.308.901,1
11	962.500,00	$3.271.401,1
12	50.309,28	$3.321.710,38
⊟ Smart Home		
1	2.048.285,52	$2.048.285,515
2	827.287,98	$2.875.573,495
3	995.522,56	$3.871.096,055
4	572.351,35	$4.443.447,405
5	2.072.160,25	$6.515.607,655
6	4.576.840,43	$11.092.448,08
7	1.753.642,99	$12.846.091,07
8	160.409,34	$13.006.500,41
9	113.777,21	$13.120.277,62
10	1.797.602,21	$14.917.879,83
11	1.161.604,00	$16.079.483,83
12	268.211,90	$16.347.695,73
Total	**19.669.406,11**	**$19.669.406,11**

Figure 6-22. A running sum measure using the `ORDERBY` function

The DAX for this is as follows:

```
DAX
Window Running Sum by Year Order by Segment =
SUMX (
    WINDOW (
        1, ABS, 0, REL,
        ALLSELECTED (
            'Date'[Year],
           'Date'[Month Of Year]
        ),
        ORDERBY ( 'Product'[Segment])),
    [Total Sales]
)
```

We use the `ORDERBY` function here to determine how the data should be arranged before performing the window function calculation. This is important because, in our case, we want to process the sales data for each year and month within a specific order defined by the Segment.

Next, here are the details on the functions we use with `ORDERBY`:

`WINDOW`
: This function defines the calculation window and processes the sales data for the selected year and month.

`ORDERBY('Product'[Segment])`
: This is where we order the data by the `Segment` column in the `Product` table. The `ORDERBY` clause makes sure that the data is arranged by `Segment` before the `SUMX` calculation is performed. This ensures that the running sum is applied in the desired sequence.

`ALLSELECTED`
: This function ensures that the running sum is calculated over the selected year and month, preserving the current filters in the report.

`SUMX`
: This function iterates over the window and calculates the total sales for each row, applying the running sum logic based on the ordered data.

`ORDERBY` is great for defining the sequence for calculations inside `WINDOW`, `RANK`, and `INDEX` functions.

PARTITIONBY

We can use this function to define groups (or partitions) within data. It tells DAX, "Only compare and rank rows within the same group." This function is beneficial when you must perform calculations separately for each segment, category, or grouping dimension. It ensures that DAX treats each group as an independent entity during calculation. It's also critical when you want to perform calculations like running totals or rankings that reset for each group.

For instance, let's say you're calculating a running sum of sales over time. Without `PARTITIONBY`, the calculation would run continuously across all years. However, when you use `PARTITIONBY`, you tell DAX to reset the calculation for each new year.

Let's look at an example in which we want to partition the running sum of our sales by year (see Figure 6-23).

Running Sum Sales by Year

Year	2024		2025	
Month	Sales	Running Sum	Sales	Running Sum
1	944.112,64	$944.112,635	2.077.141,08	$2.077.141,075
2	2.266.706,22	$3.210.818,855	1.472.587,98	$3.549.729,055
3	1.381.079,01	$4.591.897,865	1.021.454,56	$4.571.183,615
4	3.893.186,48	$8.485.084,345	652.145,59	$5.223.329,205
5	4.830.122,32	$13.315.206,665	2.072.160,25	$7.295.489,455
6	5.361.405,36	$18.676.612,025	5.955.509,99	$13.250.999,44
7	2.561.238,72	$21.237.850,745	1.773.987,97	$15.024.987,41
8	808.533,09	$22.046.383,835	186.101,34	$15.211.088,75
9	1.807.938,87	$23.854.322,705	185.338,37	$15.396.427,12
10	3.228.348,30	$27.082.671,005	1.830.353,81	$17.226.780,93
11	4.676.428,04	$31.759.099,045	2.124.104,00	$19.350.884,93
12	1.853.949,14	$33.613.048,185	318.521,18	$19.669.406,11
Total	**33.613.048,19**	**$33.613.048,185**	**19.669.406,11**	**$19.669.406,11**

Figure 6-23. Running sum measure in DAX for different years

The DAX for this is as follows:

```
DAX
Window Running Sum by Year =
SUMX (
    WINDOW (
        1, ABS, 0, REL,
        ALLSELECTED (
            'Date'[Year],
           'Date'[Month Of Year]
        ),
        PARTITIONBY ( 'Date'[Year] )
    ),
    [Total Sales]
)
```

Without `PARTITIONBY`, the running sum would continue from year to year, which you may not want. For example, if you track sales performance for each year, you likely want the sum to restart every January 1, not accumulate across years. By using `PARTITIONBY`, you make that happen, ensuring that the running sum is calculated independently for each year (see Figure 6-24).

Running Sum Sales by Year

Year	Month	Sales	PARTITIONBY (Year)	No PARTITIONBY
2024	1	944.112,64	$944.112,635	$944.112,635
2024	2	2.266.706,22	$3.210.818,855	$3.210.818,855
2024	3	1.381.079,01	$4.591.897,865	$4.591.897,865
2024	4	3.893.186,48	$8.485.084,345	$8.485.084,345
2024	5	4.830.122,32	$13.315.206,665	$13.315.206,665
2024	6	5.361.405,36	$18.676.612,025	$18.676.612,025
2024	7	2.561.238,72	$21.237.850,745	$21.237.850,745
2024	8	808.533,09	$22.046.383,835	$22.046.383,835
2024	9	1.807.938,87	$23.854.322,705	$23.854.322,705
2024	10	3.228.348,30	$27.082.671,005	$27.082.671,005
2024	11	4.676.428,04	$31.759.099,045	$31.759.099,045
2024	12	1.853.949,14	$33.613.048,185	$33.613.048,185
2025	1	2.077.141,08	$2.077.141,075	$35.690.189,26
2025	2	1.472.587,98	$3.549.729,055	$37.162.777,24
2025	3	1.021.454,56	$4.571.183,615	$38.184.231,8
2025	4	652.145,59	$5.223.329,205	$38.836.377,39
2025	5	2.072.160,25	$7.295.489,455	$40.908.537,64
2025	6	5.955.509,99	$13.250.999,44	$46.864.047,625
2025	7	1.773.987,97	$15.024.987,41	$48.638.035,595
2025	8	186.101,34	$15.211.088,75	$48.824.136,935
2025	9	185.338,37	$15.396.427,12	$49.009.475,305
2025	10	1.830.353,81	$17.226.780,93	$50.839.829,115
2025	11	2.124.104,00	$19.350.884,93	$52.963.933,115
2025	12	318.521,18	$19.669.406,11	$53.282.454,295
Total		**53.282.454,30**	**$53.282.454,295**	**$53.282.454,295**

Figure 6-24. Result of a DAX measure using `PARTITIONBY` year

MATCHBY

This function was introduced to enhance the performance and precision of window functions like `INDEX`, `OFFSET`, `WINDOW`, `RANK`, and `ROWNUMBER`. It helps avoid circular dependency and duplicate row errors.

More importantly, `MATCHBY` allows you to specify a unique identifier (such as an ID or key) to determine the "current row" in your window function calculation, instead of using all columns in the table. This is particularly useful when working with large datasets. Rather than having Power BI scan all the columns, `MATCHBY` narrows them down to the specified unique identifier, significantly improving performance. For example, if you're working with a large sales table, using `MATCHBY` on a unique `SalesID` column ensures that each row is treated individually, even when calculating window functions across other columns like `Sales`. This makes the calculation more efficient and accurate.

Direct Lake

Previously, we examined how to analyze performance metrics and enhance DAX measures to improve the performance of Power BI reports. This section concentrates on a storage mode called Direct Lake, which is especially useful for enterprise-scale models. But what is it?

Direct Lake is a Power BI semantic model storage mode in Microsoft Fabric. It lets you work with large datasets stored in Delta tables, typically in lakehouses or warehouses, without importing the data into your model. Instead of refreshing or loading everything in advance, Power BI reads the data directly from storage when needed.

To see how this fits in, let's compare it to Import and DirectQuery:

- Import mode loads all data into memory and caches it locally. However, the downside is that refreshes can be slow and resource intensive, particularly with large datasets.
- DirectQuery bypasses loading data into memory and sends each query directly to the data source. While this minimizes memory load, it can result in slower performance and limited modeling features.
- Direct Lake strikes a balance between Import mode and DirectQuery. It uses the VertiPaq engine for rapid query performance (like Import mode) but only retrieves the data it needs when it needs it (like DirectQuery). This results in faster development, improved scalability, and reduced memory usage, making Direct Lake an ideal solution for environments with frequent data changes or massive datasets that are impractical to replicate.

Implementing and Configuring Direct Lake

To use Direct Lake, you must work within a Microsoft Fabric workspace and connect to supported sources—specifically, Delta tables from Fabric lakehouses or warehouses. When you create a semantic model in Power BI within Fabric and link it to a lakehouse, Direct Lake is applied automatically if the connection and data meet the requirements.

The setup process is straightforward. You connect to your lakehouse or warehouse through Power BI, and Direct Lake will be used as long as the data is in Delta format. You don't need to manually enable it unless you're switching from another storage mode.

DirectQuery as a Fallback for Direct Lake

You also need to understand that Direct Lake isn't always available. Certain scenarios can cause Power BI to use DirectQuery mode as a fallback, even when the underlying data is still in Delta format. For instance, if a semantic model queries a view in the SQL analytics endpoint or a table that enforces row-level security (RLS), Direct Lake will not be applied and DirectQuery mode will be applied instead. Additionally, Power BI may use DirectQuery as a fallback if the Delta table exceeds capacity guardrails (e.g., if it has too many parquet files or row groups). This can occur even if the data is in Delta format and the semantic model is within the same workspace.

The use of DirectQuery as a fallback occurs automatically and without notice, so end users may not immediately recognize it. Indications that it has happened include increased latency and reduced data modeling options.

Refreshing Direct Lake Models

A key feature distinguishing Direct Lake from Import mode is how refreshes operate. In Import mode, a refresh operation involves copying all relevant data into Power BI, which can be resource intensive and slow, especially with large datasets. Direct Lake manages refreshes differently. Instead of transferring data, it refreshes the metadata. This is often referred to as *framing*.

During a refresh, Power BI updates its reference to the latest version of the Delta tables in OneLake. The actual data isn't moved or reloaded; only the structure and references are updated. This process typically completes in seconds and puts minimal load on the system, and that's a significant advantage for organizations that deal with constantly updating data. It means new data becomes available to users much faster, without waiting for scheduled refresh cycles or triggering complex data movement operations.

There are two different Direct Lake modes: Direct Lake on OneLake and Direct Lake on SQL. While both provide fast, query-over-files access, Direct Lake on OneLake allows tables from multiple Fabric items in a single model, whereas Direct Lake on SQL is limited to one Fabric item. You can create models that use Direct Lake on OneLake in Power BI Desktop, but you must create Direct Lake on SQL models in the Fabric interface first. This distinction can impact how you structure your data and develop your models.

Incremental Refresh for Semantic Models

While improving DAX query performance is a key optimization strategy in Power BI, optimizing the semantic model itself is equally important. Performance might not be a concern for smaller datasets, but keeping the model fast and responsive becomes increasingly challenging as the dataset grows. For example, if you're working with a large dataset that grows by millions of rows every night, reloading all the data during each refresh can slow down both the refresh process and the performance of your Power BI report.

One effective way to address this is by implementing *incremental refresh*, which involves only refreshing specific data instead of reloading the entire dataset. This significantly reduces refresh times and improves resource utilization, which becomes crucial as your semantic model scales. By implementing incremental refresh, you can ensure that even large, enterprise-scale models remain efficient and performant.

Let's look at how incremental refresh works and how to set it up in Power BI.

Incremental refresh works by partitioning data into two categories: data that needs frequent refreshing and data that doesn't require frequent updates. In Power BI, this is done with Power Query, where the table is filtered based on date/time parameters, specifically the `RangeStart` and `RangeEnd` parameters. Only the rows within the defined refresh period are updated with each refresh. The data outside this period becomes part of the historical data and is no longer refreshed, and that ensures more efficient use of resources and faster refresh times, especially for large datasets.

Requirements

Before you can set up incremental refresh in Power BI, you need to understand the prerequisites:

Licenses
: You need to use Fabric stock-keeping units (FSKUs) for incremental refresh in Fabric workspaces. You can also use Power BI Pro or Power BI embedded analytics, but incremental refresh for real-time data (using DirectQuery) is only supported in FSKUs and Power BI embedded models.

Data source
: The data source you want to load incrementally must support filtering data by date/time.

Implementing Incremental Refresh in Power BI

To implement incremental refresh in Power BI, we must start by defining two parameters: `RangeStart` and `RangeEnd`. We initially use these parameters, which are specified in the Manage Parameters dialog box in Power Query Editor, to filter the data loaded into the Power BI Desktop model table to include only those rows with a date/time that's within the time period we are interested in. `RangeStart` represents the earliest date/time, and `RangeEnd` represents the most recent date/time. After we publish the model to the service, the service automatically overrides `RangeStart` and `RangeEnd` to query data defined by the refresh period specified in the incremental refresh policy settings.

For example, say your `Sales` table gets new rows every night and you want to limit the number of rows loaded into the model to the last seven days. Here's what you do:

1. Open Power Query (Transform Data)
2. Go to Home
3. Click on Manage Parameters
4. Click on New Parameter

Figure 6-25 shows what the Manage Parameters pop-up looks like.

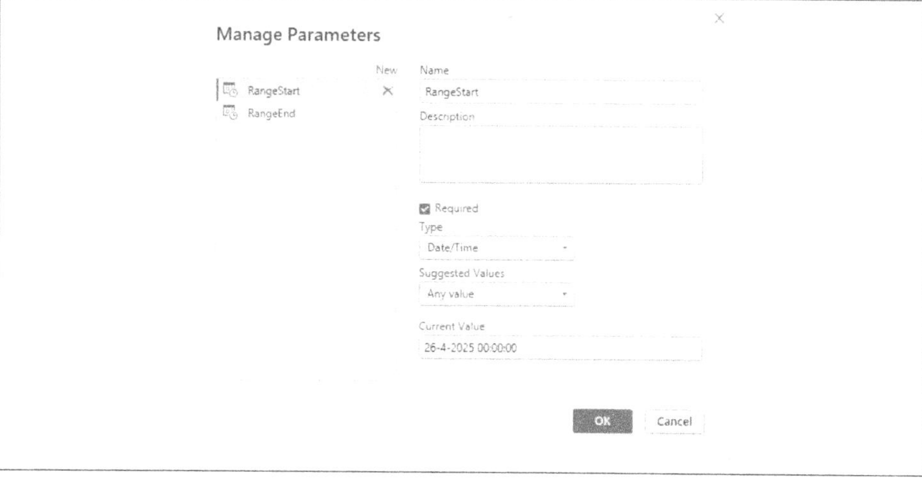

Figure 6-25. Configuring the range start and end for incremental refresh

Next, you'll use these two parameters in your Sales table's `Date/Time` column. Make sure you're referring to the parameters you have created. Figure 6-26 shows where you should click.

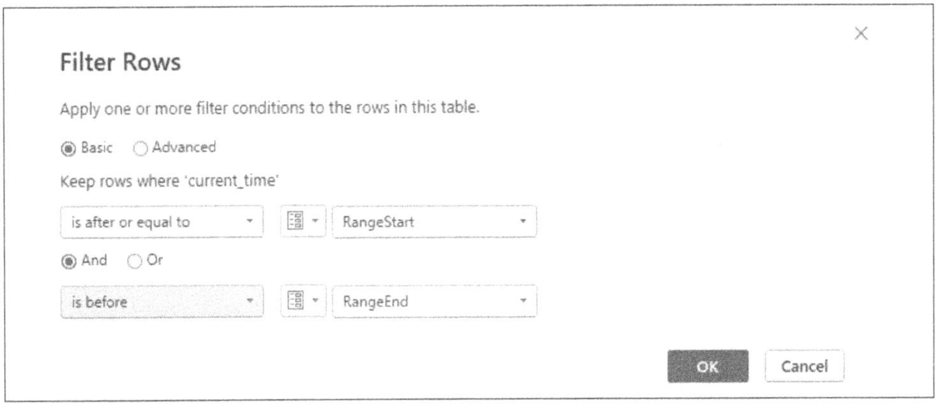

Figure 6-26. Filtering the `Date/Time` column based on the range parameters

Now, you need to create a policy that will be used after the model is published. Having this policy is essential for creating and managing table partitions and performing refresh operations. To define the policy, you open the model view in Power BI and either right-click on your table or click on the three dots. You'll see an option labeled "Incremental refresh," and when you click on it, a pop-up window will open (see Figure 6-27).

When you're configuring incremental refresh, several options are available:

Archive data starting _____ before refresh date
: Here, you define how much historical data you want to keep (e.g., five years' worth). Older data will get removed automatically.

Incrementally refresh data starting _____ before refresh date
: Here, you define how much recent data you want refreshed (e.g., the last seven days' worth).

Get the latest data in real time with DirectQuery (Premium only)
: You can check this box to add a DirectQuery partition to fetch the latest changes beyond the refresh period.

Only refresh complete days
: You can check this box to ensure that only full days are refreshed. This prevents partial updates, which is important if your metrics rely on complete daily data.

Detect data changes

You can check this box to make Power BI refresh only periods where changes have happened, based on a separate `Last modified` column. This reduces refresh time even more if the data is stable.

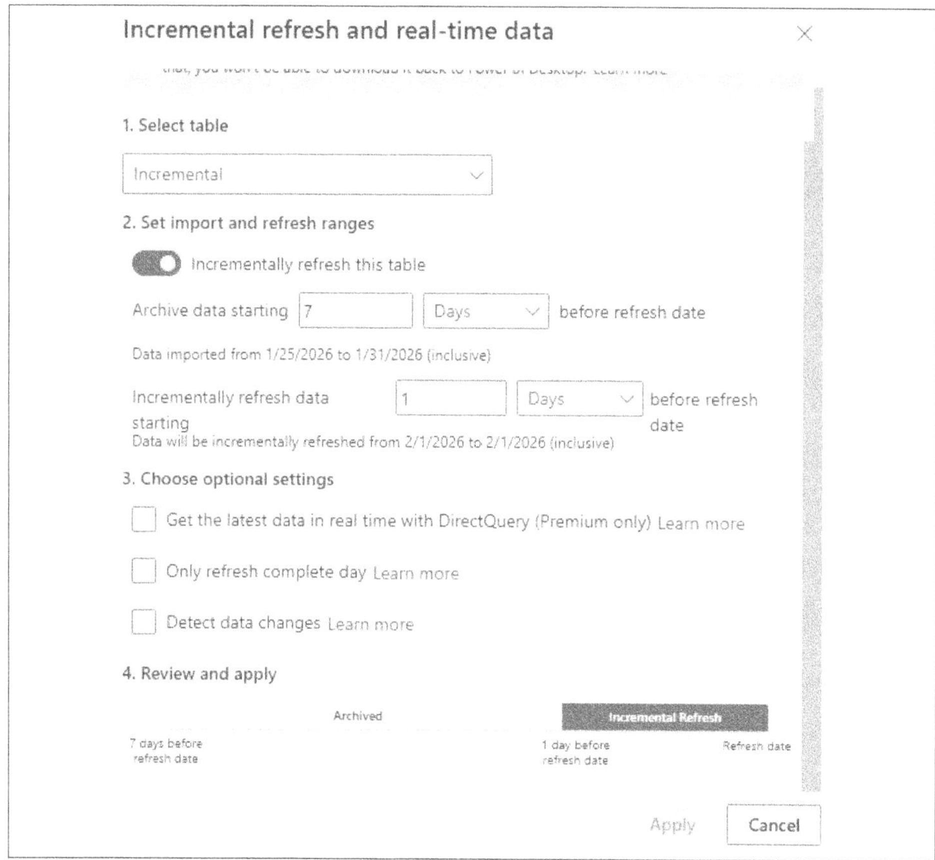

Figure 6-27. Configuring incremental refresh

Publishing

After you set up incremental refresh, you publish the model to the Power BI service. You should perform the first refresh manually so you can monitor its progress. This initial refresh can take a while because partitions are created, historical data is loaded, relationships and hierarchies are rebuilt, and calculations are processed. After the first refresh, refreshes will be much faster since only the incremental partitions will be updated.

Limitations

When using incremental refresh in Power BI, there are a few important things to keep in mind. Once a semantic model is published to the Power BI Service, it can no longer be downloaded as a *.pbix* file. However, when you use Power BI project files (*.pbip*), this limitation doesn't apply in the same way. Power BI project files can be downloaded from the service because they don't include the physical partitions; they only include the refresh policy definitions. This means that even with incremental refresh configured, you can open and manage the project locally without losing the model structure.

If you republish a *.pbix* file with incremental refresh, the model in the service will be overwritten, and all partitions and previously loaded data will be removed and rebuilt during the next refresh. This means refresh operations can be resource-intensive. In fact, in Power BI Pro workspaces, a refresh can run for up to two hours, and in Fabric capacities (FSKUs), the limit increases to five hours for scheduled refreshes. However, when a refresh is triggered through the XML for Analysis (XMLA) endpoint, this limit does not apply.

Finally, real-time data using DirectQuery is only supported in Fabric capacity workspaces. It isn't available in noncapacity workspaces, even if incremental refresh is enabled.

Summary

In this chapter, you learned how to improve the performance of large semantic models in Power BI. You started by using `INFO.VIEW` functions to check your model's metadata and spot potential bottlenecks. You also used the performance analyzer in Power BI Desktop to measure how long visuals take to load and where delays happen. You practiced refining DAX measures to make them faster. You also explored Direct Lake storage mode, which is useful for big models because it reduces memory pressure and speeds up queries. Finally, you learned how to set up incremental refresh so that only new data is updated, thus avoiding unnecessary full refreshes and saving time.

PART III

Maintaining a Data and Analytics Solution

In a data-driven world, data is one of an organization's most valuable assets. However, this value comes with a great responsibility: ensuring that the data is secure and that only the right people can access it. In a platform as comprehensive as Microsoft Fabric, where a wide range of users from different teams interact with various data items, controlling access is critical. It's not just about preventing data breaches; it's about meeting regulatory compliance, maintaining data integrity, and fostering a culture of trust.

Managing access across an entire organization may seem like a huge task, but Microsoft Fabric provides a robust set of tools and features to handle this effectively. Implementing a sound security architecture is foundational to maintaining a reliable and compliant data environment.

In this part, we will walk you through these essential security and governance features.

In Chapter 7, we'll begin by exploring how to implement workspace-level access controls, which manage who can access and work within your Fabric workspaces. Next, we'll move on to more granular control by implementing item-level access controls and managing access control to compute resources. Then, we'll dive deeper into advanced data security with row-level, object-level, and file-level access controls that ensure users can only see the specific data they're authorized to view. After that, we'll learn how to apply sensitivity labels to classify and protect your most sensitive data items. Finally, we'll cover endorsing items, a process that builds trust and promotes the use of high-quality, validated data throughout your organization. Building on this secure foundation, Chapter 8 shifts focus to maintaining the analytics development lifecycle to ensure your solutions remain reliable as they evolve. We begin with version control, which helps you track changes and keep your work organized within a workspace. Next, we explore the Power BI project (*.pbip*) file format and reusable assets, such as template files (*.pbit)*, data source files (*.pbids*), and shared semantic models, to streamline development and promote consistency. We then move on to deployment pipelines, which provide a structured way to promote content among development, test, and production stages. Then, we examine impact analysis tools like the lineage view to identify downstream dependencies before making changes, and finally, we conclude with the XMLA endpoint for advanced management and automation of your semantic models.

CHAPTER 7

Implementing Security and Governance

Microsoft Fabric provides a robust set of tools and features to help you handle security and governance effectively, and in this chapter, we'll walk you through them. We'll begin by exploring how to implement workspace-level access controls, which manage who can access and work within your Fabric workspaces. Next, we'll move on to more granular control by implementing item-level access controls and managing access control to compute resources. Then, we will dive deeper into advanced data security with row-level, object-level, and file-level access controls, ensuring users only see the specific data they are authorized to view. After that, we will learn how to apply sensitivity labels to classify and protect your most sensitive data items. Finally, we'll cover how to endorse items, a process that builds trust and promotes the use of high-quality, validated data throughout your organization.

Implementing Workspace-Level Access Controls

You can configure access to every workspace in Microsoft Fabric. Consider the scenario in Figure 7-1.

It's a demo setup where you have five different workspaces (Workspaces A through E) and user groups with five different access control requirements (User groups 1 through 5). This setup is nonexhaustive and only shows a subset of the possible different combinations. User group 1 has read access to Workspace A and Workspace B, User group 4 has the access it needs to create items in Workspace B and Workspace D, etc.

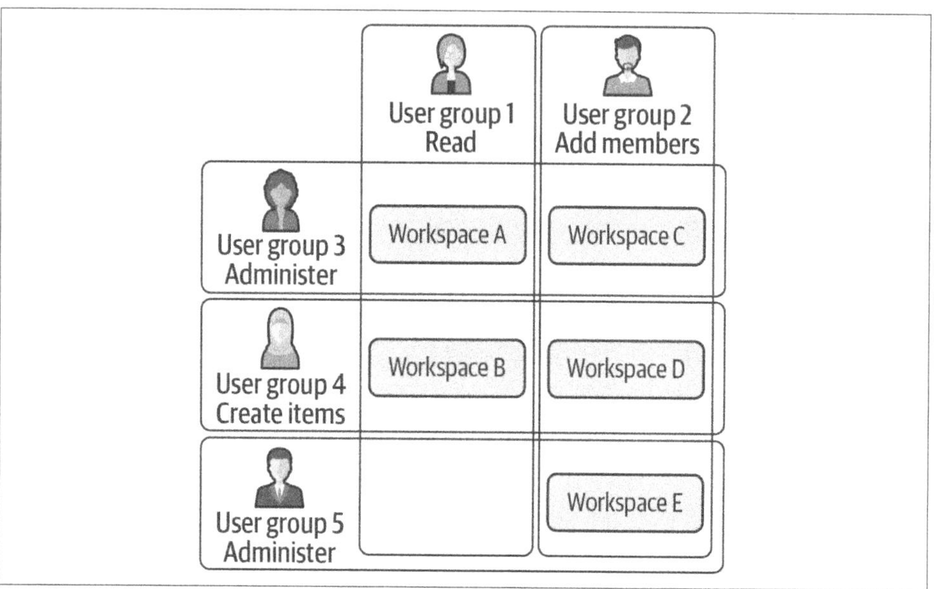

Figure 7-1. Example scenario of workspace access setup

As a best practice and rule of thumb, you should grant access to workspaces by using groups from Entra ID. In this way, you move the maintenance of access to the IT department, which has processes in place for this. Then, you, as the developer, will be able to focus on setup and content creation.

When setting up workspace access control, you have four main roles to choose from:

- Administrator
- Member
- Contributor
- Viewer

Most of these roles have some out-of-the-box limitations on what they can do. Table 7-1 summarizes these limitations, and the list after the table goes into the details.

Table 7-1. The four main roles in a workspace and their high-level access

	Administrator	Member	Contributor	Viewer
Maintaining and deleting workspaces	✓	✕	✕	✕
Adding members to a workspace	✓	✓	✕	✕
Writing data to items and OneLake	✓	✓	✓	✕
Creating new items in a workspace	✓	✓	✓	✕
Reading data from the items in a workspace	✓	✓	✓	✓

Maintaining and deleting workspaces

This capability is only available to the administrator of a workspace. It enables the user to maintain all aspects of the workspace, from the workspace settings (as mentioned in Chapter 1) to the configuration of all four roles in the workspace. This also implies the ability to delete a workspace and change the icon, description, etc.

Adding members to a workspace

This capability is a part of the member role, and access to it is the one difference between the member role and the contributor role. It enables the user to maintain the roles in a workspace (except the administrator role) by adding and removing the defined members of these roles. This capability also includes the ability to define sharing items inside the workspace with other users. (Also, see the "Implementing Item-Level Access Controls" section later in this chapter).

Writing data to items and OneLake

The "Write data" capability lets the user create or modify items inside databases, database mirrors, lakehouses, and warehouses in a workspace. It also lets the user read data from shortcuts, lakehouses, and warehouses through the Fabric API and subscribe to OneLake events.

Creating new items in a workspace

This capability lets the user create and delete items in a workspace and set up executions and job schedules.

Reading data from the items in a workspace

This capability is the one with the least privileges. Users who are in any of the four roles can read data from items in a workspace, connect to SQL Analytics endpoints, and read data from lakehouses, warehouses, and shortcuts using the TDS endpoint.

Configuring Role Access in a Workspace

You use the same tools to configure the roles in a workspace as you use to configure all other roles. At the top of each workspace, you'll find the "Manage access" setting (see Figure 7-2).

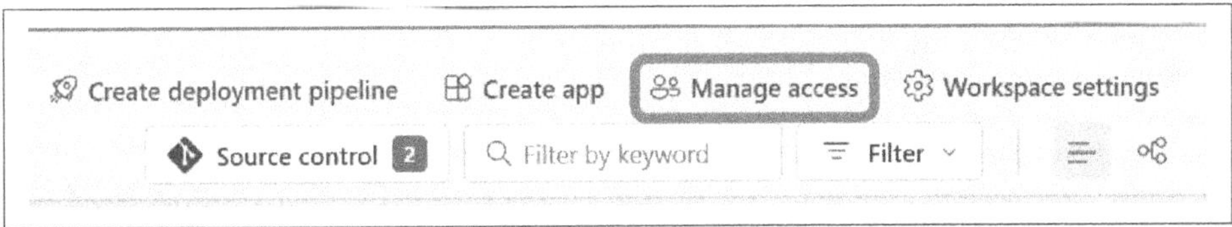

Figure 7-2. "Manage access" setting in each workspace

Click it to bring up the settings pane for roles (see Figure 7-3).

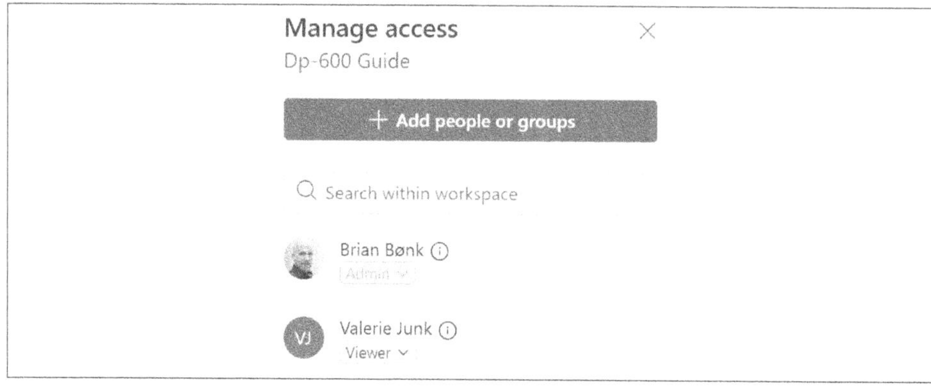

Figure 7-3. Settings pane for roles in the workspace

It will show you the list of existing roles and an "Add people or groups" button you can click to do just that.

Changing Existing Roles in a Workspace

To change existing access controls in a workspace, you can select the role for each member or group by clicking their current role and selecting a new one. The list of roles is the same as shown in area 3 of Figure 7-4.

Adding People or Groups to a Role in a Workspace

Clicking the "Add people or groups" on the screen shown in Figure 7-3 brings up a screen with the options shown in Figure 7-4.

We've highlighted some key areas on this screen (numbered 1–4):

The area where you can add new people or groups (area 1)
: Here, you can type in the people or groups you want to add to the workspace. You can only create one role at a time, but you can then add more people or groups to that role.

The default selection of the role for the listed users or groups (area 2)
: This is always the role with least privileges: viewer. To choose a different role, click the default role name to bring up the list in area 3.

The list of possible roles to select from (area 3)
: This list has all four roles to choose from, but if you are a member of this workspace, you cannot select the admin role because you don't have the rights.

The Add button (area 4)
: You click this to submit the new roles to the workspace.

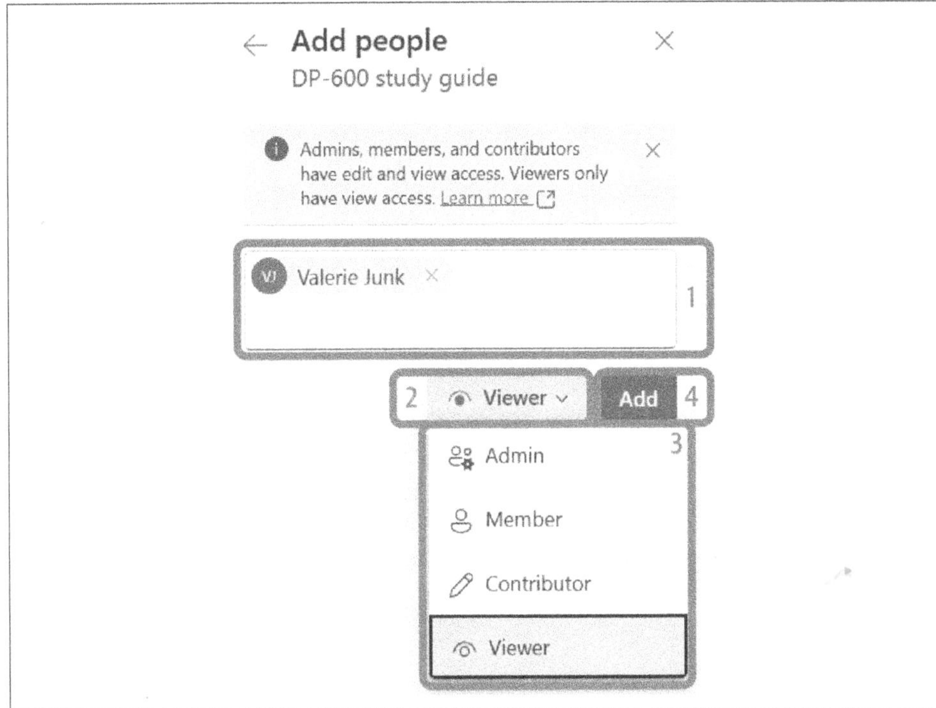

Figure 7-4. Add new people or groups to a workspace

The First Administrator of the Workspace

Anyone who creates a workspace through the Fabric UI on the web experience will be the first administrator, and they can add other people or groups to the roles after creating the workspace creation.

If you are using the API for Fabric to create the workspace, the process can be performed without the creator being the first administrator. This is out of scope for this exam, though.

Workspace access control is limited to four roles and easy to maintain and develop. The additional option of item-level access control adds complexity, and we'll get into that in the next section.

Implementing Item-Level Access Controls

While workspace-level access control is foundational, it often proves too coarse-grained for enterprise-level security. The core principle of a robust security architecture is the principle of *least privilege*, which dictates that users should only be granted the minimum permissions they need to perform their tasks.

Item-level access control in Microsoft Fabric is the primary mechanism for enforcing this principle. It allows for precise, surgical management of permissions on individual items within a workspace. It represents a significant step beyond the predefined workspace roles (administrator, member, contributor, and viewer), and it provides you with the flexibility to build a highly secure and compliant data environment.

Permission Types

Item-level permissions are distinct from workspace roles and can be assigned to individual users, security groups, or distribution lists. These permissions can either supplement or, in some cases, override the default access granted by a workspace role. The key permission types are as follows:

Read
: This is a consumption-focused permission. A user with Read access can view an item, such as a Power BI report or a lakehouse. Read access also allows a user to view a report built on a semantic model but not to connect to it in Power BI Desktop or create a new report from scratch. In a lakehouse, users with Read access can view tables and files but cannot query or write data.

Build
: This is a critical permission for enabling self-service and downstream analytics. Granting Build permission on a semantic model allows users to connect to that model in tools like Power BI desktop, Excel, and other reporting applications. It also enables users to create new reports and visuals from the curated data model. In a lakehouse, Build permission allows users to connect to the SQL endpoint, enabling them to write SQL queries against the lakehouse tables and use them as a source in their own data pipelines. A user can have Read access without Build access, but they cannot have Build access without Read access.

Write
: This permission is for creators and developers, and it allows a user to modify or delete an item. For example, a user with Write permission on a Power BI report can open it in the Power BI desktop, make changes, and republish it. In a Dataflow Gen2, Write permission allows a user to edit the data transformation logic.

Reshare
: This powerful permission gives a user the ability to share an item with other users. For example, if a report consumer has Reshare permission on a specific report, they can share a link to that report with their colleagues. However, this can be a double-edged sword, and you should be careful whom you grant Reshare permission to in order to maintain control over data dissemination.

Configuring Item-Level Access for Users or Groups

If you click the three-dot menu (also known as the *context menu*) that you'll find in most items in a workspace, you'll see the "Manage permissions" option in the drop-down list (see Figure 7-5).

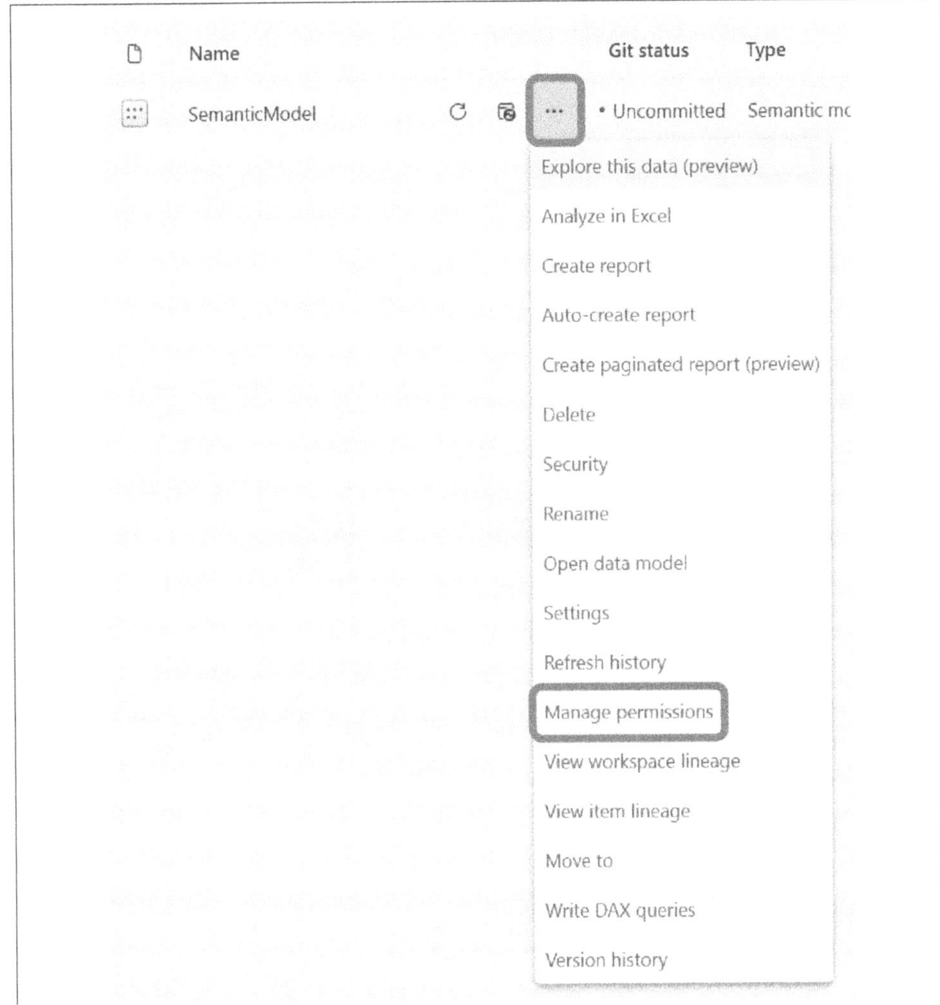

Figure 7-5. Context menu of a semantic model

Note that the context menu varies across items in a workspace, so "Manage permissions" may appear in different places in the drop-down list.

Also note that some items (e.g., Dataflow Gen1, Dataflow Gen2, eventstreams) do not have this option, so you can't share them individually to users. The user must be in one of the roles listed in the "Implementing Workspace-Level Access Controls" section.

When you select the "Manage permissions" option, it will bring up the window shown in Figure 7-6.

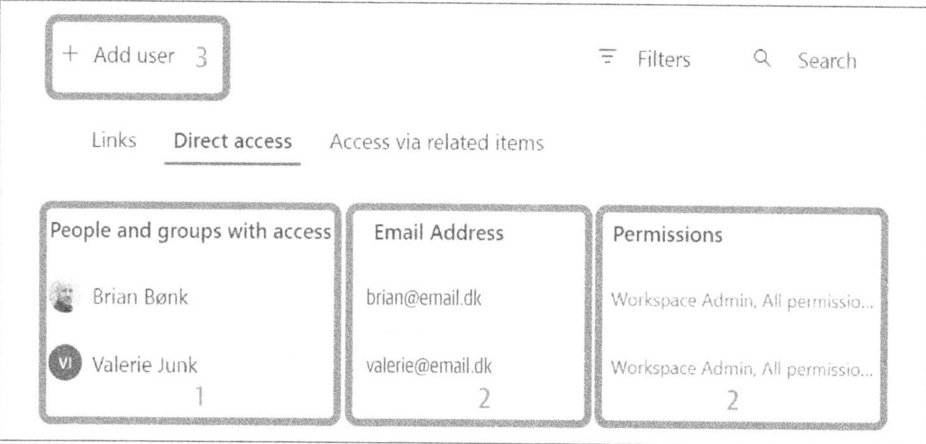

Figure 7-6. "Manage permissions" window and options

The window may vary depending on the item type, but it will include three areas that we've numbered 1–3 in the figure. You'll see the list of people who currently have direct access to this item (in area 1). You'll also see the list of permissions for this item (in area 2). In this case, both users listed in area 1 have access to the item because they have the admin role for the workspace.

If you want to share this item with other users or groups, you must click the "+ Add user" button (in area 3), which will bring up the pop-up in Figure 7-7.

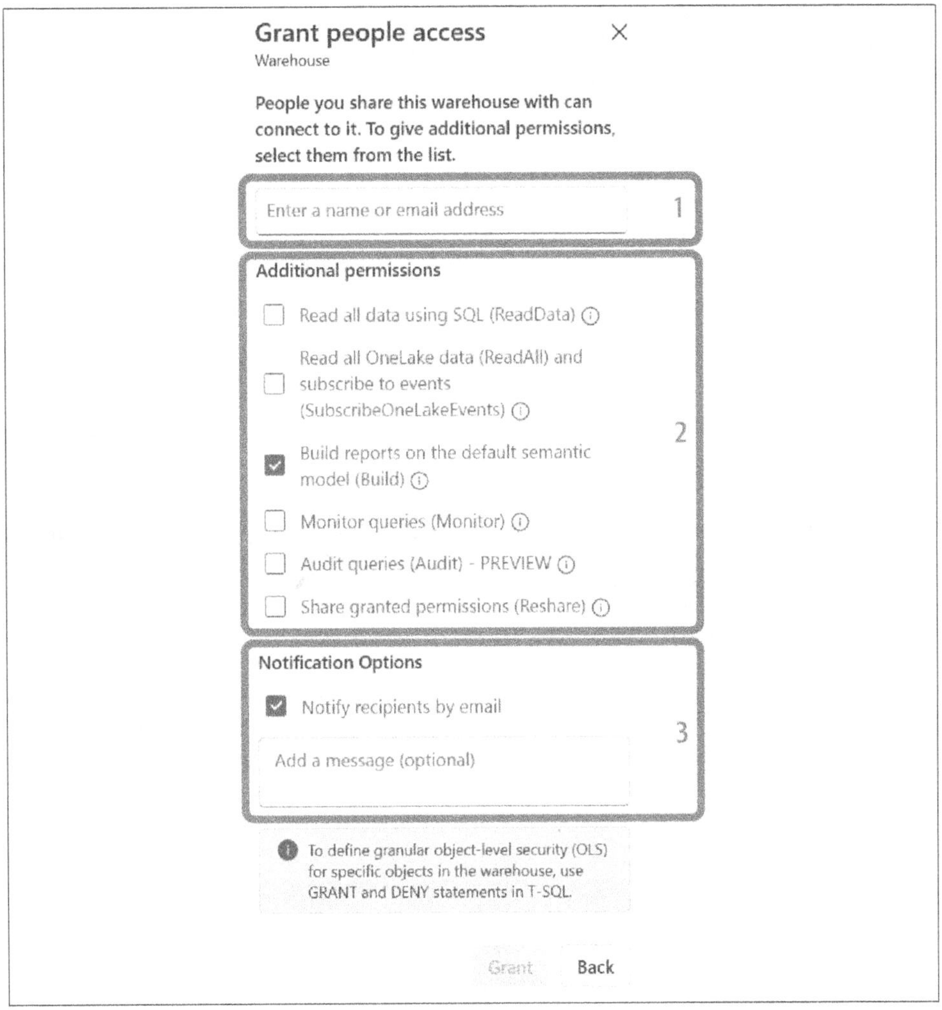

Figure 7-7. Settings for sharing an item

This pop-up is from the warehouse item, and it has all the possible settings for an item. (Note that other items from the workspace can have different settings windows). We've highlighted three main areas in the pop-up (numbered 1–3):

Input field (area 1)
: You use this to add the users or groups who should have access to this individual item.

List of options for sharing this item (area 2)
: Notice here the option to Reshare, which we said earlier you should be careful about granting. Unfettered resharing by users could make you lose control of resharing in the organization and of governance of the access policy.

Notification options (area 3)
: Here, you can determine whether the added users or groups will get an email notification of any sharing along with a custom text.

Permissions for an Item

As mentioned earlier in this chapter, item-level access control differs from item to item in the workspace. Table 7-2 provides a consolidated list of the different permissions for item-level access control.

Table 7-2. Permissions for item-level access control

Permission granted while sharing	Effects
Read	The recipient can discover the item in the data hub, open it, and connect to the warehouse or SQL analytics endpoint of the lakehouse.
Edit	The recipient can edit the item or its content.
Share	The original recipient can share the item and grant to the new recipient some or all of the same permissions that they (the original recipient) have. For example, if the original recipient has Share, Edit, and Read permissions, then the original recipient can at most grant Share, Edit, and Read permissions to the new recipient.
Read All with SQL analytics endpoint	The recipient can read data from the SQL analytics endpoint of the lakehouse or warehouse data through TDS endpoints.
Read all with Apache Spark	The recipient can read lakehouse or data warehouse data through OneLake APIs and Spark, and they can also read lakehouse data through lakehouse explorer.
Subscribe to OneLake events	The recipient can subscribe to OneLake events for lakehouses, data warehouses, mirrored databases, SQL databases, and KQL databases.
Build	The recipient can build new content on the semantic model.
Execute	The recipient can execute or cancel execution of the item.

In summary, item-level access control is a powerful tool for implementing a scalable, secure, and manageable data environment. By combining it with the broader workspace roles, you can effectively govern who sees what in your Microsoft Fabric tenant.

However, it also adds complexity to the entire setup. You can configure explicit access to an item in a workspace without the granted user having access to the workspace. Imagine an enterprise setup with these access controls configured and you can quickly envision the effects on governance and maintenance of the setup.

Controlling Access to Compute

Access to workspaces and specific items in one thing, but you can also allow specific users access to the underlying compute, meaning the capacity units of Fabric.

You have two options for accessing the compute engine in Fabric:

Through the SQL Analytics endpoint
: The SQL analytics endpoint provides direct SQL access to tables in OneLake, and you can configure security there natively through SQL commands. These permissions only apply to queries made through SQL.

Through the Spark engine for the lakehouse
: Access to the Spark engine gives access to the underlying data through the Fabric API or the Spark engine when you're working with notebooks.

Currently, OneLake data access control level is in preview, and it provides a central place to control access to data. Since it's in preview for now, we won't cover it in this book. Instead, we'll refer you to Microsoft Learn (*https://oreil.ly/YZONs*), which includes this information:

> OneLake security uses role assignments to apply permissions to its members. You can either assign roles to individuals or to security groups, Microsoft 365 groups, and distribution lists. Every member in the user group gets the assigned role. If someone is in two or more security groups or Microsoft 365 groups, they get the highest level of permission that is provided by the roles. If you nest user groups and assign a role to a group, all of the contained users have permissions.

Implementing Row-Level, Column-Level, Object-Level, and File-Level Access Control

When giving your end users access to data across your entire data estate, you have four specific access methods to choose from, based on your specific needs and requirements:

Row-level access control
: End users are subject to an enforced and nonchangeable filter on the rows of the data. Such users may be sales representatives, each of whom is only allowed to see their own personal sales and clients.

Column-level access control

End users are only allowed to query or get insights to specific columns in your database that include information like Social Security numbers, credit card numbers, etc.

Object-level access control

End users may be completely blocked from accessing a specific object in the database. This could apply to a group of end users who are not allowed to see the personal identification information on the employees table, which is configured to be seen and used only by the HR department.

File-level access control

This is specific to targeted users who can access the underlying files in OneLake: the delta parquet files. Here, you have the option to grant or remove access to a specific file, a set of files, or folders in the OneLake structure.

At the time of this writing, you can't create column-level and object-level security in Power BI through the application itself. You can do it with third-party tools, but those are not a part of the exam and thus not a part of this book.

Power BI Security

While Microsoft Fabric provides a robust security layer for the entire data estate, Power BI requires a specialized approach to ensure that the right insights reach the right people without compromising sensitive information. Securing Power BI is not just about who can open a report; it is about defining exactly what data they see once they are inside.

In this section, we focus on the mechanisms that protect your Power BI assets. We begin by exploring row-level security (RLS) and object-level security (OLS), which allow you to filter data and hide specific tables or columns based on a user's identity. We will then look at how to manage these roles in the Fabric portal to ensure seamless enforcement across both the web and desktop experiences. Finally, we will cover the use of *sensitivity labels*, which provide an extra layer of protection by classifying and encrypting content to ensure that your organization's most critical data remains secure, even when it is exported or shared outside of the workspace.

Row-Level Security in Power BI

As stated previously, row-level security involves enforcing a specific filter (though it doesn't have to be just one filter) on a group of users on the rows of the data. This also doesn't have to be on just one table, since you can enforce the filter throughout the entire semantic model based on the relationships in the model.

An example of this could be a semantic model with a fact table of sales and a dimension table of sales representatives. The two tables are related to each other based on a key, so we configure the sales representative table to enforce a filter based on the end user's credentials. From this, the entire semantic model will force all the end users to have their own username filtered on the sales representative table. Also, from the relationship, the sales table will be filtered. The end user will not be able to change this implementation. Figure 7-8 illustrates this setup of row-level security in a semantic model.

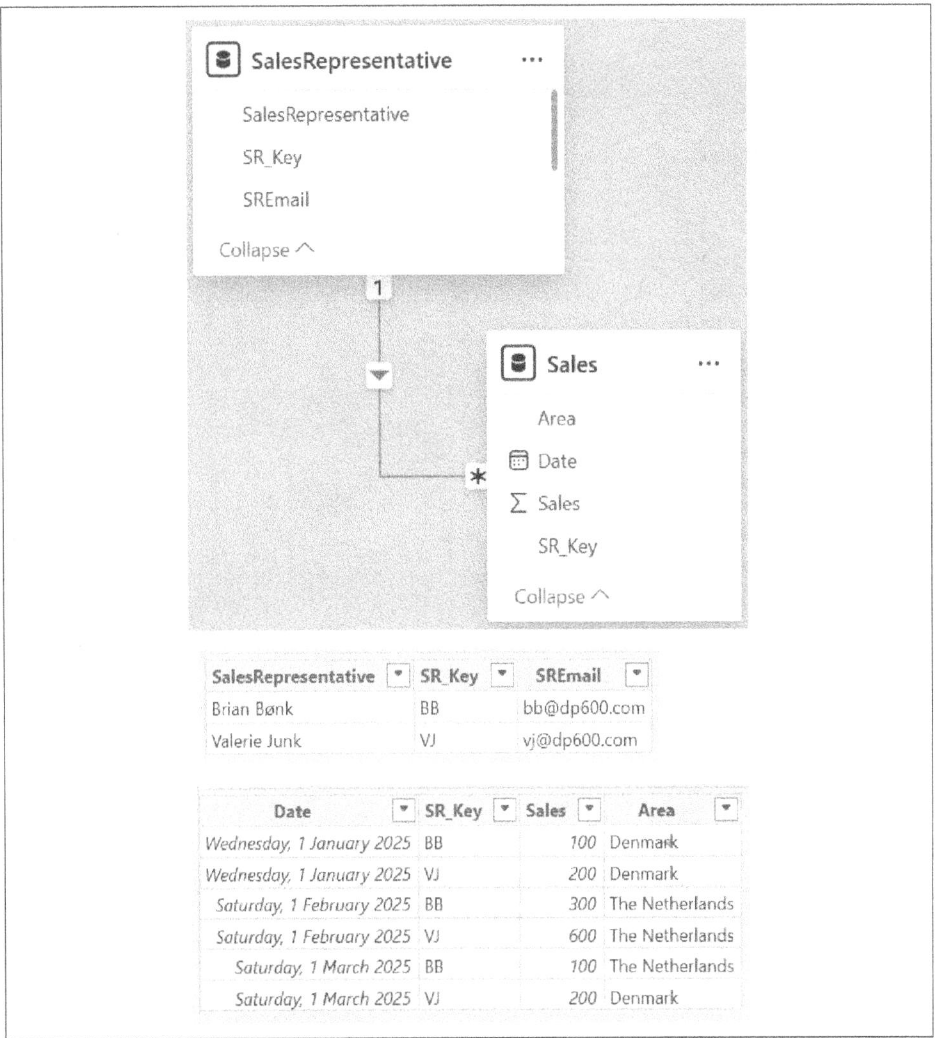

SalesRepresentative	SR_Key	SREmail
Brian Bønk	BB	bb@dp600.com
Valerie Junk	VJ	vj@dp600.com

Date	SR_Key	Sales	Area
Wednesday, 1 January 2025	BB	100	Denmark
Wednesday, 1 January 2025	VJ	200	Denmark
Saturday, 1 February 2025	BB	300	The Netherlands
Saturday, 1 February 2025	VJ	600	The Netherlands
Saturday, 1 March 2025	BB	100	The Netherlands
Saturday, 1 March 2025	VJ	200	Denmark

Figure 7-8. A `SalesRepresentative` dimension table and a `Sales` fact table in a simple semantic model, plus a snapshot of the demo data we're working with in this section

In this figure, you can also see the relationship between the two tables. It's in the SR_Key column, which is the key for the sales representative in each table.

To create a row-level security on the semantic model after this change in the relationships, you must find the Security section of the main menu at the top of the Power BI desktop screen (see Figure 7-9).

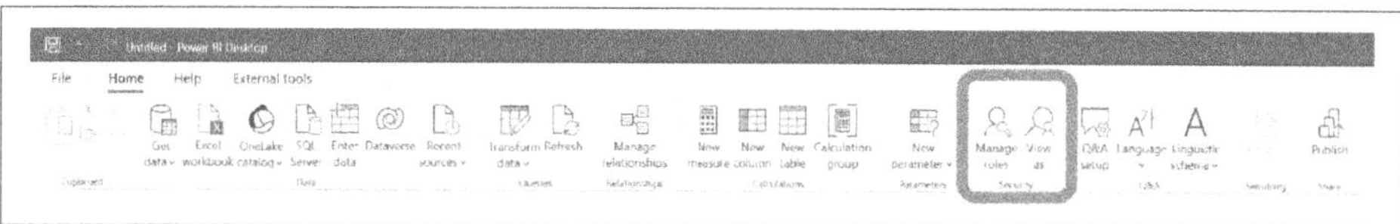

Figure 7-9. Security section of main menu in Power BI Desktop

Next, click "Manage roles" to open the pop-up shown in Figure 7-10.

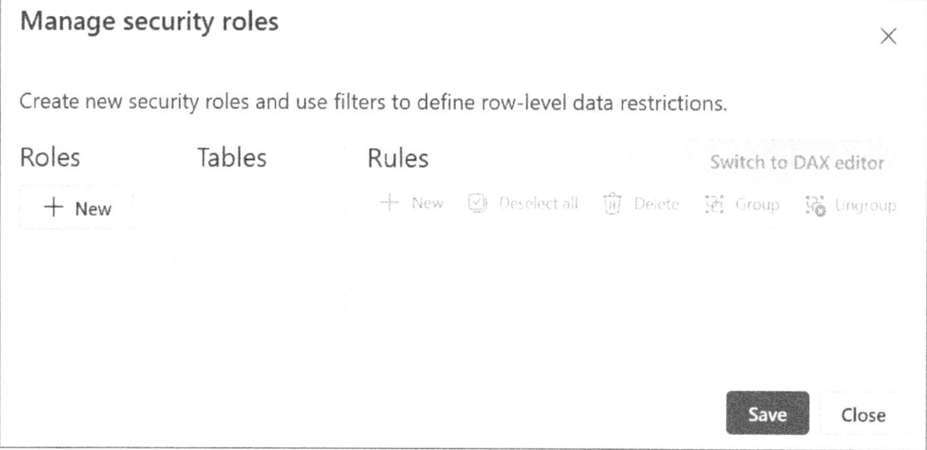

Figure 7-10. "Manage roles" popup in Power BI Desktop

Then, you'll be ready to create row-level security on the model.

You have two options for creating row-level security: fixed or dynamic. Fixed row-level security uses a fixed filter based on a DAX expression in the editor. Dynamic row-level security filters the data based on the current user's login credentials. We'll delve into both of these approaches in the following sections.

Fixed row-level security

You can create fixed row-level security on the "Manage security roles" screen (see Figure 7-11).

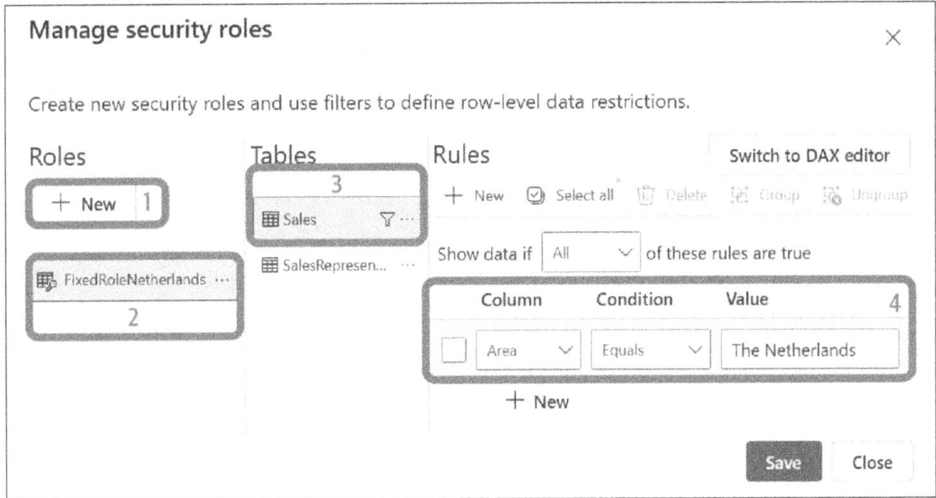

Figure 7-11. Creating a fixed row-level security role in Power BI

We've highlighted the areas in the figure (numbered 1–4) that you use in the creation process:

+ New button (area 1)
: Click this button to create a new fixed row-level security role.

Role name box (area 2)
: By default, the name of the role is Untitled, but you can change it by double-clicking the box or selecting "rename" from the three-dot-menu. In the figure, we've entered "FixedRoleNetherlands" as the new name of the role.

Table selection box (area 3)
: Here, you can select the tables you want to filter. In our example, we want to filter the sales table to only show data from The Netherlands.

Column, condition, and value selection area (area 4)
: Here, you can add the needed business logic to the security setup. You configure the rule by selecting the column and choosing the condition and type in the value for the filter. From the top menu in this area, you can also group elements together for grouped logic, and in this way, you can create both as simple and complex logic for security as needed.

  Here, we've selected Area from the Column drop-down menu and Equals from the condition menu, and we've typed "The Netherlands" into the Value field.

Once you've filled in these areas, you can click Save to create a fixed row-level security role named FixedRoleNetherlands.

To test the role, you can go back to the Power BI window and click the "View as" button from Figure 7-9 to bring up the window shown in Figure 7-12.

Figure 7-12. "View as roles" window from Power BI desktop

This window will display the role you just created, and you can select that role and click OK to produce the filtered report shown in Figure 7-13.

SalesRepresentative	Area	Sum of Sales
Brian Bønk	The Netherlands	400
Valerie Junk	The Netherlands	600
Total		**1000**

Figure 7-13. Results from the fixed role in Power BI Desktop

You can see that the report is filtered to only show data from the area of The Netherlands.

After you complete deployment to a workspace in Microsoft Fabric, you can add a user or a security group to the row-level security group (see Figure 7-14).

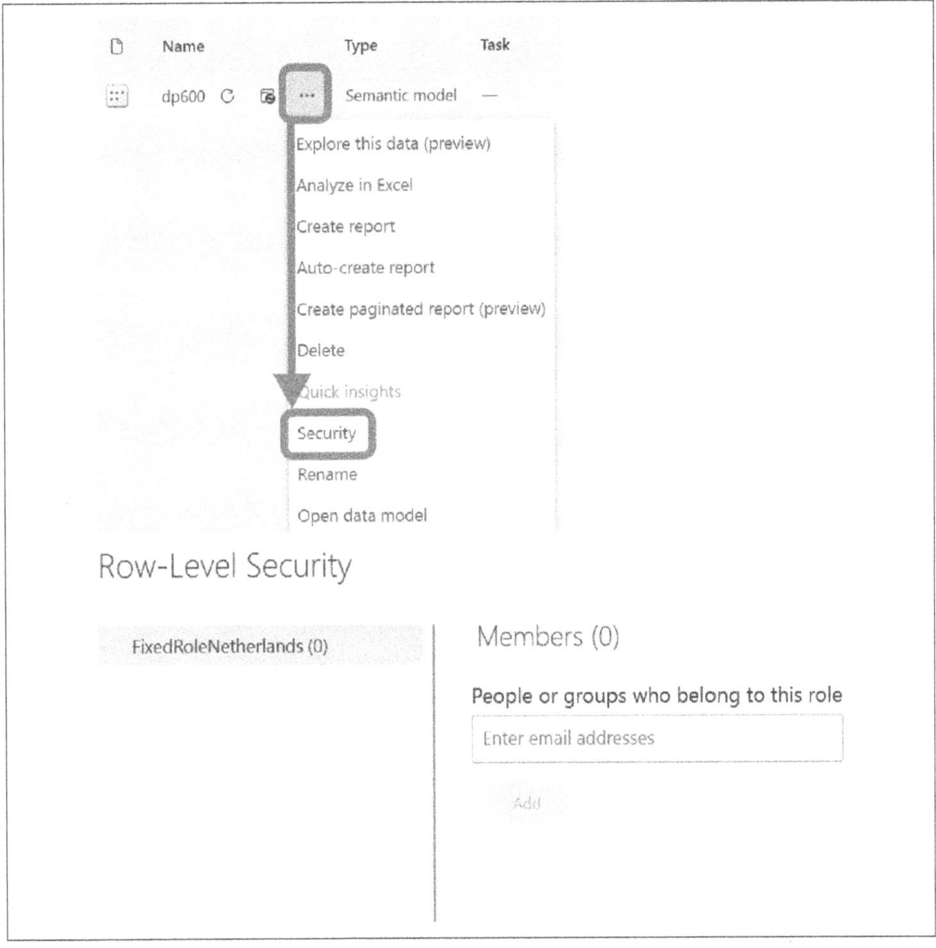

Figure 7-14. Setting up security on a report after deployment

In this figure, you can see the context menu option named Security and also the option to add users or security groups to the roles in the semantic model. The text box on the right is where you type in the users or security groups who should have access to the data, based on the marked role.

You can also create a similar role to filter only data from Denmark, if you wanted to.

In this book, we teach you how to create roles in a simple way. However, the UI also gives you options to group elements together and apply "any" or "all" logic to the groups of filters in the entire setup. This can involve extensive setup of roles and determination of what data each role has access to. As you might expect, manually creating such roles in a semantic model will take a lot of time if you have just a few users, areas, or other elements you need to filter the data on.

That's where dynamic row-level security comes to play.

Dynamic row-level security

To create dynamic row-level security, you make selections on and enter data into the "Manage security roles" screen (see Figure 7-15).

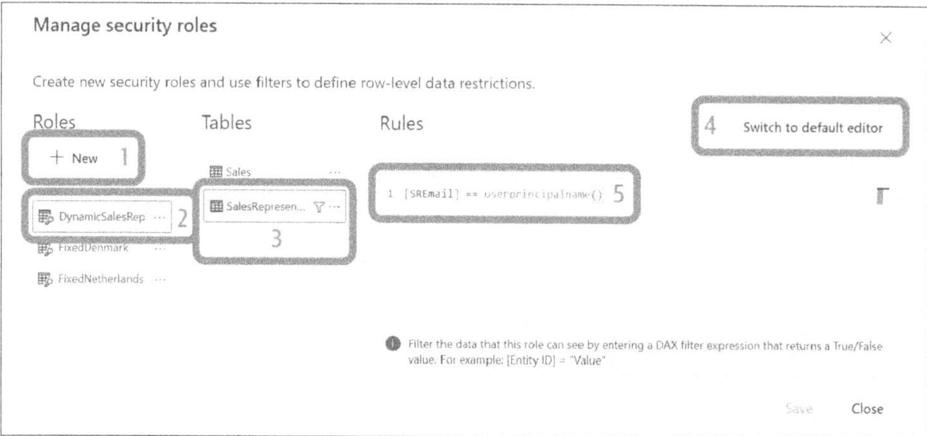

Figure 7-15. Creating a dynamic row-level security role

We've highlighted the areas in the figure (numbered 1–5) that you use in the creation process:

+ New button (area 1)
: Click this button to create a new dynamic row-level security role.

Role name box (area 2)
: By default, the name of the role is Untitled, but you can change it by double-clicking the box or selecting "rename" from the three-dot-menu. In the figure, we've entered "DynamicSalesRep" as the new name of the role.

Table selection box (area 3)
: Here, you can select the tables you want to filter. In our example, we want to filter the `SalesRepresentatives` table based on the current user's login information.

Switch to DAX editor button (area 4)
: The easiest way to implement this dynamic approach is to create the expression as a DAX expression, so we click the "Switch to DAX editor" button.

  Note that when in the default mode, as you saw in the approach before, this button says "Switch to DAX editor." However, when we click it, the text changes to " Switch to default editor." This is shown in Figure 7-15, which depicts the screen after we have clicked the button.

DAX expression window (area 5)
: Here, you can type in the DAX expression to filter your data.

The DAX expression that's typed into area 5 in the figure uses the `UserPrincipalName()` expression from Power BI. In Power BI, we have two options to get the user's login information: from the `UserName()` expression or the `UserPrincipalName()` expression. These two expressions (or functions) return the user's login information in two ways: `UserName()` returns the UserID (the user's information in the `<domain>\<username>` format), and `UserPrincipalName()` returns the username (the user's information in the `<username>@<domain>` format). In this case, we have the email from the sales representatives, so we can use the `UserPrincipalName()` function to grab the current user's information in the filter context. This gives us the DAX expression from area 5 in the figure:

```
[SREmail] == userprincipalname()
```

To test this role, we can go back to the Power BI window and click the "View as" button from Figure 7-9 to bring up the window shown in Figure 7-16.

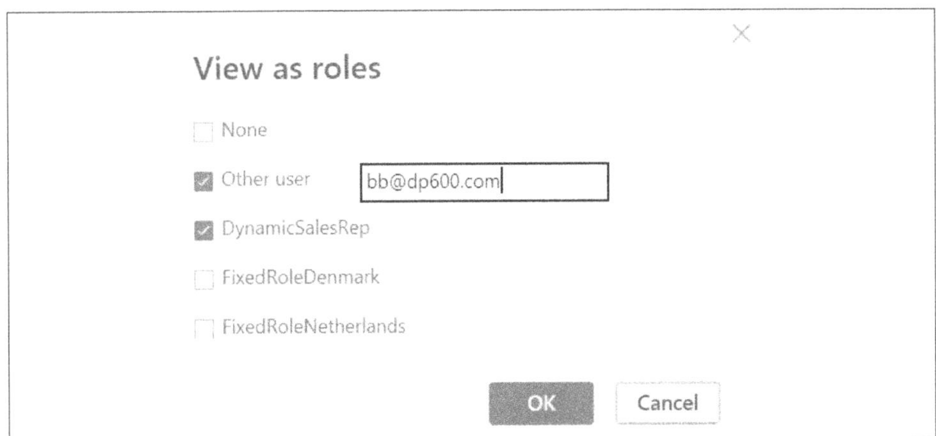

Figure 7-16. "View as" window from Power BI desktop

We need to check the "Other user" box so we can type in the email of the user we want to test the report with. We also need to check the box for the "DynamicSales-Rep" role to test using that role. Then, we can click OK to generate a report with only the data from the sales representative with the email of *bb@dp600.com* (see Figure 7-17).

SalesRepresentative	Area	Sum of Sales
Brian Bønk	Denmark	100
Brian Bønk	The Netherlands	400
Total		**500**

Figure 7-17. Report generated with dynamic filter based on current user

After we finish deploying to the workspace, we can add more people and users to the role by following the same process shown in Figure 7-15.

You can also alter the simple approach with the `UserPrincipalName()` as the single filter expression and modify it to fit your exact needs. The expression does not have to refer to a single table. It can be as complex a DAX expression as you need.

These examples represent only the tip of the iceberg of row-level security in Power BI. There are numerous mechanisms and methods of implementation. You can have a full semantic model with dozens of tables and relationships, and the setup and implementation can quickly become complex and require deep analysis of the approach. Which approach is the "correct" one depends on your organization's needs and requirements.

Warehouse Security

Implementing security in a warehouse in Microsoft Fabric is entirely different from doing it in Power BI. We do it with a *security policy* that uses the SQL analytics endpoint. The security policy is a set of T-SQL statements that, together, define access to one or more tables when using the SQL analytics endpoint. The approach is almost the same as with the semantic model, though the scenario needs a lot more code because the relationships between tables are not enforced in the security functions themselves. The developer needs to handle everything explicitly, based on their own knowledge.

Row-Level Security in a Warehouse

The security policy is made up of a `SECURITY POLICY` statement and a predicate. The *predicate* is a function that filters the data on a specific table, based on the user that is currently logged in. We create this function as a `SCHEMA` bound function, and we set the relationship between the predicate and the user with the `SECURITY POLICY` statement.

For example, a `SCHEMA` bound function looks at the `User_Name()` to filter rows, and this function is then bound to a table with the `SECURITY POLICY` statement. The main takeaway here is that you need to be very explicit. If a user has a role that allows them to see a specific set of data in one table, and if this data is related to another table, then you must implement the security on both tables. There is no automatic cascading of security.

Here's a simple example. First, you'll need to create the function that will act as the predicate. This function will filter rows based on the current user's name:

```
CREATE FUNCTION Security.fn_user_security_predicate(@Username AS sysname)
RETURNS TABLE WITH SCHEMABINDING AS
RETURN SELECT 1 AS result WHERE @Username = USER_NAME();
```

Next, you'll create the security policy itself, binding it to the predicate function and the table you want to protect:

```
CREATE SECURITY POLICY Product.ProductSecurityPolicy
ADD FILTER PREDICATE Security.fn_user_security_predicate(
    CAST(USER_NAME() AS sysname)
)
ON Product.DimProduct;
```

With these two statements, you've created a policy that ensures users can only see rows in the DimProduct table where the `UserName()` matches their own.

The row-level security in a Fabric warehouse is evaluated at query time. This means that every time a user runs a query, the security predicate is applied as a filter. This is different from what happens in a Power BI semantic model, where the security roles are applied when the model is refreshed and deployed and the data is then filtered based on the role assigned to the user.

This process involves creating the function, then creating the policy, and finally applying it to the tables. It is also possible to add multiple policies to a single table. It's not just a single security policy that defines the access. It's the combination of all policies that are active on the table.

The benefit of this approach is that it's very flexible and that you can use it to implement very complex security models. The downside is that it requires you to have a deep understanding of T-SQL and the security model of the warehouse itself.

Column-Level Security in a Warehouse

With the warehouse, you can also explicitly handle column-level security.

While row-level security is about filtering which rows a user can see, column-level security is about controlling which columns they can access. You handle this by using standard SQL GRANT, REVOKE, and DENY statements: GRANT lets you give users access to a column, REVOKE lets you remove GRANT statements, and DENY lets you specifically deny access to columns in a table. This means you can grant specific users or groups of users access to specific columns of a table. For example, you might want to grant a group of users access to a sensitive column like CreditCardNumber or hide it from them, depending on whether or not they need to see it.

This is a straightforward approach, but it requires you to perform a careful analysis of the data model and the user roles because you must explicitly define every user and every column they should have access to. This approach is powerful, but it can be a bit of a burden to manage when you have a lot of tables and users.

Here's a simple code example of granting and denying access to a column:

```
-- Grant SELECT permission on the DimProduct table to a user
GRANT SELECT ON Product.DimProduct TO [john.doe@contoso.com];
-- Deny SELECT permission on the Cost column to the same user
DENY SELECT ON OBJECT::Product.DimProduct(Cost) TO [john.doe@contoso.com];
```

This process is very different from the way you handle row-level security. With column-level security, there's no need for functions or security policies. You use a simple GRANT or DENY statement. The key is to be very precise and ensure you have a clear understanding of your user roles and data. The management of this security needs to be part of your overall governance strategy.

Object-Level Security in a Warehouse

Object-level security is about controlling access to entire data objects. This is the broadest level of security you can implement in a warehouse, and you handle it with the same GRANT and DENY statements you use in column-level security. But while column-level security is about a specific column, object-level security is about the whole object, like a table, a view, or even a schema.

The most basic object-level security scenario is giving a user or a group access to a table. If they don't have this permission, they can't even know whether the table exists. Implementing object-level security is a simple and effective way to manage broad access rights. You can grant different permissions, such as SELECT, INSERT, UPDATE, or DELETE, to give yourself very granular control over what a user can do with an entire object.

Here's a code example showing how to grant and deny access to an entire table:

```
-- Grant SELECT permission on the FactSales table to a role
GRANT SELECT ON FactSales TO SalesTeamRole;
-- Deny all permissions on the sensitive Customers table to a user
DENY ALL ON Customer.DimCustomer
```

The approach is simple but powerful. By combining object-level, column-level, and row-level security, you can build a very robust security model that can fit almost any scenario. It is a bit of a burden to manage, but it gives you complete control over your data.

Lakehouse Security

In the Microsoft Fabric ecosystem, not all security is handled at the SQL or semantic model layer. A core part of the platform is the lakehouse, which sits on top of OneLake.

Here, the data is just files, plain-old files in folders. This is where you'll do your data engineering, load raw data, and transform it before it ever sees a SQL endpoint. And because it's just files, you handle the security at a much lower level.

The security model here is all about access to files and folders, and it's a lot simpler than the complex T-SQL statements we've been looking at. You're not defining complex predicates or `GRANT` statements for individual columns. Instead, you're granting permissions at the file or folder level.

You manage this security through the Fabric user interface by assigning permissions to users or groups. The permissions themselves are pretty straightforward and are built around the three core rights:

Read
: With this permission, a user can see a file or folder and read its contents. They can't make any changes, rename anything, or delete anything. This is the simplest form of access and is often used for consumers who only need to read a dataset.

Read and write
: This permission gives a user the ability to not just read the data but also to create new files, modify existing ones, or delete them. It's a key permission for data engineers and developers who are responsible for maintaining the data in the lakehouse.

Read, write, and execute
: The term *execute* might seem odd when we're talking about files, but think of it as *full control*. A user with this permission can do everything a read and write user can do, but they also have permission to execute other commands like managing permissions on the files. This is often reserved for administrators or owners of the data.

You assign these permissions directly in the lakehouse files and folders, and you'll typically manage this through the main Fabric portal. You can find the permissions dialog for any file or folder in the UI, and it's a quick process of assigning users and their roles.

It's important to remember that these permissions are different from the workspace roles (administrator, member, contributor, and viewer). While a workspace role provides overall access to the items in a workspace, file-level access controls what a user can actually do with the files inside the lakehouse. A user with a viewer role in a workspace, for example, might be given "Read and write" access to a specific folder in the lakehouse, allowing them to load data but not modify other items in the workspace.

You manage the permissions directly on the objects. Simply navigate to the object (like a folder) in the lakehouse explorer and set the permissions. This contrasts with the semantic model, where security is defined by roles and is a part of the model itself. In the lakehouse, the permissions are a separate layer that sits on top of the files. The two layers of security work together to give you a very robust model, but they're completely independent of each other.

Applying Sensitivity Labels to Items

While row, column, and object security are all about controlling who can see what data, there's a whole other layer of security that deals with the data itself, no matter where it is. This is where *sensitivity labels* come into the picture. Think of sensitivity labels as a way to classify your data and apply a set of rules and policies to it.

The concept is simple: you label data based on how sensitive it is, and then, the label enforces protection settings. It's about data governance and ensuring that sensitive information is treated correctly throughout its entire lifecycle. This isn't just a Fabric-only thing; these labels are part of a broader platform called Microsoft Purview Information Protection, which means the labels you use in Fabric are the same ones your organization uses in SharePoint, Teams, and Power BI. The goal is to have a consistent and unified approach to data classification.

The Different Sensitivity Labels

The labels you can apply aren't on a fixed list from Microsoft. They are defined by your organization's governance team, and they reflect your company's specific needs for data classification. A typical set of labels might look something like this:

Public
: This is for data that can be shared freely, such as a public-facing report or a dataset that has no sensitive information.

General
: This is the default label for most internal data. It's for everyday business data that isn't highly sensitive but shouldn't be shared with external parties.

Confidential

This is for data that contains information that is not for general consumption, such as internal financial reports and personal data.

Highly confidential

This is for your most sensitive data, such as trade secrets, employee records, and business acquisition plans. This label often comes with strict protection rules.

Some of these labels may even have sublabels. For example, a Confidential label may have sublabels like Confidential - Finance or Confidential - HR that allow for even more granular classification without creating a long list of top-level labels. The key here is that the labels are tools a developer can use to tag data, and the rules are then enforced by the system.

How to Use Them

The process of applying a sensitivity label is very straightforward, and it's a fundamental step that a developer should perform whenever they create a new item. For example, when you create a new semantic model in your workspace, there will be a drop-down box in the properties where you can choose a sensitivity label. It's a simple, manual process.

The magic happens behind the scenes. Once you label an item, that label "cascades" down to all connected items. If you create a semantic model and label it Confidential, any reports you build on top of that semantic model will automatically inherit the Confidential label. This is a critical point. A developer might not even need to think about applying a label to a report; it's inherited from the underlying data source.

This inheritance is what makes sensitivity labels so powerful for governance. If an organization has a policy that a Confidential report can't be exported to a PDF file or printed, Fabric will enforce that rule for all items tagged with that label. The developer's job is to apply the correct label, and the platform will take care of the rest. This creates a very robust governance model that is hard to circumvent.

Sensitivity labels are all about classification and governance. They do not replace row-level or column-level security. A label can enforce a policy that prevents a user from exporting a report, but it will not filter the data that the user can see. The two layers of security work together: one controls who can see what, and the other controls how the data can be used.

Endorsing Items

In an organization where everyone is creating reports, datasets, and other items, it can quickly become hard to figure out what's what. How do you know if a specific report is the "official" one you should be using for your business decisions? How do you know it's accurate and trustworthy? This is where endorsements come in.

Endorsements provide a way to signal the quality and reliability of an item in Fabric. They are simple visual cues that tell users this specific report, semantic model, or other artifact has been vetted and approved. Think of them as stamps of approval from the person or team who owns the data. They make it a lot easier for other users to discover and use the right data, without having to guess or ask around. They're a crucial part of data governance and building trust within the organization.

The Different Endorsements

There are three types of endorsements you can apply to an item in Microsoft Fabric: Promoted, Certified, and Master Data. They have different meanings and are used for different purposes:

Promoted
: This is the most common endorsement, and it's a way for a user to officially recommend an item. You'll use this on items that are a good starting point for your team or that your team regularly uses. Applying a Promoted endorsement is a way for a data creator to say, "Hey, this is the one you should be using. It's ready for general use." For example, you can promote a report or a semantic model that has been tested and is ready to be shared with a wider audience. The key here is that the item is recommended by its owner or a team member.

Certified
: This endorsement carries a lot of weight. An item can only be certified by a team that has been given certification authority, such as the data governance team or a Center of Excellence. Certification means the item has met the organization's strict quality standards and has been verified for accuracy, security, and performance. You'll apply this to the most critical and trusted datasets, the ones that are used for official reporting and business-critical decisions.

Master data
: When an item has the Master data badge, it means the data in the item is a core source of organizational data. The Master data designation is often used to indicate that a data item is to be regarded as the authoritative, single source of truth for certain kinds of organizational or business data, such as product codes and customer lists. You can only apply the Master data label to items that contain data, such as lakehouses and semantic models. Only users who are specified by the Fabric administrator can label data items as Master data.

The differences among these endorsements come down to a matter of trust and authority. A Promoted item is recommended by a user, while a Certified item is officially approved by the organization.

While an endorsement doesn't change any of the permissions on the item, it does change the item's discoverability. Endorsed items are prioritized in search results and are easier for other users to find and use. A user may not be able to see a report due to a lack of permissions, but if they're granted access, they'll easily be able to see that it's Promoted or Certified.

How to Use Them

The process of applying an endorsement is simple, and you do it directly in the item's settings. You can find the endorsement option in the item's details pane or in its settings. It's a manual process in which you select the item and then choose either Promoted or Certified from the endorsement options. It's a straightforward action, but it also means that you're responsible for ensuring the data meets the standards you're claiming it does.

If you're the owner of an item, you can promote it. To certify an item, you must be a member of the certified endorsement group that your admin has set up. This ensures that only the right people can certify an item. The goal is to make sure that users can trust the data they're using and that there's a clear line of authority and responsibility for every item in the organization. The use of endorsements is an essential part of a good data governance strategy.

Summary

In a data-driven world, an organization's data is one of its most valuable assets. But with this value comes a great responsibility to ensure that it's secure and only the right people can access it. In a platform as comprehensive as Microsoft Fabric, where a wide range of users interact with various data items, controlling access is critical. You can't just rely on good intentions; you need robust tools to handle it.

This chapter walked you through those essential security and governance features. We started with how to handle workspace and item-level access, and then, we moved on to the deeper, more granular controls you need to secure data itself, including row-level, object-level, and file-level access. We then explored how to classify and protect sensitive data using sensitivity labels and how to build a trustworthy environment by using endorsements.

Knowing how to implement these security and governance features is a key part of your role. It will help you meet compliance requirements, maintain data integrity, and foster a culture of trust within your organization.

CHAPTER 8

Maintaining the Analytics Development Lifecycle

After a Power BI report is published to a workspace, it rarely stays the same. It gets updated, data models change, and new needs often come up. This is a good thing because it means users are working with the report, and we can improve it to provide better insights.

However, while making changes to a single report may seem easy, in large organizations, we often manage many reports or data models. We can't just keep all the changes in our head. It's important for the organization to track changes in a clear and organized way, so that even if we leave and come back again after a year, we understand what was done to the reports in our absence. Also, we sometimes need to move reports or datasets to other workspaces. For example, we may have separate workspaces for development, testing, and production. In addition, reusing parts of reports or models saves us time and effort because we don't need to start from scratch every time.

In this chapter, we'll explore how to handle all these tasks.

We begin with version control in a workspace, which helps us track changes and keep work organized. Next, we explore the Power BI project (*.pbip*) file format, which allows us to manage report files and related assets more efficiently. After that, we look at reusable assets such as template files (*.pbit*), data source files (*.pbids*), and shared semantic models. Then, we move on to deployment pipelines, which help promote content from development to test and production environments in a controlled and reliable way. We also cover impact analysis, so you can determine which downstream items will be affected by changes you make before you make them, like lakehouses, warehouses, dataflows, and semantic models. Finally, we explore how to deploy and manage semantic models using the XMLA endpoint.

Configuring Version Control for a Workspace

When working with data over a longer period of time or with several coworkers, version control is incredibly handy. Let's imagine we're editing a report or data model, and at some point, something breaks or behaves unexpectedly. In addition to wanting to know what happened, we want to find out if it happened before (like during the last change). We may also want to know who made the changes that caused the problem and discuss with them why they made those changes, instead of just rolling them back.

With version control, not only can we save the changes we make, but we can also see which changes have been made and roll back changes that are not what we or our coworkers intended. Version control is also a great documentation method and a way of making sure, even after a long period of time, that we know what was done and by whom.

In Fabric, you have two options for version control: Azure DevOps and GitHub. You can choose which one to use for each workspace and set it up according to your preferences or your organization's standards. Both options let you apply familiar source control tools and processes to your Fabric items, making it easier to keep work organized, safe, and ready to roll back if you need to.

Setting Up GitHub and Azure DevOps Version Control

We can configure version control at the workspace level in Fabric. To do this, we open the workspace where we want to enable version control and go to "Workspace settings." Then, in the settings menu, we'll find a section called "Git integration," where we can choose and set up either GitHub or Azure DevOps (see Figure 8-1). We can link each workspace to only one of these options at a time, so we'll need to pick the one that best fits our environment or organization.

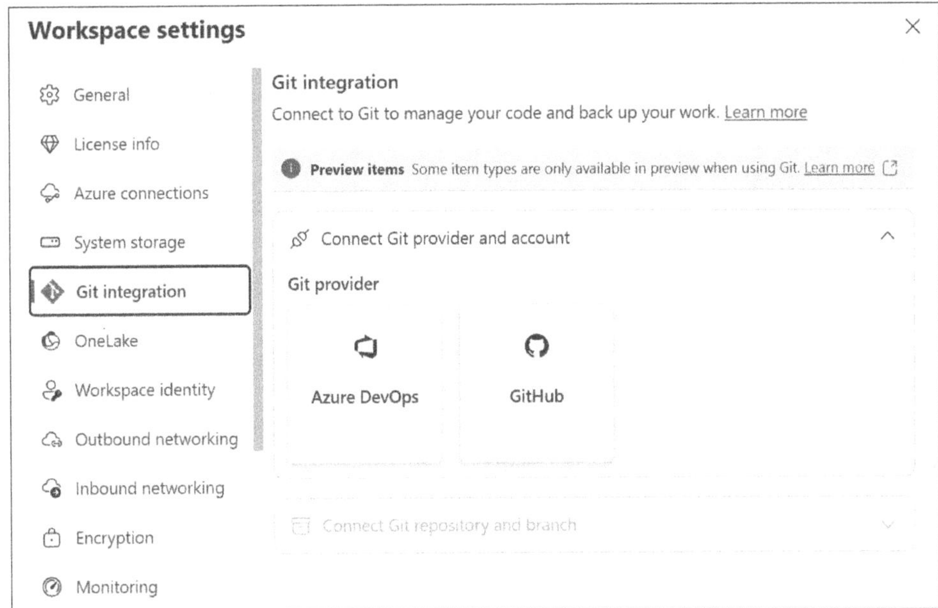

Figure 8-1. Git integration section of the Fabric workspace settings

We'll start with setting up GitHub integration.

Setting up GitHub version control

When we open the Git integration menu for the first time, the GitHub icon may be grayed out since that happens by default (see Figure 8-2).

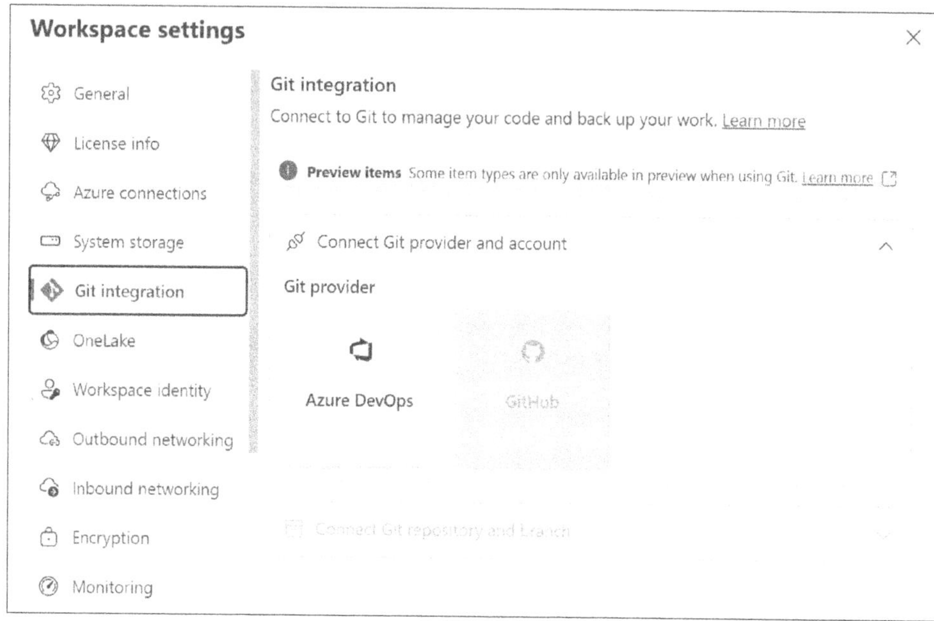

Figure 8-2. GitHub integration is grayed out by default in the workspace settings

If we hover over the grayed-out GitHub option, we'll see a message telling us to contact our Fabric administrator to enable GitHub for us. To do this, the administrator needs to go to the Admin portal and search for the Git integration section. The last option, "Users can sync workspace items with GitHub repositories," is disabled by default in each tenant, but the Fabric administrator can turn this setting on for specific users or for the entire organization (see Figure 8-3). Once they do this, it can take up to 15 minutes before the change becomes visible, so there's no need to worry if the button is not immediately available to you.

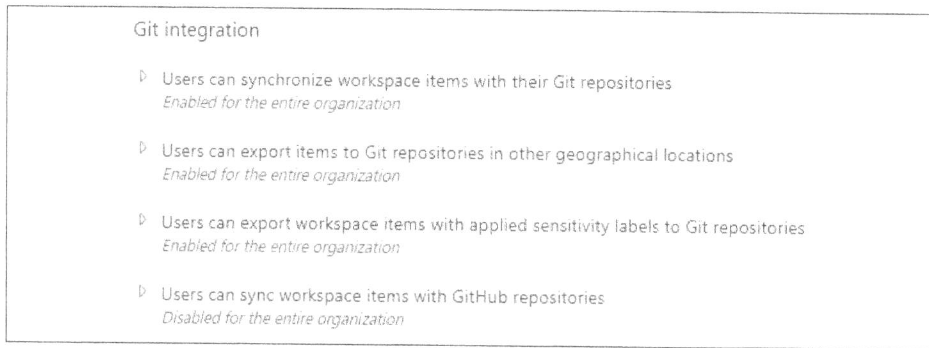

Figure 8-3. Synchronization with GitHub is disabled by default in the admin settings

Figure 8-4 shows the specific options under "Users can synchronize workspace items with GitHub repositories" for enabling GitHub integration.

Users can synchronize workspace items with their **Git** repositories

Enabled for the entire organization

Users can import and export workspace items to **Git** repositories for collaboration and version control. Turn off this setting to prevent users from syncing workspace items with their **Git** repositories. Learn More

Enabled

Apply to:

The entire organization

Specific security groups

Except specific security groups

Delegate setting to other admins

Select the admins who can view and change this setting, including any security group selections you've made.

Capacity admins can enable/disable

Workspace admins can enable/disable

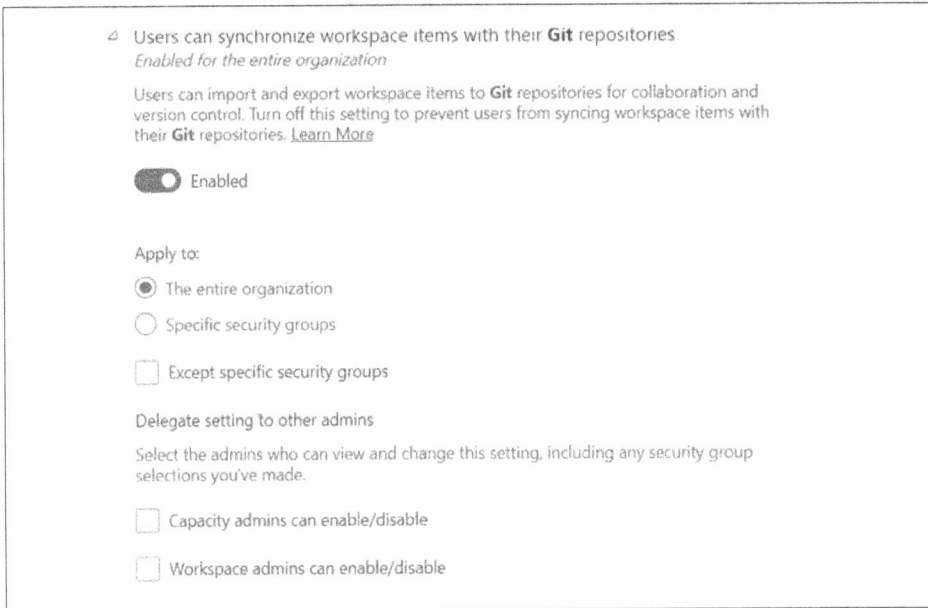

Figure 8-4. Specific options under "Users can synchronize workspace items with GitHub repositories" for enabling GitHub integration

An admin can apply the Git integration settings to the entire organization, limit them to a specific security group, and even exclude certain security groups. Depending on the structure of the organization, one approach might be more practical than another.

There is also the option to delegate these settings to other administrators, such as capacity admins or workspace admins. This can be useful in larger environments where responsibilities are shared.

Once the GitHub Git integration button becomes clickable, we can add an account. We can add any GitHub account here, even a personal one, so it's important to be careful that only the right people are granted access and allowed to connect a GitHub account. Figure 8-5 shows the screen we see when we click on the GitHub option in the Fabric workspace settings.

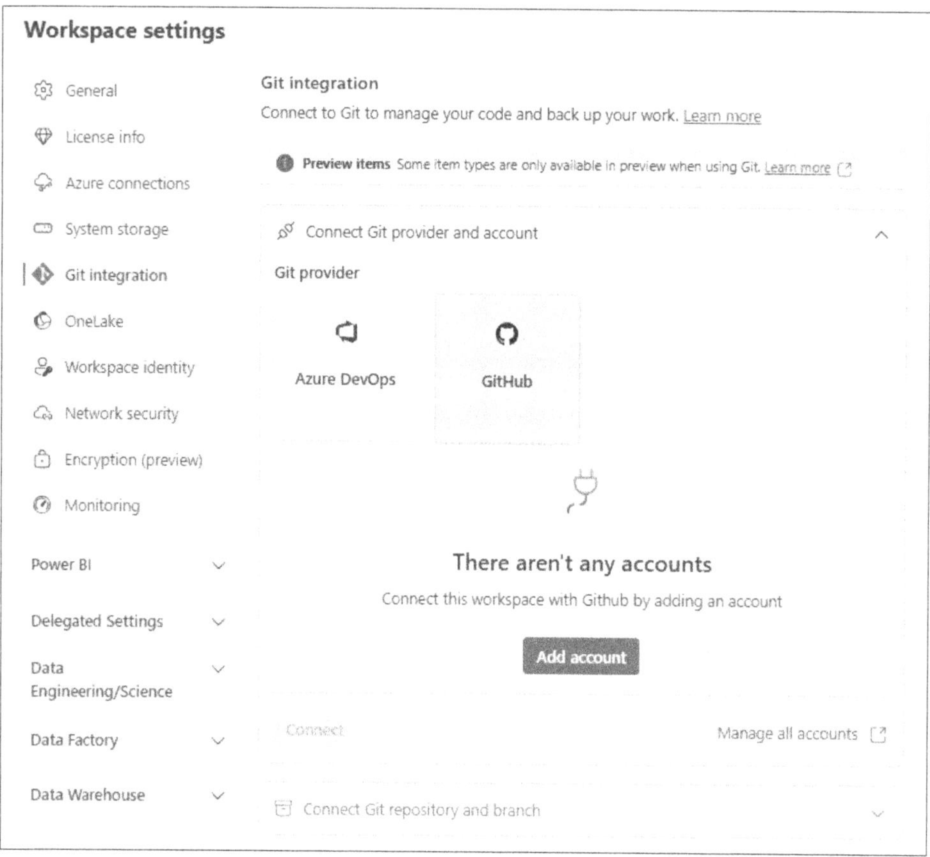

Figure 8-5. Adding a GitHub account to connect in the workspace settings

After we click on "Add account" we need to provide some information for Fabric to be able to connect to GitHub. First, we choose a display name, just for reference within Fabric. Next, we add a personal access token from GitHub, which we can generate in the developer settings in GitHub. This token authorizes Fabric to connect to our GitHub account securely. Finally, we provide the URL of the repository we want to link to this workspace. Figure 8-6 shows a screenshot of the information that we need to provide. Once we've filled in all the details, we can save and connect the workspace to GitHub.

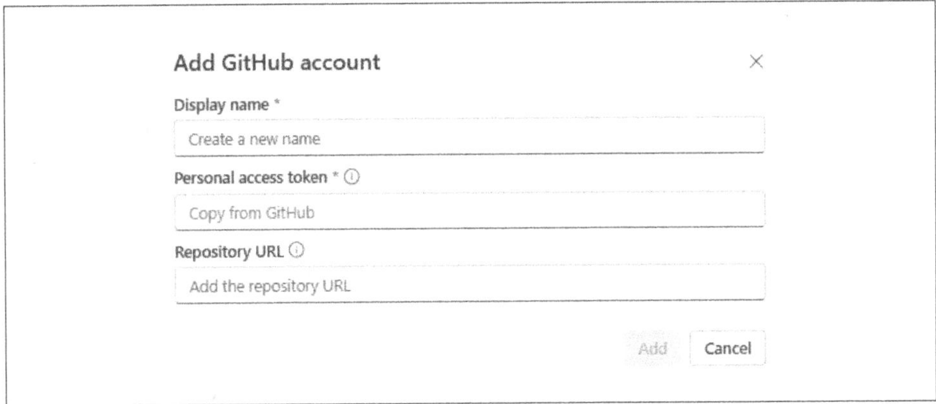

Figure 8-6. Screen where we provide an access token and repository URL to connect a GitHub account

Once we click on Add, the content of the workspace will be synced from the workspace to Git. From that point on, any changes made in the workspace can be synced and tracked in Git. Figure 8-7 shows the confirmation message we receive right after clicking Add, indicating that the syncing process has started.

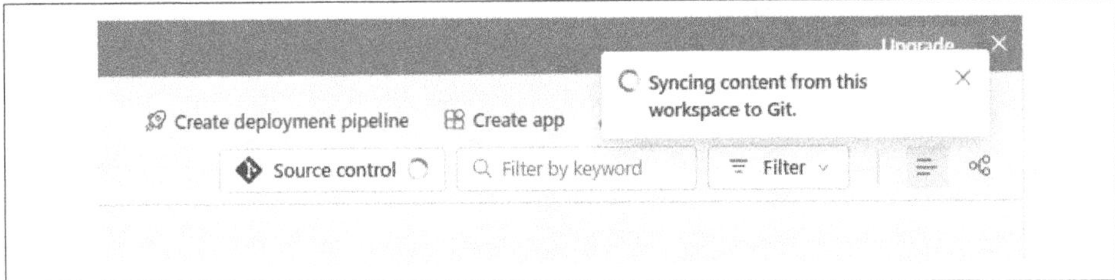

Figure 8-7. Message we receive after clicking Add, confirming that changes made to content of the workspace will be synced and tracked in Git

Setting Up Azure DevOps version control

Using Azure DevOps for version control works much like using GitHub, with the main difference being the setup process. In Azure DevOps, you need to specify your organization, project, Git repository, branch, and (optionally) Git folder. Figure 8-8 shows the setup screen where you enter this information. Once you finish configuring them, the syncing and version tracking work just like with GitHub.

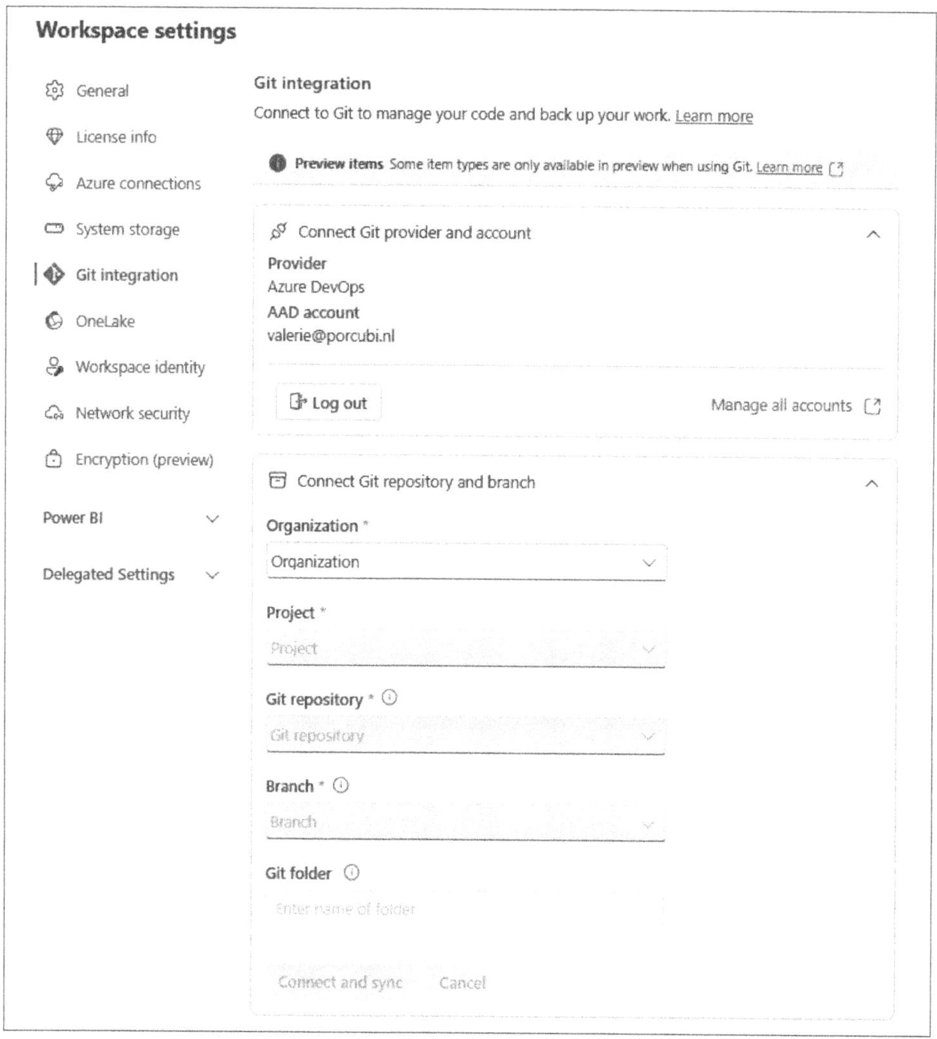

Figure 8-8. Configuring Azure DevOps as Git integration in the Fabric workspace

To perform this configuration, we must have access to the Azure DevOps organization. We need to select the organization, the project, the Git repository within that project, and the branch we want to work with. We can also select a Git folder, but it's optional. Once we've set everything, we click "Connect and Sync." That will bring up the same confirmation message in the top-right corner of our screen that we get when we complete a GitHub connection.

Working with Version Control in Fabric

After version control is configured, it works the same in Azure DevOps and in GitHub. We'll see a new "Source control" button in the upper right-hand corner of our Fabric workspace (see Figure 8-9.), and it provides us with important information.

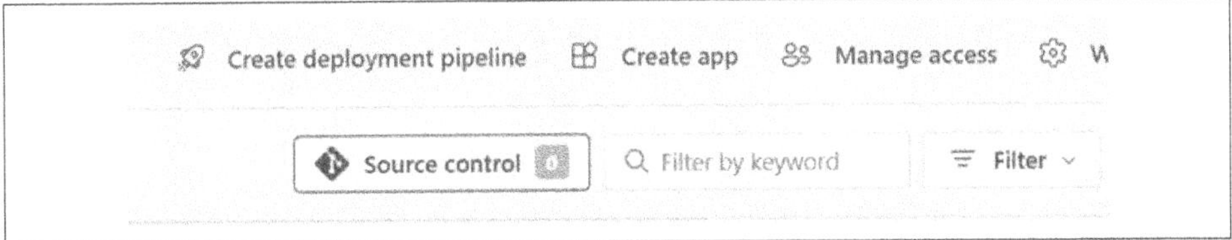

Figure 8-9. "Source control" button that appears after a successful Git integration

The number in the "Source control" button tells us how many changes have been made but are not yet synced. Inside the workspace, we can also see whether each item is synced or whether it has unsynced changes. Figure 8-10 shows an example where all items are fully synced, so the "Source control" button shows 0.

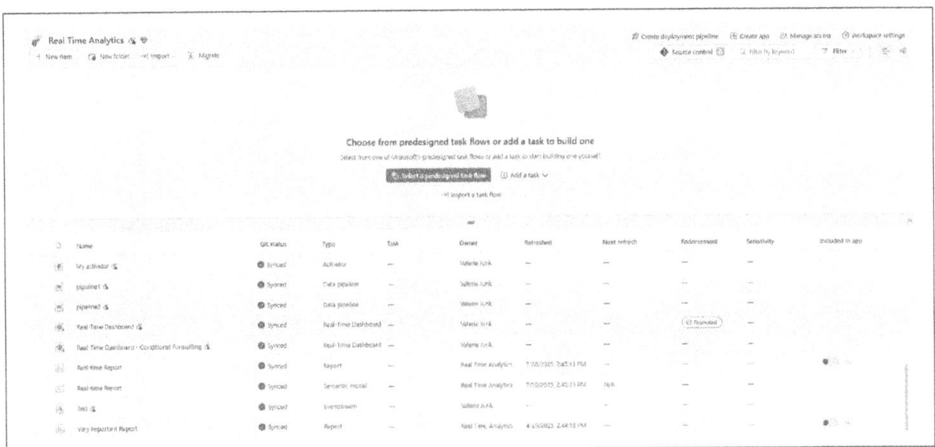

Figure 8-10. Screen with a "Source control" button showing all items in the workspace are synchronized

When you make a change to an item, like editing a notebook in the workspace, the "Source control" button updates to show how many changes are not yet committed. You'll also see a message next to the item itself, indicating it has uncommitted changes. Figure 8-11 shows an example of a notebook file marked with Uncommitted changes.

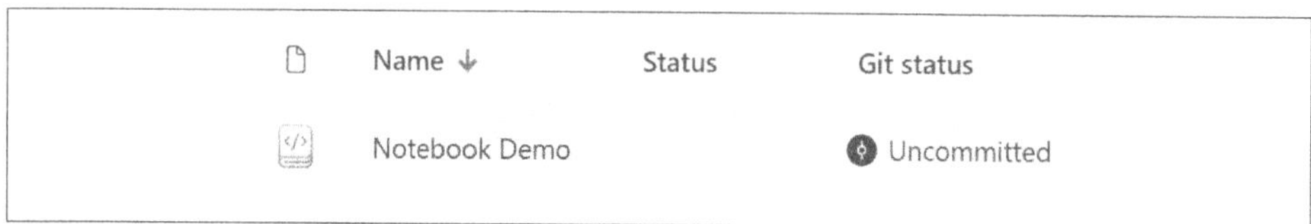

Figure 8-11. A notebook file with uncommitted changes

Figure 8-12 shows the "Source control" button displaying a 1. Even if we don't yet know exactly which item was changed, this tells us there is something new or updated that needs our attention. It's a clear signal that changes are pending synchronization, so we can review and commit them before moving on.

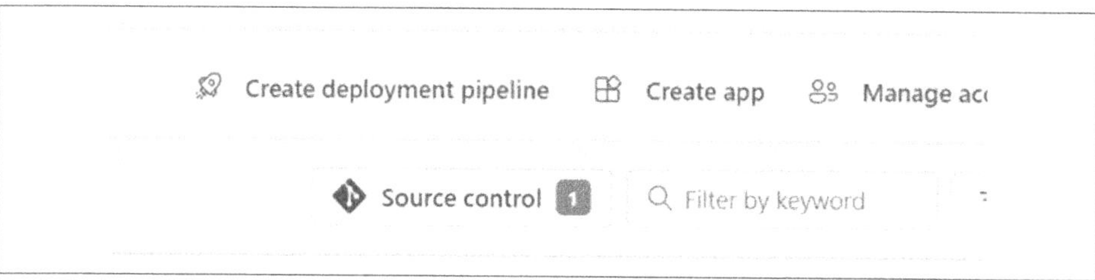

Figure 8-12. "Source control" button showing one uncommitted change in the Fabric workspace

When we click the "Source control" button, a side window called "Source control" opens in the workspace. There, we'll see the current branch, which is "main" in this example but could be any branch that was chosen. Below that, there's a free text field where we can write a commit message describing the changes we're about to commit. This is important, especially when working with others, because it helps everyone understand what each synchronization includes. We'll also see a list of the items and their status (see Figure 8-13).

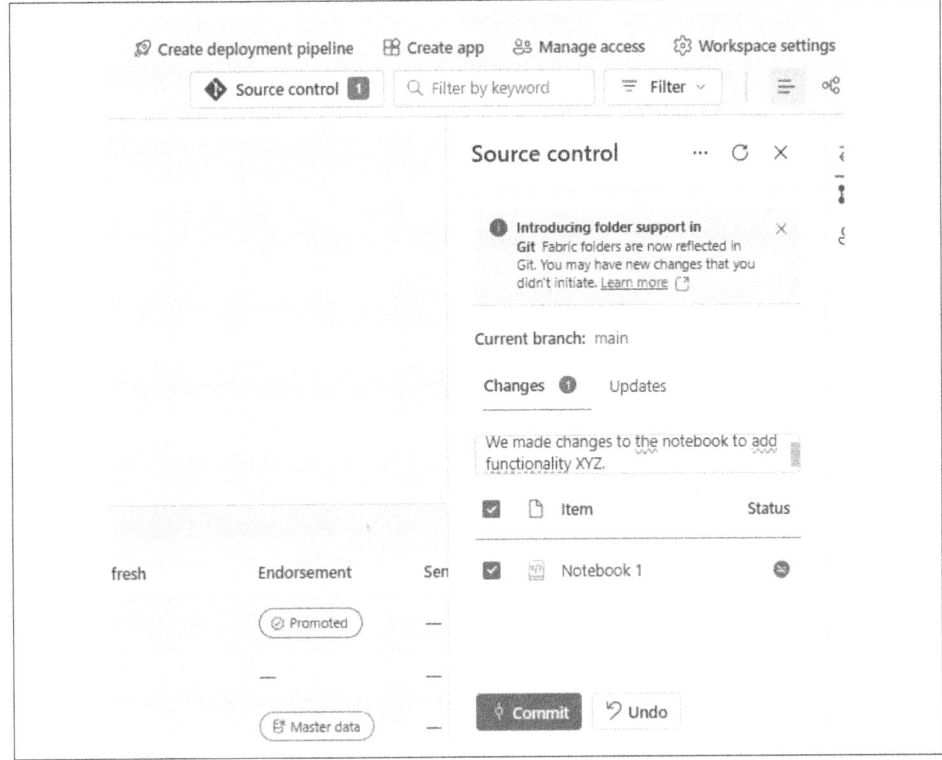

Figure 8-13. "Source control" window where we can see all items that have been changed

When we click Commit, the changes are saved to the Git repository. From that moment on, the commit, with all its details and changes, is stored in version control. This means we can review what was changed, when it was changed, and by whom. Figure 8-14 shows an example of a commit in a Git repository.

Commits
Notebook-1-Dev...
All users
All time
Commits on Aug 10, 2025
Committing 18 items from workspace 9efdec90-d04e-456e-9695-af4a3cc87b2b
ed83a34
Porcu-BI committed 41 minutes ago

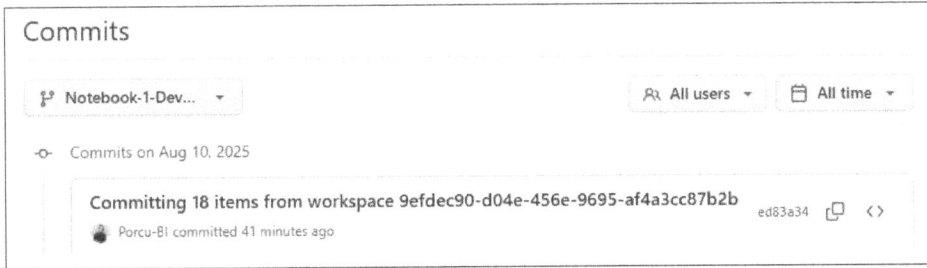

Figure 8-14. Commit made in a Git repository

Benefits and Limitations of Version Control

Version control is not just a nice-to-have. It's important for collaboration, auditing, and maintaining quality in Power BI and Fabric projects. Knowing who changed what and when makes troubleshooting faster and keeps everyone aligned. Even if we're the only ones working on a project, over time, just keeping notes in our head will not be enough. Version control acts as a built-in history and documentation system that will save us time and headaches down the road.

But before we finish this section, we need to also look into the limitations of version control in Fabric:

- In GitHub, only cloud versions are supported; on-premises setups aren't. Also, you can't commit files larger than 50 MB all at once. If your changes are bigger than that, you need to split them into smaller commits. Also, GitHub doesn't support cross-geo checks, which can cause issues if your team works in different regions.
- In Azure DevOps, the user you connect with must be the same one you use in Fabric. This connection also won't work if your company uses certain security policies like IP Conditional Access. If your workspace and Git repositories are in different regions, your admin must allow data to move between them. The commit size limit is 125 MB.

Table 8-1 provides an overview of these limitations.

Table 8-1. Comparison of limitations of version control in GitHub and Azure DevOps

Limitations	GitHub	Azure DevOps
Cloud or on-premises	Only available in the cloud version	Available as cloud and on-premises
Max commit size	50 MB	125 MB (25 MB with connector)
Cross-geo support	No cross-geo validation	The admin must enable cross-geo exports
User account	Any Git account will work	The user must be the same in Fabric and Azure DevOps
IP Conditional Access policy	Supported	Not supported if enabled

When you're setting up version control in Fabric, keep in mind that only workspace admins can connect or disconnect Git repositories. Once they're connected, anyone with access to the workspace can work on the content. Also, workspaces with template apps installed can't use Git integration.

Being aware of these limitations helps you plan version control better and avoid surprises during collaboration and deployment.

Power BI Project Files

Working with data and analyzing it is not just about building a report and publishing it. You need to manage changes, keep track of what's been done, and make sure multiple people can work on the same solution without breaking anything. You may also already know that it's not possible for multiple people to work simultaneously on the same Power BI *.pbix* file. That's where Power BI Project files (*.pbip*) come in. They separate the report and the semantic model into different files, which makes it much easier for multiple people to work on the same thing at the same time, improves version control by making changes more visible, allows reuse of parts of a project, and generally makes collaboration more efficient.

Saving a Power BI Project File

We have three options for how to save a Power BI file in Power BI Desktop: as a Power BI file (*.pbix*), as a Power BI template file (*.pbit*), or as a Power BI project file (*.pbip*). We'll cover these options in this section. Figure 8-15 shows the menu that appears when you save a Power BI file, where you can choose from these options.

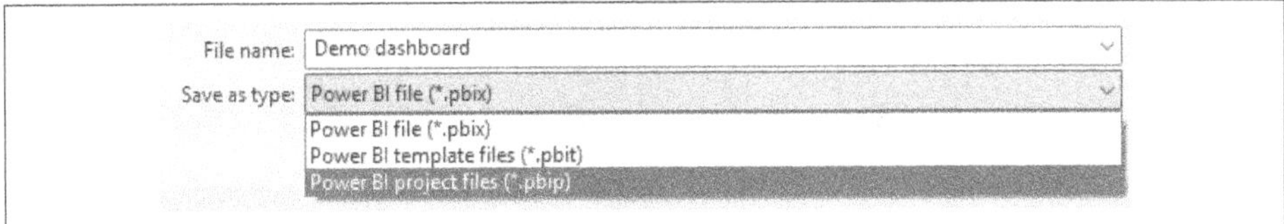

Figure 8-15. The three options for saving a Power BI file

Saving a Power BI report as a *.pbix* file creates a single file in which the report and its semantic model are combined. Power BI projects work differently. Saving one as a Power BI project file creates a folder that contains two subfolders, one for the report and one for the semantic model, along with a *.gitignore* file and the *.pbip* file itself (see Figure 8-16).

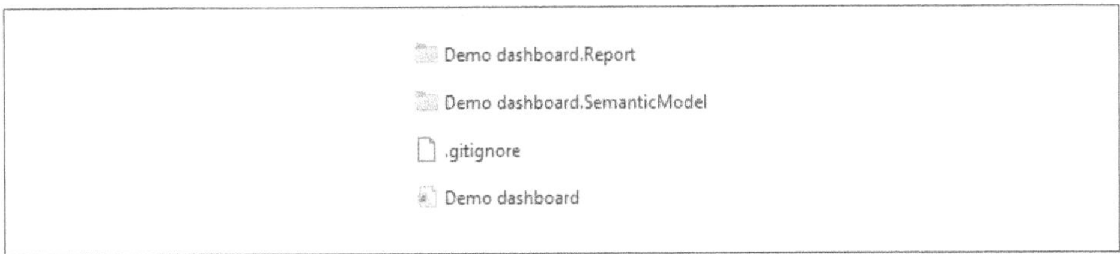

Figure 8-16. Content of a folder that's created when you save a report as a Power BI Project file

In our example, the project is named "Demo dashboard," and this name is automatically applied to the report and model subfolders. Each part of the folder structure represents a separate component of the project, which allows for more flexible management of the files.

Before we look further into *.pbip* files, you need to know that this feature is still in preview. This means you first need to activate it in Power BI Desktop by going to File > Options and settings > Options > Preview features. Then, in the features list, select "Power BI Project (.pbip) save option" and save the changes. Then, restart Power BI Desktop and save your work as a project file (see Figure 8-17).

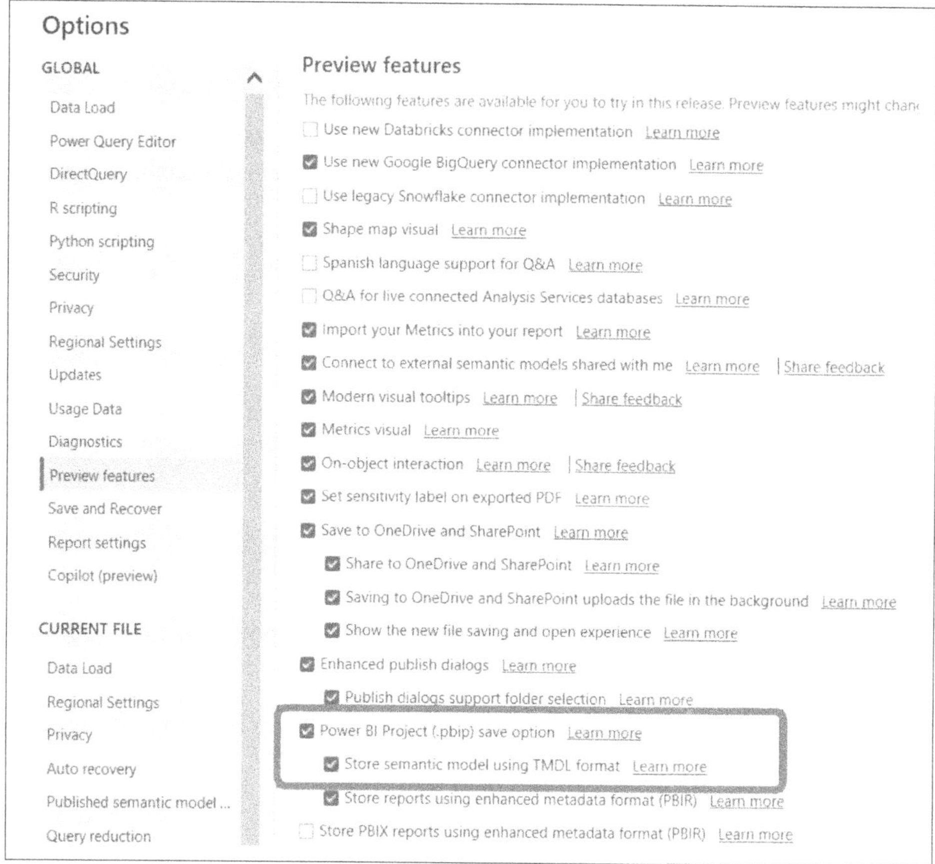

Figure 8-17. Activating Power BI project files in the Power BI settings because they're in preview

After you save a Power BI report as a Power BI project and open the file again (for example, by clicking on the *.pbip* file in the folder you created), at the top of the screen, you'll see at the end of the line of text at the top of the Power BI Desktop screen a parenthetical note: "(Power BI Project)." This indicates that a Power BI project file has been opened (see Figure 8-18).

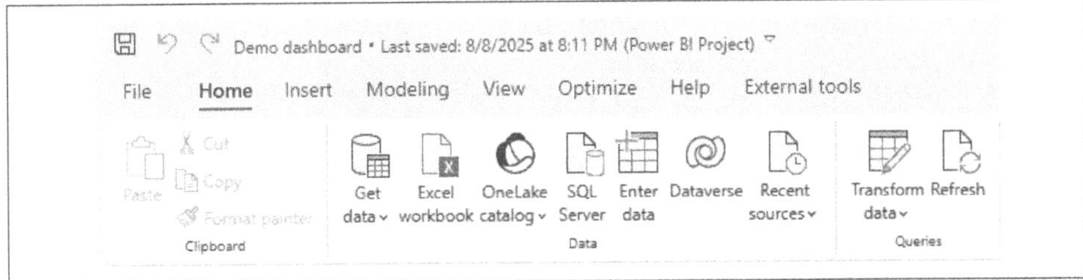

Figure 8-18. What we see at the top of the page if we open a Power BI project file

Clicking the small arrow to the right of the parenthetical note reveals additional details about the file, including the locations of the report and the semantic model (see Figure 8-19). Clicking any of the file paths directly opens the folder location.

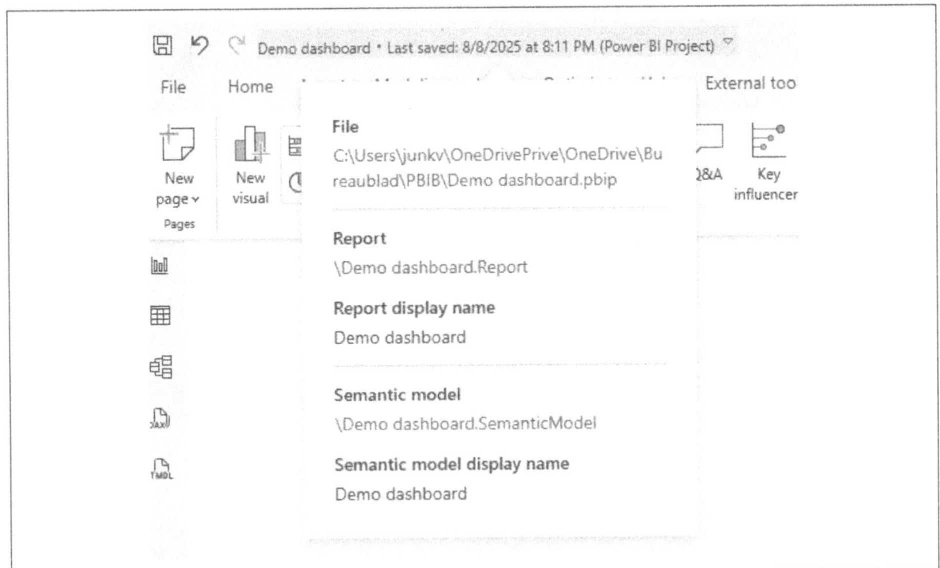

Figure 8-19. Clicking the project name to open a pop-up with file and folder details

Benefits of Using Power BI Project Files

So why use Power BI project files? One of the main benefits is that they let you make changes outside of Power BI Desktop. Because the report and semantic model are stored separately, you can use tools like Visual Studio Code (VS Code) to edit the text definitions directly. This is particularly useful when you're updating multiple measures or making widespread changes, because you won't have to click through all items individually in Power BI Desktop.

Another benefit is that the folder structure makes version control easier. When everything is in one *.pbix* file, tracking small changes in Git is not really possible. But with Power BI projects, the files are split, and that makes it easier for you to see what exactly changed in a commit: the model, the report, or both.

Finally, using project files makes reuse more straightforward. You can copy parts of the project, like a report page or model object, into another project without having to rebuild it from scratch.

It's also important to note that using project files doesn't change the end-user experience. A report saved as a *.pbix* file and another saved as a *.pbip* file will look and behave the same in Power BI Desktop and the service. The difference lies in how the files are stored, managed, and maintained, which is especially relevant for developers.

Limitations of Power BI Project Files

You also need to be aware of several practical limitations when you're working with Power BI project files. Power BI Desktop does not automatically detect changes made with external tools, so any edits you perform outside of Desktop will only appear after you restart the application. Features like sensitivity labels and report page synonyms are not supported, and that can affect governance and metadata management. The *.pbip* files also have a maximum path length of 260 characters by default, so you need to use short folder paths to avoid save errors. Additionally, you can't save *.pbip* files directly to OneDrive or SharePoint; doing so can create syncing problems and potentially cause failed save operations.

Reusable Assets in Power BI

When working with Power BI, we often create multiple reports, build different semantic models, and set up data connections repeatedly. Many of these don't need to be rebuilt each time, and we also want to avoid starting from scratch every single time.

A better approach involves using *reusable assets*, which are files or objects that capture parts of our work, such as report templates, data source definitions, and existing semantic models. We can reuse these assets in other projects, and that not only saves us time but also maintains consistency across teams and environments.

In this section, we'll explore three types of reusable assets: Power BI template files (*.pbit*), Power BI data source files (*.pbids*), and shared semantic models. Each one serves a different purpose, but all of them make developing in Power BI more efficient and organized.

Power BI Template Files

In Power BI Desktop, we can save a report as a template file. A *template* captures the structure of a report, allowing us or others in our organization to use it as a starting point for new reports. This is helpful when we need to use the same layout, model, or queries repeatedly. When we save a Power BI report as a Power BI template, we get a single file (*.pbit*) that includes the following parts of our report:

- Report pages, visuals, and other visual elements
- The semantic model definition, including schema, relationships, and measures
- Power Query definitions (including parameters)

A template contains the structure of the report (pages, visuals, model, and queries), but not the data itself. When we open a Power BI template file, Power BI asks us to connect to the data source to load data. Templates are therefore useful for reuse and standardization.

Creating a Power BI Template File

To create a template file from a Power BI report, you simply save it as a *.pbit* file instead of a *.pbix* file. This doesn't overwrite the *.pbix* file, but it creates a new file. Figure 8-20 shows the menu option you see when saving the report.

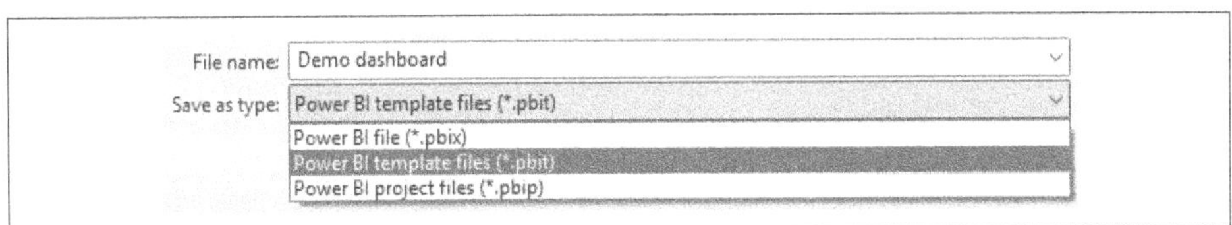

Figure 8-20. The Power BI option for saving a template file

Then, you click Save, and Power BI will bring up a screen where you can write a description of the template before the system saves it (see Figure 8-21). As always, we recommend that you write a clear description, for the sake of both your coworkers and yourself, since it might be a year or more before you look at the file again.

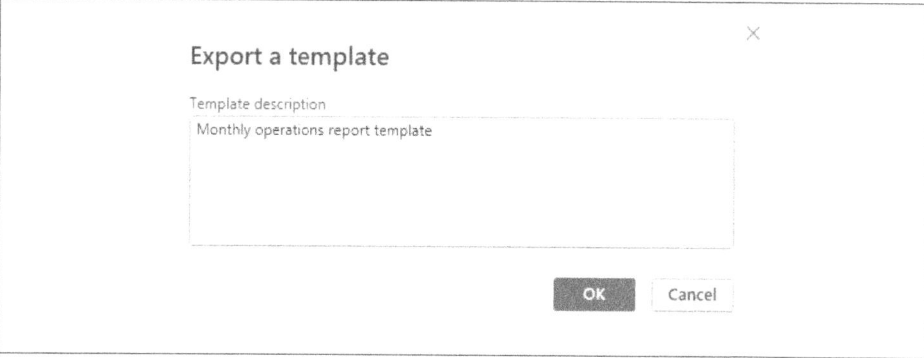

Figure 8-21. Screen where you can write a description of a template file before it's saved

Using Report Templates

To use a Power BI report template, you can open the file in Power BI Desktop either by launching Power BI Desktop itself or by double-clicking on the file. If any parameters were used in the Power BI file that you saved as a Power BI template, the first message you'll see will direct you to fill in the parameter value (see Figure 8-22).

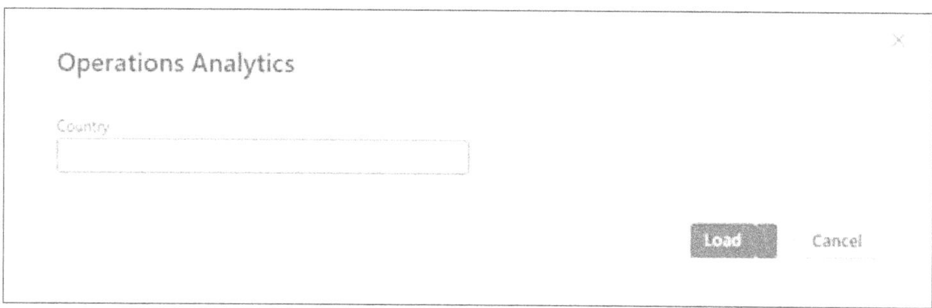

Figure 8-22. Screen where you can fill in parameter values if any parameters were used in the source file

After you fill in the parameter, Power BI will ask for the location of the data source. At this point, you can connect to the data by using your own credentials. Figure 8-23 shows a prompt for credentials for a web source.

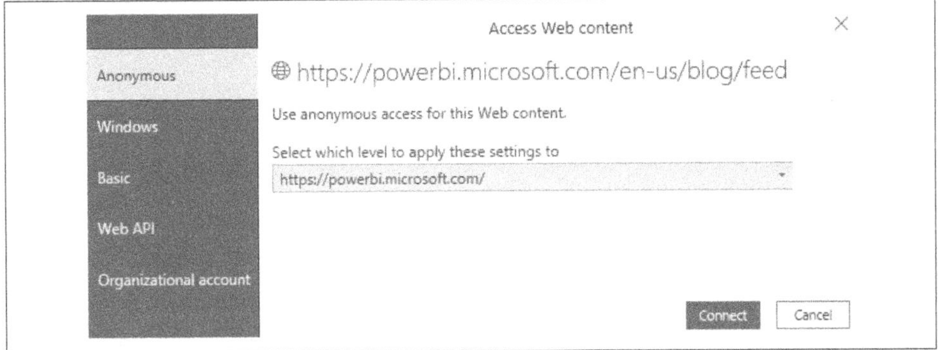

Figure 8-23. Filling in your own user credentials when opening a file and connecting to a Power BI template

You should know that when you try this with your own file, Power BI may not ask for your credentials if the original data source connection permission is still present. To test this whole process, remove the data source permission from the source file and then export the template. After that, Power BI will prompt you to enter credentials when you open the template.

Using report templates is an easy way to reuse report structures without copying the data. It saves time, helps maintain consistency, and simplifies sharing a standard starting point with others. In our daily work, we primarily use *.pbix* files, but *.pbit* templates are handy when we need to use the same layout, model, or queries repeatedly.

Power BI Data Source (.pbids) Files

Power BI template files are very useful for reusing the same report layout and semantic model relationships, but sometimes, we only want to reuse the connection from a Power BI file. We can do this by saving and then importing the data source connection as a Power BI Data source file (*.pbids*).

In a *.pbids* file, we don't have any visuals like in a Power BI template file; a *.pbids* file is a JSON text file that holds the data source connection. It doesn't contain data or queries, just the following connection information:

- The type of data source (for example, Excel or SharePoint)
- The connection details (such as a database or file path)
- Optional authentication settings, depending on the data source

Here's an example of what a *.pbids* file looks like:

```
{
  "version": "0.1",
  "connections": [
    {
      "details": {
        "protocol": "sharepoint-list",
        "address": {
          "url": "https://[url]"

        },
      }
    }
  ]
}
```

This code is from a Power BI data source file with a sharepoint list as a data source.

Creating a Power BI Data Source File

To create a Power BI data source file, we can export an existing data source connection from one of our files. To do this, we need to open a Power BI report in Power BI Desktop, go to Home > Transform data, and then select "Data source settings" (see Figure 8-24).

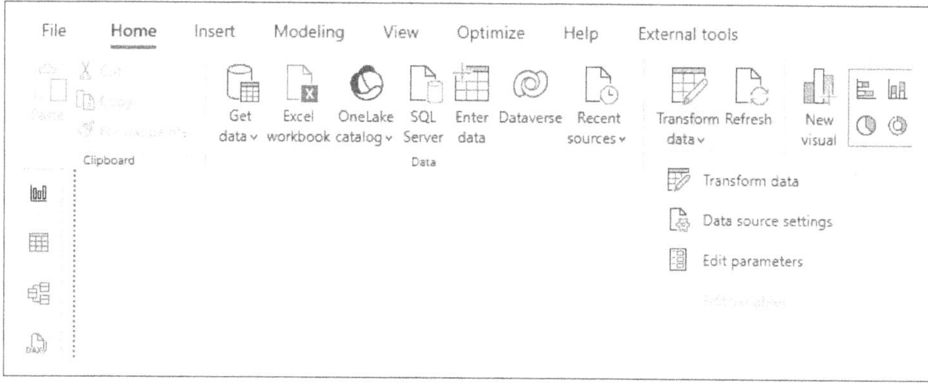

Figure 8-24. Opening the Data source settings to create a .pbids file

That will bring up all the data sources in the current file and the global permissions. If we want to export a data source in our current file, we can click on the data source and then click the Export PBIDS button at the bottom of the page (see Figure 8-25).

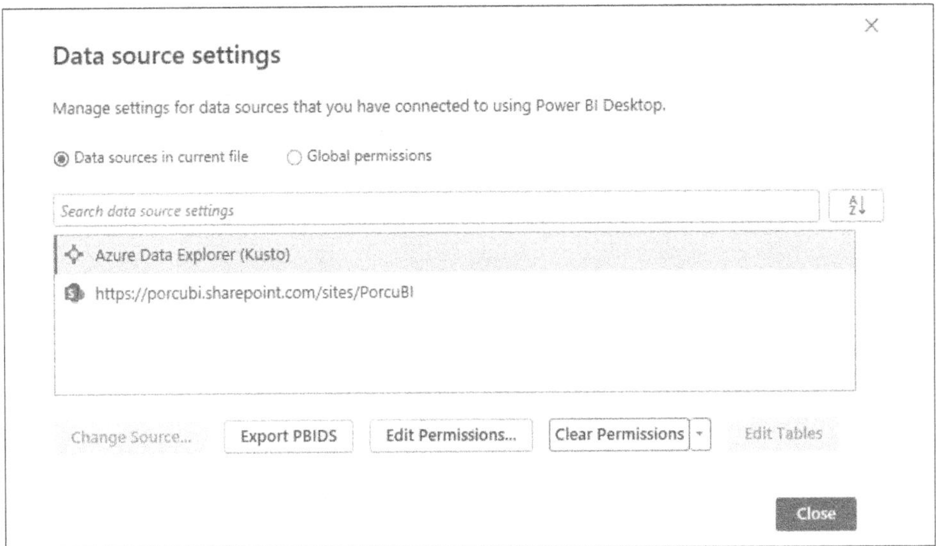

Figure 8-25. Exporting a .pbids file in the data source settings

Once you save the export, it will be stored as a *.pbids* file. An example of such an export is shown in Figure 8-26. If you open the file in a text editor, you'll see its JSON structure, which defines the connection information for the data source.

Figure 8-26. What a .pbids export looks like in a folder

After performing the export, we can easily reuse the *.pbids* file by double-clicking it. Even though, in our case, the *.pbids* file may not look like a typical Power BI file, we can double-click it and select Power BI as the tool. Then, Power BI will automatically establish the connection that's defined in the file, so we won't need to set it up manually.

Using Power BI data source files is a simple way to share and reuse data source settings. However, there are some limitations. Currently, a *.pbids* file can only contain a single data source, and trying to include more than one data source in a file will result in an error.

Power BI data source files make it easy to reuse and share data source connections across multiple reports. They save time, ensure consistency, and reduce the chances of errors when setting up connections.

Shared Semantic Models

Now that we have looked into Power BI template files and Power BI data source files, let's briefly explore another type of reusable asset: shared semantic models. While these models have the look and feel of a Power BI template, the data source connection is with the data source file. But a shared semantic model allows multiple reports to use the same underlying data model, including tables, relationships, and measures. This not only helps you avoid duplicating work but also ensures consistency across reports. For example, a shared semantic model can serve as the "one source of truth" within a company, where everyone creating a report connects to the same semantic model.

Connecting to a Shared Semantic Model

If you're wondering where to find a shared semantic model, note that you can use and import all semantic models published to a Power BI workspace where you have access and editing rights. To see which semantic models are available, go to Home > Get data > Power BI semantic models (see Figure 8-27).

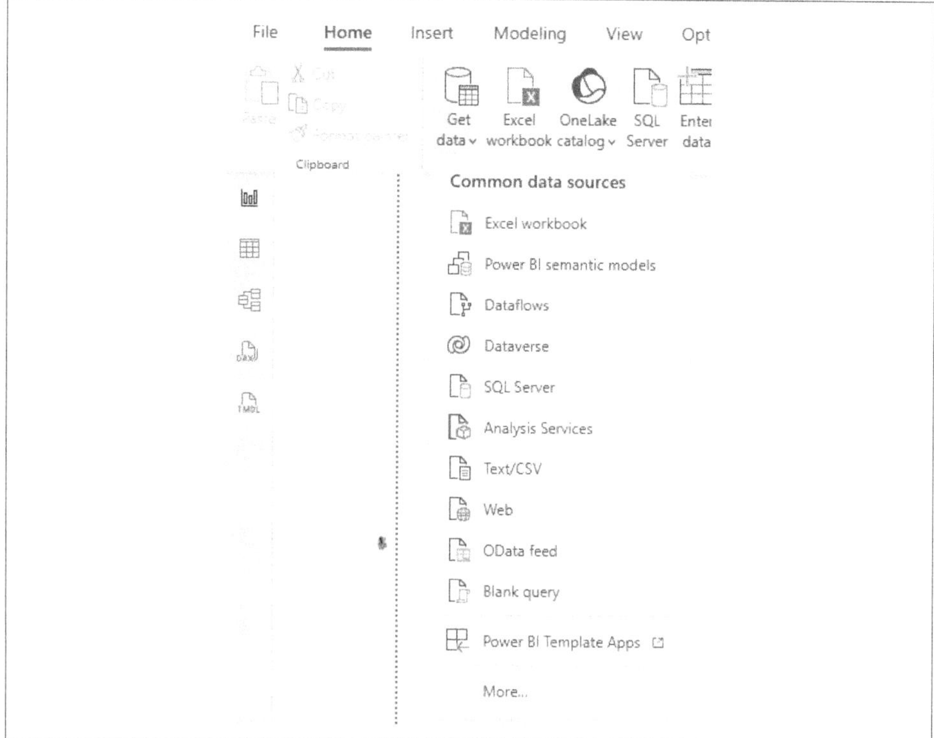

Figure 8-27. Clicking Get data > Power BI semantic models

This will display all the semantic models that are available to connect to. In our example, some models have a "Master data" endorsement (see Figure 8-28). As we mentioned in Chapter 7, this endorsement indicates that the model is considered core, trusted data within the organization. Only users or groups authorized by the administrator can assign this endorsement, which indicates that the model is reliable and approved for use across reports.

OneLake catalog

Discover data from your org and beyond and use it to create reports

All | My data | Endorsed in your org | External data | Filter by keyword | Filter(1)

Name	Owner	Refreshed	Location	Endorsement	Sensitivity
Demo File	Valerie Junk	8/17/25, 11:30:38 A...	Test Workspace	Master data	—
RSS Feed	Valerie Junk	5/10/25, 11:00:10 P...	Live Workspace	—	—
Examples	Valerie Junk	9/7/24, 3:22:27 PM	Live Workspace	—	—
Power BI Action Driven Design Ideas	Valerie Junk	2/14/24, 7:12:15 PM	Portfolio	—	—
Burn Down Chart Tutorial	Valerie Junk	12/29/24, 3:40:13 P...	My Workspace	—	—
Before - After Dashboard	Valerie Junk	8/17/23, 3:27:12 PM	Portfolio	—	—
Social Media Dashboard 2022	Valerie Junk	8/16/23, 2:10:44 PM	Portfolio	—	—
Sales Accessibility	Valerie Junk	2/24/24, 7:05:20 PM	Portfolio	—	—

Connect | Cancel

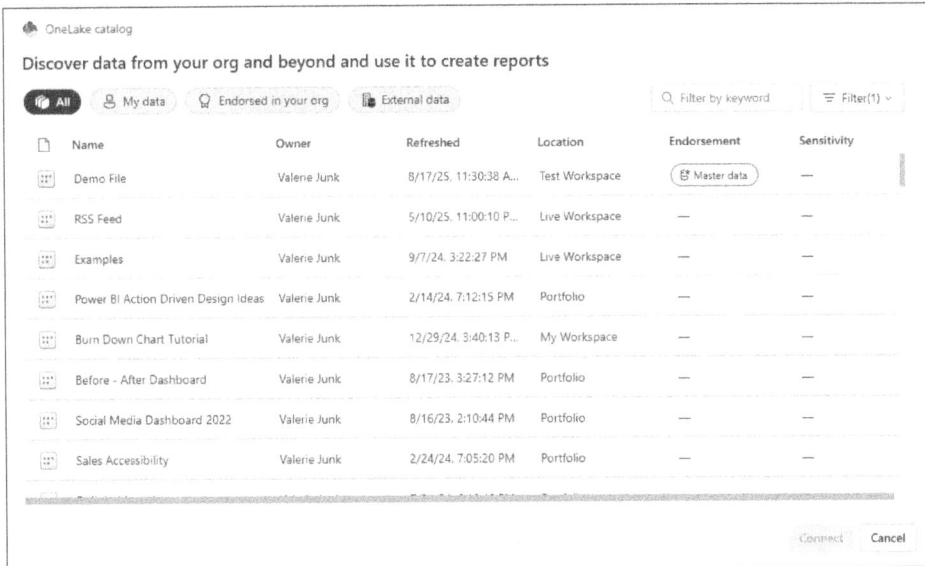

Figure 8-28. Available semantic models, one of which has a "Master data" endorsement

Also remember from Chapter 7 that semantic models can also have other endorsements, like Promoted or Certified, which help users identify models that are recommended or meet organizational quality standards (see Figure 8-29).

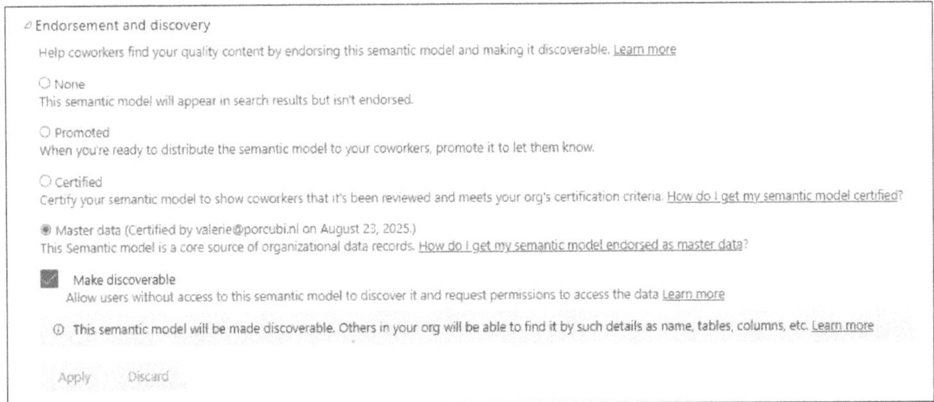

Figure 8-29. Different endorsement types that can be assigned to each semantic model

Using shared semantic models, teams can quickly build reports and visuals without recreating the underlying data logic. The models ensure consistency in tables, relationships, and calculations across multiple reports. We can create additional measures if we need to, but changes don't affect the original model.

On the other hand, we'll encounter some limitations when using a shared semantic model. Because the connection is live, we can't edit the model itself—we can't change relationships, queries, or existing calculations. We can create additional DAX measures in our report, but these changes are not saved back to the original model. Adding too many measures this way can slowly turn the report into a separate version, which reduces consistency.

Deployment Pipelines

Creating items in a workspace is just one part of the equation. Another part is working in a development environment, where you'll have a different workspace for each stage in the development cycle. This could be, for instance, one workspace each for development, testing, and production.

You can move and deploy items among workspaces with built-in deployment pipelines in Microsoft Fabric. If you have any experience in Azure DevOps, you'll notice that deployment pipelines in Fabric and Azure DevOps work in almost the same way. The main difference is that you build deployment pipelines in Fabric through a UI and configure them with a mouse, while you configure pipelines in Azure DevOps mainly with YAML code.

Example Scenario

To help you understand how a deployment pipeline works, we've created the following development scenario that consists of three-steps: development, testing, and production. In the testing and production steps, you must deploy the items from the previous step to move the process towards putting the final version into production. Figure 8-30 provides an illustration of this scenario.

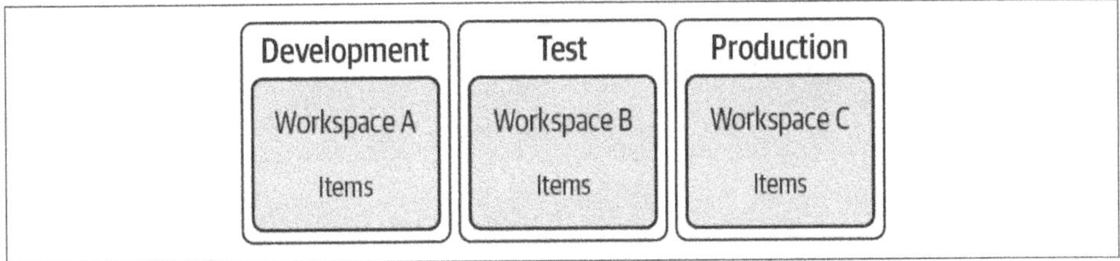

Figure 8-30. Example scenario for deployment pipelines

We use workspaces A, B, and C for development, testing, and production, respectively. Initially, only workspace A contains the following items:

- A semantic model
- A copy job
- A lakehouse

We'll use this scenario throughout this section to help you understand how to create, configure, and use deployment pipelines in Microsoft Fabric.

Creating a Deployment Pipeline

You create a deployment pipeline in Microsoft Fabric "outside" a workspace. A deployment pipeline cannot exist inside a workspace because it copies items and content from a workspace. If it existed inside a workspace, it would copy itself in each deployment.

You can find the "Deployment pipelines" button in the main menu in Microsoft Fabric (see Figure 8-31).

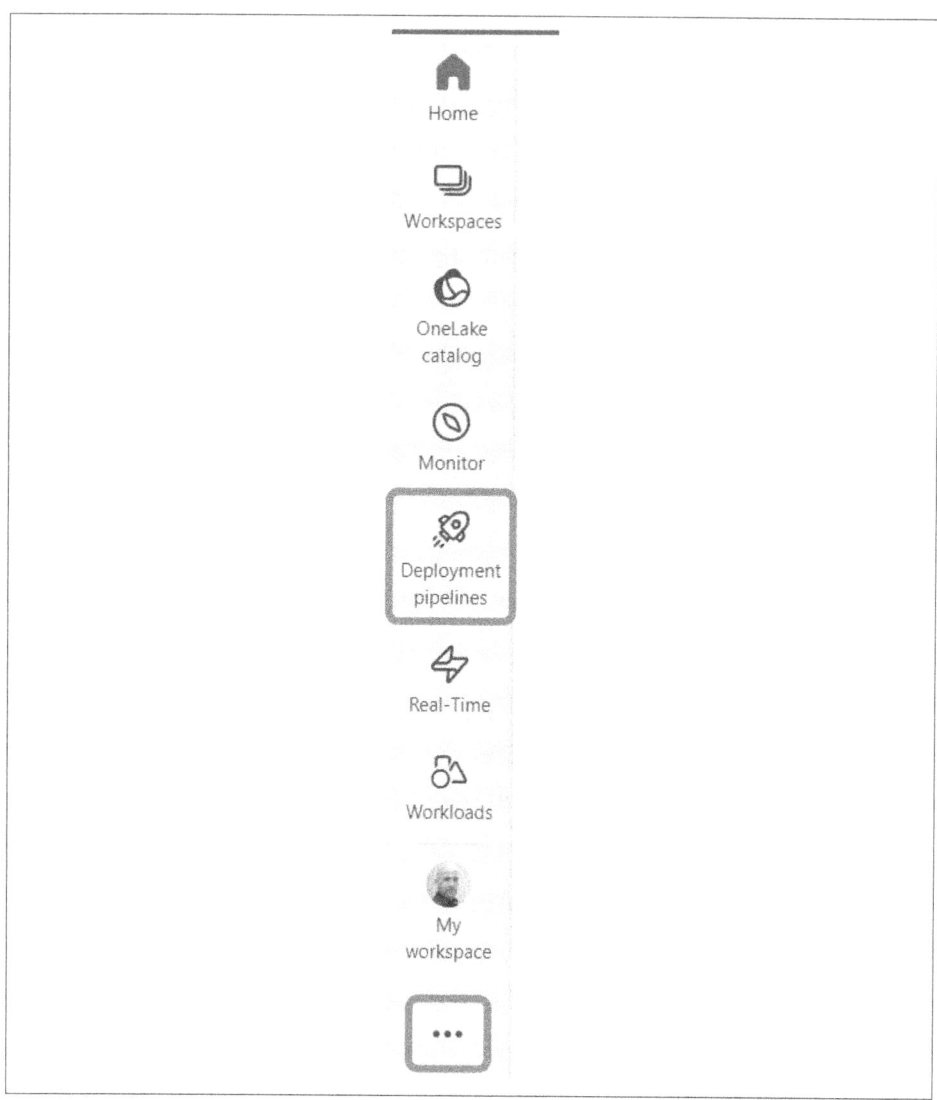

Figure 8-31. "Deployment pipelines" button in the main menu of Microsoft Fabric

If you can't see the "Deployment pipelines" button, click the three-dot context menu at the bottom. Clicking either one will bring up the splash screen shown in Figure 8-32, unless you've already created deployment pipelines. In this case, you'll see a list of them instead of the splash screen.

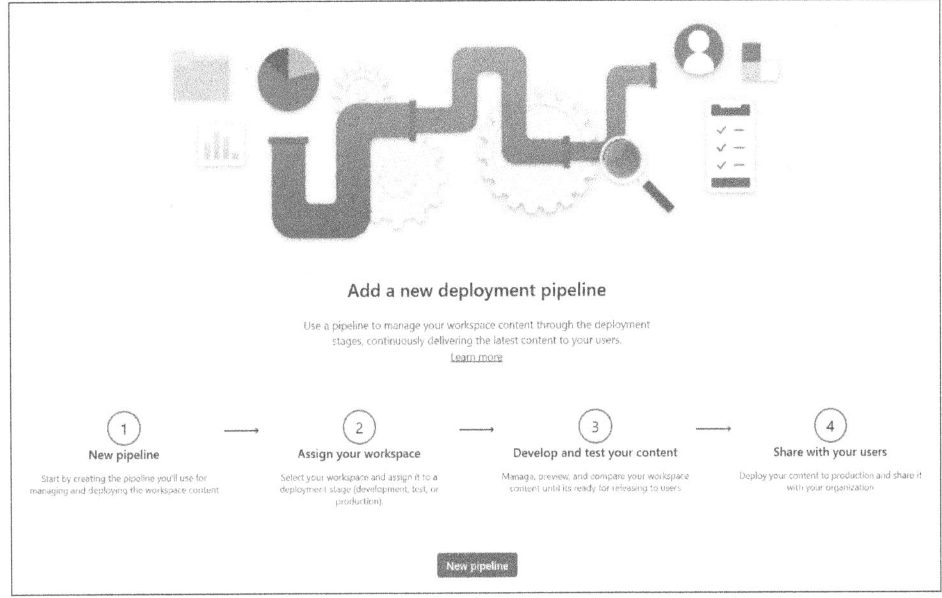

Figure 8-32. Splash screen you'll see if you haven't created a deployment pipeline

The splash screen details the four steps you must go through to build your deployment pipeline:

1. New pipeline: create a new deployment pipeline.
2. Assign your workspace: select the workspaces to assign to each stage in the process.
3. Develop and test your content: do your daily work and develop the items and content you need to support your business requirements.
4. Share with your users: deploy the items and content to the workspaces to share them with your users.

Step 4 implicitly acknowledges that you do not share your development workspace with your users—they'll only have access to the testing and production workspaces.

To start the process, click the "New pipeline" button in Figure 8-32. It will take you to the screen shown in Figure 8-33.

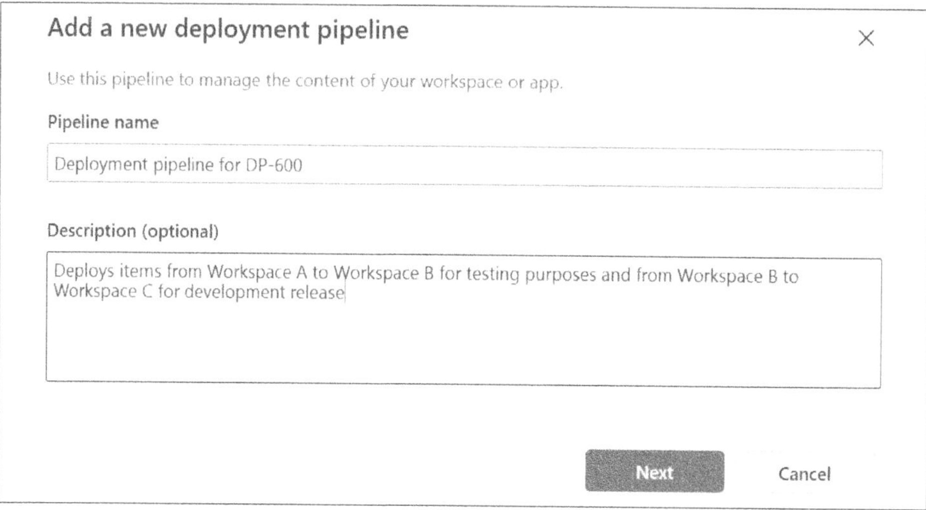

Figure 8-33. Creating a new deployment pipeline

Then, type in a name and a description for the pipeline in the respective boxes. In our example, we've typed in a demo name and description that adhere to the format in this training guide, but you should use your own name and description.

Then, click the Next button to go to the deployment pipeline configuration screen (see Figure 8-34).

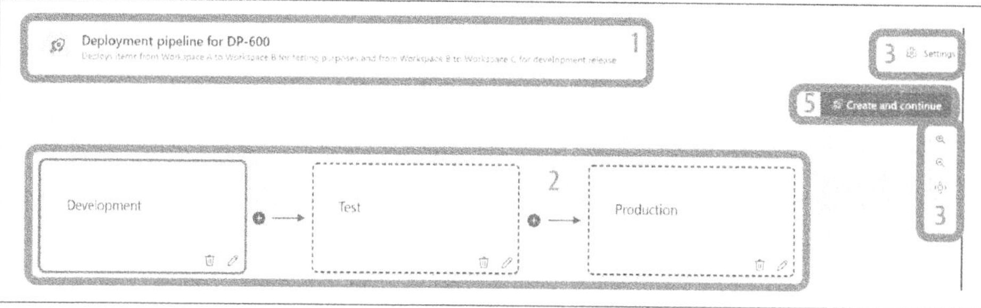

Figure 8-34. Deployment pipeline configuration screen

We've highlighted some important areas (numbered 1–5) in the figure:

Pipeline name and description (area 1)
: These are the ones we just typed when we created the deployment pipeline.

Stages of the deployment pipeline (area 2)
: These are the three default stages in the deployment pipeline, and in each stage, there's a trash can and an editing pencil. You can click the trash can to delete the

stage, and you can click the editing pencil to take you to the screen where you can change the settings for each stage (see Figure 8-35).

Settings (area 3)
: Here, you can only change the pipeline's name and description of the deployment pipeline.

Zoom and pan buttons (area 4)
: You can use these to zoom in and out of and pan over the deployment pipeline canvas.

"Create and continue" button (area 5)
: You click this to complete the pipeline creation process.

Each deployment pipeline must have at least 2 stages and a maximum of 10 stages. So, if you delete one stage from the default three stages and don't add a new one, you won't be able to delete a second one.

Figure 8-35. Screen where you can edit stage settings

The stage settings screen includes fields where you can view and change the stage's name and description, plus a "Set as public" slider you can use to make the stage viewable or not viewable by the public. By default, the final stage of a pipeline is public. A consumer of a public stage who doesn't have access to the pipeline sees it as a regular workspace, without the stage name and deployment pipeline icon on the workspace page next to the workspace name. You can have as many public stages as you want or none at all.

In our example, we're not changing any of the settings, so we just click the "Create and continue" button to create the deployment pipeline and make it visible (see Figure 8-36). Next, we can begin to configure the stages and the deployment process.

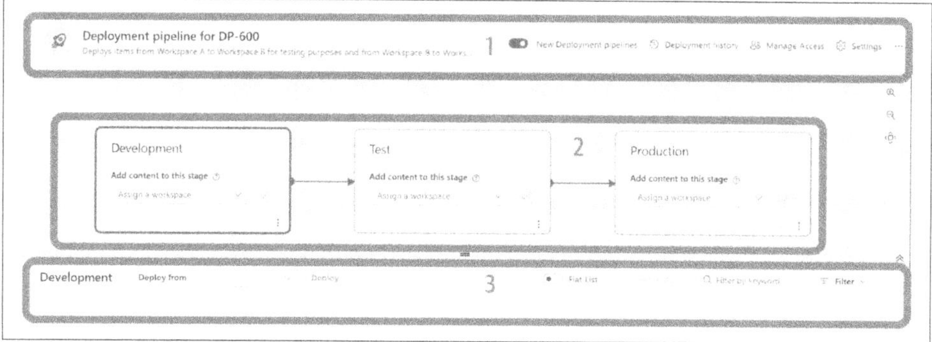

Figure 8-36. Deployment pipeline, ready for stage configuration

In the figure, we've highlighted some areas (numbered 1–3) to focus on. We'll go into them in detail in the following sections.

Top menu (area 1)

In the top menu, you can find the options and main settings for the deployment pipeline, including Deployment history, Manage Access, Settings, and Delete pipeline (the last of which is in the overflow context menu to the right).

New deployment pipelines. This option is available at the time of this writing, and when it's enabled, you have access to an updated UI for handling and configuring the deployment pipeline. We expect this option to be removed from future versions of Microsoft Fabric.

Deployment history. Click this option to view the usage history of this specific deployment pipeline. Later in this section, we will dive into the details of the content.

Manage access. Click this option to go to a screen where you can configure who has access to the deployment pipeline (see Figure 8-37).

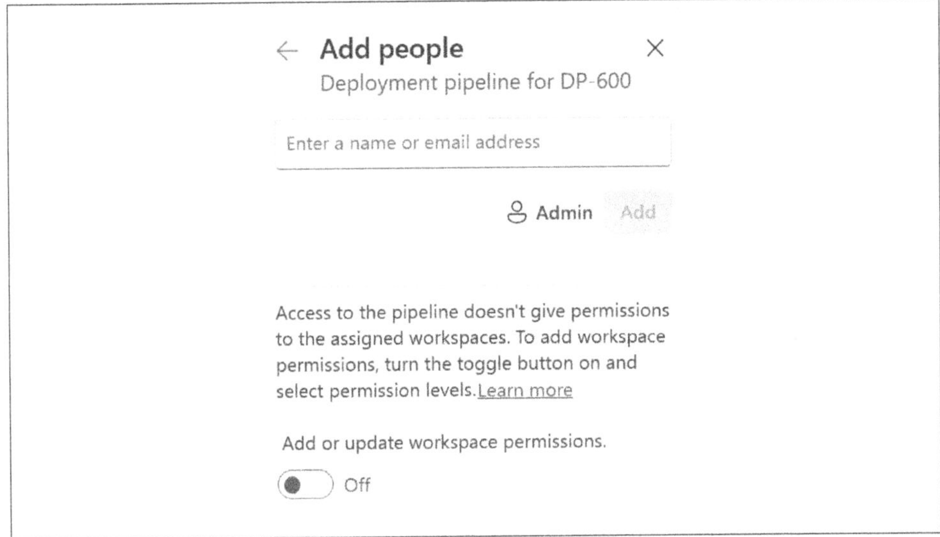

Figure 8-37. Deployment pipeline access control

This screen also gives you the option to add new people or groups to the deployment pipeline. Notice that there is only one role (Admin) for a deployment pipeline.

In addition, there's an "Add or update workspace permissions" slider that lets you grant access to the workspaces from the deployment pipeline. This setting is off by default, which means admins can manage the deployment pipeline without having access to the underlying items or data in each of the workspaces. If you want admins of this deployment pipeline to also have access to the workspaces from the same deployment pipeline, then set the slider to the On position when you add those admins.

Settings. Click this option to change name and description of the deployment pipeline.

Canvas (area 2)

This area displays the three configured stages: Development, Test, and Production. However, no workspaces have been configured for each stage yet, so you can configure them by using the drop-down menu in each stage (see Figure 8-38).

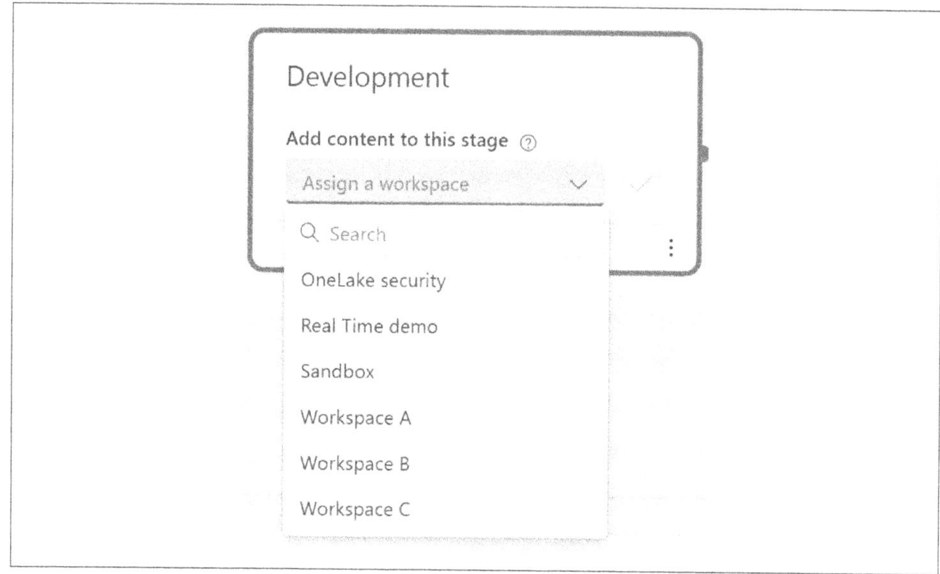

Figure 8-38. Drop-down menu for selecting a workspace for the development stage in a deployment pipeline

This figure includes a list of six workspaces, and we choose Workspace A because it's the one from the scenario we need to use.

Then, we click the checkmark, which will bring up a warning (see Figure 8-39).

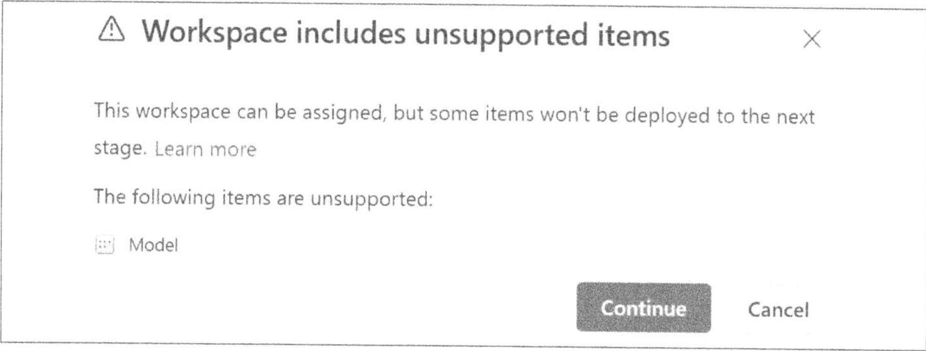

Figure 8-39. Warning that there are unsupported deployment pipeline items in the workspace

This warning indicates that some items are not supported by the built-in deployment pipelines in Microsoft Fabric. In Workspace A, we have three items as listed in the beginning of this subsection. But the semantic model named "Model" is not supported by the deployment pipeline.

The list of supported items in the deployment pipelines can be found in the Introduction to Deployment pipelines link from Microsoft Learn (*https://oreil.ly/vXTxp*). In this link, we can read that semantic models are only supported (at the time of writing this book and in preview) if they originate from a *.pbix* file and if they aren't Push datasets. Also note that we created this specific semantic model from the scenario directly in the Fabric UI to give you examples of some of the items that are not currently supported.

Development stage details (area 3)

When you click the Continue button on the warning screen, area 3 from Figure 8-36 gets updated with the information shown in Figure 8-40.

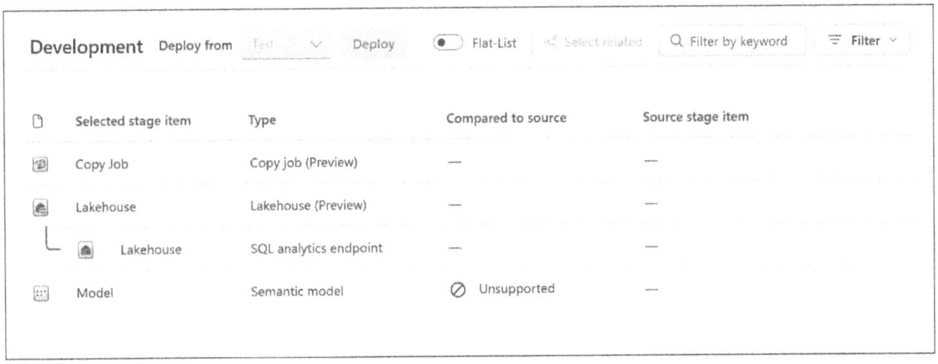

Development Deploy from Test Deploy Flat-List Select related Filter by keyword Filter

	Selected stage item	Type	Compared to source	Source stage item
	Copy Job	Copy job (Preview)	—	—
	Lakehouse	Lakehouse (Preview)	—	—
	└ Lakehouse	SQL analytics endpoint	—	—
	Model	Semantic model	Unsupported	—

Figure 8-40. Development stage details area for a stage with assigned workspace

Area 3 displays the items from Workspace A, with a status of Unsupported in the "Compared to source" column for the semantic model.

The options at the top of area 3 let you show all items in the entire deployment pipeline, with a new column to give you the location (workspace). You can find this in the Filter drop-down menu to the far right in the top menu. You can also search for an item by name in the field right next to the Filter menu. In addition, you can use the Filter option to find an item by its type and by its status in the current stage, compared to its status in the previous stage (which is also known as the *source*).

Perform all the same steps to assign Workspaces B and C to Test and Production and finish creating your deployment pipeline.

Configuring a Deployment Pipeline

We've already covered some high-level aspects of configuring a deployment pipeline, such as security and stages. But we also have the option to configure rules for each stage, use the deployment pipeline to copy items among stages, and promote them for the next development stage. For example, we can give each stage different databases or different query parameters. The development stage might query sample data from the database, while the test and production stages might query the entire database.

When you deploy content among pipeline stages, configuring deployment rules enables you to allow changes to content while keeping some settings intact. For example, you can define a rule for a semantic model in a production stage to point to a production database. Once you've successfully defined or changed a rule, you redeploy the content. The deployed content inherits the value defined in the deployment rule and always applies the rule as long as it is unchanged and valid.

Only a subset of items from a workspace is eligible to have rules applied to it. Table 8-2 lists these items.

Table 8-2. Items that can and can't have specific deployment pipeline rules applied to them

Item	Data source rule	Parameter rule	Default lakehouse rule	Details
Dataflow Gen1	✓	✓	×	Use this to determine the values of the data sources or parameters for a specific dataflow Gen1.
Semantic model	✓	✓	×	Use this to determine the values of the data sources or parameters for a specific semantic model.
Paginated report	✓	×	×	This is defined for the data sources of each paginated report. Use it to determine the data sources of the paginated report.
Mirrored database	✓	×	×	This is defined for the data sources of each mirrored database.
Notebook	×	×	✓	Use this to determine the default lakehouse for a specific notebook.

To work with rules in the deployment pipelines, you must be the owner of the item in the workspace you are trying to configure. This is a minor limitation to being the admin of the deployment pipeline.

When you're creating a new rule, you'll see a small lightning icon in the stage (see Figure 8-41).

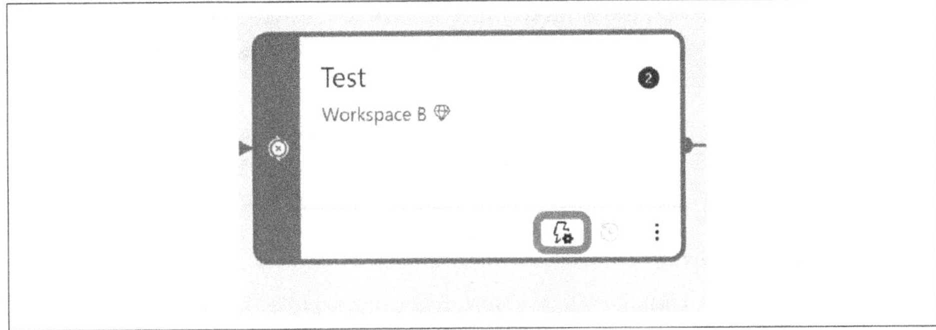

Figure 8-41. Rules setting in a stage from a deployment pipeline

Click the icon to bring up the "Set deployment rules" screen (see Figure 8-42).

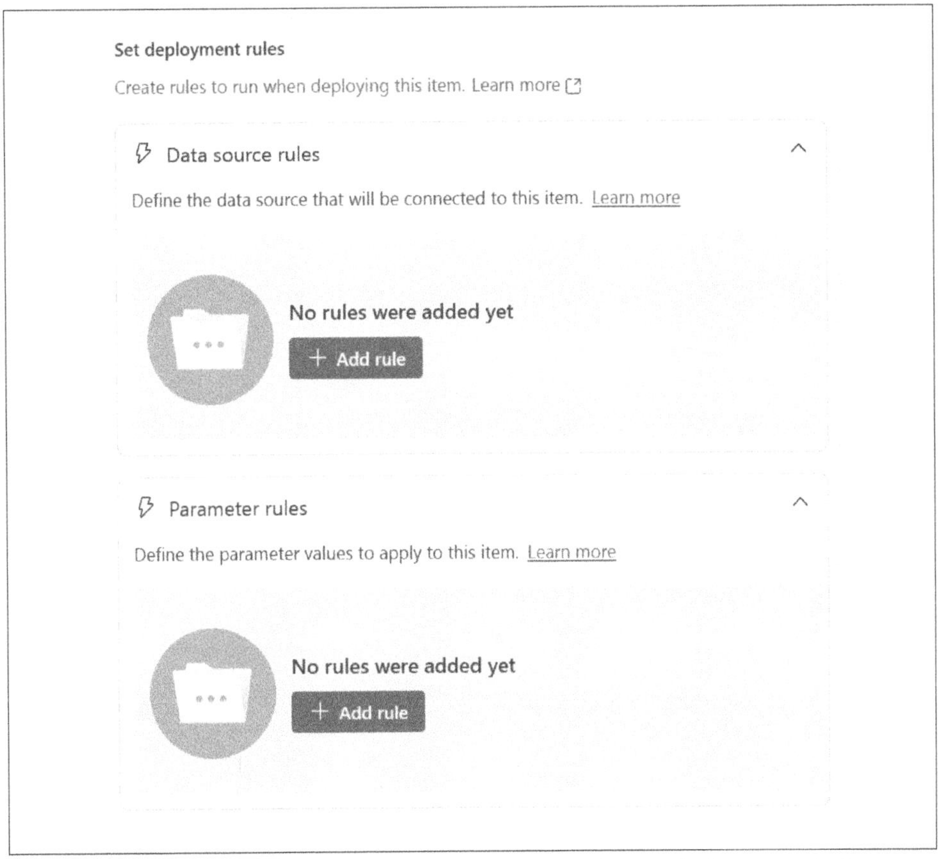

Set deployment rules

Create rules to run when deploying this item. Learn more

Data source rules

Define the data source that will be connected to this item. Learn more

No rules were added yet

+ Add rule

Parameter rules

Define the parameter values to apply to this item. Learn more

No rules were added yet

+ Add rule

Figure 8-42. Screen where you can add rules to an item from a deployment pipeline

Here, you can start adding the rules to the item. We've created a new semantic model from a *.pbix* file to show you the settings for this specific item. The setting for each supported item will be different.

There are two types of semantic model rules you can add: data source rules and the parameter rules. To add and define a data source rule, click the "+ Add rule" button in the "Data source rules" area of the screen and then do one of the following:

- Select a data source from a list.
- Select Other and manually add the new data source. Note that you can only select a data source of the same type.

To configure a parameter rule, follow the same process: click the "+ Add rule" in the "Parameter rules" section of the screen in Figure 8-42, select a parameter from the list of parameters, and select a parameter value to apply after each deployment (see Figure 8-43). The screen will show the current parameter value, and you can change it to whatever value you want to take effect after each deployment.

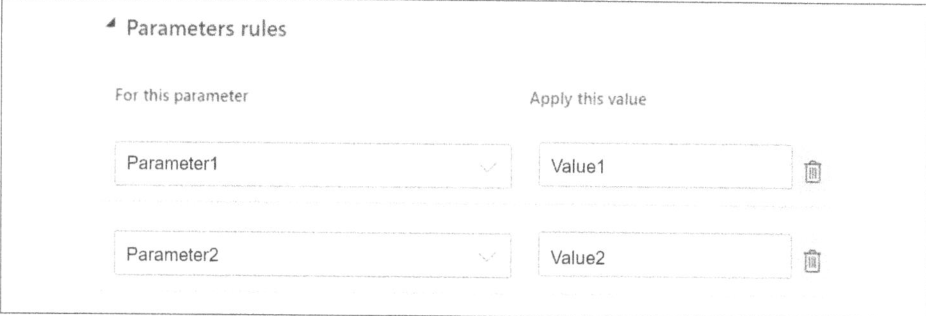

Figure 8-43. Configuring a parameter rule in a deployment pipeline

The DP-600 Exam does not cover how to define parameters for items, so just know that you can set parameter values in the deployment pipeline on each stage.

Once you've set the deployment rules, the deployment pipeline will be fully configured and ready for use. The next section will cover how to use the deployment pipeline, and it will also dive into the history of the deployment pipeline's execution.

Deploying Among Stages

Once you've created the deployment pipeline, you can begin to use it to promote items. You can do this in an all-in process or a cherry-picking process, in which you select only the specific items you want to deploy.

For example, you can select the Test stage from the deployment pipeline to bring up the screen shown in Figure 8-44.

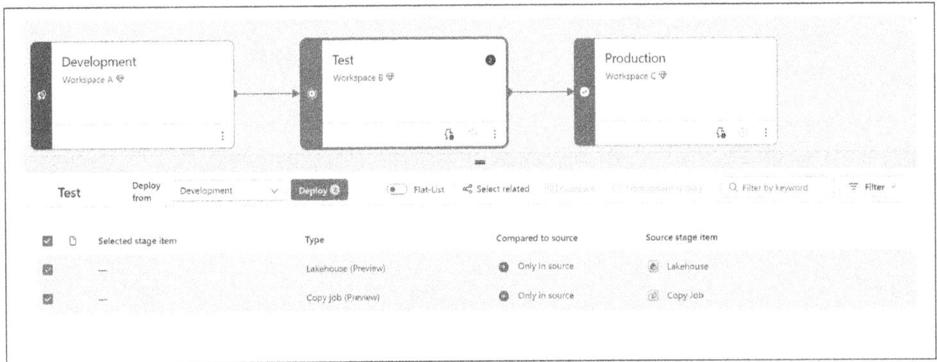

Figure 8-44. Test stage selected for deployment

Then, you can select the items you want to deploy, and that will make the Deploy button change to be clickable. (This is already done in the figure). Selecting only some of the available items is known as *cherry-picking*.

Notice the small, circled 2 in the Test stage. It indicates that the Test stage is unsynchronized on the number of items between the prior stage (Development) and the current stage (Test).

In the "Deploy from" drop-down menu, you can choose from which stage you want the deployment to read the items. In this case, you want to deploy from the Development stage to the Test stage.

Then, click the Deploy button to go to a screen like the one shown in Figure 8-45.

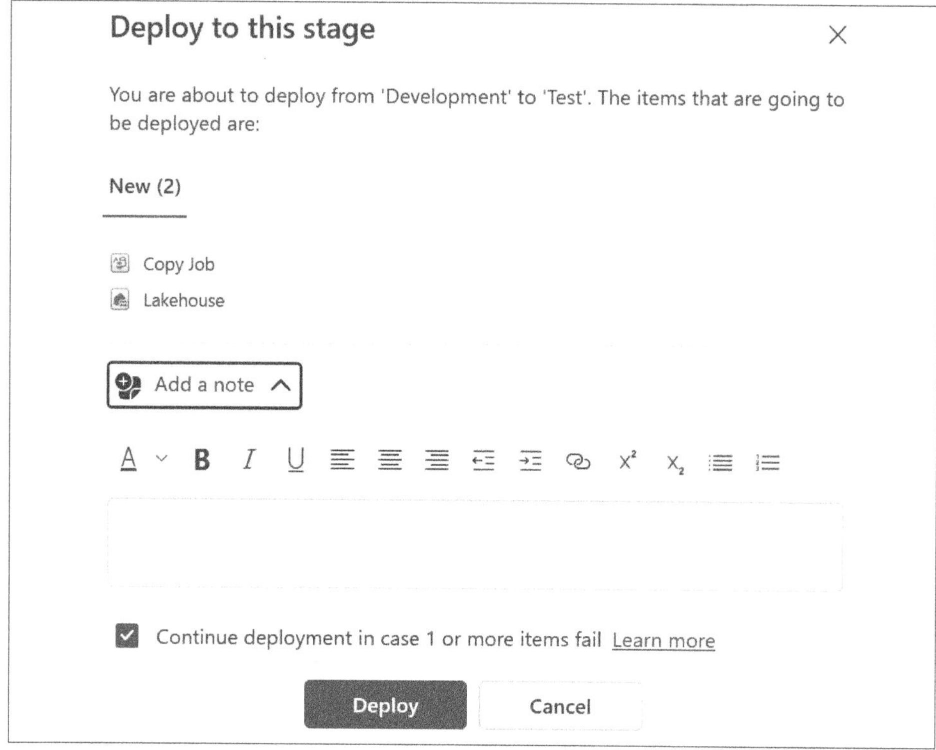

Deploy to this stage
You are about to deploy from 'Development' to 'Test'. The items that are going to be deployed are:
New (2)
Copy Job
Lakehouse
Add a note
Continue deployment in case 1 or more items fail
Learn more
Deploy
Cancel

Figure 8-45. Defining the deployment

Here, you can type in any notes you want to make about the deployment. If you wish, you can also check a box to indicate that you want the deployment to continue if one or more items fail. Whether or not you should check that box depends on your business needs and the requirements for your deployment.

Then, click the Deploy button to start the deployment pipeline and move the items from the source stage to the destination stage.

Deployment will take a few minutes, and then, Workspace B in our scenario will have the two supported items from the setup: the copy job and the lakehouse (see Figure 8-46).

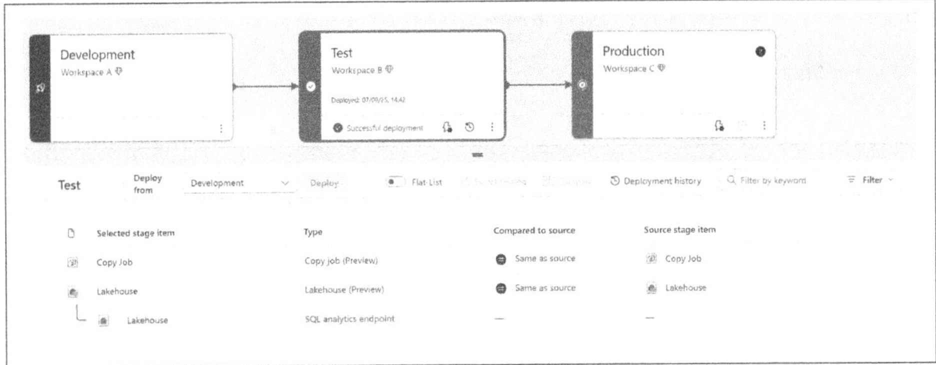

Figure 8-46. Screen showing a successful deployment pipeline

The screen shows that the status of the deployment to the Test stage is "Successful deployment," and it also shows the option to deploy from Test to Production.

Deployment History

Each time a deployment pipeline is executed, a row in the history is added for later governance and log analytics.

Figure 8-47 depicts a "Deployment history" screen showing the history of the deployment we just made.

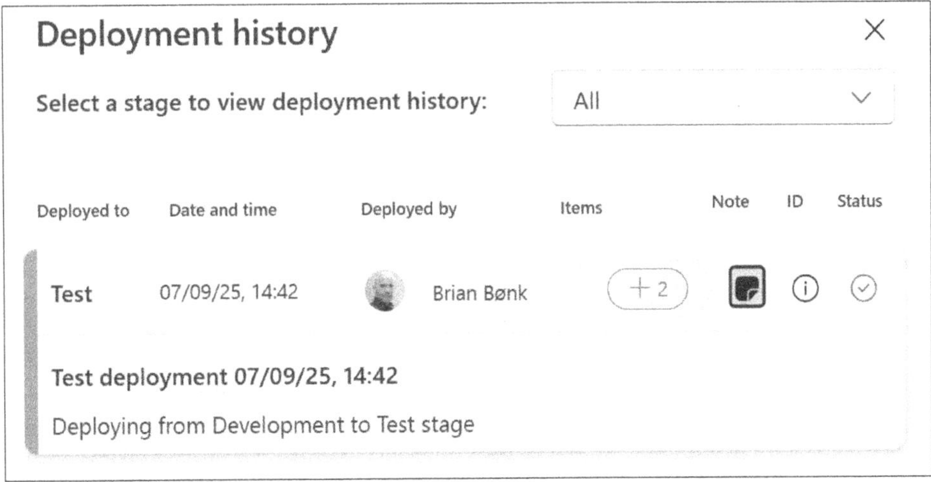

Figure 8-47. History of the current deployment pipeline

On the "Deployment history" screen, you can see the following:

- What stage the items have been deployed to
- The date and time of the deployment
- Who made the deployment
- An icon you can click to view the list of items that were deployed
- An icon you can click to view the notes from the deployment (e.g., "Deploying from Development to Test stage," per the figure)
- The unique ID (name) of the deployment
- The deployment status

You can also use the drop-down list at the top right to filter the history by selecting "All" or a specific destination stage.

At this point, you've created a full deployment pipeline, configured it, and executed the first deployment from the Development stage to the Test stage.

Deployment pipelines are good assets to use when working with the development cycle of items in workspaces. You can outsource the deployment among stages and remove the manual work of handling the different stage versions. As soon as you've created the deployment pipeline, the end user will be able to execute the deployment with just a few clicks of their mouse.

Performing Impact Analyses of Downstream Dependencies

It's helpful to think of every single item in your workspace, from a dataflow to a semantic model, as a piece of a larger puzzle. They all depend on each other, and changing one piece of a puzzle may cause problems if it doesn't fit or looks wrong. So when you update one piece, you need to understand which other pieces are going to be affected—or you might fix one small thing and unintentionally break ten others. This is a crucial skill for the DP-600 exam, but even more so for your real-world work as a Fabric professional.

The good news is that Microsoft Fabric gives you a great tool to help with this: the *lineage view*, which is a way to visualize all the dependencies within your workspace. You can see which dataflow feeds a lakehouse, which lakehouse feeds a semantic model, and which semantic model is used in which report. The lineage view shows you the connections among your data items so you can view the full picture before you make a change.

Let's go through a list of a few simple changes that can have big impacts:

Changing a dataflow
: Imagine you have a dataflow that's used to pull in sales data. You decide to change the name of a column from `customerid` to `customerId` to match a new naming convention. This may seem like a small cosmetic change, but it could break every semantic model, report, and dashboard that depends on that specific column name. Lineage view will show you every item that references that dataflow, so you'll know exactly where to check for broken dependencies.

Modifying a semantic model
: Let's say you have a semantic model with a bunch of measures that are used to calculate profits. You decide to adjust the DAX formula for one of those measures, but if a report or another semantic model is using that measure, the numbers will change—and that could lead to incorrect analyses.

Deleting a column from a lakehouse or data warehouse
: This is probably the most potentially harmful change you can make. If you delete a column from a data warehouse that's being used by a report, that report will simply break and show an error. But with the lineage view, you can identify all the affected items and create a plan to either update them or notify the people who own them.

Ultimately, performing an impact analysis is all about anticipating the consequences of your actions. So before you click Apply or Publish, you need to ask yourself, "What else is going to be affected by this change?" The lineage view in fabric is designed to help you answer that question in a simple, visual way.

Using the Lineage View

In every workspace in Microsoft Fabric, you have two options for viewing items: as the default list or as a lineage view.

The lineage view button is in the top-right corner of the workspace. Figure 8-48 shows you the full lineage view.

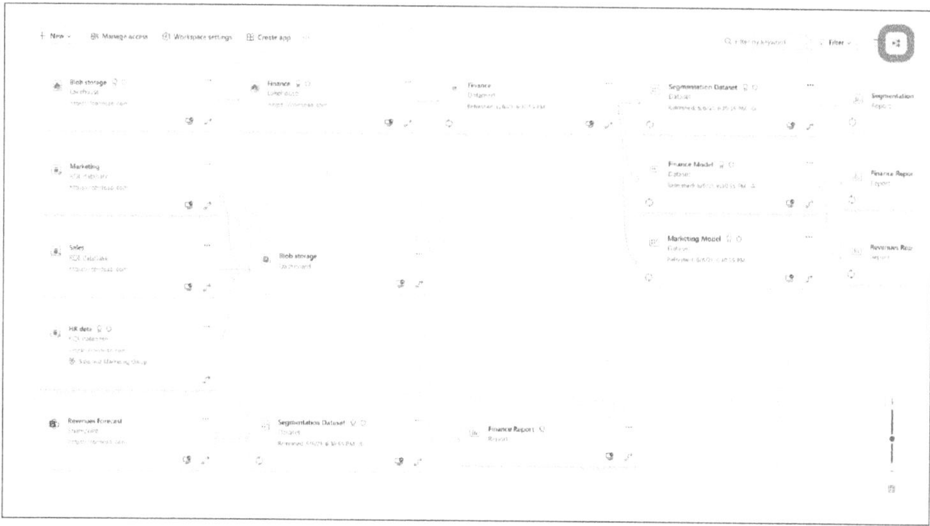

Figure 8-48. Lineage view in Microsoft Fabric

The lineage view shows you each item in the workspace, and their dependencies on each other. For instance, the Blob storage in the upper lefthand corner feeds data to the Finance lakehouse to its right.

You can select any item in the lineage view to highlight its connections and dependencies (see Figure 8-49).

In the figure, we've selected the Blob storage item we mentioned before, and the lineage view shows us the entire stream of dependencies from it. At least eight items are dependent on the Blob storage, so changing it could potentially impact all eight items that are downstream from it.

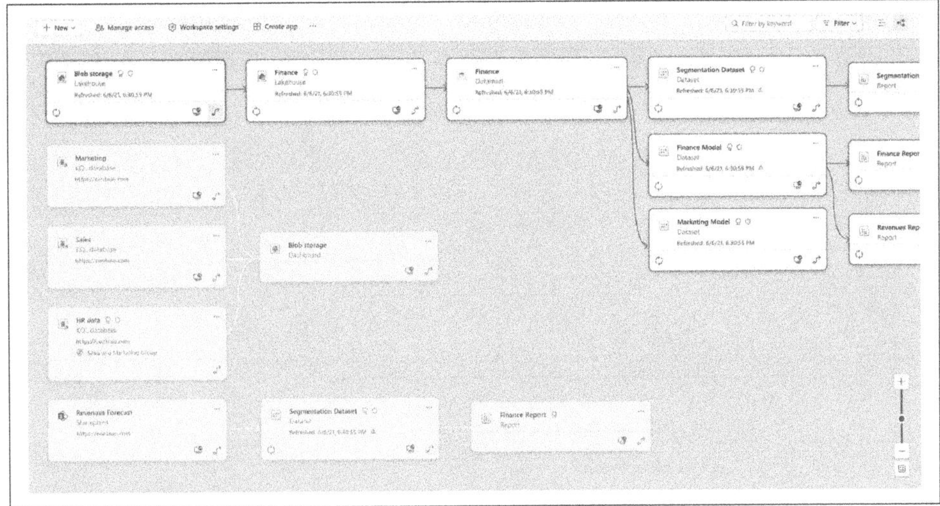

Figure 8-49. Selecting a specific item in the lineage view

Using Impact Analysis

Sometimes, the lineage view can be overwhelming, and you may prefer to view a simple list of the items that are impacted by a specific item. To get this list for a specific item in the lineage view, you can click the impact analysis icon in that item (see Figure 8-50).

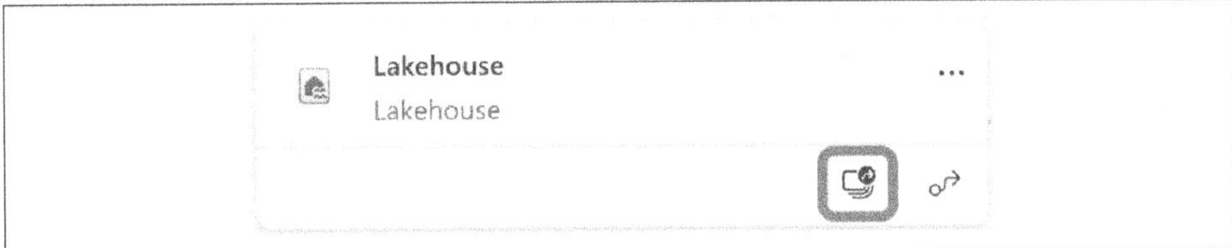

Figure 8-50. Impact analysis icon in an item in the lineage view

Clicking the icon will bring up the impact analysis overview in Figure 8-51.

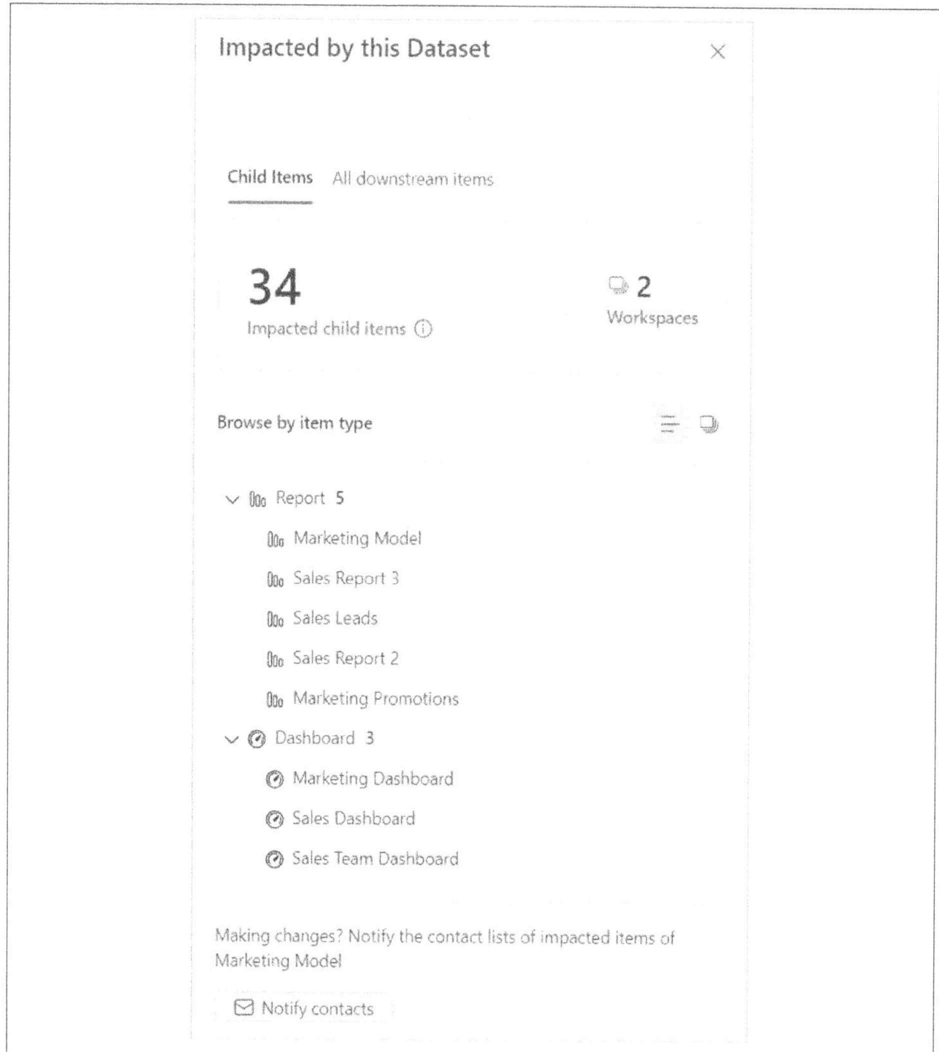

Figure 8-51. Impact analysis by item type

Here, we can see that the semantic model has 34 child items that use it as a source.

This example shows the items by item type, but you can also choose to view the same list by workspace by clicking the icon to the far right of "Browse by item type" on the screen shown in Figure 8-51. Figure 8-52 shows the results of clicking this icon.

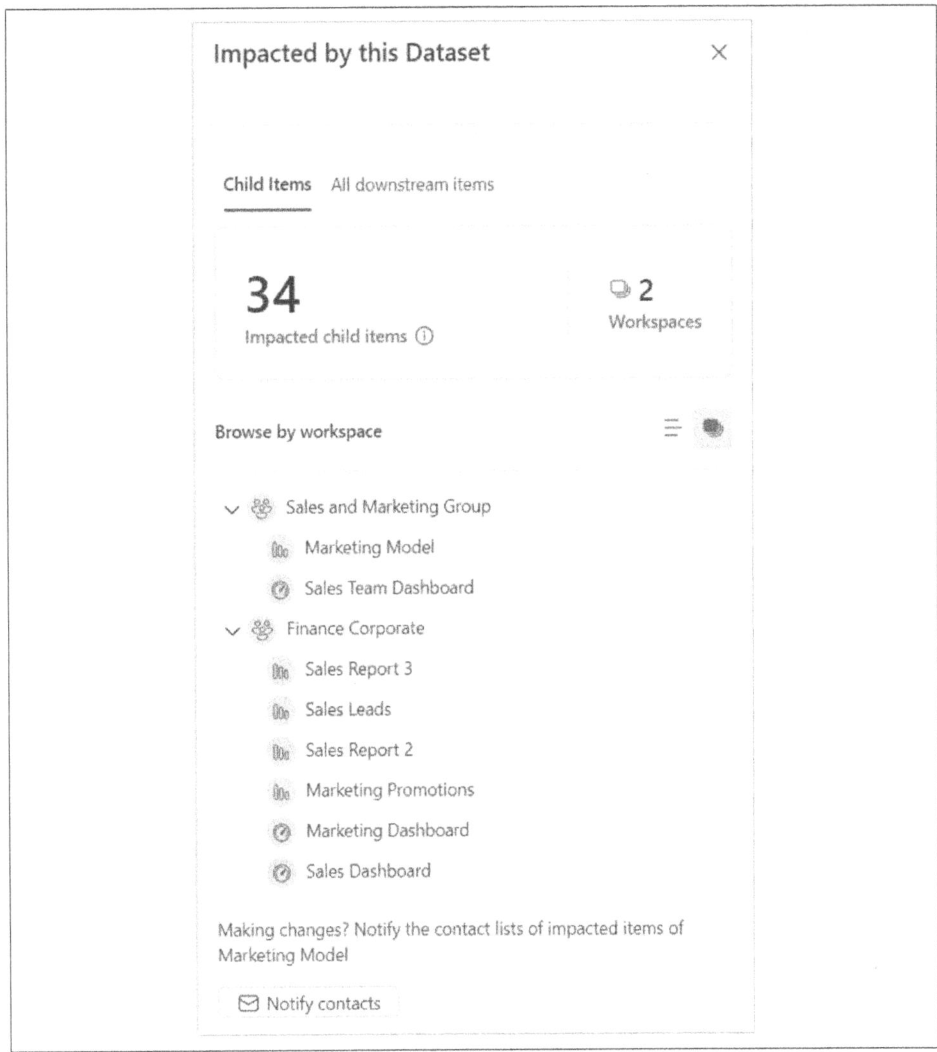

Figure 8-52. Impact analysis by workspace

On the screens shown in both Figures 8-51 and 8-52, you can click the "Notify contacts" button to notify contacts of any future changes. This will bring up the screen shown in Figure 8-53.

Notify contacts

An email notification will be sent to all the contacts for all impacted workspaces, including workspaces you don't have access to. Learn more

Notification message (required)

Add a note (required)

ⓘ The email may have many recipients, depending on the number of contacts and workspaces.

Send Cancel

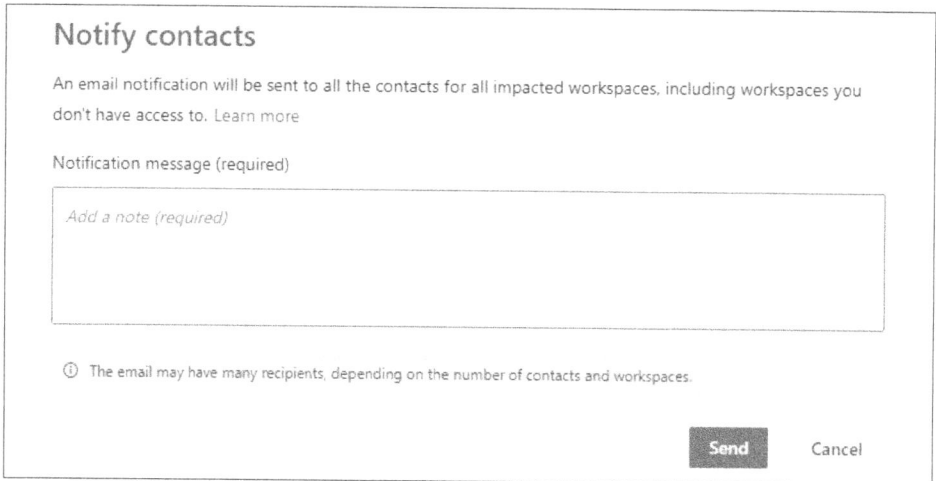

Figure 8-53. "Notify contacts" screen

Here, you write your notification message to your contacts and click the Send button to notify all contacts of any changes to workspaces.

You should configure one or more contacts for each specific Microsoft Fabric workspace in the workspace settings or when you create the workspace. This is a general governance issue, so it's out of scope for this book.

Deploying and Managing Semantic Models Using the XMLA Endpoint

When you build a semantic model in Microsoft Fabric, you use a UI to create your tables, relationships, and measures. This is great for development, but what if you need to perform more advanced tasks? What if you need to automate a deployment or process a single partition of a table? This is where the XMLA endpoint comes in.

Simply put, the *XMLA endpoint* is a communication protocol used by Microsoft Analysis Services. It's like a direct line to the semantic model's core engine. In Fabric, this endpoint allows you to connect to your semantic model from external tools that are designed for advanced management and development. Figure 8-54 shows you how this could look.

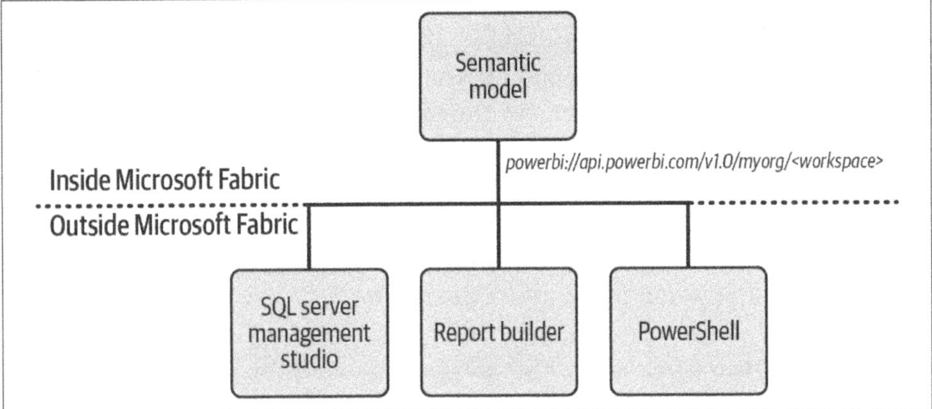

Figure 8-54. Schematic usage of the XMLA endpoint

In Figure 8-54, you can also see that the default connection string to your workspace is built with this syntax:

```
powerbi://api.powerbi.com/v1.0/myorg/<workspace>
```

> You may ask why you don't see the organization name or username in the connection string. This is because of the nature of the underlying API, which automatically filters the objects you have access to based on your credentials. So, even though you may have a workspace with the same name as a different organization, you'll only get access to your own workspace.

The XMLA endpoint opens a world of possibilities, including the following:

Advanced deployment
: While using Fabric deployment pipelines is a great way to move items among workspaces, the XMLA endpoint gives you more control. You can use tools like Visual Studio with the Analysis Services projects extension or Tabular Editor to develop a semantic model and then deploy it to a Fabric workspace via the endpoint. This is a common practice in enterprise environments.

Scripting and automation
: You can use tools like SQL Server Management Studio (SSMS) to write and execute XMLA scripts against your semantic model. This is perfect for automating tasks like data refreshes, backing up your data, and performing a partial refresh of a single table partition. For example, if you have a massive table, you can use XMLA to refresh only the data for the most recent month, instead of refreshing the entire table.

Third-party tools
: The XMLA endpoint is what allows powerful third-party tools like Tabular Editor and DAX Studio to connect to your semantic model in the service. These tools offer advanced functionalities for editing your data model, managing your DAX expressions, and troubleshooting performance issues that aren't available directly within the Fabric UI.

In a nutshell, the XMLA endpoint is what takes your work from simple development to professional management. It's the bridge that connects the easy-to-use Fabric interface with the powerful capabilities of external tools.

Many people use external tools for Fabric every day, but they're out of scope for the DP-600 exam. You'll only get questions that are based on Microsoft standard applications and software.

Setting Up the XMLA Endpoint

The XMLA endpoint enables you to use third-party tools and perform offline work with Microsoft Fabric. It's the communication protocol that lets client applications and the underlying engine handle semantic models, governance, lifecycles, and data management. All communication in this process is fully encrypted.

By default, the XMLA endpoint is set to "read only" for the semantic models workload, which means you can only query the data and not alter it. But here's a list of steps you can follow to enable the XMLA endpoint to *read and write* in your local environment after you've created your Fabric capacity (or started your Fabric trial):

1. In the Fabric portal, click the Settings options in the top right corner.
2. Select "Admin portal."
3. Select "Fabric capacity."
4. Click on your capacity name.
5. Expand the "Power BI workloads."
6. Find the "XMLA Endpoint" setting.
7. Select "Read Write."

The Admin portal contains a lot of Fabric capacity settings, preview features, and more. These settings are out of scope of this book and the certification exam, and we won't cover them in depth here.

Managing Semantic Models from the XMLA Endpoint

In this example, we'll be using SSMS to show you how to manage a semantic model.

First, we need to connect to the endpoint from the workspace settings. In SSMS, the connection to the XMLA endpoint is an Analysis Services connection, so you choose that server type and type in your information on the Connect to Server screen (see Figure 8-55).

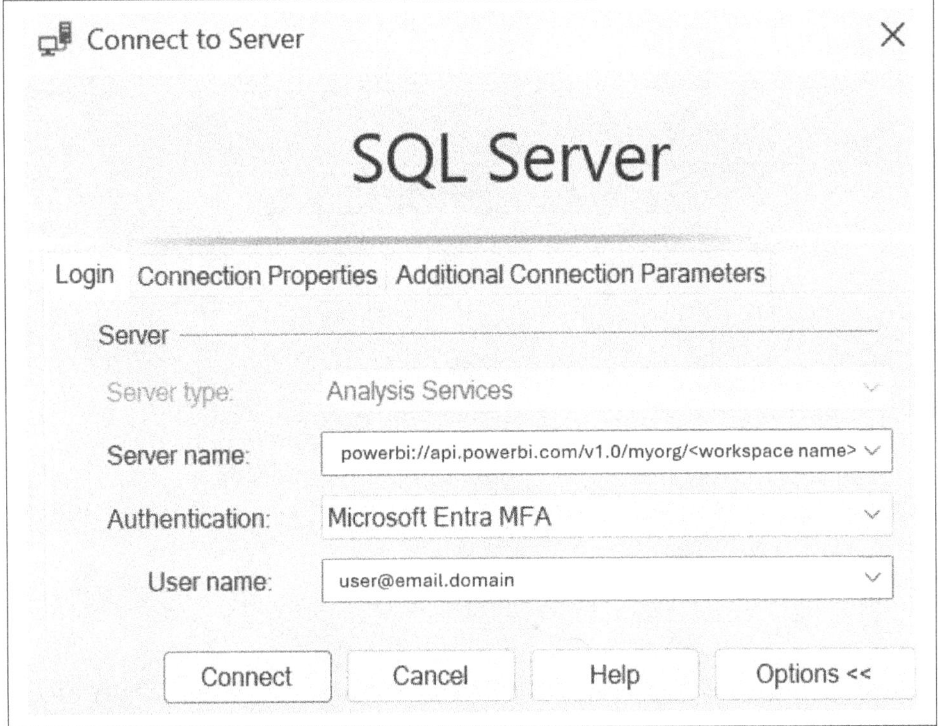

Figure 8-55. Logging in to the XMLA endpoint from SSMS

In the figure, we've entered generic text into the input fields for security reasons. You should enter your own information into the Server name and User name fields.

If you're prompted for user authentication using Microsoft standard multifactor authentication (MFA), follow the screen prompts.

After you make a successful connection to the XMLA endpoint, a list of databases will appear in the pane to the left. These are not actual databases but the models you have access to.

If you have lakehouses in your workspace, those will also show up as databases, even though they don't contain any analytics services database objects.

Figure 8-56 shows the contents of the left pane when you connect to a workspace named Workspace A.

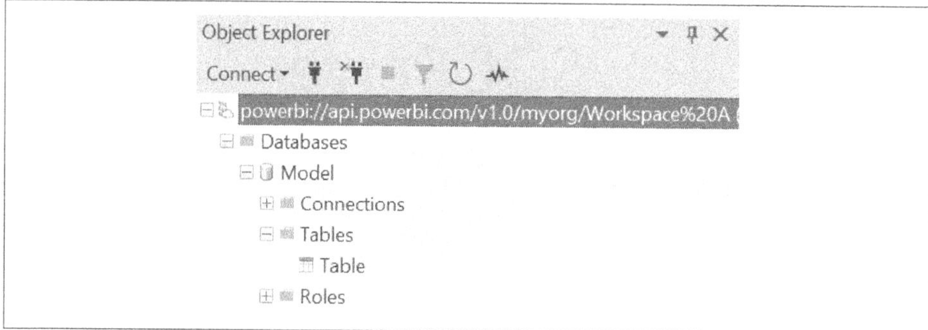

Figure 8-56. Content of a workspace with a semantic model

In the left pane, you can now begin to manage the semantic model directly in the SSMS application.

Processing a Semantic Model

If we want to process the model (if it is an import mode model), we can do that by right-clicking Model and selecting Process Database in the left pane (see Figure 8-57).

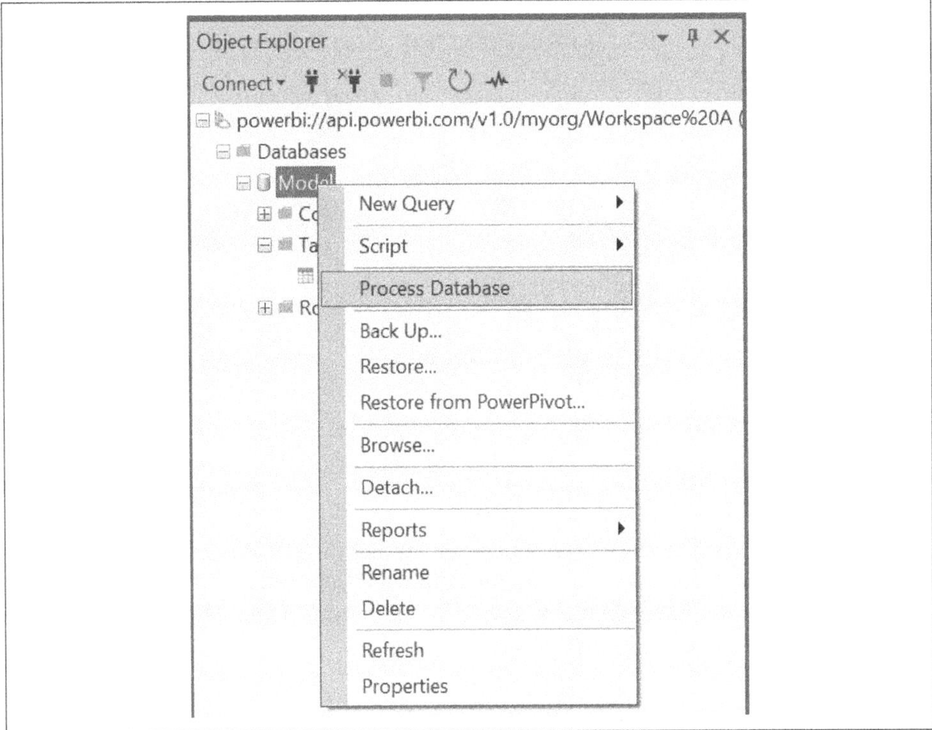

Figure 8-57. Selecting the Process Database option in SSMS

This brings up the screen shown in Figure 8-58.

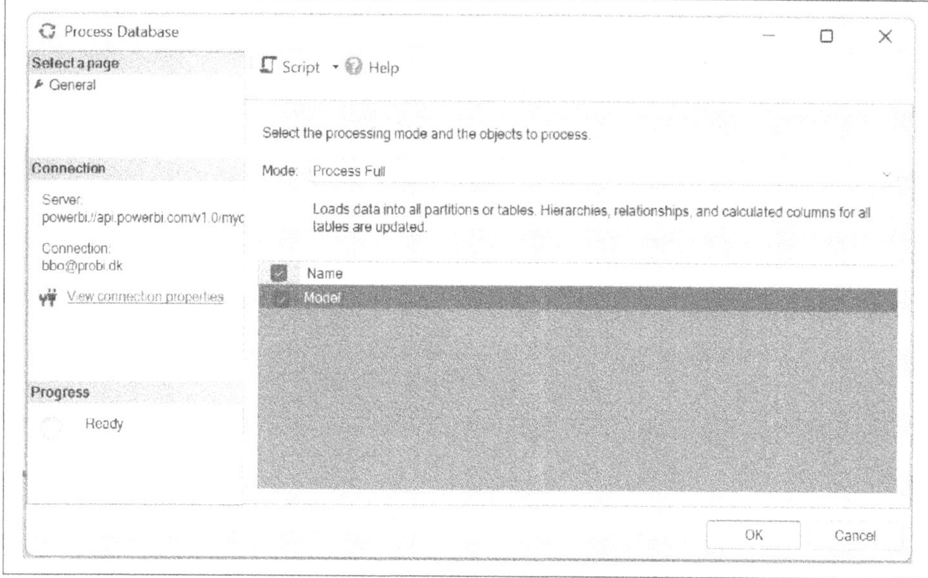

Figure 8-58. Process Database screen in SSMS

In the Mode field, select the Process Full option or the model will only process the metadata and not load new data into the semantic model. Then, click the OK button and the semantic model will start to load new data.

You can use the XMLA endpoint to automate almost every process involved in developing semantic models. We can't cover them all, but as long as you know that the XMLA endpoint and options to work with these features exist, you should be good to go for the exam.

Summary

Once a Power BI report is published to a workspace, it usually keeps evolving. Reports get updated, data models change, and new requirements appear. This is a good sign because it means people are using the report and we can improve it to deliver better insights.

Updating one report is straightforward, but in larger organizations, you often work with many reports and semantic models. You can't rely on memory alone to keep track of changes, so you need to have a clear and structured way to document them so that even a year later, you'll understand what was done.

In some cases, you also need to move content among workspaces, such as from development to testing and then to production. Also, reusing parts of reports or semantic models lets you save time and avoid having to start from scratch every time.

This chapter introduced version control using GitHub and Azure DevOps, which helps teams document and roll back changes. We explored Power BI project (*.pbip*) files, which separate report and model components to support collaboration and versioning. We also covered Reusable assets like template (*.pbit*) files, data source (*.pbids*) files, and shared semantic models to streamline development and promote consistency.

We then looked at deployment pipelines, which allow structured promotion of content among development, test, and production stages. We also covered Impact analysis tools such as the lineage view, which helps you identify downstream dependencies before making changes. Finally, we examined the XMLA endpoint, which enables advanced management and automation of semantic models using external tools.

Knowing how to maintain the analytical lifecycle will help you standardize your work, share it among projects, and save time when building new reports.

CHAPTER 9

Question Bank

This chapter includes questions we've written for you. They're similar to the types of questions you'll get on the actual exam, but keep in mind that we can't cover all the types of questions you may see there, and you can't read your way to passing the exam either. Some of what you'll be tested on are things you can only learn through experience and hands-on work with the entire Microsoft Fabric suite. Therefore, the answers to some of these questions are not found in this book and can only be learned through hands-on practice.

Also note that while the wording of the questions and the way they're structured can seem strange at first glance, that's how they'll look on the exam, and we want to help you get used to them now so you'll be as prepared as possible on exam day.

Questions

1. You have a Fabric tenant that contains a workspace that's assigned to a Fabric capacity. You need to create a solution that gives developers the option to publish custom Direct Lake semantic models using third-party tools. What should you do?

   a. In the Capacity settings, set the XMLA endpoint to Read Write.

   b. Enable users to create items from the tenant settings.

   c. Enable users to edit data models in the Power BI service from the tenant settings.

   d. In the Tenant settings, set "Allow XMLA Endpoints" and "Analyze in Excel with on-premises semantic models" to Enabled.

   e. In the Tenant settings, enable "Publish to Web."

2. You're creating a semantic model in Microsoft Power Bl Desktop, and you've developed changes to a semantic model in the TMDL format. Which file format should you use for the Power BI Desktop file?

   a. *.pbip*

   b. *.pbit*

   c. *.pbix*

   d. *.pbids*

3. In a Fabric Warehouse, you have a table named FactSales that has one billion rows. You run the following T-SQL statement:

   ```
   CREATE TABLE mirror.FactSales AS CLONE OF dbo.FactSales;
   ```

   Select the statement or statements that are true.

   a. A replica of `dbo.FactSales` is created in the mirror schema by copying the metadata only.

   b. Additional schema changes to `dbo.FactSales` will also apply to `mirror.FactSales`.

   c. Additional data changes to `dbo.Factsales` will not apply to `mirror.FactSales`.

4. You have a lakehouse in Fabric that contains a table. This table is currently unpartitioned, and you plan to implement partitioning by a specific column by using a Copy activity from a pipeline. What do you need to do first?

   a. In the Destination tab, select the partition column.

   b. In the Destination tab, set Mode to Append.

   c. In the Destination tab, set Mode to Overwrite.

   d. In the Source tab, select "Enable partition discovery."

5. You're planning to implement the ingestion of a CSV file from an Azure Store account. The implementation must support the Power Query (M) language and be executable from a pipeline. Which activity should you choose?

   a. Script

   b. Dataflow

   c. Notebook

   d. Copy data

6. You have a Fabric tenant that contains two workspaces named Workspace1 and Workspace2.

   Workspace1 contains a lakehouse named Lakehouse1. Lakehouse1 contains a table named `dbo.ClientCases`.

   Workspace2 contains a lakehouse named Lakehouse2. Lakehouse2 contains a table named `dbo.Clients`.

   You need to ensure that you can write queries that reference both `dbo.ClientCases` and `dbo.Clients` in the same SQL query, without making additional copies of the tables.

   What should you use?

   a. A shortcut

   b. A view

   c. A dataflow

   d. A managed table

7. You're working with Dataflow Gen2 to implement a solution designed to make sure the system ignores the spaces in the values when performing a join between two tables.

   What should you do?

   a. Use a lookup table.

   b. Use fuzzy matching.

   c. Use fuzzy grouping.

   d. Use a reference table.

8. You're working in Dataflow Gen2, and you want to merge two queries into one. You need to ensure that the query returns all the rows that are present in both tables. Which type of join should you use?

   a. LEFT OUTER JOIN

   b. LEFT ANTI JOIN

   c. RIGHT OUTER JOIN

   d. FULL OUTER JOIN

   e. INNER JOIN

9. You have a Fabric workspace that's allocated to an F-128 capacity. The workspace contains a KQL database with a table named `DeviceLogs`.

   `DeviceLogs` contains 25 columns named `c1` through `c25` and 10 billion rows. Column `c1` contains identifiers ranging from 1 to 15 that are equally distributed.

   You have the following query:

   ```
   DeviceLogs
   | project c1, c2, c3
   | where c1 == 1
   ```

   You modify the query as follows:

   ```
   DeviceLogs
   | where c1 == 1
   | project c1, c2, c3
   ```

   How will the execution time of the query be impacted?

   a. The execution time will not change.

   b. The execution time will be shorter.

   c. The query will fail.

   d. The execution time will be longer.

10. You have a semantic model named Model1. Model1 contains a single table named `Orders` with the following columns:

    ```
    Order Date
    Product Name
    Quantity
    ```

    You have a report that contains a page named Orders, which contains a slicer for the Product Name field and a clustered column chart that shows Quantity by Order Date.

    You need to allow users the option to choose between Quantity by Product Name and Quantity by Order Date in the column chart. The solution must minimize development effort.

    What should you do?

    a. Create a measure.

    b. Create a field parameter.

    c. Create a dynamic format string.

    d. Create a calculation group.

11. You have a Fabric workspace with a warehouse named Warehouse1. You have a user named User1 who has the viewer role for the same workspace. You need to delegate permissions to User1 to meet the following requirements:

    - User1 must be able to share the warehouse to other users.
    - The solution must follow the principle of least privilege.

    Which permission should you assign to User1?

    a. The member role in the workspace
    b. The admin role in the workspace
    c. The contributor role in the workspace
    d. The `db_owner` role in the warehouse

12. You have a Fabric workspace named Workspace1 that contains a lakehouse and includes a user named User1.

    You need to ensure that User1 can read all the data in the lakehouse but not any other items or data from the workspace. Which two actions should you perform?

    a. Share the lakehouse by using item permissions.
    b. Select "Read all Apache Spark data."
    c. Add User1 to the viewer role.
    d. Add User1 to the contributor role.
    e. Add User1 to the member role.

13. Your task is to connect a Fabric workspace to a GitHub repository. What information do you need to accomplish this?

    a. A PAT and the URL for the repository
    b. A SAS token and the branch name for the repository
    c. An access key and the branch name for the repository
    d. An access key and the URL for the repository

14. You have a workspace in Fabric with a warehouse and a lakehouse.

    The warehouse contains a table named `dbo.FactSalesSmall`, and the lakehouse contains a Delta table named `dbo.FactSalesConsolidated`.

    Your task is to copy the data from `dbo.FactSalesSmall` to `dbo.FactSalesConsolidated`, using a low-code solution.

    What should you do?

    a. Use a notebook to read the data from Table1 and insert the data into Table2.

    b. Use a Dataflow Gen2 to read the data from FactSalesSmall and insert the data into FactSalesConsolidated.

    c. Use a stored procedure to read the data from FactSalesConsolidated and insert the data into FactSalesSmall.

    d. Use a notebook to read the data from FactSalesConsolidated and insert the data into FactSalesSmall.

15. In a Fabric workspace, you have a Dataflow Gen2 with complex business logic implemented. You need to persist the output to a lakehouse in the workspace. What two options do you have to configure the destination?

    a. Configure the default destination.

    b. Configure the destination for the current flow.

    c. Configure the destination as a new step in the flow pane.

    d. Configure the destination using a notebook.

    e. Configure the destination using a pipeline.

16. You're working in Microsoft Fabric, and you have a workspace with several reports and a semantic model that contains information about a future acquisition to be made.

    You need to make sure that data from the items does not fall into the wrong hands, and the solution must ensure that future items in the workspace inherit the settings. What should you do?

    a. Plan a configuration of tags.

    b. Plan a configuration of sensitivity labels.

    c. Plan a configuration of endorsement.

    d. Split the report and semantic model into two workspaces.

17. An analytics engineer is designing a new data solution in Microsoft Fabric. The solution will involve a central data store that is frequently accessed for T-SQL and Spark queries. The data engineers need to be able to access semi-structured and unstructured data, and the data store must also support row-level security for users executing T-SQL queries. Which type of data store is the most appropriate choice for this solution?

    a. A data lake

    b. An external Hive metastore

    c. A warehouse

    d. A lakehouse

18. You're creating a report visual in Power BI that displays a customer's average satisfaction score based on surveys submitted over the past 12 months. The data needs to update as soon as the source data changes and be as fast as possible.

    Which storage mode should you configure for the semantic model to meet this requirement?

    a. DirectQuery

    b. Direct Lake

    c. Import

    d. Live Connect

19. An analytics team needs to implement row-level security (RLS) on a table in a semantic model to restrict data visibility based on the user accessing the report.

    Which of the following DAX functions is most often used to define RLS rules?

    a. `FILTER`

    b. `LOOKUPVALUE`

    c. `USERPRINCIPALNAME`

    d. `CALCULATE`

20. You have a data warehouse in Microsoft Fabric that contains a table named `Stage.Customers`, which receives incremental updates from a CRM system. You need to write a T-SQL query that returns the single most recent update for each customer. Which T-SQL function should you use to achieve this efficiently?

    a. `ROW_NUMBER`

    b. `RANK`

    c. `DENSE_RANK`

    d. `GROUP BY`

21. A data analyst needs to create and share semantic models with other data analysts within a Fabric workspace. The analyst needs to have full control over the models and reports and must use the least-privilege approach.

    Which of the following workspace roles would provide the necessary permissions?

    a. Administrator
    b. Member
    c. Viewer
    d. Contributor

22. Which of the following describes the purpose of a calculation group in a semantic model?

    a. To perform row-level security (RLS) by grouping users into roles
    b. To create a composite model by grouping tables from different sources
    c. To group multiple measures and apply a common calculation modifier to them
    d. To create new columns in a table based on a single DAX expression

23. A data engineer has a table in a lakehouse that contains sales data, but some of the records have NULL values in the CustomerID column. What is the most effective and low-code way to identify and resolve these missing values using the data transformation capabilities in Microsoft Fabric?

    a. Create a T-SQL view that filters out the NULL values.
    b. Use a Python notebook to fill the NULL values with a default value.
    c. Configure incremental refresh on the semantic model to ignore the bad data.
    d. Use the data profiling tools in a Dataflow Gen2 to check column quality and fill in missing values.

24. Which of the following is the primary purpose of a deployment pipeline in Microsoft Fabric?

    a. To monitor the performance of report visuals and queries to help optimize the performance of the platform
    b. To schedule a data refresh for a semantic model to keep the data as fresh and up-to-date as possible
    c. To manage the continuous integration and continuous deployment (CI/CD) of analytics solutions
    d. To create a copy of a workspace for backup purposes in case of a need for disaster recovery

25. A data engineer is designing a data model for a new analytics solution in Microsoft Fabric. The model will be used by various reports and must be easy to navigate and understand for business users.

    Which schema design is the most appropriate for this goal?

    a. A snowflake schema

    b. A flat schema

    c. A star schema

    d. A normalized schema

26. You're creating a DAX measure that needs to calculate the total sales for the previous year, based on the user's selected date. Which DAX function is the most efficient and recommended for performing this time intelligence calculation?

    a. `CALCULATE`

    b. `TOTALYTD`

    c. `PREVIOUSYEAR`

    d. `DATEADD`

27. A data analyst is building a Power BI report using a semantic model in Microsoft Fabric. They want to create a measure that calculates the total sales for the same period in the previous year. The measure must be able to respect any time filters the user applies to the report. Which of the following DAX functions should the data analyst use for this purpose?

    a.
    ```
    CALCULATE(SUM('Sales'[SalesAmount]), SAMEPERIODLASTYEAR('Date'[Date]))
    ```

    b.
    ```
    SAMEPERIODLASTYEAR(SUM('Sales'[SalesAmount]))
    ```

    c.
    ```
    CALCULATE(SUM('Sales'[SalesAmount]), DATESYTD(DATEADD('Date'[Date],
    -1, YEAR)))
    ```

    d.
    ```
    CALCULATE(TOTALYTD(SUM('Sales'[SalesAmount]),
    SAMEPERIODLASTYEAR('Date'[Date])))
    ```

28. A data engineer is preparing data from a SQL database for a lakehouse in Microsoft Fabric. The source table contains a column named `Price` with some empty string values that need to be replaced with 0. The engineer wants a low-code solution that they can easily integrate into a data pipeline. What is the most appropriate action for the data engineer to take?

    a. Write a Spark notebook with PySpark to read the data and replace the values.

    b. Add a dataflow to the data pipeline and use its transformation capabilities to replace the empty strings.

    c. Use a T-SQL query with an `UPDATE` statement to replace the empty strings.

    d. Use a `COPY INTO` command to load the data and handle the transformation.

29. An analytics engineer is designing a new Power BI semantic model that needs to handle a very large dataset from a Fabric data warehouse. The report must provide fast interactive performance for aggregations and queries. The data warehouse is scheduled to refresh nightly, so data freshness is not a major concern.

    Which storage mode should the analytics engineer choose for the semantic model?

    a. Import
    b. DirectQuery
    c. Direct Lake
    d. Live Connect

30. A data team uses a single Microsoft Fabric workspace named Analytics for development and testing. The team needs to transition its work to a Production workspace, and also ensure that the business users can deploy their semantic models and reports from Analytics to Production in a controlled manner.

    Which tool should the team use?

    a. A data pipeline
    b. Git integration
    c. A deployment pipeline
    d. A notebook

31. You're creating a dimensional model for a new analytics solution. The model contains a Sales fact table and several dimension tables, including Supplier and Customer. To improve query performance and simplify the model for business users, you want to combine the Supplier and Customer dimension tables into a single table.

    Which of the following is the most appropriate way to achieve this?

    a. Denormalize the data by creating a single, wide table that combines data from all dimension tables into the Sales fact table.
    b. Create a conformed dimension by combining the tables and ensuring all columns are in a single, well-defined table.
    c. Create a role-playing dimension by aliasing one of the tables.
    d. Create a new view in the data warehouse by joining the Supplier and Customer tables.

32. A team of data analysts is preparing to transform data from a source database. It needs to create a measure that calculates the number of days since the last order for each customer. The team wants a solution that allows for a step-by-step approach to data transformation and is easy to debug.

    Which of the following is the best tool to use for this task?

    a. A data pipeline with a lookup activity

    b. A T-SQL script in the SQL query editor

    c. A Dataflow Gen2 using Power Query

    d. A Spark notebook with PySpark

33. A data engineer has a semantic model in Power BI with a Sales fact table that is joined to a Date dimension table. The engineer wants to ensure that a user who has access to only one specific product category can only see the sales data for that category. The solution must use the least-privilege principle.

    Which of the following is the most appropriate action to take?

    a. Create a new semantic model for each product category with a filtered Sales table.

    b. Implement object-level security (OLS) on the Sales fact table.

    c. Implement row-level security (RLS) on the Sales fact table to filter the rows.

    d. Implement column-level security (CLS) on the Sales fact table to hide the SalesAmount column.

34. A data engineer is working on a data warehouse in Microsoft Fabric. They need to ensure that the data loading process is as efficient as possible. To do this, they decide to use a `MERGE` statement. What's the primary purpose of using a `MERGE` statement in this scenario?

    a. To join two or more tables together to produce a single results set

    b. To perform a bulk load of new data from a single source file

    c. To combine `INSERT`, `UPDATE`, and `DELETE` operations into a single statement

    d. To create a new table from the results of a query

35. You're developing a new semantic model in Power BI, and you want to use a DAX measure to calculate the total sales for a specific product category. To make the DAX code more readable and easier to debug, you want to store the results of an intermediate calculation in a temporary variable. Which DAX keyword should you use for this purpose?

    a. `VAR`

    b. `SET`

    c. `DEFINE`

    d. `LET`

36. A data engineer is designing a dimensional model for a new analytics solution. The model contains a fact table with measures such as `SalesAmount` and a `Product` dimension table that contains attributes like `ProductCategory`. The engineer wants to make the model as simple and efficient as possible for a semantic model.

    Which of the following best describes the relationship between the fact and dimension tables?

    a. The fact table contains the measures, and the dimension table contains the primary keys.

    b. Both the fact table and the dimension table contain measures and attributes.

    c. The fact table contains the primary keys, and the dimension table contains the measures.

    d. The fact table contains the foreign keys and measures, and the dimension table contains the attributes and a primary key.

37. A data analyst is working with a large sales dataset in a Fabric data warehouse.

    The analyst needs to apply a series of simple transformations, such as changing a column's data type, renaming columns, and removing duplicates.

    They want to use a low-code approach that is easy to repeat.

    What is the most appropriate tool to use?

    a. A SQL notebook with Python code

    b. A SQL query in the SQL query editor

    c. The visual query editor in the Fabric data warehouse

    d. A data pipeline with a copy activity

38. A data engineer is designing a dataflow to ingest and transform data. To ensure data quality and integrity, they want to enforce a rule that rejects any rows where the value in the `ProductID` column is `NULL`. Where can the data engineer enforce this data quality rule?

    a. In the data source's properties

    b. In a SQL `WHERE` clause in the target table

    c. In the data destination's schema

    d. In a data quality feature within Dataflow Gen2

39. An analytics engineer is designing an incremental refresh policy for a large semantic model. The model contains a `Sales` fact table that is partitioned by month. The team wants to keep the last three years of data and only refresh the current and previous month's data. Which two parameters must the analytics engineer configure to achieve this?

    a. `DateFrom` and `DateTo`

    b. `RangeStart` and `RangeEnd`

    c. `DateTimeFrom` and `DateTimeTo`

    d. `RefreshInterval` and `HistoricalPeriod`

40. A data analyst needs to create a DAX measure that calculates the sales for the previous month. The measure should respect any filters on the `Date` table. Which of the following DAX functions should they use?

    a. `SAMEPERIODLASTYEAR`

    b. `PREVIOUSMONTH`

    c. `TOTALMTD`

    d. `DATEADD`

41. A data analyst is building a Power BI report using a large dataset that is split across a lakehouse and an external Azure SQL database. To provide a unified view for reporting, they need to create a semantic model that can query both sources directly without importing the data. Which feature of a semantic model should the analyst use?

    a. A live connection

    b. Import mode

    c. DirectQuery mode

    d. A composite model

42. A data engineer has a warehouse with a table that contains sensitive financial data, including a `Salary` column. The engineer wants to ensure that a specific group of users can see the table but can't see the `Salary` column. Which security measure should the data engineer implement?

    a. Dynamic row-level security

    b. Column-level security (CLS)

    c. Object-level security (OLS)

    d. Row-level security (RLS)

43. A data team needs to analyze streaming log data from an application. The logs are high volume and semi-structured, and they require quick, ad hoc queries. Which of the following is the most suitable approach to storing and querying this data in Microsoft Fabric?

    a. Ingesting the data into a data warehouse and querying it with T-SQL

    b. Ingesting the data into a lakehouse and querying it with T-SQL

    c. Ingesting the data into a KQL database and querying it with KQL

    d. Storing the data in a Data Lake and querying it with a Spark notebook

44. An analytics engineer is designing a new data solution in Microsoft Fabric. The solution will involve a central data store that is frequently accessed for T-SQL and Spark queries.

    Data engineers need to be able to access semi-structured and unstructured data, and the data store must also support row-level security for users who are executing T-SQL queries.

    Which type of data store is the most appropriate choice for this solution?

    a. A data lake

    b. A lakehouse

    c. A warehouse

    d. A KQL database

45. You have a Fabric workspace named Workspace1 that contains a lakehouse named Lakehouse1. You need to ensure that only members of GroupA can access sensitive columns in the lakehouse. The solution must use built-in Fabric governance features and follow least-privilege principles.

    Which two actions should you perform?

    a. Apply a sensitivity label to the sensitive columns in Lakehouse1.
    b. Configure row-level security in Lakehouse1.
    c. Configure column-level security in Lakehouse1.
    d. Endorse Lakehouse1 as trusted content.
    e. Use workspace-level access controls to restrict GroupA.

46. You have a Fabric workspace named Workspace1 with a SQL warehouse named Warehouse1 and a semantic model named Model1. You need to deploy updated semantic model changes to production using code-based CI/CD from a third-party tool. What should you do to deploy the changes?

    a. Configure version control for Workspace1.
    b. Deploy the semantic model using the XMLA endpoint.
    c. Create a deployment pipeline between development and production.
    d. Publish Model1 directly from Power BI Service.
    e. Use *.pbids* files in the workspace.

47. You have data coming from multiple sources, and you need to select the appropriate Fabric storage method that supports both querying and file-based transformations. Which storage option should you choose?

    a. A lakehouse
    b. A warehouse
    c. An eventhouse
    d. An SQL database

48. You want to analyze and query data using Fabric KQL and DAX. Which two capabilities should you ensure are supported?

    a. Semantic models supporting DAX
    b. Lakehouse queries using SQL
    c. Eventhouse queries using KQL
    d. Dataflows supporting DAX
    e. Warehouses supporting KQL

49. You have a Fabric workspace, and you need to ingest real-time streaming data into your analytics solution while integrating with OneLake. Which component should you use?

    a. A lakehouse
    b. A warehouse
    c. An eventhouse
    d. A dataflow
    e. A semantic model

50. You're building a semantic model, and you want to support dynamic formatting and calculation flexibility. Which two features should you implement?

    a. Calculation groups
    b. Dynamic format strings
    c. Field parameters
    d. Star schema relationships
    e. Incremental refreshes

51. You're working with a lakehouse table named `SalesTransactions` that contains millions of rows. The table includes rows called `TransactionDate`, `CustomerID`, and `Amount`.

    You need to create a view that filters out transactions with `NULL` amount values and calculates the total amount per customer per month.

    How should you complete the T-SQL statement?

    a. Use `SELECT INTO` with a `HAVING` statement to create the summary table.
    b. Create a `VIEW` that uses a `WHERE` statement and `GROUP BY`.
    c. Create a `PROCEDURE` that uses `GROUP BY` to return the results set.
    d. Use `MERGE` with `PARTITION BY` to combine rows into a single dataset.

52. A data engineer needs to join two tables in a lakehouse: `Orders` and `Products`. The `Orders` table contains a `ProductID` column, and the `Products` table contains `ProductID` and `Category` columns.

    What type of join should the data engineer use to include all orders, even if the product category is missing?

    a. An INNER JOIN
    b. A LEFT OUTER JOIN
    c. A RIGHT JOIN
    d. A FULL OUTER JOIN

53. You're designing a Dataflow Gen2 that ingests data from a CSV file and transforms it into a dimensional model. During transformation, you need to remove duplicate rows and ensure column types are consistent.

    Which two transformation steps should you apply?

    a. Remove duplicates from the source table.
    b. Change column data types to match the dimensional model.
    c. Merge queries by using fuzzy matching to enrich product names.
    d. Fill missing values in numeric columns with zeros.
    e. Trim leading and trailing spaces from text columns.

54. You're building a pipeline that ingests data from an external SQL database into a lakehouse. The data includes a `Price` column that contains empty strings and `NULL` values. You want to replace the empty strings with 0 using a low-code solution, without affecting the `NULL` values.

    What should you use?

    a. A Spark notebook with PySpark
    b. A Dataflow Gen2 transformation
    c. A stored procedure in the warehouse
    d. A T-SQL `UPDATE` statement in the pipeline

55. You're working in a Dataflow Gen2 that ingests product data from a CSV file. The file contains inconsistent formatting, including leading and trailing spaces in product names and numeric columns imported as text. You need to clean the data before loading it into a lakehouse.

    What two things should you do?

    a. Remove duplicates from the source table.
    b. Trim leading and trailing spaces from text columns.
    c. Fill missing values in numeric columns with zeros.
    d. Merge queries using fuzzy matching.
    e. Change column data types to match the dimensional model.

56. You're working with a KQL database that contains a table named `MeterReadings`. You need to calculate the difference in reading values between each row and its previous row, grouped by area. Which KQL function should you use?

    a. `prev()`

    b. `row_rank_min()`

    c. `summarize()`

    d. `window_session()`

57. The `TaxiTrips` lakehouse table contains millions of rows, including columns named `TaxiCompany` and `tripDistance`. Your goal is to identify the top three taxi companies based on total miles traveled. If there's a tie for total miles, you should include both or all tied companies.

    Which T-SQL statements do you need to use to calculate the total miles per company before limiting the results?

    a. `TOP (3)`

    b. `FETCH NEXT 3 ROWS ONLY`

    c. `ORDER BY SUM(tripDistance) DESC`

    d. `GROUP BY TaxiCompany`

58. You're working with a lakehouse table named `ProductSales` that includes the columns `ProductID`, `SaleDate`, and `Revenue`. You need to create a view that returns the total revenue per product for the current year only.

    Which T-SQL clause should you use to filter the data?

    a. `HAVING YEAR(SaleDate) = YEAR(GETDATE())`

    b. `WHERE YEAR(SaleDate) = YEAR(GETDATE())`

    c. `GROUP BY YEAR(SaleDate)`

    d. `FILTER BY CURRENT_YEAR`

59. As a data engineer, you're working with a Fabric warehouse that contains a table named `CustomerTransactions`. You need to create a T-SQL statement that returns the total transaction amount per customer for the current year.

    Which combination of clauses should you use?

    a. `GROUP BY CustomerID, WHERE YEAR(TransactionDate) = YEAR(GETDATE())`

    b. `GROUP BY YEAR(TransactionDate), HAVING SUM(Amount) > 0`

    c. `ORDER BY CustomerID, TOP (100)`

    d. `PARTITION BY CustomerID, ROW_NUMBER()`

60. As a data analyst, you're preparing a report that shows the number of orders per region. The `Orders` table contains columns named `OrderID`, `Region`, and `OrderDate`. The `Regions` table contains all possible regions, including those with no orders.

    You need to prepare a report that shows the number of orders per region, and you also need to make sure that regions with no orders are included.

    Which combination of clauses should you use?

    a. `SELECT Region, COUNT(OrderID) FROM Orders GROUP BY Region`

    b. `SELECT r.Region, COUNT(o.OrderID) AS OrderCount FROM Regions r LEFT JOIN Orders o ON r.Region = o.Region GROUP BY r.Region`

    c. `SELECT Region FROM Orders WHERE OrderDate IS NOT NULL`

    d. `SELECT DISTINCT Region FROM Orders`

61. As a data engineer, you're working with a KQL database that contains a table named `EnergyReadings`.

    The `EnergyReadings` table contains columns named `Area`, `Timestamp`, and `Energy`. You need to calculate the difference in energy usage between each row and the previous row, separately for each area, sorted by timestamp.

    Which KQL statement should you use?

    a. `extend Delta = Energy - prev(Energy) by Area`

    b. `summarize Delta = sum(Energy) - sum(prev(Energy)) by Area`

    c. `sort by Timestamp desc`

    d. `project Area, Energy, Delta`

62. As a data engineer, you're working with a lakehouse table named `SalesData` that contains columns named `ProductID`, `SaleDate`, and `Revenue`. You need to create a reusable transformation that calculates monthly revenue per product and stores the results in a new table.

    Which Fabric item should you use to implement this with minimal code and easy scheduling?

    a. A Dataflow Gen2

    b. A Spark notebook

    c. A SQL stored procedure

    d. A Copy activity in a pipeline

63. A data pipeline ingests data from multiple sources into a lakehouse. The process must do the following:

    - Load raw data.
    - Perform cleansing and transformation.
    - Populate the dimensional model.

    Which Fabric item or items let you guarantee this sequence across different tasks?

    a. A Dataflow Gen2 with multiple transformations
    b. Spark notebooks chained manually
    c. A pipeline with activity dependencies
    d. Dataflow triggers

64. You're working in a Fabric workspace that contains a lakehouse named Lakehouse1. You create a data pipeline named Pipeline1 to ingest CSV files from Azure Storage. You need to add an activity to Pipeline1 that copies data into Lakehouse1 and supports Power Query M transformations.

    Which type of activity should you add?

    a. A Copy data
    b. A script
    c. A Dataflow Gen2
    d. A notebook
    e. A stored procedure

65. As a data analyst, you're developing a semantic model in Power BI. You want to simplify time intelligence calculations such as year-to-date, previous-month, and quarter comparisons across multiple measures.

    What is the best option to do so without too many additional steps?

    a. Calculation groups
    b. Field parameters
    c. Composite models
    d. Dynamic format strings
    e. Aggregation tables

66. You're designing a dimensional model for a new analytics solution in Fabric. The model includes a fact table with measures such as `SalesAmount` and a `Product` dimension table with attributes like `ProductCategory`. You want to ensure the model is efficient and easy to use in semantic models.

    Which statement best describes the relationship between the fact and dimension tables?

    a. The fact table contains primary keys and measures; the dimension table contains attributes.

    b. The fact table contains foreign keys and measures; the dimension table contains attributes and a primary key.

    c. Both tables contain measures and attributes.

    d. The dimension table contains foreign keys; the fact table contains attributes.

    e. The fact table contains calculated columns; the dimension table contains hierarchies.

67. As a data engineer, you're working on a Microsoft Fabric project involving data transformation. You need to ensure that your solution is optimized for performance, maintainability, and reuse across multiple pipelines.

    Which approach should you follow?

    a. Using default settings and relying on automatic optimization

    b. Applying best practices for transformation logic and modular design

    c. Avoiding advanced features to keep the model simple

    d. Focusing only on visual design and ignoring backend configuration

    e. Using notebooks for all transformation logic, regardless of complexity

68. As a data analyst, you're designing a semantic model for a retail company. The model includes a `Sales` fact table and `Date`, `Product`, and `Store` dimension tables. You want to ensure that the model is easy to navigate and performs well in Power BI. Which schema design should you use?

    a. Snowflake

    b. Star

    c. Flat

    d. Hybrid

    e. Normalized

69. You're developing a semantic model that includes both `Import` and `Direct Query` tables. You need to combine them in a single report while maintaining performance and flexibility. Which approach is the best choice?

    a. Using a composite model

    b. Using dual storage mode with an aggregation table

    c. Using a calculation group

    d. Using a field parameter

    e. Using dual storage mode

70. You're creating a semantic model that will be reused in multiple reports. You want to allow report authors to dynamically switch among different dimensions (e.g., Region, Product, Customer) in visuals. Which features should you implement?

    a. Calculation groups

    b. Field parameters

    c. Composite models

    d. Dynamic format strings

    e. Role-playing dimensions

71. As a data analyst, you're designing a semantic model that will be reused in multiple reports. You want to ensure that the model supports consistent logic and centralized maintenance and also avoids duplication. Which approach should you use?

    a. Creating a separate semantic model for each report

    b. Using a single shared semantic model

    c. Duplicating the model and customizing it per report

    d. Deploying the model separately for each report

    e. Using composite models with DirectQuery

72. You're building a semantic model for financial reporting that includes multiple measures, some of which already have specific formatting (e.g., currency, percentage). You want to apply consistent formatting across all measures, without duplicating measures or manually changing each one. What would you apply?
    a. Calculation groups
    b. Dynamic format strings
    c. Field parameters
    d. Composite models
    e. Aggregation tables
73. You're designing a semantic model that includes a `Sales` fact table and a `Date` dimension table. You need to create a measure that calculates the total sales for the same period in the previous year, respecting any filters applied in the report.

    Which DAX expression should you use?
    a. `CALCULATE(SUM(Sales[Amount]), PREVIOUSYEAR(Date[Date]))`
    b. `SAMEPERIODLASTYEAR(SUM(Sales[Amount]))`
    c. `TOTALYTD(Sales[Amount], Date[Date])`
    d. `CALCULATE(SUM(Sales[Amount]), SAMEPERIODLASTYEAR(Date[Date]))`
    e. `DATEADD(Date[Date], -1, YEAR)`
74. As a data engineer, you're designing a semantic model that includes a `Customer` dimension table and a `Sales` fact table. You want to ensure that users with access to only one customer can only see the sales data for that customer.

    Which kind of security should you implement?
    a. Object-level security (OLS)
    b. Row-level security (RLS)
    c. Column-level security (CLS)
    d. Calculation groups
    e. Composite models

75. You're designing a semantic model that includes both `Import` and `DirectQuery` tables. You want to allow users to query both sources in the same report while maintaining performance. What should you use?

   a. A composite model and dual storage mode

   b. Calculation groups and Import mode

   c. Field parameters and Direct Lake

   d. Aggregation tables and DirectQuery

   e. A composite model and dynamic format strings

76. As a data engineer, you're designing a semantic model that includes a `Sales` fact table and a `Date` dimension table. You want to allow users to analyze sales by fiscal year, fiscal quarter, and fiscal month. The fiscal calendar does not align with the calendar year. What should you do?

   a. Use a calculation group to define fiscal periods.

   b. Create a custom fiscal calendar table and relate it to the fact table.

   c. Use built-in time intelligence functions with the calendar table.

   d. Add fiscal columns directly to the `Sales` table.

   e. Use a calculation group with YTD, QTD, and MTD to simulate fiscal periods.

77. As a data engineer, you're designing a semantic model for a logistics company. The model includes a `Shipments` fact table and `Date`, `Customer`, and `Carrier` dimension tables.

   You want to ensure that the model supports intuitive navigation and fast performance in Power BI. Which design principle should you apply?

   a. Use a snowflake schema to normalize all dimensions.

   b. Use a star schema with clear relationships and surrogate keys.

   c. Flatten all tables into a single wide table.

   d. Use composite models with Direct Query for all dimensions.

   e. Create calculated columns in the fact table for all dimension attributes.

78. As a data engineer, you're designing a semantic model that includes a `Sales` fact table and a `Customer` dimension table. You want to ensure that relationships are stable and not affected by changes in business keys.

    What should you use to define relationships?

    a. Natural keys
    b. Composite keys
    c. Surrogate keys
    d. Foreign keys in the fact table
    e. Role-playing dimensions

79. You're designing a semantic model that includes a `Sales` fact table and a `Date` dimension table. Users need to analyze sales by multiple date types, such as order date, ship date, and invoice date.

    Which modeling approach is best practice for this scenario?

    a. Role-playing dimensions
    b. Duplicating the `Date` table for each date type
    c. Using calculation groups to switch between date types
    d. Using field parameters to select the date type in visuals
    e. Using a composite model to combine multiple date tables

80. As a data analyst, you're creating a semantic model that will be used by nontechnical users in many departments. You want to ensure that the model is intuitive and easy to navigate and that it supports consistent terminology. Which three design principles should you apply?

    a. Use friendly names for tables and columns.
    b. Hide unused columns and tables.
    c. Use technical naming conventions for consistency.
    d. Create hierarchies for common drill paths.
    e. Avoid relationships to simplify the model.

81. You're designing a semantic model that includes a `Sales` fact table and a `Date` dimension table. You want to allow users to drill down from year to quarter to month in visuals. What should you implement?

   a. Field parameters
   b. Calculation groups
   c. Hierarchies
   d. Composite models
   e. Aggregation tables

82. As a data engineer, you're optimizing a semantic model that includes a large `Sales` fact table. The model is used in multiple reports and must support fast performance for aggregations and filters.

   Which storage mode should you choose to maximize performance?

   a. DirectQuery
   b. Import
   c. Dual
   d. Direct Lake
   e. Live Connection

83. You're working with a semantic model that includes a large dataset and is refreshed daily. You want to reduce refresh time and improve performance by only refreshing recent data. What should you implement?

   a. Composite mode
   b. Incremental refresh
   c. Aggregation tables
   d. Dual storage mode
   e. Partitioning the fact table manually

84. You have a large `Sales` fact table in a semantic model. Reports query this data frequently. You want fast performance for user queries, but the dataset is too large to load entirely into memory.

   Which storage mode is most suitable?

   a. Import
   b. DirectQuery
   c. Dual
   d. Composite
   e. Live Connection

85. You have a `Sales` fact table with millions of rows and a `Date` dimension table. Reports only need to display data from the last two years, but historical data must be retained.

    You want to reduce refresh time and limit processing to recent data. What would you implement?

    a. Aggregation tables
    b. Incremental refresh
    c. Calculation groups
    d. Field parameters
    e. Creation of a separate table for the last two years

86. As a data analyst, you're reviewing a report that uses several complex DAX measures. The report is slow to load and interact with. Which tool, provided in Power BI, should you use to identify which visuals or measures are causing performance issues?

    a. `INFO.VIEW`
    b. The performance analyzer
    c. Tabular Editor
    d. Query Diagnostics
    e. The SQL profiler

87. You're designing a semantic model that uses Direct Lake mode. You want to ensure that users can query large datasets with low latency and without preloading data into memory.

    Which benefit does Direct Lake provide?

    a. Real-time streaming
    b. Query folding
    c. Direct access to Parquet files in OneLake
    d. Automatic aggregation
    e. Built-in incremental refresh

88. As a data engineer, you're configuring incremental refresh for a semantic model. You want to ensure that only the current and previous month are refreshed, while keeping three years of historical data. Which two parameters must you configure?

    a. `DateFrom` and `DateTo`

    b. `RangeStart` and `RangeEnd`

    c. `RefreshWindow` and `RetentionPeriod`

    d. `PartitionStart` and `PartitionEnd`

    e. `HistoricalStart` and `HistoricalEnd`

89. You're optimizing a semantic model that includes a large `Sales` fact table and multiple dimension tables. You want to reduce memory usage and improve query performance. Which strategy should you apply?

    a. Using Import mode for all tables

    b. Removing unused columns from the model

    c. Creating calculated columns for all measures

    d. Using DirectQuery for dimensions

    e. Reducing column cardinality to improve compression

90. As a data analyst, you're reviewing a semantic model that includes multiple calculated columns. You notice that report performance is poor and refresh times are long. Which two actions should you consider?

    a. Replacing calculated columns with measures

    b. Using Direct Lake mode for all tables

    c. Removing unused columns from the model

    d. Switching to Import mode

    e. Using field parameters to reduce model size

91. You're configuring incremental refresh for a semantic model that includes a `TransactionDate` column. You want to ensure that only the last 60 days are refreshed and that historical data is retained for 3 years. Which configuration should you apply?

    a. `RangeStart = Today - 60 days, RangeEnd = Today.`

    b. Refresh policy: Keep data for 3 years, refresh the last 60 days.

    c. Partition by year and month.

    d. Use DirectQuery for recent data.

    e. Use a composite model with Import and DirectQuery.

92. A Fabric workspace contains a semantic model that must be deployed across development, test, and production environments. The team also requires all model changes to be versioned and tracked over time.

    Which approach should you use?

    a. Saving the semantic model as a *.pbix* file and manually uploading it to each workspace
    b. Storing the semantic model in *.pbip* format and connecting it to Git for version control
    c. Exporting the model as a *.pbit te*mplate and sharing it with developers
    d. Configuring deployment pipelines without source control
    e. Publishing directly from Power BI Desktop to the production workspace

93. You're managing a Fabric workspace with multiple developers. You want to ensure that semantic models and reports are deployed consistently across development, test, and production environments. What should you use?

    a. GitHub integration
    b. Deployment pipelines
    c. Workspace cloning
    d. Manual export and import
    e. Power BI APPS

94. As a data analyst, you're working in a shared workspace, and you want to reuse a semantic model across multiple reports. You also want to ensure that updates to the model are reflected automatically. Which approach should you use?

    a. Duplicating the model in each report
    b. Using shared semantic models
    c. Exporting the model as *.pbids*
    d. Using field parameters to switch models
    e. Creating a composite model for each report

95. As a data engineer, you're preparing a semantic model for deployment. You want to ensure that the model is modular, version controlled, and compatible with external tools. Which file format should you use?

    a. *.pbix*
    b. *.pbip*
    c. *.pids*
    d. *.xlsx*

96. A Fabric workspace contains multiple semantic models and reports. To guide report authors and ensure that only trusted models are used in production dashboards, you need to highlight which models are certified.

    Which governance feature should you apply?

    a. Sensitivity labels
    b. Endorsements
    c. Workspace-level permission
    d. Deployment pipelines
    e. Git integration

97. A Fabric workspace contains a semantic model with sensitive financial information, including salary and bonus data. You need to ensure that this data is properly classified and protected, even when exported to Excel or accessed outside of Power BI.

    Which governance feature should you apply?

    a. Sensitivity labels
    b. Endorsement
    c. Workspace-level permission
    d. Deployment pipelines
    e. Git integration

98. You're managing a Fabric workspace, and you want to automate the deployment of semantic models and reports from development to production. You also want to apply environment-specific rules during deployment. Which two features should you use?

    a. Deployment pipelines
    b. Git integration
    c. Workspace cloning
    d. Parameter rules
    e. Sensitivity labels

99. A Fabric workspace hosts multiple semantic models and reports. The team requires both of the following:

   - All changes to models must be versioned and tracked over time.
   - Content must be automatically deployed across development, test, and production environments.

   What do you need to configure?

   a. Deployment pipelines
   b. Git integration
   c. Workspace cloning
   d. Parameter rules
   e. Sensitivity labels

100. A Fabric workspace contains a semantic model with a `Sales` fact table and a `Customers` dimension table.

   You need to restrict access so that sales managers can only see data for the region they are assigned to, based on their login identity. Which security feature should you implement?

   a. Column-level security (CLS)
   b. Row-level security (RLS)
   c. Object-level security (OLS)
   d. Sensitivity labels
   e. Workspace permissions

Answers

1. Correct answer: A

   To use third-party tools in conjunction with the Microsoft Fabric environment, you have to enable the XMLA endpoint. You can read more about this in Chapter 8 and also in this Microsoft Learn resource (*https://oreil.ly/FGpij*).

2. Correct answer: B

   The only format from the Power BI formats that supports the TMDL language format is Power BI Template (*.pbit)*.

3. Correct answers: A and C

   Cloning a table by creating a meta-data copy of an existing table does not alter the table and the underlying data structures. When data in the new cloned table is updated, inserted or deleted, the engine will create a new set of files to support that specific table and the changes will only apply to `dbo.FactSales`.

4. Correct answer: C

   When you're working with specific tables in a lakehouse that don't have any partitions, the first thing you need to do is to overwrite the table. You do this to create the new file structures you need for the underlying filesystem in a way that supports the necessary portioning implementation.

5. Correct answer: B

   The only activity from the list of items that supports the Power Query (M) language is the dataflow.

6. Correct answer: A

   To create a link to an existing table from a lakehouse, you must use a shortcut. This shortcut is merely a pointer to the data, which then enables you to write queries against it and use it like any normal table in the list of tables when you develop your queries. The shortcut does not copy data between the lakehouses.

7. Correct answer: B

   In the join operation from Dataflow Gen2, you can automatically skip the spaces in the join by using a fuzzy-matching method. We described this in Chapter 2, but for a more detailed description, you can also refer to Microsoft Learn's documentation on the fuzzy-matching method (*https://oreil.ly/czPo5*).

8. Correct answer: D

   When working with joins in any data platform, the way to get all the rows from both tables is to use the FULL OUTER JOIN. Refer back to Chapter 3 to see the diagrams of join types and the results for each join type.

9. Correct answer: B

   When working with the Kusto Query Language (KQL), you must help the engine perform as well as it can. You can do this in many ways. In this question, the change in the query will make the execution faster, as it helps the engine filter earlier in the stage of execution.

   You might remember from Chapter 4 that when we described the use of KQL, we also talked about ways you can help the engine perform as well as possible by placing your statements in the optimal order.

10. Correct answer: B

    When working with Power BI, creating a field parameter is the easiest way to fulfill the specific requirement to make users able to select between measures in a report. You select the measures (or columns) you want to give to the end user, and then Power BI creates the list for you and the new measure to use.

11. Correct answer: A

    In workspaces, we have the four roles from Chapter 7. In this case, the member role gives the user the ability to share items from the workspace with other people.

12. Correct answers: A and B

    In Chapter 7, we talked about item sharing and the ability to avoid having to access the workspace to share data for specific items. Here, you can leverage this option, make sure to share the lakehouse by using item permissions, and also make sure the user can read the underlying data by using "Read all Apache Spark data."

13. Correct answer: A

    When working with GitHub in Microsoft Fabric, you need to use a personal access token (PAT) and the URL for the repository. The PAT is created from the GitHub portal, and the URL is the full https string to the repository.

14. Correct answer: B

    The low-code solution from Microsoft Fabric for moving data is Dataflow Gen2. This is the only way to implement full UI data movement between a source and a destination.

15. Correct answers: A and B

    In Chapter 3, we talked about the Dataflow Gen2 options for creating destinations. Here, we have two options: either create a default destination or create a destination for the current flow of data.

16. Correct answer: B

    The sensitivity labels that we discussed in Chapter 7 let you make sure that a specific item and its downstream items are locked for (re)sharing. This implements a good governance practice for a solution in Fabric.

17. Correct answer: D

    When working with both semi-structured and structured data, the best option in Microsoft Fabric is to use a lakehouse. It can handle both data structures, and it also supports the T-SQL and Spark languages that you need to manipulate the data.

18. Correct answer: B

    You have two options for implementing live updates of data in a semantic model: the DirectQuery mode and the Direct Lake mode. The DirectQuery mode creates live queries when you use the report toward the underlying datastore. The Direct Lake mode also makes live queries, but it uses the much faster logic from a mix of the xVelocity engine and the OneLake capabilities.

19. Correct answer: C

    When you're implementing RLS in a semantic model, the `USERPRINCIPALNAME` function returns the current user's email, which you can then use for filtering in the report. See Chapter 7 for the details.

20. Correct answer: A

    When you're writing T-SQL queries, you can use the `ROW_NUMBER` function in conjunction with the (`over ... partition by....`) window function to efficiently retrieve the latest row from a subset of data based on a specific order and bucket creation.

21. Correct answer: B

    In Chapter 7, we talked about the four roles in a workspace. The member role is the one that gives access to all the reports and models in the workspace while adhering to the least-privilege approach to the solution.

22. Correct answer: C

    Calculation groups are DAX methods that can apply reusable calculations against a set of measures (or all of them) from a semantic model.

23. Correct answer: D

    You have two options for working with the data quality of any table in Microsoft Fabric: the notebook and PySpark approach and the Data profiling option from a Dataflow Gen2.

    Here, you must select the low-code option, which is Dataflow Gen2.

24. Correct answer: C

    In Chapter 8, we talked about deployment pipelines, which are built-in tools that support the process of CI/CD between workspaces and promoting some or all of the items from development through test to production.

25. Correct answer: C

    In Chapters 5 and 6, we discussed the implementation of semantic models and how to help the engine perform as well as possible. Using a star schema is the optimal way to implement a semantic model.

26. Correct answer: C

    The `PREVIOUSYEAR` function gives you an out-of-the-box functionality to "move" the calendar filter back to previous years.

27. Correct answer: A

    Here, we need to move the window of dates to the previous year and also respect the user's current filter context. To do that, we must use the `SAMEPERIODLASTYEAR` function.

28. Correct answer: B

    You use a dataflow to implement a low-code data movement in Microsoft Fabric with the ability to transform the data on the fly.

29. Correct answer: A

    The Import mode of a semantic model enables the data analyst to schedule the import of data to the model. In this scenario, the data is updated once a day and the data freshness is not a major concern to the end user. The Import mode is the way to go here.

30. Correct answer: C

    Using the built-in deployment pipelines we discussed in Chapter 8 fulfills the needed requirements. The deployment pipeline enables the end users to deploy all or some of the items using an easy approachable UI.

31. Correct answer: C

    The role-playing option in a semantic model can use the same table for more than one relationship between dimensions and facts. The downside is that only one relationship can be the active one, and you must implement the measures for the inactive one with the `USERELATIONSHIP` function in the DAX code.

32. Correct answer: C

    The dataflow option is the only one you can use to implement the requirement as a step-by-step solution for each transformation in the flow. In Chapter 3 , we talked about the step pane on the right-hand side of the dataflow and the ability to debug it with a simple approach using the mouse and the formula bar.

33. Correct answer: C

    To ensure a forced filter on specific rows in a semantic model, we can use the RLS option. This forces a defined filter that cannot be changed by the end user. Please refer to Chapter 7 for more information on this topic.

34. Correct answer: C

    The `MERGE` approach for data loading combines the `INSERT`, `UPDATE`, and `DELETE` operations into one statement.

35. Correct answer: A

    When working with DAX, you can create new internal variables by using the `VAR` function. This makes the code more readable and lets you reuse the variables with just one declaration of the DAX logic.

36. Correct answer: D

    When you're creating relationships in a semantic model, the fact table has foreign keys to one or more dimension tables. A foreign key is the pointer and identifier of the row from which the attributes can be collected in the dimension table. The dimension table contains both the primary key and the attributes for this dimension. Refer to Chapter 5 for more details.

37. Correct answer: C

    When working with the Fabric warehouse, you have the option to use the visual query editor, which gives you a UI approach to manipulating the data. In Chapter 4, we talked about this, and we also provided behind-the-scenes knowledge that the query is actually a Power Query that is translated into T-SQL when you save the query as a view in the warehouse.

38. Correct answer: D

    Within the Dataflow Gen2 item, we have the data quality option of controlling and viewing the metrics behind each column. We can also remove any rows from the dataset that contain a `NULL` value by right-clicking columns and filtering the data.

39. Correct answer: B

    When working with incremental refresh on a semantic model in import mode, you must declare the `RangeStart` and `RangeEnd` parameters. These are locked names that the semantic model uses to read the data from the source.

40. Correct answer: B

    The `PREVIOUSMONTH` function enables the DAX measure to respect the current filters that are applied to the date table, and it can also help with the "movement" of the window in which data is displayed.

41. Correct answer: D

    Only with a composite model can a developer and an analyst make use of two (or more) sources for a single table in the model.

42. Correct answer: B

    In Chapter 7, we talked about the different implementations of security in a semantic model. The CLS option is the method to use here because it lets us force access or no access to specific columns in the model. This approach is feasible even though it's not available in out-of-the-box tools.

43. Correct answer: C

    You can analyze log data and streaming data with the eventhouse, a KQL database, and the KQL language. The other services can handle bulk loads with ease, but the only services in Microsoft Fabric that can handle both semi-structured and structured streaming data are the KQL database and the KQL language.

44. Correct answer: B

    Spark queries are performed in a lakehouse in Microsoft Fabric for both semi-structured and structured data. This also lets you use both T-SQL and Spark queries to manipulate and query the data. We discussed this in Chapter 2.

    You implement RLS in the database for T-SQL through the SQL analytics endpoint, as we discussed in Chapter 7.

45. Correct answers: A and C

    Applying a sensitivity label from Fabric and configuring column-level security in the lakehouse meets the correct security requirements. You must implement column-level security in the SQL analytics endpoint as `DENY SELECT` or `GRANT SELECT` in a T-SQL statement with the needed columns as the requirement specifies.

46. Correct answer: B

    When using a code-based CI/CD implementation from a third-party provider to update and maintain a semantic model, you need to enable the XMLA endpoint, as we discussed in Chapter 8. This enables a connection from a third-party tool to the semantic model, where XMLA commands can be executed.

47. Correct answer: A

    The only file-based transformation in Microsoft Fabric is done through a lakehouse, which uses the underlying OneLake Delta Parquet storage format to store data for each table.

48. Correct answers: A and C

    The semantic model is the only service that can use the DAX language to query the data.

The eventhouse and the KQL database are the only services in Microsoft Fabric that use the KQL language.

49. Correct answer: C

    We need to handle streaming data in real time, and the only service from Microsoft Fabric that does that out-of-the-box is the eventhouse with the underlying KQL database. We discussed this in Chapter 2.

50. Correct answers: A and C

    Inside the calculation groups, you can define specific format strings for each measure and the selected element from the calculation group. The field parameters enable the end user to select specific elements in a list of measures (or dimension attributes).

51. Correct answer: B

    We use a `VIEW` because it lets us save a query we can reuse anytime without creating a new table. This is useful for large tables like `SalesTransactions`, where copying millions of rows would be inefficient. The `WHERE` clause removes transactions where the amount is `NULL`, and the `GROUP BY` clause calculates the total per customer per month.

52. Correct answer: B

    The answer is `LEFT JOIN`. We want to keep all orders from the `Orders` table, even if the corresponding `ProductID` in the `Products` table has no matching category. The `LEFT JOIN` keeps every row from the left table (`Orders`) and fills in `NULL`s for missing matches from the right table (`Products`).

53. Correct answers: A and B

    We apply these two steps because they directly address the requirements: removing duplicate rows ensures data integrity, and changing column types guarantees that the data matches the dimensional model for consistent analysis.

54. Correct answer: B

    A Dataflow Gen2 transformation provides a low-code, visual way to clean and transform data. In this case, we can replace empty strings with 0 without affecting `NULL` values directly in the pipeline. Using Dataflow Gen2 keeps the source data untouched while ensuring the ingested data is clean and ready for analysis.

55. Correct answers: B and E

    We apply these steps to clean the data before loading it into the lakehouse. Trimming spaces fixes inconsistent text formatting to ensure that product names are standardized. Changing column types ensures that numeric columns imported as text are converted to the correct type so that they match the dimensional model, which enables accurate analysis.

56. Correct answer: A

    You should use the `prev()` function because it lets you access the value from the previous row within a specified partition, which in this case is grouped by area. This makes it possible to calculate the difference between the current and previous `MeterReadings`.

57. Correct answers: C and D

    Before limiting the results to the top companies, you need to calculate the total miles per company. The `GROUP BY TaxiCompany` clause aggregates the trip distances for each taxi company, and `ORDER BY SUM(tripDistance) DESC` sorts the companies by total miles in descending order so we can identify the top performers.

58. Correct answer: B

    You use a `WHERE` clause to filter rows before aggregation. In this case, `WHERE YEAR(SaleDate) = YEAR(GETDATE())` selects only sales that occurred in the current year.

59. Correct answer: A

    You use `WHERE` to filter the rows to only include transactions from the current year. Then, you use `GROUP BY CustomerID` to calculate the total transaction amount per customer. This combination ensures that the aggregation is done only on relevant rows and that it therefore gives correct totals per customer.

60. Correct answer: B

    Use a `LEFT JOIN` from the `Regions` table to the `Orders` table because it ensures that all regions are included, even those with no orders. The `COUNT(o.OrderID)` will return 0 for regions without any matching orders, which is what the report requires.

61. Correct answer: A

    You should use `extend Delta = Energy - prev(Energy) by Area` because it calculates the difference between each row and the previous row separately for each area, sorted by timestamp.

62. Correct answer: A

    A Dataflow Gen2 provides a low-code, visual way to transform data, aggregate revenue per product per month, and load the result into a new table. It's also reusable and easy to schedule in Fabric.

63. Correct answer: C

    A pipeline with activity dependencies ensures that each step runs in the correct order: load raw data, clean and transform it, and then populate the dimensional model. Each task only starts after the previous one is finished. This approach makes sure the process always happens in the right sequence, which is important for obtaining accurate results.

64. Correct answer: C

    You should use a Dataflow Gen2 because it can copy data from sources like CSV files into a lakehouse and also apply Power Query M transformations during the process. This makes it suitable for both ingestion and data cleaning in a single, low-code activity.

65. Correct answer: A

    We use calculation groups to simplify time intelligence calculations in Power BI. They allow us to define reusable logic for operations like year-to-date, previous month, and quarter comparisons and apply it across multiple measures. This reduces repetition and improves model maintainability.

66. Correct answer: B

    In a dimensional model, the fact table stores numeric measures (like `Sales Amount`) and foreign keys that link to dimension tables. The dimension table stores descriptive attributes (like `ProductCategory`) and a primary key that matches the foreign keys in the fact table.

67. Correct answer: B

    You follow best practices and modular design to make the solution performant, maintainable, and reusable. Modular design breaks complex transformations into smaller, reusable components, making it easier to manage and optimize.

68. Correct answer: B

    You should use a star schema because it organizes the model with a central fact table (`Sales`) that's connected directly to dimension tables (`Date`, `Product`, and `Store`). This design is easy to navigate and intuitive for users, and it performs well in Power BI because queries can access dimension attributes without multiple joins.

69. Correct answer: A

    You should use a composite model because it allows you to combine Import and DirectQuery tables in a single Power BI model. This approach provides the flexibility to leverage fast in-memory queries for imported data while still querying live data for tables in DirectQuery mode.

70. Correct answer: B

    You should use field parameters because they allow report authors to dynamically switch between different dimensions in visuals, such as `Region`, `Product`, and `Customer`, without changing the underlying model. This makes the model flexible and reusable across multiple reports.

71. Correct Answer: B

    You should use a single shared semantic model because it ensures consistent logic across reports, allows centralized maintenance, and avoids duplicating calculations or tables. Report authors can connect to the shared model, and that reduces errors and improves efficiency.

72. Correct answer: B

    Dynamic format strings allow you to apply consistent formatting across multiple measures without duplicating them or manually changing each one. This is especially useful in financial reporting, where measures may have different formats, such as currency and percentages.

73. Correct answer: D

    This DAX measure calculates total sales for the same period last year and keeps any filters applied in the report, like specific months or products. `CALCULATE` applies the filter, and `SAMEPERIODLASTYEAR` moves the dates to the previous year.

74. Correct answer: B

    RLS is used to restrict access to specific rows in a table based on user permissions. In this scenario, it ensures that a user who's assigned to a particular customer can only see sales data for that customer. Using RLS is the correct approach in Power BI because it provides row-by-row access control, which ensures that sensitive customer data is protected while allowing users to interact with the model normally for the data they are allowed to see.

75. Correct answer: A

    A composite model allows you to combine Import and DirectQuery tables in the same Power BI model. Using dual storage mode for tables lets some tables use Import for fast in-memory queries while others use DirectQuery to access live data. This approach provides both flexibility and performance in the same report.

76. Correct answer: B

    A custom fiscal calendar table allows you to define a fiscal year, quarter, and month according to the company's fiscal calendar, which may not align with the standard calendar. By relating it to the `Sales` fact table, users can analyze sales by fiscal periods correctly.

77. Correct answer: B

    A star schema organizes the model with a central fact table (`Shipments`) that's linked directly to dimension tables (`Date`, `Customer`, and `Carrier`) using surrogate keys. This design provides intuitive navigation for report authors and fast query performance in Power BI.

78. Correct answer: C

Surrogate keys are unique identifiers used in dimension tables. Using them to define relationships ensures that links between the `Sales` fact table and the `Customer` dimension table remain stable, even if business keys (like `CustomerID` from source systems) change over time.

79. Correct answer: A

Role-playing dimensions allow a single `Date` table to serve multiple purposes (providing the order date, ship date, and invoice date) by creating separate relationships from the fact table for each role. This avoids duplicating tables and keeps the model efficient and easy to maintain.

80. Correct answers: A, B, and D

These practices make the model intuitive and easy to navigate for nontechnical users. Using friendly names ensures terminology is understandable and consistent across departments. Hiding unused columns and tables reduces clutter and focuses users on relevant data. Creating hierarchies supports natural drill-down paths and thus improves usability in reports.

81. Correct answer: C

Implementing hierarchies in the `Date` dimension allows users to easily drill down from year to quarter to month in visuals. This makes navigation intuitive and improves the user experience in Power BI reports.

82. Correct answer: B

Import mode loads the data into Power BI's in-memory engine to provide fast performance for aggregations, filters, and visuals. This is ideal for large fact tables used across multiple reports.

83. Correct answer: B

Incremental refresh updates only recent or changed data, instead of refreshing the entire dataset, which reduces refresh time and improves performance for large tables.

84. Correct answer: B

DirectQuery keeps the data in the source system and queries it on demand, allowing users to work with very large datasets without loading everything into memory. This provides access to the full dataset while avoiding memory limitations.

85. Correct answer: B

Incremental refresh allows you to refresh only the most recent data (e.g., the last two years) while keeping historical data intact. This reduces refresh time and processing load without losing historical records. Therefore, incremental refresh is the most efficient and maintainable solution for large datasets with mostly historical data.

86. Correct answer: B

    The performance analyzer is the Power BI tool that's designed to measure the performance of each visual and DAX measure in a report. It breaks down the time spent querying data, rendering visuals, and displaying results to help you identify which elements cause slowness.

87. Correct answer: C

    Direct Lake lets Power BI read large datasets directly from Parquet files in OneLake without loading everything into memory. This makes queries fast and efficient, even for very big tables.

88. Correct answer: B

    `RangeStart` and `RangeEnd` define the filter on the `Date` column used by incremental refresh. Power BI uses these parameters to determine which rows to refresh (e.g., current and previous month) while keeping historical data intact.

89. Correct answer: B

    Removing unused columns reduces the size of the model and improves query performance because Power BI stores less data in memory.

90. Correct answers: A and C

    Replacing calculated columns with measures reduces memory usage because measures are calculated on the fly rather than stored in the model. Removing unused columns reduces model size, which improves both query performance and refresh times.

91. Correct answer: B

    The refresh policy lets you define how much historical data to retain and which recent data to refresh. In this case, setting it to keep 3 years of historical data and refresh only the last 60 days ensures that historical data is preserved while reducing refresh time.

92. Correct answer: B

    Saving the model in *.pbip* format and connecting it to Git allows the team to track changes, manage versions, and collaborate across development, test, and production environments. This approach supports proper source control and ensures reproducibility.

93. Correct answer: B

    Deployment pipelines in Fabric allow you to promote semantic models and reports from development to test to production in a controlled, consistent way.

This ensures that changes are applied systematically, and it reduces the risk of errors.

94. Correct answer: B

    Shared semantic models allow multiple reports to connect to a single model, ensuring that any updates to the model are automatically reflected in all reports. This avoids duplication and maintains consistency.

95. Correct answer: B

    The *.pbip* format is designed for modular, version-controlled semantic models. It can be stored in Git or other source control systems, it supports collaboration, and it is compatible with external tools for development and deployment.

96. Correct answer: B

    Endorsements allow you to mark semantic models as certified or promoted, which signals to report authors which models are trusted and recommended for production dashboards.

97. Correct answer: A

    Sensitivity labels classify and protect sensitive data, such as financial and personal information. They travel with the data even when exported to Excel or accessed outside Power BI, to ensure compliance and security.

98. Correct answers: A and D

    Deployment pipelines provide a structured way to move content (semantic models and reports) from development to test to production environments. Parameter rules allow you to apply environment-specific settings (like connection strings and data sources) during deployment.

99. Correct answers: A and B

    Using Git integration allows the team to track all changes to semantic models, maintain version history, and collaborate effectively. Every update is stored and can be reviewed, which ensures that no change is lost and the development process is auditable. Deployment pipelines enable the automatic promotion of content from development to test and then to production environments. This ensures that changes are applied consistently across environments and reduces the risk of errors from manual deployment.

100. Correct answer: B

    RLS restricts access to data based on user identity, allowing sales managers to see only the rows that are relevant to their assigned region. It works dynamically with login credentials and ensures that each user sees only the data they're permitted to see.

Index

A

B

C

I

J

K

P

Q

T

V

W

X

About the Authors

Brian Bønk is a senior principal consultant and has worked with SQL Server for more than two decades, varying from projects on both size and complexity. He has been a part of the Power BI and analytics universe since the beginning and also knows his way around Fabric from both an engineering approach and analytics approach. Brian is a FastTrack Recognized Solution Architect and holds several certifications related to the Microsoft Data Platform and Business Intelligence. He blogs at *brianbonk.dk*, and he loves data and is always trying to glue the business and tech together using his knowledge and experience.

Valerie Junk is a Fabric & Power BI consultant and Microsoft Data Platform MVP with a strong focus on data modeling, visualization, and dashboard design. She helps businesses create actionable reports and optimize their data strategies. Valerie is an active contributor to the data community, sharing her expertise through blog posts on *porcu.bi*, YouTube videos, and conference sessions. She has spoken at various international events and enjoys mentoring others in the field of data analytics and public speaking. Her approach is hands-on and practical, aiming to bridge the gap between technical solutions and business needs.

Colophon

The animal on the cover of *Microsoft Fabric Analytics Engineer Associate Study Guide* is a black stork (*Ciconia nigra*). A widespread species, these strikingly large birds can be found across Europe (from Spain to Portugal) and Northern Asia to China, as well as in sub-Saharan Africa during the winter seasons.

Black storks are easily distinguished by their sleek black plumage, which reflects tints of green and purple. While they share a silhouette with white storks, black storks possess a deep red bill and long legs that provide a sharp contrast to their dark feathers. On average, an adult black stork stands about 38 to 40 inches tall, with a wingspan stretching nearly 57 to 61 inches. They generally weigh around 6 pounds, though larger males can reach slightly higher.

Unlike white storks, which nest on chimneys and live near humans, black storks are solitary forest-dwellers. They prefer secluded forests with access to marshlands, rivers, or hilly terrain. They are primarily carnivorous, stalking through shallow water to hunt for fish, small reptiles, crabs, and insects. These birds are known for being cautious around humans and often nest high in large trees or on remote cliff ledges. They are generally quiet birds, though they may engage in soft whistling during breeding season.

Currently, the black stork is listed as Least Concern on the IUCN Red List due to its massive global range. However, their populations remain vulnerable to habitat loss, specifically deforestation and the drainage of wetlands. Many of the animals on O'Reilly covers are endangered; all of them are important to the world.

The cover illustration is by Monica Kamsvaag, based on an antique line engraving from *British Birds*. The series design is by Edie Freedman, Ellie Volckhausen, and Karen Montgomery. The cover fonts are Gilroy Semibold and Guardian Sans. The text font is Adobe Minion Pro; the heading font is Adobe Myriad Condensed; and the code font is Dalton Maag's Ubuntu Mono.

www.ingramcontent.com/pod-product-compliance
Lightning Source LLC
Chambersburg PA
CBHW080706220326
41598CB00033B/5325

9798341634817